PRAISE FOR
CITIES AND THRONES AND POWERS

"In recent years, Stephen R. L. Clark has done more than any scholar before him—at least, any of whom I am aware—to rescue Plotinus from the casual but persistent misrepresentations to which he has been subjected down the centuries (usually for tendentious reasons, utterly unrelated to the actual texts of the *Enneads*). This book brilliantly demonstrates that Plotinus's thought is profoundly social, cultural, and political (and benignly so) not only in its implications, but in its direct intentions. For this alone, we owe Clark a great debt of gratitude. But the pleasure of this book goes beyond that afforded by the mere rectification of an injustice; it lies also in the experience of reading a writer who is also a great and exquisitely original philosopher in his own right engaging with a thinker with whose thought he enjoys a particular and profound sympathy."

—**DAVID BENTLEY HART**, author of *Kenogaia (A Gnostic Tale)* and *Roland in Moonlight*

"Seeking to call into question modernity's smugly embraced verities, Stephen Clark draws on his exceptional understanding of Plotinus's own work and his own provocative insights into political philosophy to bring Neoplatonic thought into conversation with contemporary concerns while helping unsettle our instinctive responses to those concerns, employing logical argument and allusive, evocative reflection. As always elegant, graceful, and learned, Clark is alert to the pronounced differences between earlier epochs and our own even while turning a skeptical eye on the temporal chauvinism that treats our own ways of seeing, judging, feeling, and acting as self-evidently superior. Linking politics with metaphysics, history, literature, and religion, this book will rightly engage the attention of historians, classicists, and political theorists along with others intent on fruitfully exploring the nature and destiny of what Clark calls 'Lifekind.'"

—**GARY CHARTIER**, Distinguished Professor of Law and Business Ethics, La Sierra University

"This wide-ranging, brilliant book by the leading expert on Mediterranean thought in antiquity is highly relevant to our own today. Clark has done ground-breaking work on Plotinus's philosophy of politics, values, culture, and the divine. This should be of interest not just to historians of ideas and culture, but to readers interested in nothing less than the meaning of life."

—**CHARLES TALIAFERRO**, Professor Emeritus of Philosophy and the Oscar and Gertrude Boe Distinguished Professor, St. Olaf College

"This book canvasses possibilities of a genuinely Neoplatonic politics, such as an organic understanding of the polis, and an ethics that arises out of a metaphysical system where taxonomies are posterior to original unity. Stephen Clark is unique, both in his combination of scholarly competence and the will to think seriously about the deeper, spiritual ramifications of Neoplatonic thought, as well as in the beauty and richness of his prose."

—**PAULIINA REMES**, Professor in Theoretical Philosophy, Uppsala University

CITIES AND THRONES AND POWERS

Cities *and* Thrones *and* Powers

Towards a Plotinian Politics

STEPHEN R. L. CLARK

Angelico Press

First published in the USA
by Angelico Press 2022
Copyright © Stephen R. L. Clark 2022

For information, address:
Angelico Press, Ltd.
169 Monitor St.
Brooklyn, NY 11222
www.angelicopress.com

Paper   978-1-62138-855-5
Cloth   978-1-62138-856-2
Ebook   978-1-62138-857-9

Book and cover design
by Michael Schrauzer

There must not be just one alone—for
then all things would have been hidden,
shapeless within that one, and not a single
real being would have existed if that one
had stayed still in itself, nor would there
have been the multiplicity of these real
beings which are generated from the One,
if the things after them had not taken
their way out which have received the
rank of souls. (*Ennead* IV.8 [6].6, 1–6)

CONTENTS

PREFACE

IT IS WIDELY SUPPOSED THAT PLOTINUS (AND perhaps most other Neo-Platonists) had little concern for this-worldly woes and problems, and offered even less advice about the proper ordering of civil society than Plato and his immediate successors.

> Although Plotinus may hold that the civic or ethical virtues are products of the contemplative ascent of the philosopher, such virtue remains present in the philosopher only as an unactivated potentiality. Genuine happiness requires that the sage transcend these virtues by assimilating himself to the contemplative life of the gods and this is a project that is possible for the philosopher alone. Plotinus holds that the wise person will transcend political concerns.[1]

But does it follow, even if this were exactly true, that Plotinus had no views about political concerns, nor any interest in promoting civil virtue? Does it even follow that, because sages must have other motives than the commonplace, they will make no contribution to the common good, or insist on walking away from the messy business of ordinary human life without offering any advice?[2]

John Dillon famously summed the matter up as follows:

> [Plotinus] would, of course, observe the vulgar decencies; it is just that they would be subsumed into something higher. One feels of Plotinus that he would have gladly helped an old lady across the road—but he might very well fail to notice her at all. And if she were squashed by a passing wagon, he would remain quite unmoved.[3]

---

1   Christopher Bobonich, *Plato's Utopia Recast* (Oxford: Oxford University Press, 2002), 4. So also James V. Schall, "Plotinus and Political Philosophy," *Gregorianum* 66, no. 4 (1985): 687–707. "No one studies the political philosophy of Plotinus because, strictly speaking, there was no such thing in his system." Schall's (not untypical) insistence that Plotinus's concentration on the One precludes any concern for all the myriad things is, so it seems to me, unwarranted—as my following remarks aim to demonstrate.
2   As Theodore Sabo ("The Politics of the One," *Acta Classica* 58 [2015]: 209–16) seems to suggest.
3   Dillon, "An ethic for the antique sage," *Cambridge Companion to Plotinus*, ed. Lloyd Gerson (Cambridge: Cambridge University Press, 1996), 324.

Can this really be correct? Does Plotinus proffer, as Dillon suggests,[4] an "uncompromisingly self-centered and otherworldly" ethic, despite insisting that we should live by the god in each of us, that we should struggle to bring that god back "to the god in the all"?[5] Surely not.

> It does no good at all to say "Look to God," unless one also teaches how one is to look.... In reality it is virtue which goes before us to the goal and, when it comes to exist in the soul along with wisdom, shows God; but God, if you talk about him without true virtue, is only a name. Again, despising the universe and the gods in it and the other noble things is certainly not becoming good.... For anyone who feels affection for anything at all shows kindness to all that is akin to the object of his affection, and to the children of the father that he loves. But every soul is a child [specifically, a daughter] of That Father.[6]

"It is obvious," he says, "that we are angry not only over whatever *our* bodies suffer, but over the sufferings of anyone closely connected to us, and in general over anyone's improper behavior."[7] Plotinus, after all, did *not* disregard old ladies, nor Emperors, nor orphan children, even if he thought that there were higher and better goals than worldly health and success. A good man (*spoudaios*) "would like all men (*anthropoi*) to prosper and no one to be subject to any form of evil," even though—and surely this must be obvious—he is himself no less *eudaimon* because, as he knows, they don't and aren't.[8] He helped the children with their homework, swiftly identified a thieving slave (and so spared the rest from torture), was "gentle [*praos*], and at the disposal of all who had any acquaintance with him."[9] He spotted Porphyry's terminal depression and intervened to help him.[10] He even hoped, we are told, to establish or re-establish

---

4 Ibid., 331. Suzanne Stern-Gillet discusses the issue in "Dual Selfhood and Self-Perfection in the *Enneads*," *Epoche: A Journal for the History of Philosophy* 13, no. 2 (2009): 331–45.

5 Porphyry, *Life of Plotinus* 2.26–7. That the god in each of us is one and the same, Plotinus says, is common doctrine: *Ennead* VI.5 [23].1, 2–4; see also Aristotle, *Nicomachean Ethics* 7.1153b32, "everything has something divine in it."

6 Ibid., II.9 [33].15, 33–16.10.

7 Ibid., IV.4 [28].28, 23–5.

8 Ibid., I.4 [46].11, 12–14.

9 Porphyry, *Life*, 9.19–20.

10 Ibid., 11.12–20.

a city in Campania, and was defeated, so Porphyry tells us, only by the envy of the Emperor Gallienus's courtiers—though I shall have more to say about this imagined project later.[11] He strongly objected to Diophanes' argument, after Plato's Alcibiades, that students should offer sex for philosophical instruction,[12] and rebuked those (later called "Gnostics") who thought themselves so superior to all earthly powers as rightly to ignore all usual authorities.[13] Amongst the many things that properly excite our love and admiration, he says, are good laws and well-ordered societies.[14] Philosophical moralists in general did not *only* suggest that we refrain from positive wrongdoing; they also objected to our neglect of those to whom or about whom we had some duty of care. "We ought to fly away from earth to heaven as quickly as we can; and to fly away means to become like God, as far as this is possible; and to become like him, means to become holy, just, and wise," so Socrates insists to Theaetetus.[15] To "fly away" is not to forsake our friends: the point is rather to "wake another way of seeing."[16] So Seneca, also advancing the duty of being "godlike":

> Would you win over the gods? Then be a good man. Whoever imitates them, is worshipping them sufficiently. Then comes the second problem—how to deal with men. What is our purpose? What precepts do we offer? Should we bid them refrain from bloodshed? What a little thing it is not to harm one whom you ought to help! It is indeed worthy of great praise, when man treats man with kindness! Shall we advise stretching forth the hand to the shipwrecked sailor, or pointing out the way to the wanderer, or sharing a crust with the starving? Yes, if I can only tell you first everything which ought to be afforded or withheld; meantime, I can lay down for mankind a rule, in short compass,

---

11   Ibid., 12.3–13.
12   Ibid., 15.7–18, drawing on Plato, *Symposium*, 218d.
13   Plotinus, *Ennead*, II.9 [33].
14   Ibid., I.6 [1].1, 41–4; 4, 4–13.
15   Ibid., I.2 [19].1, 3–6, after Plato, *Theaetetus* 176a; see also I.8 [51].6, 10–13. I have followed Plotinus's lead in addressing the apparent paradox that to be godlike requires us to be thus virtuous despite the fact that the gods themselves *aren't* virtuous, at least in the same sense (that, as Aristotle says, would be a lame or vulgar compliment: *Nicomachean Ethics* 10.1178b7–18): "Plotinus and Godlike Virtues," in *Quietism, Agnosticism and Mysticism*. Edited by Krishna Pathak (New York: Springer, 2022), 15–76.
16   Plotinus, *Ennead*, I.6 [1].8, 26–8.

for our duties in human relationships: all that you behold, that which comprises both god and man, is one—we are the parts of one great body. Nature produced us related to one another, since she created us from the same source and to the same end. She engendered in us mutual affection, and made us prone to friendships. She established fairness and justice; according to her ruling, it is more wretched to commit than to suffer injury. Through her orders, let our hands be ready for all that needs to be helped.[17]

Virtue is shown not simply in not hurting or harming others, but also, importantly, in *helping* them. The point Plotinus and Seneca both make is not that we shouldn't care for and help the needy, but that we should be careful what their real needs are. They do not need, for example, to be permanently in our care, dependent for their lives and livelihood on the will or whim of others. We may all profit from remembering the dour lesson that our mortal troubles are indeed merely mortal. It does not follow that we would not, if we were wise, attempt to help each other. The games that children—and adults— play aren't finally and absolutely serious—but also, in a sense, they are: "Toys too are taken seriously by those who do not know how to be serious and are toys themselves."[18] Precisely because possessions are no more than toys, they should not be stolen: who steals their toys from children? Plotinus—as was said of other philosophers in a like position—took care of the orphans in his charge, and their inheritance, "in case they turned out *not* to be philosophers," and arbitrated in many people's disputes about matters that he himself would consider trivial.[19] "Yet though he shielded so many from the worries and cares of ordinary life, he never, while awake, relaxed his intent concentration upon the intellect."[20]

Porphyry meant something stronger or stranger than Armstrong's translation quite conveys: Plotinus, he says, never, while awake, relaxed his orientation towards *Nous* (*ten pros ton noun tasin oudepot'*

17 Seneca, *Moral Epistles*, 95.50–2.
18 Plotinus, *Ennead*, III.2 [47].15, 55–7.
19 Porphyry, *Life*, 9.6–23; see also Diogenes Laertius, "Crates the Cynic," in *Lives of Eminent Philosophers*, vol. 2, trans. R. D. Hicks (Cambridge, Mass: Loeb Classical Library, Harvard University Press, 1924-25), 5.88.
20 Porphyry, *Life*, 9.16–19: A. H. Armstrong, *Plotinus: The Enneads*, vol. 1 (Cambridge, Mass: Loeb Classical Library, Harvard University Press, 1966–88), 31. All other passages of Plotinus cited here are drawn from Armstrong's translation (with occasional disagreements).

an egregoretos ekhalasen): he never let himself forget Reality. Even the reference to his waking state is less banal than merely a contrast to his nightly sleep. Purification is a waking up from inappropriate images,[21] and consequent enthusiasm: *Egersis*, as Sourvinou-Inwood observed, is often *arousal* rather than simple awakening, *getting up* and not just waking up.[22] Our concern for others must not weaken our own grip on something greater, better, than the fallen world around us. The world that most of us inhabit is, as Marcus Aurelius said, a dream and a delirium,[23] structured by fears and fantasies.

> The chief enemy of excellence in morality (and also in art) is personal fantasy: the tissue of self-aggrandizing and consoling wishes and dreams which prevents one from seeing what is there outside one.[24]

Waking up to reality is not a matter of blandly "facing facts," but of a renewed engagement with reality, and with its origin. Our experience is linear, partial and parochial, and most of us only rarely recall the *real* world.

It is true that Plotinus declares that there is a higher and better life than that required by the "civic virtues," and this passage has often, illegitimately, been taken to prove that he did not care himself at all about those less demanding lives:

> [One who has reached higher principles] will not make self-control [*sophrosune*] consist in that former observance of measure and limit, but will altogether separate himself, as far as possible, from his lower nature and will not live the life of the good man which civic virtue requires. He will leave that behind, and choose another, the life of the gods: for it is to them, not to good men, that we are to be made like.[25]

---

21 Plotinus, *Ennead*, III.6 [26].5, 23ff.

22 Christiane Sourvinou-Inwood, *Hylas, the Nymphs, Dionysos and Others* (Stockholm: Åströms Förlag, 2005), 235–40.

23 Marcus Aurelius, *Meditations*, 2.17.1.

24 Iris Murdoch, *The Sovereignty of Good* (London: Routledge & Kegan Paul, 1970), 59; see also ibid., 86: "Good art shows us how difficult it is to be objective by showing us how differently the world looks to an objective vision." "Objectivity," here, is quite different from any merely "neutral," "abstract" or "merely material" description (on which, more below).

25 Plotinus, *Ennead*, I.2 [19].7, 22–28; see Aristotle, *Nicomachean Ethics*, 10.1177b26–34; Plato, *Theaetetus* 176b. *Sophrosune* is better translated "self-possession" than "self-control" (which would be *enkrateia*) or even "temperance."

But this defines the motives and manners of the more god-like sort, without suggesting that such a godly person will forget all her real responsibilities here-now. Even if such a person does, like Rogatianus,[26] abjure his civic duties and his property, it does not follow that such a life is for all:[27] it has rarely been supposed that Christ's suggestion to a rich young man that he give up all his possessions is binding on *all* Christ's followers![28] And those who do not follow that example may still manage, unlike another of Plotinus's companions, Serapion of Alexandria, at least to "free [themselves] from the degradation of finance and money-lending."[29] Being a good man even of a less-than-godlike kind and a good citizen are not at all the same thing.[30] There is a real, practical question: when is it right to involve oneself in business or politics or any other "active" life with a view to making things better, and when would it be better simply to walk away from corruption? Indeed, if all that we could mind about were the ills of this mortal life we should very soon be driven to despair by our inevitable failure to correct or ameliorate them all.

So how might Plotinus, or a devout Plotinian, recommend that our lives here-now be ordered? Might it be enough to speak of *personal* virtue, and of what is required of anyone? Or must not this have further implications for *public* life, and the proper ordering of any civil community? The very same virtues are needed for the public as for the personal: they may indeed be better seen at work on the larger canvas, as Plato proposed.[31] In what follows I aim to address the assumptions that we ourselves

---

26 Porphyry, *Life*, 7, 32–47.

27 See Emperor Julian, "Letter to Themistius, 255cd," in *Complete Works*, vol. 2, trans. Wilmer C. Wright (London: Loeb Classical Library, Heinemann, 1913–23), 207: "We are told that Socrates dissuaded from the statesman's profession many who had no great natural talent."

28 Matthew, 19.16–22; Mark, 10:17–31; Luke, 18:18–30.

29 Plotinus, *Life*, 7. 47–50. I have not tried to work out what Plotinus's *economic* theory might have been, except to note the obvious: he would, like Aristotle, have considered usury "unnatural," and as a practice likely to lead to damaging inequality and oppression (Aristotle, *Politics*, 1.1258b; see also Aristotle, *Nicomachean Ethics*, 4.1121b31–5). But wealth, even inequality of wealth, does not directly concern anyone who understands what is really worth having: Plotinus, *Ennead*, II.9 [33].9, 1–9. Fortunately, perhaps, there are other people who can be induced to provide the limited necessities of "the better sort" (Ibid., 10–12)!

30 Aristotle, *Nicomachean Ethics*, 5.1130b28–9.

31 Plato, *Republic*, 2.368d–369a.

too often bring to the study, whether of Plotinus or of political theory, and develop a Plotinian answer to how best we may hope to build "Jerusalem"—taking that title as emblematic of the many visions humankind has had of a divinely ordered city. Or maybe, rather than our building that great city, we may instead expect to see it coming down from Heaven, or emerging from a terrestrial chaos. Since Plotinus himself did not write explicitly on the proper ordering of the *polis* (or Porphyry, at any rate, did not include such a treatise in his edition of the *Collected Works of Plotinus*), let alone of the empire or of the whole earth, my enterprise must rely on passing remarks, on the canonical texts to which he and his followers openly or riddlingly refer, and on the implications of his overall ontology and ethics.[32] I shall also take note of later Arabic and European developments of the Neo-Platonic theme, and of what might be amended in those themes by more recent discoveries and inventions.[33] As I emphasized in an earlier volume, Plotinian philosophy should not be treated as a dead and finished object: it is and always has been part of a living tradition of enquiry and innovation, even if one that must constantly look back to its founding fathers for their imagined approval.[34] So what follows is, admittedly, my own extrapolation of a *Plotinian* set of suggestions, and not *necessarily* what Plotinus himself proposed in his discussions with either the emperor Gallienus or his closest friends.

---

32 So also Dominic J. O'Meara, "Aspects of Political Philosophy in Iamblichus," in *The Divine Iamblichus: Philosopher and Man of God*," ed. H. J. Blumenthal and E. G. Clark (Bristol: Bristol Classical Press, 1993).

33 Walzer's translation and commentary on Al-Farabi's *Virtuous State* is a good resource for any extrapolation of a Neo-Platonic political theory, despite Walzer's conviction that Al-Farabi must have borrowed his political theory from an otherwise unknown Neo-Platonist. Richard Walzer, *Al-Farabi on the Perfect State: Abu Nasr al-Farabi's Mabadi' ahl-madīna al-fadila* (Oxford: Clarendon Press, 1982). See also Ralph Lerner, "Beating the Neoplatonic Bushes. *Al-Farabi on the Perfect State* by Richard Walzer," *The Journal of Religion* 67, no. 4 (1987): 510–17 for gentle mockery of this notion.

34 For similar attempts, see Asger Ousager, *Plotinus on Selfhood, Freedom and Politics* (Aarhus, Denmark: Aarhus University Press, 2005), 189–284; R. M. Helm, "Platonopolis Revisited," in *Neoplatonism and Contemporary Thought I-II*, vol. 2, ed. R. Baine Harris (New York: SUNY Press, 2001); Dominic J. O'Meara, *Platonopolis: Platonic Political Philosophy in Late Antiquity* (Oxford: Clarendon Press, 2003); Jeremiah Heath Russell, "Athens and Byzantium: Platonic Political Philosophy in Religious Empire," LSU Doctoral Dissertations, 2978.

My argument will be as follows. First, it is necessary to give some account of a Plotinian philosophy of mind and metaphysics, so as not to read his work (as is all too common) as if he thought, like most of us, that we are essentially singular, discrete human beings, weirdly autonomous but also merely "natural" products. We should rather suppose that we are entangled souls, that the freedom we should value is not simply to do as we please but to be freed from ignorance, fear and transient desire so as to manifest our own original natures: the supposed "ability to sin" is not a mark of our superior natures any more than our "ability" to catch cold or break a bone. Plotinus nicely balances the entanglement of soul-body composites (our immediate identities) with the workings of the World Soul, and the other eternal souls that animate successive bodies to see all things "from within." We must recognize that the phenomenal worlds we inhabit and create are subtly ambiguous and odd, while also displaying recurrent patterns from which we can glimpse the original, abiding order of all things. That phenomenal world is also full of ghosts and memories, *daimones* and gods, a fully "participated" cosmos rather than a merely "objective" one, which is itself a clue to the original, "real" world.

Having sketched this outline of a Plotinian worldview, I shall seek to describe the various social forms that would seem, especially to him, to be the inevitable context of our lives here-now. Philosophers of his day might expect to be "citizens of the cosmos" rather than, or at least as well as, citizens of some particular *polis*. Such a global life, though, must come second for most of us to the lives of the ordinary *polis*. The "city of philosophers" that perhaps he planned for Campania, with Gallienus's approval, turns out, unexpectedly, to be much like a typical Mediterranean *polis* under the *Pax Romana*, and to share features with Hindu (and other) caste societies. Such *poleis*, in turn, relied exactly on that *Pax*. On Plotinus's account, shared especially with later Islamic philosophers, the Empire is united, symbolically, in the figure of the Emperor, himself standing—for more esoteric sensibilities—for the One Itself, towards which all proper thought and action should be directed. Both Empire and *polis* depend for their stability on a shared "religion" or morale, and it is possible to wonder whether such a "religion" might be enough by itself to steer at least the more "philosophical" of us—that is, those for whom the discovery

xviii

and enjoyment of truth is a primary concern—in a good direction. The particular form that a Plotinian religion takes depends on taking seriously the theory and thought of reincarnating souls: this may seem to have unduly conservative and oppressive implications, which can perhaps be avoided. But though some sages may be content to consider themselves as simple wanderers in a world without geographical or taxonomic borders or settled communities, some rather followed the same path as Buddhists, Epicureans and Christians: to form communities of *friends*, having loyalty to their founder, to the rules he laid down, and the fellowship of the *Sangha*. Even those who prefer to go, almost literally, "alone to the Alone" will be part of such dispersed, unhierarchical communities.

Finally, I shall offer some cautious thoughts about our likely futures, dependent both on current technological advances and on the realistic suspicion (shared by our predecessors) that catastrophes and wholly unexpected turns are always to be expected. It may be, as Plotinus himself did *not* suppose, there will even be a singular, final irruption of the Real World into our changing worlds: but even without that Abrahamic expectation, we must acknowledge that the *phenomenal* world and all human or unhuman history is transient, ambiguous, dangerous, diverse—and also delightful. And that, if he was right, each soul may in the end revert to its eternal being within the Divine.

My thanks go to the Leverhulme Trust for grants which helped support the composition of many earlier papers, and especially my book on Plotinus's philosophical practice (Chicago, 2016), and to the Universities of Liverpool and Bristol. My more direct debts to earlier ancient and modern scholars are innumerable, but my special thanks for their encouragement and helpful insights over many years go to Tim Addey, Gary Chartier, Gillian Clark, Sarah Coakley, Kevin Corrigan, John Dillon, Michael McGhee, Pauliina Remes, Charles Taliaferro, Panayiota Vassilopoulou and to two anonymous reviewers of an earlier version of this volume.

THE METAPHYSICAL
BACKDROP

BEFORE EMBARKING ON MY VOYAGE TOWARDS
a Plotinian political philosophy—a philosophy that is not necessarily
Plotinus's own developed theory (if he had one at all)—I shall address
some other common misconceptions of the Plotinian and Platonic
endeavor. Platonists need not suppose, and mostly did not suppose,
that only human beings are significant agents or observers: it is
not only human beings that are children of the one Father, nor
only human beings for whom "nature" has implanted affection and
concern. Nor did they suppose that the complex and changeful
world we inhabit is to be ignored in favor of an abstract, merely
intellectual, reality. "Being ashamed to be in a body"—as Porphyry
(mis)interpreted Plotinus's unwillingness to identify himself with a
particular ethnic and geographical origin[1]—does not entail a total
disregard for "bodily" or "material" concerns: rather the reverse (but
that will require a longer analysis). Neither Stoic nor Epicurean
philosophies make room for real, individual agents who can take
responsibility for past and future action: Platonists insisted that
we, like other embodied souls, may make a real difference in the
world, even as we realize how much of what we seem to ourselves
to be and to do is outside our control. They also insisted—agreeing
in this especially with Stoic philosophers—that we can discover
real truths, and that the whole world, therefore, has an intelligible
order which is also the origin of our deepest intellectual intuitions.
We can, they insist, wake up—and so recognize the world from
and within which we grow as if for the first time: a world that
is not composed simply of disconnected bits, nor well described
solely in "material" terms.

Political philosophy—the attempt to examine, analyze and
perhaps prioritize the many forms of social living and decision-
making—must always occur within a larger framework, in which

---

1   Porphyry, *Life*, 1.1-2.

particular choices have already been made about the presumed nature of the world, of time, of causation, freedom and identity. We cannot even begin to decide how best to live together without having decided who and what "we" are and what can rationally be expected of "us." We must also have some notion of what the world around us might be like, how long any arrangements we might make could be expected to last and how far we can "reasonably" suppose ourselves to have any well-grounded insight into the nature of the world, or any sound judgement about what is worth doing. One way of bringing this home to ourselves is to consider how differently another thinker, of another time and place, would or could conceive the bounds of human community. What could it be like to be a sincere and almost consistent Plotinian, for example? What is it like to strip away our own most common assumptions and begin to recall or reinvent an older world, one populated not only by the many levels of natural being (as we suppose such beings to be) but also permeated by spirits, ghosts, memories and signs? My attempt to bring this world to life will make use of other sources than the *Enneads*, precisely to make those "classical" texts a little less familiar, and so to bring to light those features of Plotinus's world that most scholars routinely disregard, whether as jokes, unfortunate mistakes or popularizing fables.

The Real and Living World

SUBJECTS, OBJECTS AND ANIMALS

The first step is to identify how best to understand the status of humankind in a Plotinian system: not the best of all living beings, but one with a particular duty or opportunity.[1] This requires a radical re-examination of all-too-familiar assumptions. Most of us in the developed West[2] inherit an unexamined view that there are no non-human subjects, that everything other than the clearly human is only an object, even if we are sometimes prepared to acknowledge that some non-human animals, or at least some birds or mammals, may be, occasionally, "in pain" or have a point of view. "They act not; rather are they acted upon," as *action*, strictly so-called, requires that it be willed for some good reason, not merely "instinctually" pursued.[3] It may be that not everyone will nowadays admit to this. It may even be that some of us have genuinely begun to think that other animals than *human* animals are truly sentient beings—the European Union declared as much in the Treaty of Lisbon (2009).[4] But even those of us most concerned with such pains as "animals" can suffer will also often assume that, at best, they are *our* "subjects"

---

1   Plotinus, *Ennead*, III.2 [47].9, 20–40.

2   "Weird," by more global standards, as we are (that is, Western, educated, individualistic, rich and democratic): see Joseph Henrich, *The Weirdest People in the World: How the West Became Psychologically Peculiar and Particularly Prosperous* (London: Allen Lane, 2020), 21–2. Henrich's erudite account of the historical development of our "WEIRD" society is somewhat marred by his own historically determined conviction that *of course* "science" has "proved" that there are no gods, and that minds are wholly dependent upon brains (see ibid., 129).

3   Aquinas, *Summa Theologiae*, 2.1.6.2, citing John Damascene, *De Fide Orthodoxa*, 2.27.

4   See http://ec.europa.eu/food/animals/welfare/index_en.htm (accessed 25 March 2020), citing article 13 of Title 2: "In formulating and implementing the Union's agriculture, fisheries, transport, internal market, research and technological development and space policies, the Union and the Member States shall, since animals are sentient beings, pay full regard to the welfare requirements of animals, *while respecting the legislative or administrative provisions and customs of the Member States relating in particular to religious rites, cultural traditions and regional heritage* [my italics]." A similarly qualified declaration of *human* rights and interests would not be thought acceptable.

(in another sense) and have no real lives or opinions of their own. We may acknowledge that some "animals" have keener senses of sight, smell and hearing. They may be able to run mazes, track their prey or evade pursuit. They may, in some sense, recognize and remember past acquaintances, of their own species or another. Some of them—apes, crows, puffer fish or squids—may use or even create simple tools to help them find food or secure the attention of potential mates. But whatever they do, and however subtly they may communicate, we are convinced, at a level almost immune to argument, that only human beings are "rational" or "self-aware," even that only we are truly "sentient." Individual animals may turn a twig into a tool, but groups of animals don't cooperate in the making (unless they are eusocial insects). Some philosophers still argue the point: non-human animals cannot "speak," and so cannot be supposed to think (since "thinking" is simply speaking to oneself). Because they cannot "think" they can have no opinions, even about vital matters. They cannot identify anything as prey or predator or merely passer-by, even if they respond "appropriately" to such things (cannot "say to themselves" anything corresponding to those judgements, nor wonder whether they are correct). Their perceptions are therefore wholly unconscious.[5] An astonishing number of people, even those who may express some affection for other creatures, apparently believe that there is a greater difference between humans and chimpanzees than between apes and amoebas.[6] Is this too implausible to believe, especially as it implies that learning to speak (and so think and feel) is an unpredictable miracle, for individuals and for the human species? I shall not argue the case further here. But even if we admit that other animals are sentient or even sensible, we are likely

5   See Peter Carruthers, *The Animals Issue: Moral Theory in Practice* (Cambridge: Cambridge University Press, 1992), 170–93; Daniel Dennett, *Consciousness Explained* (New York: Little, Brown & Co., 1991), 171–226. This is, in my judgement, probably the worst argument ever advanced by serious and otherwise competent philosophers. For a lengthier rebuttal see Iain McGilchrist, *The Master and His Emissary: The Divided Brain and the Making of the Western World* (New Haven: Yale University Press, 2009), 105–10.

6   See Urgyen Sangharakshita [Dennis Lingwood], *What is the Sangha? The Nature of Spiritual Community* (Cambridge: Windhorse Publications, 2001), Kindle location 4338–39 citing, with apparent approval, Vladimir Nabokov in conversation with James Mossman, *The Listener*, 23 October 1969. Neither Nabokov nor Sangharakshita seems to have tried to investigate the feelings or motives of either apes or amoebas.

at least to be sure that only we can discover law-like regularities in what occurs or imagine hidden causes of our observations. Only we are even interested in so doing. "Man is the first *objective* animal. All others live in a subjective world of instinct, from which they can never escape; only man looks at the stars or rocks and says, 'How interesting…,' instantly leaping over the wall of his mere identity."[7] Wilson's remark, of course, is not original (though he puts it to particular use). Only we (it is supposed) are *curious* about things that don't immediately matter, as Abbé Galiani (1728–1787) wrote in 1771:

> It's a feeling particular to man, unique in him, which he has in common with no other animal. Animals don't have quite the same idea. Do in front of a troupe of sheep anything you want; if you don't touch them, they're not interested in you. If animals give some sign of curiosity, it's because they are frightened, and nothing else. One can frighten animals, one cannot make them curious. However, according to what I said, fear is opposed to curiosity. If curiosity is impossible for animals, a curious human being is therefore more of a human being than a non-curious one: and this is in fact true. Newton was so curious that he looked for the cause of the movement of the moon, the sea, etc. The most curious people therefore are more human than other people.[8]

How the notion that only human beings are curious ever survives acquaintance with cats, cows, crows or minke whales is itself a curiosity. But a case can perhaps be made for the suggestion that *human* curiosity is rather different than theirs: not simply an interest in the unusual, but a readiness to puzzle even over what is *usual,* and a drive to *understand* the order that lies behind all sense experience. It may be true, as Chesterton observed, that only human beings really notice that they resemble other creatures, and so differ from them even in their similarity. "The fish does not trace the fish-bone pattern in the fowls of the air; or the elephant and the emu compare skeletons."[9] The story goes back still

---

7   Colin Wilson, *Philosopher's Stone* (London: Barker, 1969), 129.
8   Ferdinando Galiani, letter 101, 31 August 1771, in *Lettres de l'abbé Galiani a madame d'Épinay ed Eugène Asse* (Paris: Charpentier, 1882), 268–69; see Francis Steegmuller, "Diplomacy: the Abbé Galiani: 'The Laughing Philosopher,'" *American Scholar* 57, no. 4 (1988): 589–97, for a brief life of this clearly engaging Neapolitan.
9   G. K. Chesterton, *Everlasting Man* (London: Hodder & Stoughton, 1925), 307.

further—for example, to Augustine, though he recognized more clearly than Galiani that our goal must be an *end-point*: God, not merely whatever secondary entities and causes populate the world in which—beyond our animal *Umwelt*—we live.

> If we were cattle, we should love the carnal and sensual life, and this would be our sufficient good; and when it was well with us in respect of that, we should seek nothing else. Again, if we were trees we could not, of course, be moved by the senses to love anything; but we should seem to desire, as it were, that by which we might become more abundantly and bountifully fruitful. If we were stones or waves or wind or flames or anything of that kind, we should, indeed, be without both sensation and life, but we should still not lack a kind of desire for our own proper place and order. For the weight of bodies is, as it were, their love, whether they are carried downwards by gravity or upwards by their lightness. For the body is carried by its weight wherever it is carried just as the soul is carried by love. We, however, are men, created in the image of our Creator, Whose eternity is true and Whose truth is eternal, Whose love is eternal and true, and Who is Himself the eternal, true and beloved Trinity, in whom there is neither confusion nor separation.[10]

The challenge to human beings, even if they disclaim any interest in a "supernatural" substance, is to discover and attempt to live in accordance with the world that lies behind experience, that pre-existed and will survive us and that stretches unimaginably far in space and time. That challenge, of course, is very rarely met even by those who have done most to sketch the outlines of that wider world: we are all parochial in our affections, as well as our understanding. And there is at least something odd about insisting that our essential *difference* (and by usual implication our superiority) from other creatures lies in our ability to reach beyond our immediate natural concerns to see them by the light of reason. This amounts to suggesting that we are absolutely better than the other animals because we are able to give their interests some consideration: so we won't.

---

10 Augustine, *City of God*, trans. R. W. Dyson (Cambridge: Cambridge University Press, 1998), 485–86 [11.28].

The gaze of the soul is Reason; but since it does not follow that every one who looks, sees, that right and perfect
looking, which is followed by seeing, is called Virtue, for
Virtue is rectified and perfected Reason. But that very
act of looking, even though the eyes be sound, cannot
turn them toward the Light unless three things persist:
Faith—by which the soul believes that, that toward which
the gaze has been directed, is such that to gaze upon it
will cause blessedness: Hope—by which, the eyes being
rightly fixed, the soul expects this vision to follow: and
Love—which is the soul's longing to see and to enjoy it.
Such looking is followed by the vision of God Himself,
who is the goal of the soul's gaze, not because it could
not continue to look, but because there is nothing beyond
this on which it can fix its gaze. This is truly perfected
Reason—Virtue—attaining its proper end, on which the
happy life follows. And this intellectual vision is that
which is in the soul a conjunction of the seer and the
seen: as seeing with the eyes results from the conjunction
of the sense of sight and the sensible object, either of
which being lacking, nothing can be seen.[11]

I leave aside, for now, the factors which Augustine understood to
be essential for the pursuit of Truth. It is enough for the moment
to note the familiar assumption: only human beings have any
acquaintance with, or even any interest in, a world beyond the
world defined and limited by our natural needs (the needs, that is,
that we share with any animal organism). Human beings, if they
are to be reckoned something else than "animals," must have an
eye to the whole truth, the cosmos as a living reality, rather than
the simple local worlds, the *Umwelten*, of all other creatures.[12]

Because they cannot, so we suppose, escape from their *Umwelten*,
non-human animals are not quite "individuals" in the sense we
allow for humans: particular dogs, cats, horses and the like will
only be doing what creatures of that kind do. They are *replaceable*:
even those animal-friendly theorists who have argued for some

11 Augustine, *Soliloquies*, trans. Rose Elizabeth Cleveland (Boston: Little
Brown & Co., 1910), 22 [1.13].
12 After Plotinus, *Ennead*, VI.6 [34].17, 42, as interpreted by Abolqasem Ferwerda, *La Signification des Images et des Métaphores dans la Pensée de Plotin* (Groningen:
J. B. Wolters, 1965), 33: "L'intelligence possède la sphere totale; l'animal lui est
postérieur et ne possède que la sphere de l'animal."

moral consideration of the creatures we affect, often concede the status of "irreplaceable person" only to a very few non-human animals. They are alive, indeed, but not "subjects of a life": they have no biographies. Only a very few, so many of us think, have any conception of their own identity and agency: if one is killed untimely, we need only arrange for another one to be born, and nothing important will have been lost.[13] A common, consciously virtuous, epigram asks that we "should love people, and use things (as the opposite never works)": this unthinkingly ignores all creatures that are neither "things" nor "people."[14] Why does even such a civilized theologian as Nicholas Lash unthinkingly contrast "human beings" and "things," as though these classes exhausted the terrestrial universe, saying that "there is a difference between listening to a waterfall and listening to another person, and in the natural scientist's world there are only waterfalls"?[15] And why might we not begin to wonder whether listening to waterfalls is itself a communication?

As I shall propose in a later chapter, we ought to consider the real possibility that even an "animal friendly" attitude does not go far enough. It is now evident that trees "communicate" with their

---

13   Joan Dunayer, *Speciesism* (Derwood, MD: Ryce Publishing, 2004), has pointed out that both Peter Singer and Tom Regan propose theories that, despite being overtly anti-speciesist, actually give a special status to creatures that share particular human properties, as we suppose (being "subjects of a life" or "self-aware"). Even chickens, though they should not be made to suffer, may, on these terms, be conveniently killed as long as there are *other* (contented) chickens ready to take their place. See also Descola, *Beyond Nature and Culture*, trans. Janet Lloyd (Chicago: University of Chicago Press, 2013), 193: "Singer has moved toward a position that is definitely more anthropocentric and eventually asserts that the life of certain sensitive beings is intrinsically more valuable on account of the fact that they are endowed with faculties that are clearly derived from those that naturalism imputes to humans, such as consciousness of self, a capacity to think and project oneself into the future, and the ability to communicate complex information. This affects only a very small number of animals, chimpanzees among them, which thus become invested with the status of persons by reason of their proximity to humans with regard to their interiority. The logical and strongly contested corollary to this position is that humans who lose such faculties as a result of serious cerebral lesions or malformations may not fully rate as persons and therefore have no automatic right to life."

14   See, for example, https://www.theminimalists.com/people-things/.

15   Nicholas Lash, *The Beginning and the End of "Religion"* (Cambridge: Cambridge University Press, 1996), 85.

neighbors, and even care for them, through the fungal network that binds their roots together.[16] We may, of course, continue to insist that this "communication" is merely a material exchange of chemicals, and that trees are as insentient, as dumb, as rocks. But perhaps the truth is rather that they are not "things" but "beings," children of the same Father, and that we can if we wish acknowledge their real presence.[17] Even waterfalls may have their own identities. "Whatever possesses a soul is a subject, and whatever has a soul is capable of having a point of view."[18]

There is a second shared assumption: that species are natural kinds. That is to say, members of any species have a common nature, distinct from that of any other species. Or rather—as is intimated in the passage from Galiani that I cited earlier—all members of a species share a unique identity, but in varying degrees: all and only human beings are *curious*, but some are more curious than others, and those who are *most* curious are most truly human. Analogously, all dogs, we may suppose, are more or less "canine" ("perfectly gentle to their familiars and acquaintances, and the reverse to strangers"[19]). In the older "Aristotelian" synthesis (which is not to say, in *Aristotle's* thought), there could be nothing "in between" such distinct types, nothing that could be a member of two species, or of none. Whatever isn't human must be entirely non-human, to be assessed and treated in entirely different ways. That this notion has survived the general acceptance of neo-Darwinian evolutionary theory is strange, but perhaps no odder than its being attributed to Aristotle himself. That philosopher, after all, insisted that there were always creatures "in between" any pair of biological groups. "Nature stretches without a break from lifeless objects to animals through things that are animated but not animals, so that there seems to be very little difference between one thing and the next, they are so close together."[20] He even suggested that all other earthly creatures

---

16   See Suzanne Simard, *Finding the Mother Tree: Uncovering the Wisdom and Intelligence of the Forest* (London: Allen Lane, 2021).

17   See Martin Buber, *I and Thou*, trans. Walter Kaufmann (New York: Simon and Schuster, 1996), 58–59.

18   Viveiros de Castro, "Cosmological Deixis and Amerindian Perspectivism," *Journal of the Royal Anthropological Institute* 4, no. 3 (1998): 476 (cited in Descola, *Beyond Nature and Culture*, 139).

19   Plato, *Republic*, 2.375c.

20   Aristotle, *De Partibus Animalium*, 4.681a12–15.

could be considered as descendants of more recognizably *human* creatures[21]—rather as the future inhabitants of Olaf Stapledon's Neptune are all (from superhuman to sea-squirt) descended from a human population (many millions of years removed from our particular human species).[22] Aristotle did not expect that *all* our conspecifics were distinctively rational and responsible, nor that other creatures could not display such properties in their own lives. Aristotle's account—as it must also be the Darwinian account—conceives of "species" only as roughly isolated populations, such that fertile intercourse is almost always possible within that population, and rare outside it. There is relatively little genetic mixing (as we would now call it) between animal species that have had time to grow apart—but they all retain a common inheritance, and may still infect each other. Plants and the wider (larger) prokaryotic kingdoms are even less constrained by species barriers. Every individual organism here in the terrestrial biosphere is related to every other, and there is no need to suppose that there is any particular shared nature common to all members of a "species" or of any larger taxon and wholly distinct from the nature of organisms of another species or larger taxon, though some species (including our own) are, currently, unusually homogenous.

But if species—including the modern human species—are not "natural kinds," we must abandon the easy complaint that it is unduly "anthropomorphic" to describe non-humans in terms derived from our experience of the human. It may sometimes be an error to do so: maybe trees don't really communicate; maybe slime-molds aren't really solving mazes (even if they do in fact discover the fastest route through mazes); maybe termites aren't really building cities (even if our cities are very much like termite mounds); maybe dogs aren't loyal unto death (even if they follow their master's body to the grave). But granted that almost all our own inheritance is shared with all other terrestrial life-forms it would be astounding if we did not have an immense amount in common, and also astounding if we could not immediately recognize the motives and beliefs

---

21 Aristotle, *De Generatione Animalium*, 2.733b1-10; see Stephen R. L. Clark, *Aristotle's Man: Speculations Upon Aristotelian Anthropology* (Oxford: Clarendon Press, 1975), 28-33.
22 Olaf Stapledon, *Last and First Men* (London: Gollancz, 1999); Stapledon, *Last Men in London* (New York: Dover, 2011).

of the larger eukaryotic animals with whom we have shared our lives for many thousands of years. The Wittgensteinian aphorism, that "if a lion could talk, we could not understand it," imagines an absurd disjunction.[23] Plotinus—though he too thought that human beings occupied a special place in the terrestrial economy, in between spirits and other animals[24]—insisted that "animals and plants share in reason (*logos*) and soul and life," and "none of them exist without good purpose," even the most savage.[25] Everything, indeed, "aspires to contemplation [*theoria*], and directs their gaze to this end"[26]—a notion to which I shall return.

There is a third assumption equally widely shared, and one implicit in our very language. Namely, that there are individual organisms, with clear boundaries and an identifiable particular essence. Even if *species* are not natural kinds, we suppose, it must be true that individual organisms are, exactly, identifiable as the very things they are, distinct from every other and able to endure through superficial changes. These are the fundamental entities in which Aristotle (probably) did believe: countable living entities with definite beginnings, boundaries, ends, essences and particular biographies. Unfortunately, if we are—as modernists will usually suppose—*material* entities it is clear at once that there are no such real material boundaries, ends and beginnings. The stuff that currently sustains what is commonly supposed to be my thinking and

---

23   Ludwig Wittgenstein, *Philosophical Investigations*, trans. G. E. M. Anscombe, P. M. S. Hacker, et al., ed. P. M. S. Hacker and Joachim Schulte (Oxford: Blackwell, 2009), 235 [2.327]. We may perhaps imagine a more truly "alien" creature, whose very anatomy would be a mystery: "Suppose that in some convulsion of the planets there fell upon this earth from Mars, a creature of a shape totally unfamiliar, a creature about whose actual structure we were of necessity so dark that we could not tell which was creature and which was clothes. We could see that it had, say, six red tufts on its head, but we should not know whether they were a highly respectable head-covering or simply a head. We should see that the tail ended in three yellow stars, but it would be difficult for us to know whether this was part of a ritual or simply a tail" (Chesterton, "Philosophy of Islands," in *The Venture Annual*, ed. Laurence Housman and W. Somerset Maugham [London: John Baillie's, 1903]). We might even be unsure whether one part is a head or tail. But that is to demonstrate that *lions* are not so strange (and Chesterton of course does not need to suppose that our ignorance would last).

24   Plotinus, *Ennead*, III.2 [47].9, 28–31.

25   Plotinus, *Ennead*, III.2 [47].9, 35–8.

26   Plotinus, *Ennead*, III.8 [30].1, 1–3. I suspect that "enjoyment" is a better translation of *theoria*—but that, for the moment, is another story.

feeling self is continually in flux: this thing here is barely a wave of the sea. We can also add, in greater detail than Aristotle ever could, that this thing here—the one writing these words as well as the one who is reading them—is a colony organism, compounded of unimaginably many cells and dependent, internally as well as externally, on the continued activity of cells and systems that are not even our conspecifics. We are all chimeras, and we all live within the same bacterial and viral sea as our friends and neighbors. If after all we feel and believe ourselves to be distinct selves it cannot be that those selves are simply material or biological. And even if our selves are *immaterial* they may not be utterly *distinct*, nor need they have an essential nature different from any "other." Empedocles declared that he had been "a boy and a girl, a bush and a bird and the fish that leaps from the sea,"[27] and can we rationally insist that he must have been mistaken? Plotinus too is ready to agree that the same soul may animate stars, humans, eagles, ants and trees alike.[28] And every soul is a child of the one Father.[29] The first Australians, we may note, essentially agreed:

> Since souls transcend time and death, and since like creator ancestors their number can't be infinite, there is no reason why a soul which confers one shape might not confer several, no reason why a soul leaving a fire need pass only to another fire, or a soul from one human pass only to another. On the contrary, a soul's ability to move from one chariot to another gives creation order and cohesion. It moves through the particular community of natural and supernatural things created by the same ancestor in the Dreaming. It makes each part dependent on it and each other for their existence. It makes them a congregation.[30]

And one final widespread assumption: that there are "laws" of nature, rationally discoverable and without exception, which

---

27 Robin Waterfield, "Empedocles DK31B117," in *First Philosophers: Presocratics and Sophists* (Oxford: Oxford University Press, 2000), 154.
28 Plotinus, *Ennead*, III.4 [15].2, 15-31. See Gananath Obeyesekere, *Imagining Karma: Ethical Transformation in Amerindian, Buddhist, and Greek Rebirth* (Berkeley: University of California Press, 2002) for a study of tribal, Indian and Greek approaches to the concept of reincarnation.
29 Plotinus, *Ennead*, II.9 [33].15, 33-16.10.
30 Bill Gammage, *The Biggest Estate on Earth: How Aborigines made Australia* (Sydney: Allen & Unwin, 2011), 127. I shall address the social implications of this thought in a later chapter.

somehow "compel" events.[31] What those "laws" may be, we cannot currently tell, nor wholly explain why they are just so. That they exist is to be considered a fundamental requirement of reason: if they didn't, we suppose, anything at all could happen at any time, and rational life would be impossible. "Every professed philosopher is forced to believe, without serious examination, in the existence of a Something that in his opinion is capable of being handled by the reason, for his whole spiritual existence depends on the possibility of such a Something."[32] At the same time, of course, it is just this assumption that we must conscientiously ignore, if we are to retain any notion of personal guilt or duty.

> The persuasion that he is free is the essence of man. One could even define man as "an animal who believes that he is free," and this would be a complete definition. M. [Sissous] de Valmire himself, when he writes that men are not free, why does he say it? So that people will believe it. Therefore, he thinks that other men are free and capable of deciding what they believe. It is absolutely impossible for a man to forget for a single instant, or to stop being persuaded that he is free. This, then, is the first point. Second point: is being persuaded that one is free the same thing as actually being free? I respond: this is not the same thing, but it produces the same moral effects. Man is then free, since he is intimately persuaded of being so, and since that is worth as much as freedom? This is the mechanism of the universe explained as clearly as spring water. If there were a single free being in the universe, there would be no more God, there would be no more ties between beings. The universe would fall apart; and if man were not intimately, essentially, and always convinced that he is free, human morality would not continue as it does. The conviction that one is free is enough to establish a conscience, remorse, justice, rewards and punishments. It is enough for everything, and here is the world explained in two words.[33]

---

3 1   Though Wittgenstein was right to remark that "at the basis of the whole modern view of the world lies the illusion that the so-called laws of nature are the explanations of natural phenomena." Ludwig Wittgenstein, *Tractatus Logic-Philosophicus*, 2nd ed., ed. D. F. Pears and B. F. McGuinness (London: Routledge & Kegan Paul, 1972), 6.371.

3 2   Oswald Spengler, *The Decline of the West*, vol. 1, trans. Charles Francis Atkinson (New York: Alfred Knopf, 1928), 199.

3 3   Galiani, "letter 124: 23 November 1771," in *Lettres*, 300-1.

Practically speaking, we all have to believe two different and seemingly incompatible things, that all things are contained in a single whole, and that we ourselves can somehow transcend that whole.

THE REAL AND WIGGLY WORLD

All these assumptions have historical roots in particular past philosophies—chiefly those associated with the European enlightenment, from the ancient Greek philosophers onwards. We are therefore often blind to other philosophical traditions, and even those same "classical" traditions when they don't agree with us, as well as to our fellow (non-human) creatures, or else unduly patronizing. Only "primitive" peoples, we suppose, don't share our casual anthropocentric, individualist, materialist and "rationalist" outlook. It is therefore a surprise when our merely *scientific* explorations begin to agree with primitives!

> However much it [modern society] has tried, through feats of engineering, to construct a material world that matches its expectations—that is, a world of discrete, well-ordered objects—its aspirations are thwarted by life's refusal to be contained. We might think that objects have outer surfaces, but wherever there are surfaces life depends on the continual exchange of materials across them. If, by "surfacing" the earth or incarcerating bodies, we block that exchange, then nothing can live. In practice, however, such blockages can never be more than partial and provisional. The hard surfacing of the earth, for example, is perhaps the most salient characteristic of what we conventionally call the "built environment." On a paved road or concrete foundation, nothing can grow, unless provisioned from remote sources. Yet even the most resistant of materials cannot forever withstand the effects of erosion and wear and tear. Thus the paved surface—attacked by roots from below and by the action of wind, rain and frost from above—eventually cracks and crumbles, and allows plants to grow through so as to mingle and bind once again with the light, air and moisture of the atmosphere. Wherever we choose to look, the active materials of life are winning out over the dead hand of materiality that would snuff it out.[34]

---

34   Tim Ingold, "Being Alive in a World of Objects," in *Handbook of Contemporary Animism*, ed. Graham Harvey (Durham: Acumen, 2013).

Or as a spokesman for "Californian Zen" put it: "The real wiggly world slips like water through our imaginary nets. However much we divide, count, sort, or classify this wiggling into particular things and events, this is no more than a way of thinking about the world: it is never *actually* divided."[35] And this is also a common theme amongst speculative physicists: so Richard Feynman, first citing an unnamed poet as saying that "the whole universe is in a glass of wine":

> If our small minds, for some convenience, divide this glass of wine, this universe, into parts—physics, biology, geology, astronomy, psychology and so forth—remember that nature does not know it! So let us put it all back together, remembering ultimately what it is for. Let it give us one more final pleasure: drink it, and forget it all![36]

Reality is not put together from a multitude of independently existing things, nor yet from an array of separable aspects. Nothing can be properly appreciated, let alone understood, in isolation. We may come to this understanding via modern science (both physics and biology), from a more attentive reading of the philosophical founders of the Western tradition or else from open-minded consideration of non-Western thought of the sort once characterized as "animistic" or "primitive." It may also be a sudden realization, a "stroke of insight." So Jill Balte Taylor, recovering from a (literal) stroke:

> My entire self-concept shifted as I no longer perceived myself as a single, a solid, an entity with boundaries that separated me from the entities around me. I understood that at the most elementary level, I am a fluid. Of course I am a fluid! Everything around us, about us, among us, within us, and between us is made up of atoms and molecules vibrating in space. Although the ego center of our language center prefers defining our self as individual and

---

35   Alan Watts, *The Book on the Taboo against Knowing Who You Are* (London: Souvenir Press, 2011), 59.
36   Richard Feynman, *Feynman Lectures on Physics*, vol. 1 (New York: Basic Books, 2011), 32 (chap. 3.7), cited in Mary Midgley, *Science and Poetry* (London: Routledge, 2011), 64. How seriously Feynman intended this, I am uncertain. Nor do I know whether he was aware of the Neoplatonic background to the metaphor, on which see Stephen R. L. Clark, *Plotinus: myth, metaphor and philosophical practice* (Chicago: University of Chicago Press, 2016), 91–104.

solid, most of us are aware that we are made up of trillions of cells, gallons of water, and ultimately everything about us exists in a constant and dynamic state of activity.... I was no longer isolated and alone. My soul was as big as the universe and frolicked with glee in a boundless sea.[37]

Taylor's insight or experience, I suggest, may help us to understand even those past philosophers that are popularly supposed to have been devoted to "abstract intellect." Soul (which is to say, experience) is fluid, and we live in constant interchange with our surroundings.

For the soul is many things, and all things, both the things above and the things below down to the limits of all life, and we are each one of us an intelligible universe, making contact with this lower world by the powers of soul below, but with the intelligible world by its powers above.[38]

And how to achieve a connection with the "intelligible world" (which is to say, the reality that lies behind or within experience)? Plotinus identified two intellectual activities: intellect (that is, *Nous*) in its right, ordering and analytical, mind, and also "out of its mind, 'drunk with the nectar'; then it falls in love, simplified into happiness by having its fill, and it is better for it to be drunk with a drunkenness like this than to be more respectably sober."[39] We do not best appreciate or understand the world by separating ourselves from it, nor by dividing it in pieces, however helpful these careful fictions may sometimes be.

FINDING THE RIGHT WAY ONWARD

These realizations, whether engendered by an appreciation of the abstract arguments or by strokes of insight, may themselves be rationalized away. Indeed, it is almost impossible that they not be. Either we ignore the conclusions or else they are swiftly corrupted. Ignoring them entirely is, as Plotinus said, "as if people who slept

---

37 Jill Balte Taylor, *Stroke of Insight* (London: Hodder & Stoughton, 2008), 69. Cf. McGilchrist, *Master and His Emissary*, 207: "Rather than separate entities in a vacuum we might think of individual entities as dense nodes within some infinitely stretchable or distensible viscous substance, some existential *goo*—neither ultimately separable nor ultimately confounded, though neither without identity nor without the sense of ultimate union."
38 Plotinus, *Ennead*, III.4 [15].3, 21–24.
39 Plotinus, *Ennead*, VI.7 [38].35.

through their life thought the things in their dreams were reliable and obvious, but, if someone woke them up, disbelieved in what they saw with their eyes open and went to sleep again."[40] But it is also possible to erect a vastly increased sense of self on the story I have told: apparently I am not contained within the boundaries of my skin, and everything around belongs to me! This is indeed what "drunkenness" more often signifies in the philosophical tradition: "When a man drinks wine he begins to be better pleased with himself, and the more he drinks the more he is filled full of brave hopes, and conceit of his power, and at last the string of his tongue is loosened, and fancying himself wise, he is brimming over with lawlessness, and has no more fear or respect, and is ready to do or say anything."[41] Sentimentally attributing "our own" feelings to the wider world, we guard ourselves against any real discovery: obviously everything else must be as pleased with us as we are ourselves!

But this error (as I shall consider it) arises from our *not* recalling the stroke of insight properly. What is it actually like when the barriers come down? What is it like (on good authority) to experience things "noetically," or "in the spirit"? Consider what Plotinus has to say about the noetic world, the world as truly known. We should not be misled by his referring to that world by the expression "There": it need not be a second world, alongside this one, but rather the one reality truly known, joyfully experienced. "Here below we can know many things by the look in people's eyes when they are silent; but There all their body is clear and pure and each is like an eye, and nothing is hidden or feigned, but before one speaks to another that other has seen and understood."[42] We can know many things by the look in people's eyes—and in the eyes of others:

> If the dog wants something, he wags his tail: impatient of Master's stupidity in not understanding this perfectly distinct and expressive speech, he adds a vocal expression—he barks—and finally an expression of attitude—he mimes or makes signs. Here the man is the obtuse one who has not yet learned to talk. Finally something very remarkable happens. When the dog has exhausted every

---

40 Plotinus, *Ennead*, V.5 [32].1.
41 Plato, *Laws*, 1.649.
42 Plotinus, *Ennead*, IV.3 [27].18, 19–24.

other device to comprehend the various speeches of his master, he suddenly plants himself squarely, and his eye bores into the eye of the human.... Here the dog has become a "judge" of men, looking his opposite straight in the eye and grasping behind the speech, the speaker.[43]

This sudden confrontation—the moment when we recognize Another and, perforce, admit that Other into our own experience—is at the root of Martin Buber's account of the I/Thou relationship, which he did not confine to merely human relations. Nor do we always need to see the Other's literal *eyes*:

> The tree is no impression, no play of my imagination, no aspect of a mood; it confronts me bodily and has to deal with me as I must deal with it—only differently. One should not try to dilute the meaning of the relation: relation is reciprocity. Does the tree then have consciousness, similar to our own? I have no experience of that. But thinking that you have brought this off in your own case, must you again divide the indivisible? What I encounter is neither the soul of a tree nor a dryad, but the tree itself.[44]

Is there a contradiction here, between my earlier deconstruction of the existence of distinct species and individuals and this forceful encounter with a genuine Other? On the contrary: the encounter shows us that our imperial pretensions, our sense of ourselves as masters of a world of objects, are mistaken. Suddenly, we are reminded of the underlying truth: our former perception of things is no more than a dream and a delirium, a distortion even of the sort of *Umwelt* that we had patronizingly ascribed to merely animal experience. The world, in the shape of dog or tree, is suddenly looking back at us, reminding us that we are all travelers together in what Aldo Leopold called "the odyssey of evolution,"[45] and what Platonists have called "the dance of immortal love."[46] Henry Beston: "They are not brethren, they are not underlings; they are other nations, caught with ourselves

43 Spengler, *Decline*, vol. 2, 131.
44 Buber, *I and Thou*, 58–59.
45 Aldo Leopold, *A Sand County Almanac and Sketches Here and There* (New York: Oxford University Press, 1968), 109.
46 Porphyry, *Life*, 23.26, quoting the Delphic comment on Plotinus, requested by his friend and disciple Amelius.

in the net of life and time, fellow prisoners of the splendor and the travail of the earth."[47]

Suddenly we are no longer "in control," no longer an aloof intelligence considering a world entirely outside us. Suddenly we are no longer trapped—any more than the sea itself is by a net.[48] Really to appreciate and experience this is a revelation. To remember it may require a novel narrative.

This meshes well with another of Chesterton's observations.

> Possibly the most pathetic of all the delusions of the modern students of primitive belief is the notion they have about the thing they call anthropomorphism. They believe that primitive men attributed phenomena to a god in human form in order to explain them, because his mind in its sullen limitation could not reach any further than his own clownish existence. The thunder was called the voice of a man, the lightning the eyes of a man, because by this explanation they were made more reasonable and comfortable. The final cure for all this kind of philosophy is to walk down a lane at night. Anyone who does so will discover very quickly that men pictured something semi-human at the back of all things, not because such a thought was natural, but because it was supernatural; not because it made things more comprehensible, but because it made them a hundred times more incomprehensible and mysterious. For a man walking down a lane at night can see the conspicuous fact that as long as nature keeps to her own course, she has no power with us at all. As long as a tree is a tree, it is a top-heavy monster with a hundred arms, a thousand tongues, and only one leg. But so long as a tree is a tree, it does not frighten us at all. It begins to be something alien, to be something strange, only when it looks like ourselves. When a tree really looks like a man our knees knock under us. And when the whole universe looks like a man we fall on our faces.[49]

---

47   Henry Beston, *The Outermost House: A Year of Life on the Great Beach of Cape Cod* (New York: Henry Holt & Co., 1988), 25.

48   See Plotinus, *Ennead*, IV.3 [27].9, 40–42.

49   G. K. Chesterton, *Heretics* (London: Bodley Head, 1905), 63. See also William Blake, "Letter to Thomas Butts (2 October 1800)," in *Complete Works*, ed. Geoffrey Keynes (London: Oxford University Press, 1966), 804–5: "Each grain of sand, every stone on the land, each rock and each hill, each fountain and rill, each herb and each tree, Mountain, hill, earth, and sea, Cloud, meteor, and

"Looking like a man" in this context is perhaps a misleading phrase. Dog, tree and the universe don't have the shape or even the character of *men* (nor even of human beings), nor do they look "like ourselves" (certainly not as we had supposed ourselves to be). The point is that they are *subjects*—but not *our* subjects—as well as objects: alive and constantly communicating.

> The path has a mind of its own but a body shared by hundreds. It is a way through the woods, a way made by the five-toes, the four-toes, the cloven hooves and a few big clodhoppers like mine. This is a path with a memory, a remembrance of passings, and it offers itself to the future for those who recognize a way worth taking. A raven rasps its rapid cries into a strong, south-westerly wind, which rakes through treetops of ash, small-leaved lime, beech and oak. In holly thickets the wind stirs goldcrests and they sing like jingling pockets of change. Old hulks of crashed elm speak of an older wood. When they were alive, a track to take out timber and charcoal cut across the slope. The elms are long fallen and so are the woodsmen whose ghost road leads nowhere. The path only slides down the steep bank to glance along old fragments of the track and then swerves back into the trees, as if deciding it a bit too unsafe to follow the abandoned way. The path touches on the history of the hedge bank too: its mound and ditches perhaps medieval, maybe older, are also under lost trees that have shaken loose of the hedge and risen 15m into the air. And above them a pair of crows play in the updraught, tumbling through the wind, snapping at the strings of their own ways through the sky. Midway, between the canopy and the ground, a hard whirring sound: a hornet, slow in the cool air, finds its hole in the hollow lime trees and closes itself into the darkness there. On the narrow, wandering line below, gouged out of clay by hoof, pad, claw and the occasional boot, I follow—a passing thought.[50]

There is one last possible error. Much of what I have said could be supposed compatible with a Spinozistic or even a modern

---

star, Are men seen afar." Kathleen Raine, *Blake and New Age* (London, Routledge, 2011), 116–18, identifies Swedenborg as the source of Blake's conception.
50   Paul Evans, "Down Memory Lane," *Guardian Weekly* (24 November 2006), 22, cited in Val Plumwood, "Nature in Active Voice," in *Handbook of Contemporary Animism*, ed. Graham Harvey (Durham: Acumen, 2013), 451.

materialist conception of a world that can always be described through law-like regularities. We are indeed all caught in a net, unable to do the least thing different from what must always happen, and inclined to insist, with Galiani as well as with the ancient Stoics, and Spinoza, that even the least difference would leave the cosmos in ruins. But this is where Plotinus—and also the greatest mathematician of the twentieth century, Kurt Gödel—disagreed.

> On this assumption, we are not ourselves, nor is there any act which is our own. We do not reason, but our considered decisions are the reasonings of another. Nor do we act, any more than our feet kick; it is we who kick through parts of ourselves. But, really, each [separate] thing must be a [separate] thing; there must be actions and thoughts that are our own; each one's good and bad actions must come from himself, and we must not attribute the doing of bad actions at least to the All.[51]

Gödel's disagreement was with Einstein and the Spinozistic God. For him God was *personal*, unbound by any finite regulation. "As [he] told Hao Wang, 'Einstein's religion [was] more abstract, like Spinoza and Indian philosophy. Spinoza's god is less than a person; mine is more than a person; because God can play the role of a person.'"[52] "Personhood" is not, in this context, the same as "humanoid," but rather signifies the jolt of recognition to which I have been referring: the reality of something that cannot be contained in any of our useful fictions. Suddenly the Other is real—and we too are jolted awake, and can rejoin the dance.

---

51 Plotinus, *Ennead*, III.1 [3].4, 21-29: Armstrong, *Enneads*, vol. 3, 21. Armstrong errs in saying "separate thing" (for "*hekaston*"): Plotinus does not suppose that anything is strictly *separated* from anything, but only that each element makes a free contribution to the All.

52 David P. Goldman, "God of the Mathematicians: the religious beliefs that guided Kurt Gödel's revolutionary ideas," *First Things* (August–September 2010): 45; after Hao Wang, *A Logical Journey: From Gödel to Philosophy* (Cambridge, Mass: MIT Press, 1996), 152.

2

Freedom, Evil and the Undescended Soul

THE NECESSARY ASSUMPTION

Is there some way to resolve the tension I have described, between the thought that we are free agents and the compelling fear that we cannot be? It seems that we must assume that we are free. If you deny that you have a will, as Augustine observed, you have dropped out of the conversation: "because I do not have to answer your questions unless you want to know that you are asking. Furthermore, if you have no desire to attain wisdom, there should be no discussion with you about such matters. Finally, you can be no friend of mine if you do not wish me well."[1] This argument of course does not establish that we really *do* "have a will," any more than a parallel argument establishes that there really is a world for us to share and talk about.

> For mine own part [said Henry More] I am prone to believe, that there is nothing at all to be so demonstrated. It is possible that *Mathematical evidence* itself, may be but a constant undiscoverable delusion, which our nature is necessarily and perpetually obnoxious to, and that either fatally or fortuitously there has been in the world time out of mind such a Being as we call *Man*, whose essential property is to be then most of all mistaken, when he conceives a thing most evidently true. And why may not this be as well as anything else, if you will have all things fatall or casuall without a God? For there can be no curbe to this wild conceipt, but by the supposing that we ourselves exist from some higher Principle that is absolutely *good* and *wise*, which is all one as to acknowledge *that there is a God.*[2]

---

1   Augustine, *The Teacher, the Free Choice of the Will and Grace and Free Will,* trans. R. P. Russell (Washington: Catholic University of America Press, 1968), 95 [*De Libero Arbitrio* 1.24].
2   Henry More, "An Antidote against Atheism" (1653), Bk. 1, ch. 2: C. A. Patrides, *The Cambridge Platonists* (Cambridge: Cambridge University Press,

There may really be no intelligible world, nor anyone else than my own current sensibility to enjoy it—but even to consider that possibility I shall have to assume that there is, after all, a world and at least the possibility of many colloquists. There would still, after all, be a distinction between the world *as it appears to me* and the one real world. And even in talking to myself I am at least *imagining* that someone or something may talk back. It may be that we are all bit players in a virtual drama engineered by the alien intelligences of the Very Last Days of All, but, on that very assumption, I cannot and we cannot escape the rules of the drama: we have to act and respond on the assumption that we can mean what we say, and that others may do so too. We may occasionally profit by not engaging too much in what seems to happen around us and following Plotinus's advice to "be spectators of murders, and all deaths, and takings and sacking of cities, as if they were on the stages of theatres."[3] But even then we need to be polite! "Whether it's reality or a dream, doing what's right is what matters. If it's reality, then for the sake of reality; if it's a dream, then for the purpose of winning friends for when we awaken."[4] We have to accept responsibility for what we say and do and expect a like responsibility from others. We must assume that our words and action are our own—even when we sometimes wonder how we can ever have said or done what now seems silly or wicked or wildly "out of character" (and may have seemed as silly at the time). And not to do the same for others would, at best, be patronizing.

We may still be puzzled. What is it to *will* something, or to do things *willingly*? On Plotinus's Aristotelian account, "Everything is a voluntary act (*hekousion*) which we do without being forced to and with knowledge, and in our power which we are also competent to do: *eph'emin de, ho kai kurioi praxei.*"[5] This may not be enough to show that we have, strictly, *chosen* what we do: that must depend on our being aware of many possible futures and selecting one as

---

1969), 214. I shall return to More's point later: that those who profess to *disbelieve in God* do not entirely understand what they are saying, and what they are surrendering.

3   Plotinus, *Ennead*, III.2 [47].15, 44f.

4   Calderón de la Barca, *Life's a Dream* (Boulder, CO: University Press of Colorado, 2004), 137–38: Sigismund speaks.

5   Plotinus, *Ennead*, VI.8 [39].1, 33–34; see Aristotle, *Nicomachean Ethics*, 3.1111a22–4.

the right thing to aim at. Only sane and adult humans make such choices (so we suppose), and only they, strictly speaking, *act* (that is, *prattein*): what others do may be *hekousia*, but not "deliberate." Such deliberation may depend on our supposing that each and every "possible" future is one that is "in our power," and that what *seems* possible really is. We may have to suppose this, while still acknowledging that we have no proof that we could ever have done, at that particular place and moment, the things we didn't do. Maybe our futures follow ineluctably from what has happened already, even though we can *imagine* ourselves in some non-actual futures and *imagine* that it "depends on us" which future is really realized. Maybe our will to do one thing rather than an imagined other is no more than our welcoming what is already being done. Maybe our imagining that other things were possible is no more than a memory that, in other circumstances not easily distinguished from the present, they did actually occur. And calling it the "right thing to do" really only means that we want to do it, or find that we already have. It remains unlikely, as above, that we can act without the illusion: even the Stoic philosophers who were readiest to insist that only what is real is possible were eager to offer good advice to all their auditors about what they should do, thereby assuming that what we *should* do and what we *probably will* do may be different, and that there are many *realizable* futures. After the event we may be best advised to understand that what we did had been ordained from the beginning: the wise man regrets and repents nothing—not even those acts and accidents that must, before they happened, have been condemned. Before the event we must assume our "freedom" to do both one thing and the other, even if we suspect that there may be no real choice (since we cannot choose to do the impossible).

Of course, the fact that we have to *assume* that we are free in this strong sense—the freedom of indifference—does not prove that we aren't. The fact that we must *assume* that there is a real world, that there are other creatures than ourselves with whom we can communicate, and that our own assertions, actions and hypotheses are actually ours, does not prove that we are mistaken. We—literally—*cannot* assume that we are wrong on any of these points, and any show of doing so is bound to be hypocritical. But the doubt remains.

WANTING TO BE FREE

Was Plotinus content to hope for a mere "freedom of spontaneity"? We want not to be constrained to act in ways we don't prefer, whether the constraint is by brute force or ignorance. The stream flows *freely* when there is no impediment, even if there is only one path it could take. We are free when we are not prevented from doing what naturally we would. Epictetus said as much:

> Consider now, in the case of the animals, how we employ the concept of freedom. Men shut up tame lions in a cage, and bring them up, and feed them, and some take them around with them. And yet who will call such a lion free? Is it not true that the more softly the lion lives the more slavishly he lives? And what lion, were he to get sense and reason, would care to be one of these lions? Why, yes, and the birds yonder, when they are caught and brought up in cages, what do they suffer in their efforts to escape? And some of them starve to death rather than endure such a life, while even such as live, barely do so, and suffer and pine away, and if ever they find any opening, make their escape. Such is their desire for physical freedom, and a life of independence and freedom from restraint. And what is wrong with you here in your cage? What a question! My nature is to fly where I please, to live in the open air, to sing when I please. You rob me of all this, and then ask, "What is wrong with you?"[6]

So the freedom we mind about, on this account, is being allowed and able to express our natures. Maybe it is obvious what natures birds and lions have, what they do or would do when not constrained or inhibited—though even this is uncertain: when you (my reader) and I consider this, is it clear what *our very own* significant nature is, whether or not we share it with our conspecifics? Do we yet know who and what we are?

Plotinus insisted that we were ourselves real causes, whose acts weren't simply and uncontroversially what the world or the world-soul demands, as the Stoics thought,[7] but "freedom" in this context is simply not being forced into an unnatural or inauthentic

---

6 Epictetus, *Discourses*, vol. 2, trans. W. A. Oldfather (London: Loeb Classical Library, Heinemann, 1925), 250–53 [4.1, 24-28]; cf. Plotinus, *Ennead*, I.4 [46].1, 8–11 on the pleasure that "musical creatures" have in their proper activity (*ergon oikeion*).
7 Plotinus, *Ennead*, III.1 [3].4, 25–29.

form. Acting according to our *deepest* nature is freedom, whether or not that nature arises from causes outside our control (as of course it does). We are free when we do what is right, when we are undeluded, and unfree when we are misled or enchanted. He has doubts about the possibility of the other traditional freedom—of indifference.

> Suppose you say, "I have the power to choose this or that"? But the things that you will choose are included in the universal order, because your part is not a mere casual interlude in the All but you are counted in as just the person you are.[8]

And yet it may well be that our "freedom to choose" depends not merely on a *belief* in "freedom of indifference" but on our really having such a freedom. Aristotle's account of our nature as *human* beings has been widely accepted, and routinely used to emphasize our superior standing: we are the sort of creatures that find themselves required to *choose*. We do what we do for *reasons* and not simply as what "comes naturally." We are required, as above, at least to assume that we are able to do or not to do, and that it is our choice that determines which. Even if the Stoics were right to suppose that the whole history of the world will be repeated forever (as there would otherwise have to be infinitely many souls to give the stories meaning[9]), there is at least some hope that the drama will be played out with subtle differences. Origen dismissed the notion of any exact repetition:

> What is said by these persons is much the same as if one were to assert that if a bushel of corn were poured out on the ground it could happen that the way the grain fell would be identical and utterly indistinguishable the second time [as the first], such that every individual grain would lie, on the second time, close to that grain where it had been thrown before, and scattered in the same order and with the same marks as happened in the first pouring; which, with the innumerable grains in the bushel, is certainly an impossible thing to happen, even

8   Plotinus, *Ennead*, III.3 [48].3, 1–4.
9   See Plotinus, *Ennead*, V.7 [18].1, 12–14; V.7 [18].3, 15–17. See Kenneth Wolfe, "Status of the individual in Plotinus," in *Ancient Models of Mind: Studies in Human and Divine Rationality*, ed. Andrea Nightingale and David Sedley (Cambridge: Cambridge University Press, 2010), 223.

if they were to be poured out incessantly and continually for countless ages.[10]

The life of the cosmos has the form of a *spiral* rather than a circle:[11] perhaps this was what Plotinus had in mind in suggesting that a good actor might get a better part "next time," in another age of the world.[12] We are not to suppose that we are co-creators of the drama, "as if the play was incomplete in itself and [we] filled in what was wanting, and the writers had left blank spaces in the middle."[13] But we are, perhaps, also part of the audience, with some chance of acknowledging the quality of the drama, and maybe modifying it. And yet everything that happens must be supposed to be the best that could, here now.[14] "How can there still be wickedness?"[15]

The obvious issue here—apart from any wish to go on blaming people for what we take to be their errors—is that much of the drama in which we are enrolled strikes us as very wrong, and many of the roles written into it. It is not enough simply to say that dramas need their villains too, that the evil sounds of Tartarus enhance the whole, that "the public executioner, who is a scoundrel, does not make his well-governed city worse."[16]

> So, then, there are good men and wicked men, like the opposed movements of a dancer inspired by one and the same art; and we shall call one part of his performance

---

10   Origen, *On First Principles*, vol. 1, trans. John Behr (Oxford: Oxford University Press, 2017), 167 (2.3.4). What other worlds and ages, subtly or wholly different, might be like, he confesses himself wholly ignorant, adding that "if anyone is able to demonstrate it, [he] would gladly learn."

11   Plotinus, *Ennead*, VI.3 [44].13, 27. See Giannis Stamatellos, *Plotinus and the Presocratics: a philosophical study of pre-Socratic influences in Plotinus' Enneads* (New York: SUNY Press, 2007), 131–32.

12   Plotinus, *Ennead*, III.2 [47].17, 42–53; so also Proclus, *Ten Problems*, 60, 18–22, cited by Carlos Steel, *Proclus, On Providence* (London: Bloomsbury, 2007), 13: "For in our lives the whole period of a tribe is analogous to a drama, fate to the producer of this drama, the souls the persons contributing to the drama: sometimes different souls, sometimes the same souls playing different roles on this fatale scene. Similarly on the theatre the same actors speak sometimes for Teiresias, sometimes for Oedipus."

13   Plotinus, *Ennead*, III.2 [47].18, 7–12.

14   Plotinus, *Ennead*, II.9 [33].4, 26–32; III.2 [47].3, 19.

15   Plotinus, *Ennead*, III.2 [47].16, 1.

16   Plotinus, *Ennead*, III.2 [47].17, 64–67, 86–9. See below for further examination of the apparently necessary evils of civil society.

"good" and another "wicked," and in this way it is a good performance (*kalōs echei*). But, then [so some will say], the wicked are no longer wicked. No, their being wicked is not done away with, only their being like that does not originate with themselves....There is a place for every man, one to fit the good and one to fit the bad.[17]

Alien Intelligences, of a demonic sort, might write us into a drama such as this, purely for their own delight: but we dare not believe *that* story if we are to carry on any sane conversation![18] We need to be willing and able to trust, as More insisted, that "we ourselves exist from some higher Principle that is absolutely *good* and *wise*."

How are we to affirm the essential goodness even of phenomenal existence? An interim answer may be simply that it is impossible for there to be any serious or consistent "blasphemy against the divine": "It is just as if a poet in his plays wrote a part for an actor insulting and depreciating the author of the play!"[19] More formally: either the cosmos is entirely determined by a single divine purpose or there is room, somehow, for other, contingent agencies. If the former, then any attempt to rebuke the Maker is only to do the Maker's bidding; if the latter, then our power to blaspheme is also an explanation for the evils the Maker permits. "Providence ought not to exist in such a way as to make us nothing. If everything was providence and nothing but providence, then providence would not exist; for what would it have to provide for?"[20] Similarly, the very attempt to *denounce* the world for its cruelty and injustice requires that there is some other real and absolutely better possibility.

REAL SELF AND THE WRAP AROUND

Whatever its metaphysical significance our experience is of "choosing" whether to do or not to do, of being led to do what's "beautiful (*kalon*)" or not. This feature of human existence, as I

---

17 Plotinus, *Ennead* III.2 [47].17, 9–14, 22–4.

18 Consider the traumatic effects of the realization, in Cixin Liu, *The Three Body Problem* (London: Head of Zeus, 2015), that all the seemingly consistent results of our scientific experimentation on the structure of matter have been distorted by the self-interested actions of an alien civilization intent on our destruction.

19 Plotinus, *Ennead*, III.2 [47].16, 7–11. See Stephen R. L. Clark, "God, good and evil," *Proceedings of the Aristotelian Society* 77 (1977): 247–64.

20 Plotinus, *Ennead*, III.2 [47].9, 1–3.

remarked before, is what is widely supposed to mark us as "supe-rior" to other animals. Plotinus has a different and perhaps more plausible view: "To be capable of opposites belongs to incapacity to remain with the best."[21] That we always have a choice is a sign of weakness, not of strength! "Feeling the need of reasoning is a lessening of the intellect in respect of its self-sufficiency."[22] The One itself doesn't need, as it were, to make up its mind or choose between a succession of tempting options, any more, according to Maximus the Confessor, than Christ's human will is a *gnomic* will, one dependent on unreliable judgment and careful deliberation![23]

This is not to say that human existence is not, in a way, the better option (and perhaps, as Buddhist and Egyptian thought both suggest, very much the rarer: as if a turtle swimming in the Ocean should chance to put his head up through a yoke floating on the surface[24]). "Men are not the best of living creatures," and should certainly not complain about those other things that are supposed to be inferior, but also they have, in a way, "a part [*moira*: a destiny] which is better than that of other living things."[25] He argues that the Stoic and Aristotelian account of *eudaimonia*, well-being, as "living naturally, without impediment," has the counterintuitive result (but is it so absurd?) that even plants, as well as non-human

---

21   Ibid., VI.8 [39].21, 6.

22   Ibid., IV.3 [27].18, 4–5.

23   See Andrew Louth, *Maximus the Confessor* (Oxford: Oxford University Press, 1996), 61. A similar contrast is drawn in pagan literature: "In *De Mysteriis* I.12 Iamblichus asserts that the divine will of the Good transcends a deliberately chosen life—while we have 'choice', the gods simply will" (Emma C. Clarke, *Iamblichus'* De Mysteriis: *a Manifesto of the Miraculous* [London: Routledge, 2019], 49). Clarke goes on to contrast this with Plotinus's judgement that we (or at least our real selves) are "in full possession of [our] (divine) will," whereas talk of God's "will" is bound to be misleading (Plotinus, *Ennead*, VI.8 [39].13, 47–50).

24   Majjhima Nikaya (129 Balapandita Sutta): see Kalu Rinpoche and M. Montenegro, *Luminous Mind: Fundamentals of Spiritual Practice* (Somerville, Mass: Wisdom Publications, 1997), 198; Naomi Appleton, *Narrating Karma and Rebirth: Buddhist and Jain multi-life stories* (Cambridge: Cambridge University Press, 2014), 33–34. So also, according to Herodotus, the Egyptians reckoned that souls could be born human only once in three thousand years (aka "a very long time"): *Histories* 2.132. Surviving Egyptian texts do not seem to support his claim, but it may have been an actual minority opinion.

25   Plotinus, *Ennead*, III.2 [47].9, 20–35. Armstrong's translation can too easily be read as saying that human beings have a part (namely *nous*) which is better than merely animal soul: this may, with some qualifications, be correct, but is not quite the point that Plotinus is making here.

animals, may be *eudaimones,* whereas the term or the concept should apply only to the human case.[26] We should rather insist that "the cause of living well will not be pleasure [nor survival], but the power of judging that pleasure [or survival] is good,"[27] and thence conclude that it is just this "rational" power which is essentially, not merely instrumentally, a good. The exercise of "reason" is not to be praised because it enables us to choose the greater over the lesser good (who or what could choose otherwise?): there are no better goods for us than its mere exercise, than the enjoyment of its own unchanging being—or rather, its concentration on the Good. Even such bodily necessities as even those who are "well off" want contribute nothing to their real "well-being."[28]

> Why then should [such a man] think that falling from power and the ruin of his city are great matters? If he thought they were great evils, or evils at all, he would deserve to be laughed at for his opinion; there would be no virtue left in him [he wouldn't be *spoudaios* any longer[29]] if he thought wood and stones, and (God help us!) the death of mortals were important, this man who, we say, ought to think about death that it is better than life with the body![30]

Plotinus agrees that even such a perfected human may sometimes experience some "involuntary fear... before he has time to reflect," but then "the wise man [in him] will come and drive it away and quiet the child in him."[31]

---

26   Plotinus, *Ennead,* I.4 [46].1. As an anti-Stoic argument this has some force, but we may perhaps suspect that other creatures can indeed "live well," and even "have a good *daimon*," in their own distinctive ways. How else, indeed, might their souls progress, or return again?

27   Plotinus, *Ennead,* I.4 [46].2, 21–23.

28   Plotinus, *Ennead,* I.4 [46].7, 2–4.

29   Armstrong (*Enneads,* vol. 1, 191) is too quick to speak of "virtue" here: one who is truly *spoudaios* has progressed beyond what we ordinarily call virtue: see Aristotle, *Nicomachean Ethics,* 7.1145a15–30.

30   Plotinus, *Ennead,* I.4 [46].7, 21–27. Augustine perhaps found solace in the thought, according to his biographer: Possidius, *Vita Augustini,* 28.11 (Patrologia Latina 32.177): http://www.earlychurchtexts.com/public/possidius_augustine_last_days.htm. But for a more nuanced comparison, see James J. O'Donnell, "The Next Life of Augustine," in *The Limits of Ancient Christianity: Essays on Late Antique Thought and Culture in Honor of R. A. Markus,* ed. William E. Klingshin and Mark Vessey (Ann Arbor: University of Michigan Press, 1999).

31   Plotinus, *Ennead,* I.4 [46].15, 17–21.

A man of this sort will not be unfriendly or unsympathetic; he will be like this to himself and in dealing with his own affairs: but he will render to his friends all that he renders to himself, and so will be the best of friends as well as remaining intelligent [*meta to noun ekhein*].[32]

But that last phrase "as well as remaining intelligent," in Armstrong's translation, is deeply misleading. Having *Nous* is not "being intelligent" in our usual sense—being "clever," nor even being "sensible." It is rather to be hanging on to what might be less misleadingly called "the Spirit," the Divine, the god who is in each one of us: *Nous* is King, "but we too are kings (*basileuomen*), when we are in accord with it; we can be in accord with it in two ways, either by having something like its writing written in us like laws, or by being as if filled with it and able to see it and be aware of it as present."[33] The best that most of us can even begin to imagine is simply to know the rules, and be more or less bound by them—but that is not what Plotinus would call "well-being." We can only rightly be "kings," laws to ourselves, "autonomous," when we embody the Law, and not when we make it up.[34]

Spengler, I remark in passing, spoke of the "inner mythology" that he identified among the Greeks:

---

32 Plotinus, *Ennead*, I.4 [46].17, 22–25.

33 Plotinus, *Ennead*, V.3 [49].4.1–4. Islamic Philosophers agreed that "reason" was supreme ("make reason the Caliph of your soul," say the Brethren of Purity: Yves Marquet, *La Philosophie des Ihwan al-Safa* [Algiers: Études et documents, 1973], 126–7) and some at least supposed that we could reason our way to Koranic truths, without the trouble of revelation. Others didn't—and perhaps "reason" anyway means more than simple reasoning: "The idea that we know being through inspired intuition was developed by Ibn Sina and others into mystical theology, the 'Eastern (*ishraqi*) philosophy' or 'philosophy of light.' This trend led away from empirical knowledge into mysticism": Antony Black, *The History of Islamic Political Thought: From the Prophet to the Present* (Edinburgh: Edinburgh University Press, 2011), 63.

34 Chappell points out that when Antigone is called *autonomos*, this is an (inaccurate) insult, not a compliment (Sophie-Grace Chappell, "Autonomy in Sophocles' *Antigone*," in *The Routledge Handbook of the Philosophy of Autonomy*, ed. Ben Colburn [London: Routledge, forthcoming]): "The point of the word as [the Chorus of elderly Thebans] use it is not that her attempt to 'make a law for herself' makes her a good (proto-)Kantian agent. Instead, they use the word to raise against Antigone the charge that she is acting irrationally and arbitrarily." Antigone's response is not to claim any supposedly Kantian right or duty to make her own laws for herself, but rather that she is obeying an older law, the gods', and not Creon's, command.

> For every man, whatever the Culture to which he belongs, the elements of the soul are the deities of an *inner* mythology. What Zeus was for the outer Olympus, *Nous* was for the inner world that every Greek was entirely conscious of possessing—the throned lord of the other soul-elements.[35]

Whether this was actually typical of the "Classical Culture" he identified as the principal life-form of the time is less certain: it may rather be a "Magian" assumption—but I shall defer its proper examination.[36]

Our real choice here-now is not between this and that immediate possibility, but between the life of the compound entity, our immediate (confused and transient) empirical self, and the god, our original being. Of each incarnate soul it can be said that "he himself is the god who comes Thence, and his own real nature, if he becomes what he was when he came, is There. When he came here he took up his dwelling with someone else, whom he will make like himself to the best of the powers of his real nature, so that if possible this someone else will be free from disturbance or will do nothing of which his master does not approve."[37]

Our original being has come into this world of change and chance, wishing to have things all its own way, "being bored with being together,"[38] and found itself "wrapped round" by another sort of soul. In consenting to that "other soul's affections," we lose our freedom.[39] "When the soul is altered by the external causes, and so does something and drives on in a sort of blind rush (*tuphlei tei phorai*), neither its action nor its disposition is to be called free.... When in its impulse it has as director its own pure and

---

35 Spengler, *Decline*, vol. 1, 312.
36 See Stephen Clark, "Plotinian Dualisms and the 'Greek' Ideas of Self," *Journal of Chinese Philosophy* 36 (2009): 554–67.
37 Plotinus, *Ennead*, I.2 [19].6, 8–12.
38 Plotinus, *Ennead*, IV.8 [6].4, 11–12.
39 So also Bulgakov in strongly Platonic mode: "Man is the son of eternity plunged into the stream of time, the son of freedom held captive by necessity and dependent upon the laws of nature, of the material, physical world. He creates history only in so far as he is free, and he is free in so far as he serves an ideal and rises above necessity, denying its power to determine him. But he destroys his freedom in so far as he sinks into the world of things and submits to their ruling power, which he is called upon to combat": Sergius Bulgakov, "Two Cities [1911]," in *A Bulgakov Anthology*, ed. James Pain and Nicolas Zernov (London: SPCK, 1976), 63.

untroubled reason (*logon*), then this impulse alone is said to be in our own power and free."[40] But all too easily "the soul becomes ugly by mixture and dilution and inclination towards the body and matter."[41] Falling in love, whether with some bodily beauty or even more abstract objects such as City or Nation or Grand Cause, is understood as our "consent" to that "other soul" that wraps us round[42]—a consent that we will mostly, but mistakenly, consider "rational." Our true freedom lies in being roused from sleep, in remembering who and what we are—which we don't know at the moment.[43] What counts as "reason" or "a reason" for the darkened soul is not what Plotinus means by a pure and untroubled Logos.

There is a strange coincidence and divergence between pagan and Christian (or Abrahamic) thought here. For Plotinus and other pagans,[44] the story was that our ascent to heaven would be a return from exile: we ourselves were gods before our fall. Christians rather supposed that we would only be gods "by adoption," having no existence at all before our corporeal births—identifying ourselves directly with that "composite" being that has wound itself around what Plotinus reckoned the god in us. "I live; yet not I, but Christ liveth in me," said Paul, "and the life which I now live in the flesh I live by the faith of the Son of God, who loved me, and gave himself for me."[45] The Spirit of Christ here takes

---

40 Plotinus, *Ennead*, III.1 [3].9; cf. VI.8 [39].15, 23–25: "When we ascend to this and become this alone and let the rest go, what can we say of it except that we are more than free and more than independent?"

41 Plotinus, *Ennead*, I.6 [1].5.

42 Plotinus, *Ennead*, IV.4 [28].43.

43 Lloyd P. Gerson, "Metaphor as an Ontological Concept: Plotinus on the Philosophical Use of Language," in *Logos et langage chez Plotin et avant Plotin*, ed. Michael Fattal (Paris: L'Harmattan, 2003), 269: "Whereas nature contemplates by operating according to an image of *Nous*, only a person can recognize that he himself is an image and that he is thinking with the images of *Nous*. The recognition by the perceptible Socrates that he is not the real Socrates, a recognition that must of course occur in a language that is ineluctably metaphorical, is more than mere assent to a proposition about Socrates."

44 Consider also the tradition of Tibetan Theurgy: "Not only must the practitioner visualize the deity as vividly as possible, but he must also, in any ritual of evocation (that is, whenever he generates himself as the deity), exchange for his own ordinary ego the ego of the deity, which is the subjective correlate of the exchange of ordinary appearances for the special appearance of the deity and his retinue of mandalas": Stephen Beyer, *The Cult of Tara: Magic and Ritual in Tibet* (Berkeley, CA: University of California Press, 1973), 76–77.

45 Paul, Galatians, 2:20.

the place of the pagan *daimon*—which Xenocrates long before had named as the proper source of being *eudaimon*.[46]

As long as we identify ourselves with the composite bodily being, we are carried along by "the bitter wave of this blood-drinking life."[47] Only when we are wholly freed from this can we be free—and we shall then have no need to wonder what best to do. The choice we made, perhaps, before we came to be "down here" was our deviation from the proper course of things, the choice to be enslaved, or better the *failure* to maintain our freedom. In this situation, here and now, "we are not substance in the strict and proper sense or absolute substance; and for this reason we are not masters of our own substance (*oukoun kurios ousia oud'autoousia. Dio oude kurioi tes hauton ousias*)."[48] From which it would seem to follow that we cannot now choose to wake, to return, to be what once we were (and maybe are eternally).

Or rather we could not choose were it not that there is still some part of us, of each of us, that has never consented to sin—in Dame Julian's phrase:[49] we are not wholly descended,[50] nor yet wholly corrupt—and so entirely dependent on outside assistance of the sort that later Platonists sought to invoke by ritual.

> The thesis of the partly undescended soul, typically Plotinian, is not a simple testimony of Plotinus's personal abilities to ascend on his own to the First Principle—as it has long been thought to be, for want of a better suggestion—but the reformulation of a specific doctrine, that of the Gnostic/Hermetic (sic). The soul of the Gnostic elect—the "pneumatic" soul, to be more precise—remained consubstantial to the divine Pleroma, never losing its substantial link with it, its salvation being thus guaranteed. The soul, not only akin (sic) to the divine, as Plato taught before, but in fact undescended and consubstantial to it (cf. 2 [IV 7], 10, 19), as Plotinus conceives it, grants therefore to every man what the Gnostics denied to all but a few, an uninterrupted and indissoluble link with the highest realities. The audacity of this approach, recognized by Plotinus (cf. 6 [IV 8], 8, 1–3),

---

46 Xenocrates: Aristotle, *Topics*, 112a37f; see also Aristotle, *Eudemian Ethics*, 1247a27f; Plato, *Timaeus*, 90.

47 Porphyry, *Life*, 22.33 (the Delphic oracle's reported words).

48 Plotinus, *Ennead*, VI.8 [39].12, 8.

49 Julian of Norwich, *Revelations of Divine Love*, trans. Elizabeth Spearing (London: Penguin, 1998), 93 (Long Text, ch. 37).

50 Plotinus, *Ennead*, IV.2 [4].1, 12–17.

consists in challenging, not Platonic adversaries, which in fact cannot be found, but Platonic Gnostics, "Sethians" who attend his School and who claim for themselves only the power to reach the Intelligible (cf. 33 [II 9], 9, 79), whereas, in the opinion of the Neoplatonic philosopher, "every soul is a child of That Father" (33 [II 9], 16, 9).[51]

Without that lifeline, that eternal link, how should we ever return, whether from the human or from the other forms of life to which we may be drawn? "The unity, individuality and Presence of 'every being belonging to the world of light,' depends upon the connection with the Angel, the archetype in Heaven."[52]

Is there still a problem? Rist is especially doubtful how "the soul in the beast" could return to being human, let alone trans-human.[53] The difficulty is less pressing than he supposed: beasts, after all, may have less trouble keeping to their roles, and to the rules.

> I swam in the seas; I flew in the skies; a gazelle, I took my ease in waterless deserts. Because of the light of consciousness, I reached the animal [stage]....After obeying the rules, I reached the human stage.[54]

There may sometimes be a suggestion (patently anthropocentric) that animals that submit to human use may earn a better incarnation! So in a mass slaughter of animals in 1979 the Bali Brahmins "explained that these animals were sacrificing their lives and that in return they were going to be reborn as humans."[55] Less anthropocentrically, both Jain and Buddhist tradition allow

---

51 Jean-Marc Narbonne, Abstract to "L'énigme de la non-descente partielle de l'âme chez Plotin: la piste gnostique/hermétique de l'ὁμοούσιος," *Laval Théologique et Philosophique* 64 (2008): 691: See also Narbonne, *Plotinus in Dialogue with the Gnostics. Studies in Platonism, Neoplatonism, and the Platonic Tradition* (Leiden/Boston: Brill, 2011). Narbonne follows a different convention for referring to distinct treatises: "33 [II.9]" would more usually be identified as "II.9 [33]."

52 Tom Cheetham, *World Turned Inside Out: Henry Corbin and Islamic Mysticism* (New Orleans: Spring Journal Inc., 2015), 90, after Henry Corbin, *Spiritual Body and Celestial Earth: From Mazdaean Iran to Shi'ite Iran*, trans. Nancy Pearson (Princeton: Princeton University Press, 1977), 9–10.

53 John M. Rist, "Integration and the Undescended Soul in Plotinus," *American Journal of Philology* 88, no. 4 (1967): 410–22, 414.

54 Rïza Tevfik Bölükbaşı, quoted in Thierry Zarcone, "Stone People, Tree People and Animal People," *Diogenes* 207 (2005): 40, and Thierry Zarcone, *Mystiques, Philosophes et Franc-Maçons en islam* (Paris: Jean Maisonneuve: Paris, 1993), 480.

55 Obeyesekere, *Imagining Karma*, 343, citing a personal communication from Hildred Geertz (ibid., 412).

that the bad effects which have resulted in an animal birth may simply be exhausted after a while, and the soul revert to some more human incarnation. But they also both suggest that beasts may have some moment of memory or illumination which will result in a better birth: a frog, for example, suddenly moved by overhearing the Buddha's teaching!⁵⁶ Rist might rather have been puzzled how the soul here-now in a *human* form could ever, of her own will and power, wake. We don't clearly know even what rules to keep. The contrary problem, that having an undescended soul we ought all already to be happy and righteous,⁵⁷ is correspondingly of little strength. Most of us don't at the moment have direct and unimpeded access to our real, immortal selves—any more than our ordinarily dreaming selves have access to the present bodily life we ordinarily take to be reality.

> If wisdom essentially consists in a substance, or rather in *the* substance, and this substance does not cease to exist in someone who is asleep or what is called unconscious; if the real activity of the substance goes on in him, and this activity is unsleeping; then the good man, in that he is a good man, will be active even then. It will not be the whole of him that is unaware of this activity but only a part of him.⁵⁸

The freedom that matters lies in our willingness to participate in the dance of life. To perform that dance we need to forget ourselves—and only so shall we *regain* our selves. What we now consciously intend is likely to be what the "other self" wrapped round us has seduced us into preferring. To wake we need Athena, as it were, to tug us round,⁵⁹ and so restore our forgotten freedom. Which is obviously a problem:

> Tell me, Socrates, are we to take you as serious just now, or joking? For if you are serious and what you say is really true, must not the life of us human beings have

---

56   See Appleton, *Narrating Karma*, 25–32.

57   Proclus, *Commentary on Plato's Timaeus*, ed. H. Tarrant ([Cambridge: Cambridge University Press, 2007], [III.334, 9ff]. Diehl = Fr. 87 Dillon), cited by J. M. Dillon in "Iamblichus' Doctrine of the Soul Revisited," in *Literary, Philosophical, and Religious Studies in the Platonic Tradition*, ed. John F. Finamore and John Phillips (Sankt Augustin: Akademia, 2013).

58   Plotinus, *Ennead*, I.4 [46].9, 18–25.

59   Plotinus, *Ennead*, VI.5 [23].7, 9f; cf. Porphyry, *Life*, 23.

been turned upside down, and must we not be doing quite the opposite, it seems, of what we ought to do?[60]

Well, yes.

HOW WE DISPOSED OF SPIRITS AND OTHER SPOOKY THINGS

Amongst the texts that Plotinus assigned his students were ones attributed to the Persian sage or prophet Zoroaster, which Porphyry takes care to tell us he himself had proved were later, spurious collections.[61] What exactly they said is uncertain, though we may assume that, like other "Gnostic" scriptures, they most likely blamed the evils of this world on a rival creator god. It may be, on the other hand, that they were more concerned with true religion of the sort advanced in another, ninth-century, compilation of "Zoroastrian" or Mazdean thought, now known to us as the Denkard. According to that incomplete record,

> the reason for mankind becoming doers of work of a superior kind is religion; and it is owing to it only that there is a living in prosperity through the Creator. It is always necessary to send it (religion) from time to time to keep men back from being mixed up with sin and to regenerate them. Gayomard, who was the origin of mankind and the first king of the world, was the first to accept the religion from the Creator. And Soshyant, the last bringer of religion for mankind from God and the embellisher of the world through religious deeds—he, who will make mankind walk in purity, is the chief and lord of the last men; he, in accordance with the will and desire of the Creator, will be the bringer of His religion at the time of the End, and will be the giver of perfect beauty to the work of rendering the world pure, free from harm and fit for paradise, which work was (first commenced) through Gayomard.[62]

The Zoroastrian story, recounting the one-off millennial war between the Truth and the Lie, would not have been exactly

---

60 Plato, *Gorgias*, 481c; see R. G. Edmonds, "The Children of Earth and Starry Heaven: The Meaning and Function of the Formula in the 'Orphic' Gold Tablets," in *Orfeo y el orfismo: nuevas perspectivas*, ed. Alberto Bernabé, et al. (Alicante: Biblioteca Virtual Miguel de Cervantes, 2010), 118.

61 Porphyry, *Life*, 16.6, 16.15–19.

62 Sanjana, *Denkard*, vol. 1, 29 [3.35]: http://www.avesta.org/denkard/dk3s1.htm#chap35 (accessed 15th April 2020).

Plotinus's,[63] but it is possible that Porphyry was right to suppose that he had intended to learn more of Persian thought when he joined Gordian's army,[64] and continued his interest.

The notion that he clearly did share with them was that "wise men of old," Minos[65] or the Egyptian sages,[66] laid down rules for common humanity, from their personal knowledge of the divine. Sometimes those rules could be conveyed as aphorisms, but they might also be insinuated through art and imagination. "The wise men of old . . . made temples and statues in the wish that the gods should be present to them":[67] the temples and statues that they made, as I remarked in an earlier volume,[68] were richly imagined ones, whether they were entirely "within their minds" or placed out in the world for all to see. The things they made "came alive" for them and other people: that is, their audience believed in them, without any need of "magical" or "mechanical" aid to make the statues move. This is also the explanation for the vivid brutality of the myths handed down about the relations of Ouranos, Kronos, Zeus[69] and the rest: anyone can remember them, and some few, like Euthyphro,[70] will begin to intuit their inner meaning, and even work out and prove the real truth that they convey.

---

63   Though there are traces of this duality in Plato's *Laws* (10.896e) and *Epinomis,* and there were some prepared to suggest that Plato himself was Zoroaster Redivivus. See A. J. Festugière, "Platon et l'Orient," *Revue de Philologie, de Littérature et d'Histoire Anciennes* 21 (1947): 6, 12; see Plutarch, *Isis and Osiris,* 48 (*Moralia,* vol. 5, trans. Frank Cole Babbitt [Cambridge, MA: Loeb Classical Library, Harvard University Press, 1936], 118-19), and *On the Generation of the Soul in the Timaeus,* 6-7 (Plutarch, *Moralia,* vol. 10, trans. Harold North Fowler [Cambridge, MA: Loeb Classical Library, Harvard University Press, 1936], 1014d-1015f).

64   Porphyry, *Life,* 3.13-19. See also J. M. Dillon, "Plutarch, Plotinus and the Zoroastrian Concept of the *Fravashi,*" in *Passionate Mind: Essays in Honor of John M. Rist,* ed. Barry David (Sankt Augustin: Academia Verlag, 2019). Attention has usually been given instead to a supposed interest in *Indian* thought, but Plotinus's own writings offer no clear evidence of this. That was more certainly an interest of Porphyry's.

65   Plotinus, *Ennead,* VI.9 [9].7, 23-6, after Plato, *Minos,* 319a, Plato, *Laws,* 1.624.

66   Plotinus, *Ennead,* V.8 [31].5-6.

67   Plotinus, *Ennead,* IV.3 [27].11.

68   Clark, *Plotinus: myth, metaphor and philosophical practice,* 125-26, 198.

69   Plotinus, *Ennead,* V.1. [10].4, 8-10; V.1 [10].7, 33f. See Pierre Hadot, "Ouranos, Kronos and Zeus in Plotinus's Treatise against the Gnostics," in *Neoplatonism and Early Christian Thought: Essays in Honor of A. H. Armstrong,* ed. H. J. Blumenthal and R. A. Markus (London: Variorum, 1981).

70   Plato, *Euthyphro,* 5e-6a; Plato, *Cratylus,* 396b.

The relationship [al-Farabi] postulated was rather like that between professional and popular science today. It is the same truth that they postulate, but professional science rests on mathematical demonstration, whereas popularizers resort to analogies, similes, and images drawn from the reader's everyday experience; the reader of popular science cannot actually check the arguments, but he can be swayed by the author's powers of persuasion.[71]

This is a harsher judgment on popular mythology than Neo-Platonists required, and neglects the real power of such images for the scientists themselves. Even philosophers may still be moved by the stories. Plotinus strongly objects to those "who have the insolence to pull to pieces what godlike men of antiquity have said nobly and in accordance with the truth."[72] Maybe he took to heart the Athenian Stranger's praise of Egyptian conservatism:

It appears that long ago they determined on the rule of which we are now speaking, that the youth of a State should practice in their rehearsals postures and tunes that are good: these they prescribed in detail and posted up in the temples, and outside this official list it was, and still is, forbidden to painters and all other producers of postures and representations to introduce any innovation or invention, whether in such productions or in any other branch of music, over and above the traditional forms. And if you look there, you will find that the things depicted or graven there 10,000 years ago (not loosely but literally 10,000) are no whit better or worse than the productions of today, but wrought with the same art.[73]

But perhaps he might allow that we might occasionally, unlikely as it may seem, improve upon tradition, or at least improve upon the flawed and partial memories of an earlier enlightenment. The aphorisms and stories may have been more appropriate to

---

71   Patricia Crone, *Medieval Islamic Political Thought* (Edinburgh: Edinburgh University Press, 2013), 173.

72   Plotinus, *Ennead*, II.9 [33].10, 13-14. See also Plato, *Phaedrus* 229e-230a, where Socrates dismisses attempts to rationalize the myths in naturalistic ways, in favor of accepting them as they are, and investigating his own self and nature.

73   Plato, *Laws*, 2.656de. This is not an entirely accurate account of Egyptian art and culture, but only of what *some* non-Egyptians took to be Egypt's central conservative theme: see Gay Robins, *Art of Ancient Egypt* (London: British Museum Press, 2008) for a brief survey.

an earlier age, have been distorted over time, or been radically misread by contemporary critics. But our initial assumption had probably better be that there are no *new* truths, no theory without any precedent, though what those precedents truly imply may still be a real discovery.

> Your laws being wisely framed, one of the best of your laws will be that which enjoins that none of the youth shall inquire which laws are wrong and which right, but all shall declare in unison, with one mouth and one voice, that all are rightly established by divine enactment, and shall turn a deaf ear to anyone who says otherwise; and further, that if any old man has any stricture to pass on any of your laws, he must not utter such views in the presence of any young man, but before a magistrate or one of his own age.[74]

We may nonetheless, from a later standpoint, have some doubts about whether the laws *were* rightly framed. We may be the readier to doubt because we inherit a notion that earlier times must always have been inferior, less "evolved," and less well-informed. In the standard historical perspective of Plotinus's day and earlier days, by contrast, civilization had long ago achieved a sounder knowledge of the cosmos, since preserved in popular stories which were remembered for other reasons than their cosmological truth. They are "the remnants of philosophy that perished in the great disasters that have befallen mankind, and were recorded for their brevity and wit."[75]

The Mediterranean peoples, and many others, were conscious that they lived in the aftermath of catastrophe, and that they had inherited ways of thought worn smooth: they lived, as we now often imagine our descendants yet may live, after an apocalypse, without any sense that they could now anticipate or outguess the powers-that-be. The world that Plotinus knew was full of spirits, *daimones*, gods and magical connections, though he did not trouble to emphasize their presence. He mocked suggestions that *daimones* might be responsible for physical illness and be exorcised with a word,[76] and generally refers to them simply as forms of life lying

---

74   Plato, *Laws*, 1.634de.
75   Aristotle, *On Philosophy*, fr. 8 Rose: W. D. Ross, ed., *Select Fragments*, vol. 12 of *Works of Aristotle* (London: Oxford University Press, 1952), 77 [fr. 10].
76   Plotinus, *Ennead*, II.9 [33].14.

between gods and men, parts of "the rich variety of the intelligible world."[77] On the other hand, Plato himself insisted that local gods—and *daimones*—deserved respect. In the initial assignment of land to the intended citizens of his imagined Magnesia, "the man who receives the portion should still regard it as common property of the whole State, and should tend the land, which is his fatherland, more diligently than a mother tends her children, inasmuch as it, being a goddess, is mistress over its mortal population, and should observe the same attitude also towards the local gods and *daimones*."[78] Just such instructions are sometimes now remembered as the elements of an environmentally respectful ethic, sadly destroyed by Christian refusal to honor the local gods.[79]

Is it right simply to ignore this feature of late (and early) antiquity and attend only to such arguments and claims as might be made by a conscientious modern rationalist? Or should we rather seek to learn what life was like for him, and might be like even now for those who can pay attention? As I remarked in an earlier work, after Chesterton: "It is the main purpose of historical or comparative philosophy to show that humanity can be great and even glorious under conditions, and with beliefs, quite different from our own;"[80] and perhaps also to show that our true beliefs are not in practice very different.

---

77   Plotinus, *Ennead*, III.2 [47].11, 7–9. Notoriously, but inexplicably, he accepted an Egyptian priest's offer to show him his "companion spirit" and found that it was instead a god (Porphyry, *Life*, 10.15–31). Armstrong's gloss that this god could only, on Plotinus's terms, be the One itself (Armstrong, *Enneads*, vol. 1, 35, after *Ennead*, III.4 [15].6), seems absurd: the One cannot be made manifest like that. See also M. David Litwa, *Posthuman Transformation in Ancient Mediterranean Thought: Becoming Angels and Demons* (Cambridge: Cambridge University Press, 2021), 127. What was manifested (or supposed to have been manifested) was more probably a star—though Ammianus Marcellinus distinguished the star-gods from the (superior?) guardian *daimones* that, he said, inspired Pythagoras, Socrates, Numa Pompilius, the elder Scipio (and "as some believe," Marius and Octavian), Hermes Trismegistus, Apollonius of Tyana and Plotinus (*Res Gestae* 21.14, 5; see Garth Fowden, *The Egyptian Hermes: a historical approach to the late pagan mind* [Cambridge: Cambridge University Press, 1986], 196).
78   Plato *Laws* 5.740ab.
79   This is not an entirely accurate diagnosis of the problem: respecting the local gods did not necessarily imply any great concern for the non-human life of the country, and neither did *disrespecting* them explain or excuse the damage we have done it.
80   Clark, *Plotinus: myth, metaphor and philosophical practice*, 11, after G. K. Chesterton, *Fancies versus Fads* (London: Methuen, 1923), 176.

Consider a folk-doctrine rather closer to our own time and place. Everyone—or almost everyone—agrees that there are no such things as fairies nowadays, and probably never were. They seem to belong to the class of mildly amusing, spooky things mentioned in urban fantasies for fun and in anti-religious tracts to suggest that believing in God is just as silly. To wonder what fairies are, and what it would mean to "believe in them," are questions lost in time—relevant if we wish to understand the poet W. B. Yeats, perhaps,[81] but not to a "modern" sensibility. After years of such skepticism, though, it is perhaps time to entertain another view: that banishing the little people from our lives was only a prelude to dispensing with the notions of God and the soul of man. If we *cannot* believe in fairies (which is to say, in *daimones*), we cannot properly believe in anything (as I shall seek to show below).

Of course, our fictions and even our serious thinking about the terrestrial past or the astronomical present are full of things *like* fairies. Once upon a time there were many almost-human species whom our ancestors encountered with mingled fear and wonder.[82] Nowadays we call them Neanderthals, Denisovans, *Homo floresiensis* and the like. Our immediate ancestors perhaps remembered them instead as elves, dwarves, giants, goblins and even (maybe) mermen. According to folk memory, particularly in Europe, dwarves were cunning artificers, while elves liked dance and revelry. Of course, we may be wrong to think that we truly *remembered* those long-lost almost-humans; perhaps instead they were only speculative imaginings to explain old bones and arrowheads, fossils and mysterious cave-paintings—just as our own stories about Neanderthals are also, mostly, fictions. It is also very likely that there are species out there beyond the sun as sapient as ourselves. What we imagine about them shows much more about ourselves than about biological possibility. How probable is it that we would recognize intelligence in some

---

81 See W. B. Yeats, *Fairy and Folk Tales of the Irish Peasantry* (London: Walter Scott Publishing, 1890); F. Kinahan, "Armchair Folklore: Yeats and the Textual Sources of 'Fairy and Folk Tales of the Irish Peasantry,'" in *Proceedings of the Royal Irish Academy. Section C: Archaeology, Celtic Studies, History, Linguistics, Literature* 83C (1983): 255–67.

82 "The result probably would have struck a modern observer as something more akin to a world inhabited by hobbits, giants and elves than anything we have direct experience of today, or in the more recent past" (David Graeber and David Wengrow, *The Dawn of Everything: a new history of humanity* [London: Allen Lane, 2021], 81).

utterly alien form when it takes so much effort even to acknowledge that wolves or octopus or bees have their own lives and thoughts?

Of some things at least we can be confident: the other human species are no more, and there are probably no galactic visitors here either. For now, there are only us, and the stories we tell are always of creatures who have long since gone away. Maybe they left England at the Reformation, as one of Rudyard Kipling's stories suggests?[83] But the same notion is to be found many centuries earlier, in Chaucer or even in Homer. Long ago, perhaps, there were gods as well as fairies walking secretively among us. Nowadays their very essence is to have always *gone away*, to have hidden themselves in the hills, or in an alongside universe, a Fairyland or an imagined Afterlife. Once there was open commerce between the worlds; now the passages are closed. Fairies obey other rules, and hint that the world is stranger than we think. Even the story of their having gone away is more significant than the simple explanation that there aren't any fairies nowadays, whether they tired of our company, or are straightforwardly deceased. Their very essence is that they aren't here and now—and so must be Somewhere Else.

Unravelling the significance of the stories is easier if we distinguish the four layers of interpretation identified in medieval Biblical hermeneutics: literal, moral, analogical and anagogical. *Lettera gesta docet, quid credas allegoria, moralis quid agas, quo tendas anagogia.*[84] On the literal account, the stories simply represent our own and our ancestors' best guesses about the other species with whom we shared the world (or may share the cosmos). They may even represent other, unseen inhabitants of our own world, as "natural" as ourselves, creatures of the air.[85] The moral reading rather suggests what other axioms and attitudes might be possible to us, or to creatures only a little different from us: how much is our enjoyment of the young,

---

83   Rudyard Kipling, "Dymchurch Flit," in *Puck of Pook's Hill* (London: Mac-Millan, 2016), 300–24.
84   Augustine of Dacia, *Rotulus pugillaris*, vol. 1, ed., Angelus Walz (Rome: Pontifical Institute, Angelicum, 1929); see Henri de Lubac, *The Four Senses of Scripture*, trans. Mark Sebanc (Grand Rapids: Eerdmans, 1998), 1–9, 271–77.
85   See Stephen R. L. Clark, "*The Mind Parasites:* Wilson, Husserl, Plotinus," in *Around the Outsider: Essays presented to Colin Wilson*, ed. Colin Stanley (Alresford: O-Books, 2011), for an account of the congruence between stories by Colin Wilson, C. S. Lewis and Eric Frank Russell—all postulating the existence of unseen life forms that control and prey on us, and are themselves subject to natural law.

respect for age or for authority, our sexual confusion or religious fervor rooted in biology, or old tradition? Are the "moral mysteries" species-specific (and so not strictly binding on all sapient or rational creatures)? Perhaps—many recent fantasies suggest—the fairies are bound more by *honor* than by empathy, in a hierarchical society (sociologically, a status society rather than a contract one, and moved by shame much more than guilt). Analogically, "fairy stories" encapsulate metaphysical truths or speculations: perhaps that there is no necessary "logical" connection between cause and effect, or that the universe is not, after all, homogenous and subject everywhere to the very same natural laws. Maybe we should not ignore the role of intentional action in the state of things. Maybe, on the other hand, there is a question whether everything with an "outer" life also has an "inner" (fairies, after all, in some versions, have no "souls"). But the "anagogical" interpretation is perhaps most useful: fairies represent forgotten human possibilities and strange philosophies that we might grow to understand, to transcend, to reject entirely or to embrace. What is it that we have dismissed in imagining or insisting on the fairies' long-drawn-out departure? Are we certain that it wasn't subterfuge, and that they may not linger still?

> Spirits functioned as basic hermeneutical devices that helped thinkers to understand the structure of the created world: they represented a vast array of motivating forces, invisible impulsions, and unseen inspirations that helped endow the often-confusing, chaotic material realm with meaning and coherence. Thus, investigation into the natures of spirits and demons was embedded within rationalist and analytical forms of inquiry. Natural philosophers as well as demonologists and theorists of spiritual discernment all employed empirical evidence drawn from the sensory world in order to make inferential arguments about the nature of abstract spirits. Though their conclusions are not ones we would accept today, their methods were proto-scientific in many ways, beginning from the certain and known in order to extrapolate information about the unknown. To seek to know spirits was to engage in forms of logical inquiry.[86]

---

86 N. M. Caciola, "The Science of Knowing Spirits: Rationality and the Invisible World," in *Knowing Demons: Knowing Spirits in the Early Modern Period*, ed. Michelle D. Brock, et al. (London: Palgrave MacMillan, 2018), 295.

The first and most obvious thought is that in imagining them away we are seeking to purify our experience, to come closer to the real world by stripping away emotional projections and hierarchical assumptions. Thomas Sprat, writing in his *History of the Royal Society* (founded to facilitate new scientific discovery at the end of the seventeenth century), announced the grand expulsion.

> The poets of old to make all things look more venerable than they were devised a thousand false Chimaeras; on every Field, River, Grove and Cave they bestowed a Fantasm of their own making: With these they amazed the world.... And in the modern Ages these Fantastical Forms were reviv'd and possessed Christendom.... All which abuses if those acute Philosophers did not promote, yet they were never able to overcome; nay, not even so much as King Oberon and his invisible Army. But from the time in which the Real Philosophy has appear'd there is scarce any whisper remaining of such horrors.... The cours of things goes quietly along, in its own true channel of Natural Causes and Effects. For this we are beholden to Experiments; which though they have not yet completed the discovery of the true world, yet they have already vanquished those wild inhabitants of the false world, that us'd to astonish the minds of men.[87]

According to the "Real Philosophy" we should find out the truth of things by careful measurement and bold experiments, not reading our own preoccupations and bad habits into the world of nature. The Enlightenment project had its origins in a theological judgement: both that King Oberon and his army were not to be trusted, and that we should not hope to identify any "final causes" in our investigation of nature. That latter rejection was to lead in the end to Darwin's insight, that even the organs and practices of living creatures could be explained without a direct appeal to teleology. All we can safely do is *describe*, in the least moralistic terms, what happens, without expecting to understand why it should. Whether this project is entirely safe, or even entirely helpful, for our understanding, is one of the questions raised by rumors of fairies. When Sprat dismissed "false Chimeras" he was not merely denying the existence of a biological taxon, as we might

---

87 Thomas Sprat, *History of the Royal Society*, 3rd ed. (New York: Elibron, 2005), 340.

nowadays insist that there are no yetis, nor yet a "Beast of Bodmin," nor even saying that they were now extinct, like Neanderthals or dinosaurs. MacIntyre remarks that "to believe in God is not to believe that in addition to nature, about which atheists and theists can agree, there is something else, about which they disagree. It is rather that theists and atheists disagree about nature as well as about God."[88] The same is true for those who believe (or not) in fairies, or moral truisms, or operative final causes.

Sprat sought to oppose a certain kind of fantasy but himself fell prey to it. Most of us feel confident that the world is both terrible and beautiful, and is even meant to be so. Most feel unnerved by the whisper of woods in solitude, or fascinated by rainbow sparkles in a waterfall. Most feel awe as well as terror in the face of natural marvels. We happily admire an *imaginary* world more readily than we admire what is called "reality" (especially when we cannot do much to change or improve that "real world"). Sprat himself was moved by a great dream—the dream of building a better world than the old. And such a hope rests on an unproven axiom, that human intelligence can surpass what Nature does. Oddly enough, that axiom—which earlier and more Stoic philosophers reckoned absurd and dangerous—encapsulates exactly that dream of another, better and more malleable world which is otherwise called Fairyland, the place where wishes can come true.

The unproven axiom which allowed Sprat to dismiss the old "fantastical forms" was a version of the Christian, and earlier Abrahamic, gospel: we can purify our thoughts and dedicate our efforts to discovering real truths not dependent on our whim or fancy. Sprat's words, in fact, echo the words of Athanasius in the fourth century AD, in his essay on the Incarnation:

> In former times every place was full of the fraud of oracles, and the utterances of those at Delphi and Dodona and in Boeotia and Lycia and Libya and Egypt and those of the Kabiri and the Pythoness were considered marvelous by the minds of men. But now since Christ has been proclaimed everywhere, their madness too has ceased, and there is no one left among them to give oracles at all. Then, too, demons used to deceive men's minds by

---

88 Alasdair MacIntyre, *God, Philosophy, Universities: a selective history of the Catholic philosophical tradition* (London: Rowman and Littlefield, 2009), 47.

taking up their abode in springs or rivers or trees or stones and imposing upon simple people by their frauds. But now, since the Divine appearing of the Word, all this fantasy has ceased, for by the sign of the cross, if a man will but use it, he drives out their deceits.[89]

The Church was similarly disposed to condemn not merely the *worship* of celestial bodies, but even any recognition of the stars (including the sun and moon) as living. Plato thought this rash:

> When you and I try to prove the existence of the gods by pointing to these very objects—sun, moon, stars, and earth—as instances of deity and divinity, people who have been converted by these scientists will assert that these things are simply earth and stone, incapable of paying any heed to human affairs, and that these beliefs of ours are speciously tricked out with arguments to make them plausible.[90]

When Justinian issued an edict in 543 AD against the "errors of Origen," he blamed them on the pagan Platonic tradition that Plotinus also shared. Christians were not to agree that our souls were pre-existent as Origen indeed suggested,[91] descending into particular bodies as a punishment, nor that they might have several incarnations. They were not to agree that the stars themselves were living and visible gods, nor that our resurrection bodies were ball-shaped (that is to say, perhaps, that we could expect to rise as stars).[92] Christians really should think it right, like Plotinus's

---

89 Athanasius, *On the Incarnation* (London: Bles, 1944), chap. 8, para. 47. Cf. Minucius Felix, *Octavius*, in *Tertullian and Minucius Felix: Apology; De Spectaculis*, trans. T. R. Glover (Boston: Harvard University Press, Loeb Classical Library, 1931), 399 [27.5-7]: "All of this, as most of your people know, the demons themselves admit to be true, when they are driven out of men's bodies by words of exorcism and the fire of prayer. Saturn himself, Serapis, Jupiter, or any other demon you worship, under stress of pain, confess openly what they are; and surely they would not lie to their own disgrace, particularly with some of you standing by."
90 Plato, *Laws*, 10.886de.
91 Origen, *Principles*, vol. 2, 547 (4.3.10): "Every one of those who descend to earth is arranged, in accordance with his merits or with the position that he had had there [in an earlier or higher world], to be born in a particular place or nation or walk of life or infirmity, or to be begotten from parents who are religious, or not, so that it may sometimes happen that an Israelite descends among the Scythians, and a poor Egyptian is brought down to Judea."
92 Polycarp Sherwood, *The Earlier Ambigua of Saint Maximus the Confessor and his Refutation of Origenism* (Rome: Herder, 1955), 77-81. This notion of "astral

opponents, "to call the lowest of men brothers, but refuse, in their raving talk, to call the sun and the gods in the sky brothers and the soul of the universe sister."[93]

By one account the demons, the false chimeras, the gods above, and the rest were real creatures banished by the coming of the Word; by the other, they were phantasms that had existed only in the human imagination and were now made nothing by a new philosophy, a better way of thinking. Either way, we were now to deal with all non-human things merely as "natural objects" subject to discoverable laws of nature, without supposing that they, as individual entities, had any commands for us, or a meaning to be revered. We were also freed, perhaps, from traditional authority, from the divine right of kings and priestly manipulation.

A similar revulsion was recorded even earlier by the imperial Roman poet Virgil, who depicted an episode of the Roman civil wars as a victory of human law and ordinarily human beings over "every kind of monstrous god and barking Anubis too."[94] All that should matter to us is, on the one hand, human society, and on the other the merely natural context of our actions. So also the Hebrew prophets, demanding that the sacred groves be cut down, and Israel reject all rival gods. This process of disengagement, of detachment, was a gradual one: the Hebrews were always falling back, they said themselves, into the old idolatry; the Romans continued, mostly, to expect omens in the flight of birds and the state of a sacrificial victim's entrails, and half-persuaded themselves that their emperor was divine; many Christians still suppose that there are non-human spirits at work, for good or ill, in all the world around them. Neither Sprat nor (obviously) Athanasius intended to suggest that the created world was not a divinely sanctioned enterprise. But the eventual result of exorcising nature (as it were) was to generate an image of the natural world wholly devoid of value, the mere concatenation of events. Chesterton identified the danger, in the words of a thoroughly sane poet writing in 1929:

---

immortality" is still found among Ismāʿīlī sects, alongside more familiar expectations of reincarnation as human beings: Obeyesekere, *Imagining Karma*, 313.

93 Plotinus, *Ennead*, II.9 [33].18, 17–21.

94 Virgil, *Aeneid*, 8.699; cf. Erik Hornung, *Conceptions of God in Ancient Egypt: the One and the Many*, trans. John Baines (New York: Cornell University Press, 1982), 15–16.

Don't you see that dreadful dry light shed on things must at last wither up the moral mysteries as illusions, respect for age, respect for property, and that the sanctity of life will be a superstition? The men in the street are only organisms, with their organs more or less displayed. For such a one there is no longer any terror in the touch of human flesh, nor does he see God watching him out of the eyes of a man.[95]

---

95   G. K. Chesterton, *The Poet and the Lunatics* (London: Darwen Finlayson, 1962), 70.

3

Multiplicity in Earth and Heaven[1]

THE PHENOMENAL AND THE REAL

We are best conceived as souls rather than as particular bodily beings, and the "real world" lies behind or within the manifold phenomena with which a soul may briefly identify. Each soul, in her endless life, will know, as it were from within, what it is like to be a bush and a bird, a boy and a girl, and a fish that leaps from the sea. Each soul must somehow free herself from the illusions of sense so as to recover her one original being within the divine *Nous*. How we might then come to live (in this phenomenal world), and what social arrangements might then be appropriate, will be the topic of a later chapter: living in a world without established boundaries, whether geographical or taxonomic. But I should first begin to explore what value the phenomenal worlds might have, and what the "real world" might be supposed to be. To do so I should also seek to make it clear that we all already admit the difference between "the real" and the manifold phenomena.

Amongst the many misreadings, as I suppose, of Platonism or Neo-Platonism, is the notion that Platonists despise our present phenomenal world and prefer an etiolated, abstract order accessible only to cold and "inhuman" intellects. Real Platonism, I suggest, is otherwise, and that misreading rests on misunderstandings. There is indeed an ethical risk in neglecting the infinite detail and differences of the phenomenal world in favor of a merely "abstract" understanding, as though only "the rational," or what we suppose to be rational, were really significant.[2] But it is also difficult or impossible not to believe that there is a "real world" behind or within the phenomena,

---

1   An earlier version of this chapter appears as Clark, "Multiplicity" and is used here with the consent of Oxford University Press.
2   See Christopher Isaac Noble, "Everything in Nature is in Intellect: Forms and Natural Teleology in Ennead 6.2.21 (and elsewhere)," *Phronesis* 66, no. 4 (2021): 426–56, rebutting the notion that any natural feature is excluded from, and unknown to, Intellect.

and that we can "get in touch" with the principles from which the phenomenal worlds are made. It is indeed now becoming common-place to remark that our "brains" manufacture a phenomenal world that is not fully representative (at least) of the underlying somewhat (though those who say so continue, rather oddly, to believe in the existence of such brains, without explaining how our "intellects" can thus surpass our senses). Egyptian thought (and other traditions worldwide) imagines how those multiple principles emerge from "Nothing" and together constitute an eternal "spiritual" reality: Plato's Forms are both the heirs of earlier "gods" and the parents of later powers, existing in the divine *Nous* (the Spirit) "before" their reflection in phenomena. Rather than rely on what happens "always or for the most part," a Christian Platonist may conceive the eternal world as one far surpassing the phenomena and able to intrude upon or reform what seems to us here-now. Plotinus's Platonism, I suggest, is closer to the Christian version, despite some ambiguities, than most Christian scholars have recognized. Our phenomenal worlds do not now express all that is contained in the divine: it does not follow that they are detached from that divine. He would have agreed, I suggest, with Hopkins: "All things counter, original, spare, strange.... He fathers-forth whose beauty is past change."

Lying on the grass beneath a maple tree on a summer after-noon we can see the sparkle of different greens, of shivering lights and shadows. The grass itself is composed of multiple branching shoots, interspersed with daisies and alive with little beetles, ants and spiders. Hidden away beneath us, the soil from which grass, flowers and trees all grow is itself a medley of organic and inorganic matter, ploughed by worms and even smaller creatures and fizzing with fungi and prokaryotic life. The phenomena are disparate, ever changing, glittering with reflected light. The wind rustles the leaves. Children are playing distantly.

> Glory be to God for dappled things—
> For skies of couple-colour as a brinded cow;
> For rose-moles all in stipple upon trout that swim;
> Fresh-firecoal chestnut-falls; finches' wings.
> Landscape plotted and pieced—fold, fallow, and plough;
> And áll trádes, their gear and tackle and trim.[3]

---

3 Gerard Manley Hopkins, "Pied Beauty [1877]," in *Poems*, ed. Robert Bridges (London: Humphrey Milford, 1918), 133.

Each leaf, each grass blade, each small beast is different, and their multiplicity is at once obvious and easily neglected—so that we only (usually) carry away some memory just of trees, grass, insects that cannot be described in detail even as we experience it. The sentiment not quite accurately attributed to Ronald Reagan that "if you've seen one redwood tree, you've seen them all" (and so need not be much concerned about the loss of redwoods), may actually represent a common feeling.[4] We cannot take in the multiplicity, the "blooming, buzzing confusion" of an infant's experience,[5] and we hardly care to bother. What we mostly remember are stock pictures, stereotypes and roughly repeated features. Repeated impressions constitute experience[6]—and such memories necessarily leave out most of the unrepeated detail.

This process, thinning the original whole experience, can be continued as we examine and reflect upon the concepts we have acquired: gradually, it may come to seem to us that our understanding must be abstract. Different classes of things are folded up into genera, and what seems most important will be the widest categories of being. We notice *trees* rather than individual maples, small fluttering brown things rather than individual sparrows (finches, robins or whatever). We may come to notice only *objects* in our way, and think ourselves intelligent because we can—more or less—predict what motions usually to expect of them. Abstract understanding, sometimes expressed in merely mathematical terms, is granted an authority denied to the immediate, unrepeatable experience. "Knowledge" can only be of the wide-ranging principles that best describe the etiolated memories. Eventually we

---

4 The more accurate quotation seems to be as follows: "We've got to recognize that where the preservation of a natural resource like the redwoods is concerned, that there is a common-sense limit. I mean, if you've looked at a hundred thousand acres or so of trees—you know, a tree is a tree, how many more do you need to look at?" (speaking at the Western Wood Products Association in San Francisco on 12 March 1966): https://www.snopes.com/fact-check/if-youve-seen-one-tree/ (accessed 27 May 2020). The idea that the only reason to preserve the trees must be for the pleasure of tourists is, obviously, foolish, as is the conviction that all trees are the same. It is also a rhetorical device, illicitly dependent on the notion of abstract understanding stripped of all merely personal significance that I describe below.

5 William James, *The Principles of Psychology*, vol. 1 (New York: Cosimo, 2007), 488.

6 A. A. Long and D. N. Sedley, eds., "Aetius 4.11.3," in *The Hellenistic Philosophers*, vol.1 (Cambridge: Cambridge University Press, 1987), 238 [39E].

may hope to reduce that knowledge to some single formula, the shortest possible description of everything that ever happens: a "Schrödinger Equation" for all that is.[7] This description is inevitably one stripped of all merely "personal" or social significance, emotional affect or aesthetic appreciation. That, said Chesterton, is the "dreadful dry light" that must at last wither up the moral mysteries as illusions: "Respect for age, respect for property, and the sanctity of life will be a superstition. The men in the street are only organisms, with their organs more or less displayed."[8]

There is of course a relatively harmless, even an advantageous, reading of this story: it is not that the *real world* consists only of such abstract formulae or even of material objects stripped of their significance, nor even that these are all that we should be concerned about. The advantage of abstract understanding is merely practical: we can achieve a lot by disregarding unnecessary details. The course of a missile is unlikely to be affected by its color, any more than by whatever pet name it has been given, or whether its target is justly chosen. Even our *moral* conduct may sometimes be improved by recognizing that age, sex, gender, nationality and political associations are of no account when deciding how to treat our neighbors: it is enough that they are sentient individuals with their own distinct and unrepeated being—though for that very reason it may also be a mistake to disregard or diminish immediate attachments. Someone who (for example) trusts and cares for her child, her spouse or her parents no more and no less than she would trust and care for any random, unrelated stranger may earn a rationalist's approval, but hardly the common herd's! As Aristotle observed, if *all* men are our brothers then none will be treated as we now treat those who are presently reckoned our brothers: the scheme advanced in Plato's *Republic* "results in each citizen's having a thousand sons, and these do not belong to them as individuals but any child is equally the son of anyone, so that all alike will regard them with indifference."[9] The rational does not exhaust the real, either in ontology or ethics.

---

7   That is, a linear partial differential equation that describes the wave function or state function of a quantum-mechanical system—which might, in principle, be the totality of things.

8   Chesterton, *Poet and the Lunatics*, 70.

9   Aristotle, *Politics*, trans. Ernest Barker, ed. R. F. Stally (Oxford: Oxford University Press, 1995), 2.1262a1-3.

Is this to abandon the long tradition of Platonic (and also Stoic) intellectual theory? Plato, after all, seems to suggest that the rational and the real must be identical: what cannot be described without contradiction must be, in some sense, an illusion, "rolling around between being and non-being."[10] We may be forced here-now to rely on our perceptions and our mere unrationalized beliefs, but the truth is only available to intellect and has no flaws or even any contingencies. Knowledge, it may seem, can only be of necessary truths, and God Himself—being identically Real Knowledge—can know nothing of the merely transient, contingent features of our mortal lives, nor have any reason to be concerned with any merely local experience. The real world has no particular center (and certainly we ourselves are not central either in being or in value), nor is anything intrinsically "far away" or "near," nor yet "past" or "future." Neither is there any preferred *scale* of things, as though our human lives were more real than an earthworm's or a star's—unless we can persuade ourselves that our mere intuition of the wider, "real" world itself gives us some reason to think that human life *could* express that knowledge. The world as a whole, we can pretend, can only be for gods and humans, since only gods and humans have any notion of a world that transcends, informs, sustains the little worlds of current, flawed experience to which all other animals (we say) must be confined.

One answer to this ontological and ethical proposal is to insist instead that the real world is the sum of all phenomena: not only what appears to us, but also what appears to birds, ants, fungi, trees and prokaryotes. The world beneath, if it exists at all, is not what anyone or anything experiences.

> We may, if we like, by our reasonings, unwind things back to that black and jointless continuity of space and moving clouds of swarming atoms which science calls the only real world. But all the while the world we feel and live in will be that which our ancestors and we, by slowly cumulating strokes of choice, have extricated out of this, like sculptors, by simply rejecting certain portions of the given stuff. Other sculptors, other statues from the same stone! Other minds, other worlds from the same monotonous and inexpressive chaos! My world is but one

---

10 Plato, *Republic*, 5.479d4.

in a million alike embedded, alike real to those who may abstract them. How different must be the worlds in the consciousness of ant, cuttlefish or crab![11]

On this account it is the phenomenal detail that is real, rather than the abstract similarities and continuities. And those phenomenal details are not simply sensual: consider for a moment even the words you are now reading. You are not clumsily deciphering a set of scribbles (as might be the case if you were inspecting cuneiform without any background in Sumerian or Assyrian script), but reading (even if, occasionally, misreading) English sentences. Just so, you do not, as you look around, see merely shades of color or hear essentially unmeaning hums and crackles. You do not simply *infer* the existence of your spouse, your child, your cat from noticing sounds and colors. You see and hear real entities, according to your own personal and social history, with whatever emotional affect, and despite whatever mistakes you may make about *their* feelings. That is the world of our experience—and any theories we may have about the world beyond experience are indeed just theories (with a deliberate gesture towards the notion of *theoria* that will concern me later). "It is very strange that thousands of men easily believe in atoms without having the slightest knowledge of the facts and calculations which confirm this hypothesis, while they decline to believe in their souls, of which, at all events, they know more than of atoms!"[12]

There are further implications about the nature of past and distant worlds that are only occasionally acknowledged:[13] the actually experienced past was nothing like what we nowadays experience, and stories about the gradual evolution of our own and cognate species within a merely material, unexperienced something are as mythological as any primitive narrative about the emergence of Atum from the primordial Nothing. We may further notice, with George Berkeley, that what we shall perceive hereafter need not be "stinted to ye few objects we at present receive from some dull inlets of perception, but proportionate to wt our faculties shall be wn God has given the finishing stroke to our nature & made us fit

---

11   James, *Principles of Psychology* vol. 1, 288–9.
12   Wincenty Lutoslawski, *The World of Souls* (London: Allen & Unwin, 1924), 149 (see also ibid., 58: "Do you know more about atoms than about yourself?").
13   See Stephen R. L. Clark, "History of Appearances, or Worlds United," in *Homage to Owen Barfield*, ed. Martin Ovens (forthcoming).

inhabitants for heaven, a happiness which we narrow-sighted mortals wretchedly point out to ourselves by green meadows, fragrant groves, refreshing shades, crystal streams & wt other pleasant ideas our fancys can glean up in this Vale of misery."[14] At present we only perceive a little of God's imaginings, and all (perhaps) are dependent only on the single will of God! Creation is the manifestation to finite spirits of what always already exists in the divine imagining.[15]

ARCHAI: PRINCIPLES AND BEGINNINGS

But perhaps we should make a fresh start, exactly from those past myths, if we are to understand what a thorough-going Platonism might contribute. One familiar story of the world's beginning is indeed that everything emerged (or perennially emerges) out of Nothing. That Nothing may itself be characterized, at least in negative terms, as undifferentiated, inconceivable, unlimited and "Not Many."[16] Out of that Nothing emerges (for no particular reason) the First Thing, and from that First distinctly existing being—which is also, in a sense, no thing—all the things there are successively emerge. In Egyptian thought the One (Atum) becomes the Million, which all bear, as it were, the echo or stamp or reflection of that First. In Chinese thought, at the other end of the Eurasian continent, it is similarly from the Nameless that Heaven and Earth spring, and all their offspring. Even what at first must seem a radically different notion—that "in the beginning God [Elohim] made heaven and earth"—is difficult to distinguish from the other: what is the difference between an unknowable God and an equally unknowable non-God?[17] So David Hume, through his character Cleanthes, appositely enquires "how...mystics, who maintain the absolute incomprehensibility of the Deity, differ

---

1 4 George Berkeley, "Sermon on Immortality [1708]," in *Works*, vol. 7, ed. A. A. Luce and T. E. Jessop (Edinburgh: Thomas Nelson, 1948), 12.

1 5 George Berkeley, *Principles of Human Knowledge and Three Dialogues*, ed. Howard Robinson (Oxford: Oxford University Press, 1996), 196.

1 6 According to Plutarch, *De Ei*, 9.388e, the indestructible divinity that undergoes transformations is known as Apollo (that is, *a-polla*, not many) in the Conflagration imagined by Stoic philosophers, and as Dionysus (or cognate identities) when he is rent apart and distributed "into winds, water, earth, stars, plants and animals": Ivan M. Linforth, *The Arts of Orpheus* (Berkeley: University of California Press, 1941), 317–18.

1 7 See Stephen R. L. Clark, "Who is God," *European Journal for Philosophy of Religion* 8, no. 4 (2016): 1–22.

from Sceptics or Atheists, who assert, that the first cause of all is unknown and unintelligible?"[18] Why should it matter whether we call the ultimate, unknowable, uncaused and inexplicable origin and context of all things "God" or "Matter"? According to Plotinus the One holds being and beauty before itself like a golden veil (or like a barrier), and Matter—its absolute opposite—is "bound in golden chains":[19] if neither can be directly seen nor comprehended how do we know they are different? Does it matter whether we say that all things began from an infinite sea of possibility or from an infinite power? Apparently so: the power has purpose. And mere possibility can never be a sufficient explanation for anything.[20]

That there is or was a single beginning to all the myriad things which now make up the world of our experience may be a necessary tool of thought, a way of expressing or excusing the conviction that there are no really radical divisions: what is true here and now will also, if it is really true, be true in all the world, over however many years and light-years. There is at the same time a certain arbitrariness implicit in the story of what is: everything has emerged from Nothing—a condition without any pre-conditions, limits or definite probabilities. The primeval mound, Atum, just happens. The Lord's command is unconstrained at least by any physical conditions.[21] That all things have a single origin may not, of itself, tell us much about their nature, nor help us to identify what exactly will prove "the same" over all the years and light-years.

> Without all doubt this world could arise from nothing but the perfectly free will of God.... From this foun-tain ... [what] we call the laws of nature have flowed, in which there appear many traces indeed of wise contrivance,

18 David Hume, "Dialogues Concerning Natural Religion [1779] pt.4," in *Hume on Religion*, ed. R. Wollheim (London: Fontana, 1963), 131.

19 Compare Plotinus, *Ennead*, I.6 [1].9 and I.8 [51].15.

20 See Aristotle, *Metaphysics*, 12.1071b.

21 I attempt throughout to distinguish the "physical" from the "material": the latter refers to that strange image of reality according to which the only real and abiding properties are to do with shape or location, with no intrinsic link to any *experiential* properties. The "physical" is merely what happens *phusei*, by nature, without any commitment to its metaphysical nature. In my under-standing the physical, the realm of nature, is the whole of phenomenal reality, maintained by the World Soul and refracted in the experience of all lesser souls. "Materialists" prefer to suppose that the "physical" world is also and entirely "material," despite the epistemological and ethical problems this idea generates.

but not the least shadow of necessity. These therefore we must not seek from uncertain conjectures, but learn them from observations and experiments. He who is presumptuous enough to think that he can find the true principles of physics and the laws of natural things by the force alone of his own mind, and the internal light of reason, must either suppose that the world exists by necessity, and by the same necessity follows the laws proposed; or if the order of Nature was established by the will of God, that himself, a miserable reptile, can tell what was fittest to be done.[22]

There seems no reason, in modern cosmological theory, for certain pervasive features (the relative power of different distinct forces) to be exactly what they are. Either these features have been dictated, perhaps so as to allow the emergence of life-forms such as ourselves, or this merely happens to be the arrangement that allows for that emergence—and indefinitely many other distinct worlds or aeons, with utterly different features, somehow exist beyond all possible perception. In postulating such a "multiverse," cosmologists have moved from the Stoic conception (that only this actual world is possible) to the Epicurean (that all possible worlds are actual). The Platonic conception—that *not* all possibilities are actual—has clear ontological and ethical advantages.[23] That is another story. But at least we may now confirm that there *are* certain definite abiding and universal principles at work, beyond the mere requirement that there be *something*. Or in mythological narrative, "Atum is the god who 'in the beginning was everything,' complete in the sense of being an undifferentiated unity and at the same time non-existent, because existence is impossible before his work of creation,"[24] and who (on the Heliopolitan story preserved in the Coffin Texts[25]) then sneezes, spits or ejaculates

---

22   Isaac Newton as represented by Hooykaas, after Cotes' preface to second edition of *Principia*: R. Hooykaas, *Religion and the Rise of Modern Science* (Edinburgh: Scottish Academic Press, 1972), 49.

23   Plato does suggest in *Timaeus*, 30cd that the phenomenal world must contain reflections of all the living creatures akin to the Maker (that is, present to the divine Intellect), but it does not follow that all possible *events* occur in this one world. As Aristotle observes "the potential need not necessarily always become actual" (Aristotle, *Metaphysics*, 3.1003a2), or there would be no distinction between the possible and the real.

24   Hornung, *Conceptions of God*, 67.

25   See James P. Allen, *Middle Egyptian: an Introduction to the Language and Culture of Hieroglyphs*, 3rd ed. (Cambridge: Cambridge University Press, 2014), 175–78.

Shu and Tefnut (the dry and the moist). These latter in turn engender Geb and Nut, who are the earth and sky, or else the down below and the up above. The principles and powers that rule the world or worlds might, possibly, have been different, but are now unavoidable. These principles, it has been suggested, lie behind Plato's own account of "Forms."

> The supersensible world is an immutable hierarchy of Ideas, or Types, which throws its image upon the everflowing stream of time. Or, it is a heaven of divine souls, which impart themselves to the groups of transitory things that bear their name. The whole conception is manifestly mythical, but it is of the essence of the theory. The logical interpretation is struggling to get clear of the mythical; the Idea threatens to pass from being an indwelling group-soul to being a mere universal concept, which does not exist at all, and, if it did, could not cause the existence or becoming of particular things. Plato did not realize that he was only making an important discovery in logic; he thought he was discovering the causes—the sole, true causes—of the existence of the world.[26]

Cornford's comment is too patronizing to believe: why not instead acknowledge that Plato's Forms are indeed proposed as causally significant powers, and that they are indeed functionally identical both with Egyptian gods and with Christian angels? According to Jeremy Naydler:

> The concept of the First Time is comparable to that of the realm of being in which the Platonic Ideas exist. In Egyptian thought, though, it is not abstract ideas that are to be found here, but living gods and archetypal relationships that obtain among them. The First Time is the realm of metaphysical realities conceived in terms of symbolic images and myths. These are the patterns that are reflected in the mundane world and that need to be participated in if mundane events are to be filled with archetypal power.[27]

So also Raymond Barfield:

---

26 F. M. Cornford, *From Religion to Philosophy: a study in the origins of western speculation* (New York: Harper & Row), 257-58.

27 Jeremy Naydler, *Temple of the Cosmos: the Ancient Egyptian Experience of the Sacred* (Rochester, VT: Inner Traditions International, 1996), 93.

Proclus took the divine ideas of Plotinus and made them
into gods that can not only be known (as in Plotinus)
but can also know. Dionysius makes them into angels.
Thus it is that the Forms of Plato become the Angels
of Christendom.[28]

Barfield's error here lies in supposing that Plotinus—or his
predecessors—imagined that the divine ideas were only *objects* and
(being "abstract") causally inert. Quite otherwise: they could not
be thus disentangled from the subjects, the immortal *Nous* that
knew them, and they were imagined, exactly, as causes.

In short, the Forms postulated by Platonists are not abstract
universals but rather eternal paradigms made manifest both in the
phenomena of experience and in the mental calculations of such
finite creatures as ourselves. An *arche* is both a ruling principle and
a starting point. Even numbers and geometrical figures are more
than abstractions or human artefacts—though there is an element
of human construction in our employment of them in describing
the phenomena. Counting how many "things" there are in a given
volume, or how many temporal intervals have passed during some
experience, obviously depends on how we divide up the "real," fluid
phenomena, what "net" we employ. As before:

> The real wiggly world slips like water through our imagi-
> nary nets. However much we divide, count, sort, or classify
> this wiggling into particular things and events, this is no
> more than a way of thinking about the world: it is never
> *actually* divided.[29]

But the real *archai* are not so wiggly, though they are connected
each to each and manifest in many different ways. So how are we to
speak about these Forms, and where (as it were) can they be? The
received answer, borrowing perhaps from Aristotle's understanding
of the relation of the divine intellect and what it comprehends, was
that the Forms, the Intelligibles, existed in union with the divine,
eternal Intellect (that is, *Nous*—though the term is often better
translated as "Spirit"). Plotinus argued indeed that anything else
would make it impossible even for God to be sure that He understood them—there being, on any other hypothesis, a gap between the

28 Raymond Barfield, *The Ancient Quarrel Between Philosophy and Poetry* (Cambridge: Cambridge University Press, 2011), 97.
29 Watts, *The Book on the Taboo*, 59.

Forms and even God's understanding.[30] This is not to say that the divine Intellect contemplates *propositions*: the objects of Intellect are not propositions nor formulae but real entities bound together into a complex unity, the very things that *our* propositions are about.[31]

It should here be noted that a common distinction between real or elite philosophy and merely popularized philosophy or "religious" language cannot apply to Plotinus.

> [Alfarabi] said that both philosophy (*falsafa*) and religion (*milla*) gave you the truth, but that they did so in different versions, designed for different audiences. Philosophy, which had existed before religion, led you to things as they really were by means of proofs based on demonstration (*burhan*); religion represented the abstract truths of philosophy in symbols, images and similes that everyone could understand and secured acceptance for them by persuasion (*iqna*). For example, religion would describe the void as water or darkness. The relationship he postulated was rather like that between professional and popular science today. It is the same truth that they postulate, but professional science rests on mathematical demonstration, whereas popularizers resort to analogies, similes, and images drawn from the reader's everyday experience.[32]

---

30   See Plotinus, *Ennead*, V.5 [32]; see Stephen R. L. Clark, "A Plotinian Account of Intellect," *American Catholic Philosophical Quarterly* 71 (1997): 421–32.

31   Plotinus, *Ennead*, V.8 [31].5, 2–24: "One must not then suppose that the gods or 'the exceedingly blessed spectators' in the higher world contemplate propositions, but all the Forms we speak about are beautiful images in that world, of the kind which someone imagined to exist in the soul of the wise man, images not painted but real." It is worth adding that Plotinus's account of what the Egyptian sages intended (IV.3 [27].11; V.8 [31].6) is more accurate than classical scholars have always realized. "The mixed form of their [the Egyptians'] gods is nothing other than a hieroglyph, a way of 'writing' not the name but the nature and function of the deity in question. The Egyptians do not hesitate to call hieroglyphs 'gods,' and even to equate individual signs in the script with particular gods; it is quite in keeping with their views to see images of the gods as signs in a metalanguage. As is true of every Egyptian hieroglyph, they are more than just ciphers or lifeless symbols; the god can inhabit them, his cult image will normally be in the same form, and his priests may assume his role by wearing animal masks": Hornung, *Conceptions of God*, 124. See Jan Assmann, *Religio Duplex: how the Enlightenment reinvented Egyptian religion*, trans. Robert Savage (Cambridge: Polity, 2014), 26–33, for a brief account of the nature, and later reception, of hieroglyphs (and also hieratic and demotic script). It is likely that Plotinus saw no distinction between hieroglyphs and aesthetic tropes such as the child on the lotus, or the god in his barge (ibid., 29–30, commenting on Iamblichus).

32   Crone, *Medieval*, 173.

But Plotinus himself relies on symbols, images and similes not merely to expound a doctrine to a wider audience but to represent reality even to himself and his closest students. The contrast between "philosophers," who supposedly argue from self-evident axioms by clearly necessary steps to some abstract conclusion, and "prophets," who present a vision of reality that subverts our ordinary intuitions, is, at least, overdrawn.

Max Tegmark's inference from modern cosmological practice seems to match the older idea (and also relies on persuasion more than abstract logic):

> According to the Aristotelian paradigm, physical reality is fundamental and mathematical language is merely a useful approximation. According to the Platonic paradigm, the mathematical structure is the true reality and observers perceive it imperfectly.[33]

What flows from that reality are the phenomena of our very various experience—but the real things are eternal.

> It is already clear that the thought of a horse existed if [God] wanted to make a horse; so that it is not possible for him to think it in order to make it, but the horse which did not come into being must exist before that which was to be afterwards.[34]

Does this constitute a real difference between the Plotinian and the Christian view of God's creative activity? Maybe so—but there are clear parallels in all the Abrahamic faiths. For Jews, the Word that is the root of all things is the Torah, or the Wisdom it embodies:

> In human practice, when a mortal king builds a palace, he builds it not with his own skills, but with those of an architect. Moreover, the architect does not build it out of his head, but employs plans and diagrams to know how to arrange the chambers and the wicket doors. Thus God consulted the Torah and created the world, while

---

33 Max Tegmark, *Our Mathematical Universe: My Quest for the Ultimate Nature of Reality* (London: Allen Lane, 2014), 49.

34 Plotinus, *Ennead*, VI.7 [38].8, 6–9. What that eternal Horse may be, of course, is not necessarily much like the horses of our current, phenomenal reality (any more than the merely material horses that moderns imagine are "behind" the manifold phenomena can be much like what *we* perceive). Charles Williams attempted a poetic or literary evocation of such forms: see *The Place of the Lion* (London: Faber, 1931).

the Torah declares, "In the beginning God created" (Genesis 1:1), "beginning" referring to the Torah, as in the verse, "The Lord made me as the beginning of His way" (Proverbs 8:22).[35]

Might Wisdom be the first thing that God *made*, before the foundation of the world, and so be everlasting rather than eternal? But the logic of the story must be that it is rather *uncreated*: how, save by Wisdom herself, could even He have made Wisdom? The blueprint, or the Will and Reason expressed in the blueprint, always precedes the building or even the drawing of the blueprint. "How could the predeterminations and the divine volitions that create all existent things be themselves created?"[36] Again: "How can the Logos, being the Counsel and Will of the Father, come into being Himself by an act of will and purpose?"[37] Muslims (or at least Sunni Muslims) seem to have drawn the same conclusion: the *Koran*, as the Wisdom of God and the plan for creation, is itself *uncreated*.[38]

Plotinus notes one further implication that Abrahamic tradition has tended to ignore: the Divine Intellect, the *Logos*, contains all Forms as eternal realities: "It lived not as one soul but as all, and as possessing more power to make all the individual souls, and it was the 'complete living being,' not having only man in it: for otherwise there would only be man down here."[39] All real things, all the eternal templates, reside within the single unified Form of all Forms—from which it follows that, if Humanity is to be "in the image and likeness of God," it must also be "a lumpe where all beasts kneaded be."[40]

---

35   *Bereisheet Rabbah* [c. 500 AD] 1:10: cited in Yakov Z. Meyer, "Parashat Teruma: the primordial Torah," *Haaretz* (30 January 2014).

36   Palmer et al., *Philokalia*, vol. 4, 387.

37   G. L. Prestige, *God in Patristic Thought* (London: SPCK, 1952), 151, after Athanasius, *Against the Arians*, 3.64: "He is external to the things which have come to be by will, but rather is Himself the Living Counsel of the Father, by which all these things have come to be."

38   See a brief discussion by Shari L. Lowin and Nevin Reda, "Scripture and Exegesis: Torah and Qu'ran in historical perspective," in *Routledge Handbook of Muslim-Jewish Relations*, ed. Josef W. Meri (London: Routledge, 2016), 61. In both Christian and Muslim history the notion that it was "created" was preferred by rulers, as it suggested both that the Word as it had been previously declared might turn out to be obsolete, and—by analogy—that their own arbitrary commands were valid: see Hugh Kennedy, *The Caliphate* (London: Penguin, 2016), 114-16.

39   Plotinus, *Ennead*, VI.7 [38].8, 29-32; see also VI.6 [34].15, 11-13; VI.7 [38].12.

40   John Donne, "To Sir Edward Herbert at Julyers [1651]," in *A Critical Edition of the Major Works*, ed. John Carey (Oxford: Oxford University Press, 1990), 200-1.

Hans Urs von Balthasar summarizes the thought of Maximus the Confessor (580–662)[41] on this point as follows: "In the Logos, all the individual ideas and goals of creatures meet; therefore all of them, if they seek their own reality, must love him, and must encounter each other in his love. That is why Christ is the original idea, the underlying figure of God's plan for the world, why all the individual lines originate themselves concentrically around him."[42] Which is to repeat Plotinus's metaphor, of the circle's radii meeting in their center.[43] Maybe there is still room for a distinction between God's eternal *intention* for His creatures and the templates he had devised for them, as well as a distinction between those everlasting templates, gods, powers and principalities and their echo or reflection in the common features of phenomena? According to Von Balthasar,[44] Maximus distinguished the divine ideas, "the basic outlines, in God, of his plans for the world, the preliminary sketch of the creature within the Spirit of God," from the "created universals'" that are the immanent principles of created being. "The concentration of the ideas of the world in the Creator does not mean the dissolution of the world into God."[45] The divine essences are, perhaps, not co-eternal with God.[46] But the distinction is hard to maintain: in the one Word all things are implicit, even those things that are not, or not yet, brought out to illuminate or ground phenomena. Our own "real selves," on a Plotinian account, are eternally resident in the Word, even though our experienced selves are far removed, far fallen, from that beatitude!

According to al-Farabi, "All men [that is, all human souls] are really a single entity in many individuals."[47] Indeed, all animate entities are, in a way, one soul.[48]

---

41 See Maximus Confessor, *Selected Writings*, trans. George C. Berthold (London: SPCK, 1985).

42 Hans Urs Von Balthasar, *Cosmic Liturgy: the Universe according to Maximus the Confessor*, trans. Brian E. Daley (San Francisco: Ignatius Press, 2003), 133.

43 Plotinus, *Ennead*, VI.8 [39].18, 18; see also Ps-Dionysius, *Divine Names* [644a] in *Complete Works*, trans. Colm Luibheid and Paul Rorem (London: SPCK, 1987), 62.

44 Von Balthasar, *Cosmic Liturgy*, 116–18.

45 Ibid., 119.

46 Ibid., 152.

47 Joel Kraemer, *Humanism in the Renaissance of Islam*, 2nd ed. (Leiden: Brill, 1992), 115.

48 Plotinus, *Ennead*, IV.9 [8].4, 2–3: "But our discussion still wants to find out how they are one!"

Might the powers and principalities that govern distinct aspects of the totality themselves be fallen as we are? Plotinus thought the idea at least disrespectful,[49] and denied that such powers could simultaneously "remember" what should be well enough to help create the worlds and have "forgotten" so much as to act against what should be.[50] But of course that is exactly our own condition: why may it not apply even to those agencies that are not embodied in particular times, places and fragile bodies? Abrahamists—and even some "pagan" Platonists—have found it possible to think that *some* superhuman powers are fallen, if not literally into flesh yet into fleshly attachments.

> They themselves rejoice in everything that is likewise inconsistent and incompatible; slipping on (as it were) the masks of the other gods, they profit from our lack of sense, winning over the masses because they inflame people's appetites with lust and longing for wealth and power and pleasure, and also with empty ambition from which arises civil conflicts and wars and kindred events.[51]

Are they genuinely distinct (though unlocalized) entities, or are we to suppose instead that they are merely *images* for distinguishable powers and affections of all souls? There may be no clear answer. The "fallen" powers are echoes or reminders of their originals. Before Adam fell, "what is now gall in him sparkled like crystal, and bore the taste of good works, and what is now melancholy in man shone in him like the dawn and contained in itself the wisdom and perfection of good works; but when Adam broke the law, the sparkle of innocence was dulled in him, and his eyes, which had formerly beheld heaven, were blinded, and his gall was changed to bitterness, and his melancholy to blackness."[52] Hildegard was here repeating an ancient theme, about the corruption of what is in origin benign.

> What comes from the stars [that is from the planetary spheres through which the soul descends to earth] will not reach the recipients in the same state in which it

---

49 Plotinus, *Ennead*, II.9 [33].9, 53–64.

50 Ibid., II.9 [33].4, 8–18.

51 Porphyry, *On Abstinence from Killing Animals*, trans. Gillian Clark (London: Duckworth, 2000), 72 [2.40, 3].

52 R. E. Klibansky et al., *Saturn and Melancholy* (Edinburgh: Thomas Nelson, 1964), 80, citing Hildegard of Bingen: Kaiser ed., *Hildegardis Causae et Curae* (Leipzig 1903), 43.

left them. If it is fire, for instance, the fire down here is dim, and if it is a loving disposition (*philiake diathesis*) it becomes weak in the recipient and produces a rather unpleasant kind of loving (*ou mala kalen ten philesin*); and manly spirit, when the receiver does not take it in due measure, so as to become brave, produces violent temper or spiritlessness; and that which belongs to honor in love and is concerned with beauty produces desire of what only seems to be beautiful, and the efflux of intellect produces knavery (*panourgia*); for knavery wants to be intellect, only it is unable to attain what it aims at. So all these things become evil in us, though they are not so up in heaven.[53]

The same, perhaps, is true, on Plotinian terms, of our own selves. All souls first illuminate the heavens, and some come lower, not to their advantage.[54] We here-now are fallen both from the divine and from the stars, separated and confused, but something of us has *not* fallen, and "our heads are firmly set above in heaven."[55] Like the powers, we can ourselves contribute, for good or ill, to the constant remaking and reimagining of this grand image, this *eikon aei eikonizomene*.[56] We are not, as Stoic philosophers would have us, simply cogs within the machine, and neither are the powers above: there are many agencies at work. Indeed those many agencies are also working within in us—to the point that we cannot reasonably claim yet to be the unitary persons that we would wish to be.[57]

Those who seek to follow the Delphic instruction—so St. Hesychios was to say—find themselves, as it were, gazing into a mirror and sighting the dark faces of the demons peering over their shoulders.[58] The gods (or demons) are constantly at work in us,

---

53 Plotinus, *Ennead*, II.3 [52].11; see Stephen R. L. Clark, "Climbing up to Heaven: the Hermetic Option," in *Purgatory: philosophical dimensions*, ed. Kristof K. P. Vanhoutte and Benjamin W. McCraw (London: Palgrave-MacMillan, 2017).

54 Plotinus, *Ennead*, IV.3 [27].17, 8–11.

55 Ibid., IV.3 [27].12; IV.8 [6].8, 1–4.

56 After ibid., II.3 [52].18, 17.

57 Ibid., VI.7 [38].41, 22–24. Urgyen Sangharakshita, *What is the Sangha? The nature of spiritual community* (Cambridge: Windhorse Publications, 2001), makes much of this insistence, that most of us don't manage to be what he calls "individuals," united in our drive to some particular goal.

58 Palmer et al., *Philokalia*, vol. 1, 123. See also Plato, *Phaedrus*, 229b4–30a6, where Socrates puts aside literal, physicalist interpretations of the creatures of Greek myth, in favor of asking whether he is himself "a more complex creature and more puffed up with pride than Typhon."

as also in the world at large. Maybe, indeed, we are even less in charge of our own minds and feelings than we thought.

> Let us suppose that each of us living creatures is an ingenious puppet of the gods, whether contrived by way of a toy of theirs or for some serious purpose—for as to that we know nothing; but this we do know, that these inward affections of ours, like sinews or cords, drag us along and, being opposed to each other, pull one against the other to opposite actions; and herein lies the dividing line between goodness and badness.[59]

Two principles in particular are worth further attention: the Empedoclean duo, Love and Strife. It has been usual to reckon these, respectively, as "good" and "evil," but a better version rather acknowledges their equal force and authority. "Love" brings things together, and "Strife" separates them—but it is that separation which allows for, and creates, the promise of individual lives, while "Love," left to itself, brings everything together into an undifferentiated monad.[60] Either principle, power or angel can lead to disaster; so also many other principles, powers and angels, separated from their origin in *Nous*—or as Plotinus expresses the idea mythologically, in Kronos.[61]

THE USUAL, THE ANOMALOUS AND WHAT IS YET TO COME

The Aristotelian paradigm (which is not entirely or exactly Aristotle's) takes individual entities to be the primary substances, and true science to be the discovery and examination of "what happens always or for the most part,"[62] perhaps in the hope that all such generalities will turn out in the end to be necessities. Such generalities, or "laws," may be reliable, but they do not really explain anything that happens, but only record it. By Aristotle's own account we may more reasonably look to the *ends* that all such processes may serve: a thing's nature is the path of its growth towards its becoming what its nature needs.[63] The growth of the Whole Thing,

---

59 Plato, *Laws*, 1.644e.
60 See Peter Kingsley, *Ancient Philosophy, Mystery, and Magic: Empedocles and Pythagorean Tradition* (Oxford: Clarendon Press, 1995).
61 Plotinus, *Enneads*, V.1. [10].4, 8–10; V.1 [10].7, 33f. See Hadot, "Ouranos, Kronos and Zeus."
62 Aristotle, *Physics*, 2.198b36.
63 Ibid., 2.193b13–15.

the totality of existence, is always already complete, not something to be expected in an apocalyptic future. Platonists may take Aristotle's point more to heart: the nature of anything is rather what it *should* be than what, descriptively, it seems to be at any particular time. The world that embodies the forms, if it should ever come into being, is the real world.[64] And of course, for Platonists, that real world always already exists in the Divine Intellect.

This last point may also be where Abrahamic and ordinarily Hellenic ("pagan") Platonists diverge. For Plotinus the world of our present experience is already as good as such a world could be (granted its existence as a medley of disparate visions and expectations), and the hope of a remade world is at least disrespectful. "What other fairer image of the intelligible world could there be?"[65] Even a gradual improvement is not something we should much care about:[66] if we are always to be aiming to get more or better, "even the gods will be better off now than they were before, but they will not be perfectly well off; they will never be perfectly well off."[67] Christians, on the other hand, hoped for a better world, expected "to judge angels,"[68] and reckoned themselves superior in rank and, hopefully, in eventual virtue even to the highest of angelic spirits.[69] This, in all the Abrahamic traditions, was the sin of Satan: not to acknowledge Adam (which is to say, Humanity) as God's Chosen. The angels' fall, so tradition tells us, began in Satan's outrage that he could be expected to bow down before an animal![70]

---

64   C. D. C. Reeve, *Philosopher Kings: the argument of Plato's Republic* (Indianapolis: Hackett, 2006), 116–17.

65   Plotinus, *Ennead*, II.9 [33].4, 26–7.

66   Though he does envisage the possibility that "from adultery or the carrying off of a captive, children may come according to nature and better men, it may happen, and other better cities than those sacked by wicked men": ibid., III.2 [47].18, 16–18. And just possibly, in the next performance of the world drama we will play our parts a little better: ibid., III.2 [47].17, 45–60.

67   Ibid., I.5 [36].2.

68   1 Corinthians 6.1–4. Paul's hope (and his consequent advice to the Corinthians not to resort to Roman Law to settle their disputes) rested not on a claim to spiritual superiority, but on the presence of the Holy Spirit, made visible (perhaps) in "the gifts of the spirit" (see I Corinthians 12–13; Galatians 5.22f). See also 1 John 4.1: "Beloved, believe not every spirit, but try the spirits whether they are of God."

69   The Hermetic Corpus hints at the same idea: human beings are to stand above even the star-gods: Brian P. Copenhaver, *Hermetica* (Cambridge: Cambridge University Press, 1992), 36 [10.24].

70   "We created you and then formed you and then We said to the Angels,

That there may be, or even will be, a better world than this, and that it will be founded rather on domestic virtues than more "god-like" fantasies of control, is an idea that has survived its theological origins (without any clear justification). Someday, it is supposed, people will relate to each other as friends and family, with unlimited resources of food, drink, information, company. They will have avoided all attempts at despotic control or group-think and be happy each to explore their individual vocations. Any necessary collective decisions will be made through "democratic" procedures, allowing the Many all to contribute to the One. Plotinus was perhaps more patient and realistic than to suppose this outcome either likely or long-lasting, but some elements of the vision may still be worth recalling and incorporating in the transient and parochial arrangements of ordinary social life. But they won't last, and neither do they truly include all current mortal lives.

But "pagan" and Abrahamist can agree that there is, in some sense, a "better world" than this—namely the world eternally envisaged in the Divine Intellect—and can agree that we here-now should model our thoughts and actions, as far as possible on that ideal. We are not to think merely "mortal thoughts," but rather to "immortalize" ourselves as much as possible,[71] and remember our celestial identity.

> Even before this coming to be we were there, men (*anthropoi*) who were different, and some of us even gods, pure souls and intellect united with the whole of reality; we were parts of the intelligible, not marked off or cut off but belonging to the whole; and we are not cut off even now.[72]

"Pagan" and Abrahamist, on the other hand, disagreed about the possibility of a real transformation of this whole world, currently groaning like a woman in travail.[73] Someday there will be "a new heaven and a new earth," and "the holy city, new Jerusalem, will come

---

'Prostrate before Adam' and they prostrated except for Iblis [which is the Arabic term for Satan]. He was not among those who prostrated. God said, 'What prevented you from prostrating when I commanded you?' He (Iblis) replied, 'I am better than him. You created me from fire and You created him from clay.' God said, 'Descend from heaven. It is not for you to be arrogant in it. So get out! You are one of the abased'" (*Koran* Surah 7 [al-A`raf], 11–13).

71 Aristotle, *Nicomachean Ethics*, 10.1177b33.
72 Plotinus, *Ennead*, VI.4 [22].14, 18ff.
73 Romans 8.22.

down out of heaven from God, made ready like a bride adorned for her husband."[74] That strange possibility, of a radical invasion and disruption, cannot be predicted from within our present system, as one might predict even such catastrophes as global war, disease, volcanic eruption, meteor strike, γ-ray bursts or solar flares. On any usual pagan aesthetic it is an obvious breach of dramatic protocol, and a reminder (perhaps) that we should attend rather more to the likelihood of exceptions, irruptions, uncovenanted mercies. Rather than looking to see what happens "always or for the most part," we should instead be alert to anomalies, to the unpredicted, to what does *not* usually happen (or is supposed to happen).

> The progress of science is often described by materialists as a continuous process of disillusionment, but the truth is that the main illusion it has shattered is the notion that human beings are limited to the horizons of the ordinary everyday world as normally experienced by average people in most ages of history. By following up the odd extraordinary event that fails to fit into the framework of everyday thought, science has again and again shown that human beings can have far wider horizons and far more dimensions of experience than are dreamed of in the down-to-earth philosophies of people who pride themselves on their common sense.[75]

"Pagan" and Abrahamist can agree at any rate that there are many ways—indefinitely many ways—to be. All things may have a single origin and purpose in what Plotinus calls "the One," but for that very reason we must also acknowledge the multiplicity of manifested (and unmanifested) intelligible being—"a sphere all faces, shining with living faces,"[76] each of which has its own being and expression.

> It is a multiplicity because the beings of the universe are many, but one, that what holds them together may be one; by its manifold oneness it dispenses life to all the arts, and by its indivisible oneness it directs them wisely.[77]

---

74 Revelation 21.1–2.

75 John Wren-Lewis, "Resistance to the Study of the Paranormal," *Journal of Humanistic Psychology* 14 (1974): 42.

76 Plotinus, *Ennead*, VI.7 [38].15, 25–28; see Stephen R. L. Clark, "Sphere of Many Faces," *Dionysius* 34 (2016): 8–26. Many Egyptian gods, it is worth noting, are described as "many faced" or "lord of faces": Hornung, *Conceptions of God*, 126.

77 *Ennead* IV.1 [21].2, 45–8.

The whole phenomenal world, compounded of all the different phenomenal worlds, is unimaginably various and always open to sudden transformations and intrusions. "Million-fuelèd, nature's bonfire burns on."[78] After such a transformation and intrusion, we may perhaps look back and see the seeds of what was to come in earlier experience—but it is also possible that the seeds of the new world were held "aloft" in the eternal, "the mystery hidden for ages and generations but now revealed to his saints."[79]

Even Plotinus seems to allow, despite his disapproval of those who think themselves superior to gods, that there *might* after all be a better form of experience than the one or ones implicit in the present phenomena. Zeus (that is, Soul) is the one of Kronos's children who lives outside his Father (*Nous,* or Spirit), for a good purpose (so that there should be "a beautiful image of beauty and reality") but bound to be surpassed by those offspring that have stayed "within," the worlds that have not (yet) had temporal or phenomenal reflections.[80] And perhaps there is a clue to those so-far-unseen realities, exactly, in what is here-now *different*.

> All things counter, original, spare, strange;
> Whatever is fickle, freckled (who knows how?)
> With swift, slow; sweet, sour; adazzle, dim;
> He fathers-forth whose beauty is past change:
> Praise him.[81]

---

78 Hopkins, "That Nature is a Heraclitean Fire and of the comfort of the Resurrection," in *Poems,* 48.

79 Colossians 1.26; see also Ephesians 3.4–5.

80 Plotinus, *Ennead,* V.8 [31].12–13. See also Copenhaver, *Hermetica,* 20 [5.9]: "He is himself the things that are and those that are not. Those that are he has made visible; those that are not he holds within him....There is nothing that he is not, for he also is all that is, and this is why he has all names, because they are of one father, and this is why he has no name, because he is father of them all."

81 Hopkins, "Pied Beauty," in *Poems,* 133.

4
Keeping the Old Ways Living[1]

AN ALIEN AND UNFAMILIAR WORLD

Imagining that there are fairies (ghosts, demons, elves, dwarves, goblins, giants and the rest) is an expression of our feeling that the world is indeed both alien and unfamiliar. Our ancestors—to revert to the paleological speculation I mentioned earlier—found the European woods creepy because they could see or sense or fantasize the faces that were peering out at them. The woods had their own lives, their own indifference to the ordinarily human beings who had begun to explore them. Something was going on in them that had no respect for human lives and values, whose actions made no sense in human terms.

Understandably, we *want* them to have gone away. Folk memory— or speculative fantasy—is full of heroes, often divinely mandated, who cleared away the monsters, both the merely brutal and the mildly mischievous, and who laid the foundations of a peaceable rural landscape as well as of stone cities. Sprat wished to make the world a truly *familiar* place, one that we could come to understand by common sense and reason if we rejected anything "uncanny." Yet rather few of us are really inclined to empty the world of its significance and stop seeing "sermons in stones and books in the running brooks." Ceremonials, temples, sacred writings testify to the significance, to us and to our ancestors, of things that mattered more than food and shelter. Eliminating kings and priests, we merely assign the titles to ourselves, and imagine ourselves a royal and priestly people! We drove the fairies away because we preferred an ordinary humanity, not because we wanted to

---

1 This chapter draws on an essay published as "An Absence of Fairies," *First Things* 271 (March 2017): 33–38; see also Stephen R. L. Clark, "Elves, Hobbits, Trolls and Talking Beasts," in *Creaturely Theology*, ed. Celia Deane-Drummond and David Clough (London: SCM Press, 2009). John Milbank, in one of his Stanton lectures (2011), drew a larger moral from my earlier paper, Stephen R. L. Clark, "How to Believe in Fairies," *Inquiry* 30 (1988): 337–55, than I had seen myself: http://theologyphilosophycentre.co.uk/papers/Milbank_StantonLecture8. pdf (accessed 15th April 2020). I am grateful for his insight.

discover the real, "unhuman" truth. On the contrary, we drove away the uncanny.

We are like the citizens of Hope Mirrlees's *Lud-in-the-Mist* (written in the 1920s), who preferred simple bourgeois pleasures to the unnerving sense that something altogether different lay only a few miles away.[2] Domestic lives disguise from us, even now, our recognition that the world itself is older, vaster, weirder, more intractable than we can ever imagine. We pretend that romantic comedies or naturalistic thrillers set in the present day are more "realistic" than any that require us to remember that we live between immensities, for no more than a fraction of sidereal time in a world that we did not make. Tolkien had a point!

> The notion that motor-cars are more "alive" than, say, centaurs or dragons is curious; that they are more "real" than, say, horses is pathetically absurd. How real, how startlingly alive is a factory chimney compared with an elm-tree: poor obsolete thing, insubstantial dream of an escapist![3]

One further feature of modernity—alongside the errors I itemized in an earlier chapter—is the assumption that time is linear, and progressive. Our ancestors, we suppose, were simpler creatures, barely able to cope with their immediate environment, and quite ignorant of the larger world or their own past. We may also fantasize that there were other, alien worlds before us, but usually insist that these too were simple, ignorant and merely "animal" in nature. Dinosaurs must have been stupid because they lived a very long time ago (and now are gone). Neanderthals must clearly have been backward. A more careful account must at least acknowledge that "dinosaurs" were a very diverse kind, and endured for many millions of years, but those years, we suppose, must still have been entirely savage, "mindless" because non-human. Strictly, we do not know what civilized societies developed long ago, within our species or another, nor what the "uncivilized"—those without abiding cities—knew that we have long forgotten. After our own future (likely) collapse it will not be many centuries before most certain or easily readable traces of our passage will have vanished—and we may be correspondingly entirely ignorant of earlier

---

2   Hope Mirrlees, *Lud-in-the-Mist* (London: Gollancz, 2000).

3   J. R. R. Tolkien, *On Fairy Stories*, ed. Verlyn Flieger and Douglas A. Anderson (London: Harper Collins, 2014), 71.

passages.[4] Less disciplined, or more imaginative, fantasists like H. P. Lovecraft, a writer of cosmic horror stories, crafted wholly alien civilizations to precede (and follow) us. Alongside the fiction that the world is wholly familiar and safe exists the fear that it is in fact an incomprehensible horror, something wholly beyond the human. Lovecraft expressed this idea in a letter to his friend Farnsworth Wright in 1927:

> Now all my tales are based on the fundamental premise that common human laws and interests and emotions have no validity or significance in the vast cosmos-at-large. To me there is nothing but puerility in a tale in which the human form—and the local human passions and conditions and standards—are depicted as native to other worlds or other universes. To achieve the essence of real externality, whether of time or space or dimension, one must forget that such things as organic life, good and evil, love and hate, and all such local attributes of a negligible and temporary race called mankind, have any existence at all. Only the human scenes and characters must have human qualities. These must be handled with unsparing realism (not catch-penny romanticism), but when we cross the line to the boundless and hideous unknown—the shadow-haunted Outside—we must remember to leave our humanity—and terrestrialism—at the threshold.[5]

His advice for those too troubled by these thoughts was mainly to hold on to their own cultural traditions, echoing in this the words of a cultured Roman in a third century dialogue:

> Seeing that either chance is certain, or nature uncertain, how much more reverent and better it is to accept the teaching of our elders as the priest of truth; to maintain the religions handed down to us; to adore the gods, whom from the cradle you were taught to fear rather than to know familiarly; not to dogmatize about divinities, but to believe our forefathers who, in an age still rude, in the world's nativity, were privileged to regard gods as kindly or as kings! Hence it is that throughout wide empires,

---

4   See Schmidt and Frank, "Silurian Hypothesis."
5   Letter to Farnsworth Wright, 5 July 1927, taken from http://www.hplovecraft.com/writings/quotes.aspx (accessed 11th April 2020). See Schultz and Joshi, *Essential Solitude*.

provinces and towns, we see each people having its own individual rites and worshipping its local gods.[6]

The principal pagan attack on Christians in late antiquity was that they had abandoned their own tribes' traditions. Jews, though they stood aside from the *consensus gentium*, at least had their own, unusual, traditions: Christians, being drawn from every race and station, had betrayed their own ancestral gods, the values and distinctions in which they and their ancestors were reared. "It is impious," Celsus said, "to abandon the customs which have existed in each locality from the beginning."[7]

The intellectual assumptions of our more recent ancestors, in the Mediterranean world and also further afield in India and China, were perhaps less paranoid than Lovecraft's—but they were also much less inclined to include a belief in progress. Quite otherwise, as the Egyptian priest told Solon (according at least to Plato):

> Like the rest of mankind you have suffered from convulsions of nature, which are chiefly brought about by the two great agencies of fire and water.... The memorials which your own and other nations have once had of the famous actions of mankind perish in the waters at certain periods; and the rude survivors in the mountains begin again, knowing nothing of the world before the flood.[8]

Xenophanes of Colophon (570–478 BC) cited evidence for the suggestion:

> Shells are found inland and in the mountains, in the quarries at Syracuse the impression of a fish and seaweeds has been found; ... on Malta there are slabs of rock made up of all kinds of sea-creatures. He says that these came about a long time ago, when everything was covered with mud, and that the impression became dried in the mud. He claims that the human race is wiped out whenever the earth is carried down into the sea and becomes mud, that then there is a fresh creation.[9]

---

6   Minucius Felix, *Octavius*, 6.1 (Caecilius speaks, after briefly expounding a version of the oldest cosmological story, that all things, even the gods, have had their birth from emptiness).

7   As quoted by Origen, *Contra Celsum*, 283 (5.26).

8   Plato, *Timaeus*, 22bc; see also Plato, *Laws*, 3.677ad.

9   Waterfield, *First Philosophers*, 29 [21A33DK].

Or perhaps there has always been a remnant saved from ruin, from which the world was repopulated, indefinitely many times. We are in no better position than Diodorus to answer the question on a *cosmic* scale, even if we can now be fairly sure that humankind did, sometime, have a beginning—though long before our own recorded history. Aristotle indeed suspected that there had never been an absolute beginning, and he was not alone in this:

> One group, which takes the position that the universe did not come into being and will not decay, has declared that the race of men also has existed from eternity, there having never been a time when men were first begotten; the other group, however, which hold that the universe came into being and will decay, has declared that, like it, men had their first origin at a definite time.[10]

The generations of humankind are infinite if time had no beginning, and we can infer that they also have no end—and no radical, final alteration in their mode of being.

> Every man ought to understand that either the human race never had a beginning at all, and will never have an end, but always was and always will be, or else it must have been in existence an incalculable length of time from the date when it first began.[11]

The assumption of mediocrity[12] which modern cosmologists also use—that we do not occupy any special place in the cosmos, and that things will look much the same from any and all locations—also applies in history (and maybe, some have thought, in scale[13]). But this does not secure our present comfort: if things are

---

10 Diodorus Siculus, *Library of History*, vol. 1, trans. C. H. Oldfather (Cambridge, Mass: Loeb Classical Library, Harvard University Press, 1933), 1.6.3. Aristotle suggests that everything has already been discovered, and forgotten, an infinite—or at least an indefinite—number of times: *De Caelo*, 270b19-20, *Meteorologica*, 339b27-8, *Politics*, 7.1329b25-6. So also *Ecclesiastes* 1.10: "Is there anything of which one can say, 'Look this is new'? No, it has already existed, long ago before our time. The men of old are not remembered, and those who follow will not be remembered, by those who follow them."

11 Plato, *Laws*, 6.781e-782a.

12 "The principle of mediocrity [is] that we should assume ourselves to be typical in any class that we belong to, unless there is some evidence to the contrary": Alexander Vilenkin, "The Principle of Mediocrity," *Astronomy & Geophysics* 52, no. 5 (2011): 33-36.

13 See Plotinus, *Ennead*, VI.2 [43].4, 19-21: a body can be divided infinitely.

always "very much the same," we must conclude that catastrophes always happen—and this too is confirmed by present experience.[14]

> For nothing at all anywhere has remained in the same condition; everywhere all has been subject to change and vicissitudes. Egypt once held the sovereignty over many nations, but now is in slavery. The Macedonians in their day of success flourished so greatly that they held dominion over all the habitable world, but now they pay to the tax-collectors the yearly tributes imposed by their masters. Where is the house of the Ptolemies, and the fame of the several successors (i.e., of Alexander) whose light once shone to the utmost boundaries of land and sea? Where are the liberties of the independent nations and cities, where again the servitude of the vassals? Did not the Persians once rule the Parthians, and now the Parthians rule the Persians? So much do human affairs twist and change, go backward and forward as on the draught-board.[15]

As one of Chesterton's minor characters enquires: "Can you tell me, in a world that is flagrant with the failure of civilizations, what there is particularly immortal about yours?"[16] Whereas the assumption of linear progression at least allows, and maybe promotes, the notion that our descendants will one day and forever afterwards be "gods," the more ancient and widespread thought is that any such apotheosis would require us to step aside from

---

"Whence it appears that in the smallest particle of matter there is a world of creatures, living beings, animals, entelechies, souls. Each portion of matter may be conceived as like a garden full of plants and like a pond full of fishes. But each branch of every plant, each member of every animal, each drop of its liquid parts is also some rich garden or pond. And though the earth and the aire which are between the plants of the garden, or the water which is between the fish of the pond, be neither plant nor fish; yet they also contain plants and fishes, but mostly so minute as to be imperceptible to us": G. W. Leibniz, *Monadology and other philosophical writings*, trans. Robert Latta (Oxford: Clarendon Press, Oxford, 1898), 256. Ibid., 65–67. He was probably mistaken in supposing that existence at those different scales would be indistinguishably similar.

14 See Kathryn A. Morgan, "Plato and the Stability of History," in *Greek Notions of the Past in the Archaic and Classical Eras: History Without Historians*, ed. John Marincola, et al. (Edinburgh: Edinburgh University Press, 2012).

15 Philo, *De Iosepho*, 134–36; see Katell Berthelot, "Philo's Perception of the Roman Empire," *Journal for the Study of Judaism in the Persian, Hellenistic, and Roman Period* 42, no. 2 (2011): 181–82.

16 G. K. Chesterton, *Napoleon of Notting Hill* (Harmondsworth: Penguin, 1946), 25.

history and from our present place. And that any present public triumph will always be short-lived. The world of our experience will never be the world at large. That world therefore must always be mysterious, and our own existence finite.

Plato warned us long ago that we were living, as it were, in a puddle, or on the margins of the real world, or even trapped in a cave to watch a shadow-play.[17] What shall we find if we make our escape from the cave or from the puddle? More of the same, or something weirdly different? Is Fairyland an illusion or the dream of a wider world? Science-fictional adventures in an imaginary future, amongst extra-terrestrial intelligences or future versions of humanity, are, obviously, not accurate predictions of our future but have more truth in them than the supposition that our current social and biological order is undying. And so do fairy stories. We *know*—if we think about it—that our world is changing all the time, often in ways that may well prove catastrophic. None of our guesses about what will certainly replace our current customs and beliefs are likely to be accurate: but at least we can imagine other times and places best by subverting our own easiest illusions. Perhaps we can begin by wondering if the fairies, *daimones*, really have gone far away. Maybe things really are always much the same—including expectable catastrophe.

SPIRITS STILL AMONG US

Perhaps instead of going away, the fairies, *daimones*, spirits are living among us still and exercising their familiar glamour. They only pretended to leave, or we only pretended to have expelled them: money, nation-states, fashionable dress, fantasy heroics and celebrity culture are all phantoms.[18] One story is of some mortal

---

17 Plato, *Phaedo*, 109b; Plato, *Republic*, 7.514a–518b.
18 See Eugene McCarraher, *The Enchantments of Mammon: How capitalism became the religion of modernity* (Cambridge, MA: Harvard University Press, 2019), for a study of the way consumption, and the misery (of the exploited classes) have been moralized, and the Christian (and other) praise of poverty has been turned on its head. McCarraher aptly cites Chesterton's remark that the American employer rules mostly by fairy tales (ibid., 429, drawing on G. K. Chesterton, "Utopia of Usurers," in *Collected Works*, vol. 5 [San Francisco: Ignatius Press, 1987], 414): "Even the tyrant never rules by force alone; but mostly by fairy tales. And so it is with the modern tyrant, the great employer. The sight of a millionaire is seldom, in the ordinary sense, an enchanting sight: nevertheless, he is in his way an enchanter. As they

midwife who is called to attend a fairy birth and instructed to mark the new-born's eyes with a particular ointment. Accidentally (or perhaps with curious intent) she marks her own left eye as well and realizes—in some versions—that what had seemed to her a magnificent palace is in truth a cold and dirty cave. In other versions, it is the reverse: a ramshackle hut becomes, to her new eyes, a palace. Later, about her own business, she observes the fairy who had summoned her walking through the local market taking—unseen by others—whatever he desired. Realizing that she has seen him, he at once blinds her left eye, so leaving her subject once again to *Maya*, to illusion.[19] We may occasionally see the real world, and the real powers that move it, but we are much happier to live inside illusion, in the world of merely *human* happenings, as the fairies among us define them. To set ourselves to reject the older gods, spirits, fairies is actually to renounce all "moral mysteries" and to claim the same power of radical redescription for ourselves: if Nature no longer offers any obstacle to human projects, no threat of violence against those who slaughter the cattle of the sun or cut down sacred groves, then the world is ours to remake as we will. On the one hand, most of us prefer the domestic world. On the other, there are those who profess to have seen through those illusions and seek only their own advantage in a world stripped of all meaning. Which is the real illusion?

Athanasius and Thomas Sprat alike had a better hope than either, insisting instead that the truly real world could and should be discovered, if only we stopped imagining that poetic phantoms ruled it and us alike and that it was something more than an abyss. We would find the truth that mattered, they both thought, by cooperating in the human enterprise. We were no longer to be gulled by current convention, nor terrified by any unhuman powers, because these monsters had indeed been long defeated: Heracles, long before, had cleared away the monsters and rescued

---

say in the gushing articles about him in the magazines, he is a fascinating personality. So is a snake."

19   See W. Y. Evans-Wentz, *The Fairy Faith in Celtic Countries: the Classic Study of Leprechauns, Pixies, and Other Fairy Spirits* (Oxford: Oxford University Press, 1911), 136-37. For further details of the story's spread see Críostóir Mac Cárthaigh, "Midwife to the Fairies (ML 5070): The Irish Variants in Their Scottish and Scandinavian Perspective," *Béaloideas* 59 (1991): 133-43.

Prometheus from his torment;[20] Christ the Incarnate Word testified that illness and all misfortune existed *so as to be remedied*;[21] Baconian experimentalists claimed a similar vocation, to torment Nature into giving up her secrets.[22] Great Pan, the first-century story said, is dead, and the world is freed of its despots, so as to permit the building, or the arrival, of the New Jerusalem, the new and *better* world. But perhaps this was too romantic, too optimistic a prediction. Most of us have preferred to live without complaint in our familiar domestic world; even if there are no sacred groves, no fairy presences, no knowledgeable beasts "out there," we have little hesitation in thinking *human* lives, and our local institutions, are sacred. Even the gospel of redemption and rebirth becomes, very often, only worship of the current state of things, the resident oracles and spirits, the obviously "successful" businessmen or politicians. And the rejection of current values in its turn easily becomes a merely cynical rejection of all non-egoistic value, the world that fairies see and those "successful" people use.

Is a third possibility a real one, some way of acknowledging the power and value of "fairy" that is not simply to accept either the domestic illusion or the larger and more dreadful nihilistic fantasy? Could there be fairies whose imagination helps to serve the fully humane ideal rather than diminish or deny it? Chesterton would have thought so.

> Fairy tales are not responsible for producing in children fear, or any of the shapes of fear; fairy tales do not give the child the idea of the evil or the ugly; that is in the child already, because it is in the world already. Fairy tales do not give the child his first idea of bogey. What fairy tales give the child is his first clear idea of the possible

---

20 A story allegorized by Plotinus as Prometheus's rescue by his real, abiding self: Plotinus, *Ennead*, IV.3 [27].14, 12–14.

21 John 9.1–3: "As he went along, he saw a man blind from birth. His disciples asked him, 'Rabbi, who sinned, this man or his parents, that he was born blind?' 'Neither this man nor his parents sinned,' said Jesus, 'but this happened so that the works of God might be displayed in him.'"

22 Bacon himself did not, strictly, speak (as some have supposed) of "torturing" Nature, but rather of interrogating her (sic) to learn how best to dominate her. He made considerable use of mythical figures to explain his strategies and desires: see Carolyn Merchant, "The Scientific Revolution and *The Death of Nature*," *Isis* 97 (2006): 513–33 and Carolyn Merchant, "Violence of Impediments: Francis Bacon and the Origins of Experimentation," *Isis* 99 (2008): 731–60.

defeat of bogey. The baby has known the dragon inti-
mately ever since he had an imagination. What the fairy
tale provides for him is a St. George to kill the dragon.[23]

There is also the metaphysical question I sketched before: how
can a merely material world ever accommodate our own experience
of life? Cartesians—taking the theologically grounded refusal to
believe in spirits or worry about the influence of final causes to some
sort of plausible limit—believed that "animals" were insentient, and
that only humans, maybe only adult humans, had goals or thoughts
or feelings. The more fundamental doubts thereby gained traction:
maybe some things that look like humans aren't; maybe even clearly
human beings have no real subjective life. Even if, in some sense, I
exist, I don't know what I am—and it turns out, so some modern
materialists have begun to argue, that nothing I do or even say and
think is more than the motion of material parts (and so even the
notion of rational argument itself is subverted). No one is really
"subjectively conscious," precisely because no one could identify such
subjectivity in others (and so could have no words to describe it in
themselves), and because there could be no way that evolutionary
selection could detect or propagate this purely private "feel."[24] All
that can be ascribed to any natural being is a power to respond
"appropriately" to some current state of affairs, without any need
to suppose that there is "something it is like to be" such a creature.
Oddly, of course, this leaves the modern materialist unable to deny
that insects, trees or protists may also respond "appropriately," and
therefore be just as "objectively conscious" (which is only to say
"observably awake") as we are ourselves. Even cities, nations and
corporations must turn out to be "persons" too.

Even modern materialists, of course, have difficulty sustaining
the strange thesis that they are not themselves conscious in the old,
subjective, sense, and that their own identity is a cultural illusion
or semantic error. It seems undeniable that something is going on
in us—in me and in you my readers—that is not best described

---

23   G. K. Chesterton, *Tremendous Trifles* (London: Methuen, 1904), 102.
24   Stephen R. L. Clark, *From Athens to Jerusalem: the love of wisdom and the love of
God* (Oxford: Clarendon Press, 1984), 121–57. When I made the point in the
early 80s at a Thyssen conference, the philosophers present professed not to
understand what "consciousness" could refer to, and the paper was excluded
from the conference proceedings. Times have changed a little!

in merely material terms: we have thoughts and feelings denied (or so we mostly suppose) even to the cleverest chess-playing computer program. We do have an "inner" life. Maybe consciousness is an emergent property? But this is only to say that we have no idea how it happens, nor any way of equating the felt reality of our own being with other, measurable, features. It is as much as to believe in magic, in the arbitrary conjunction of events. So panpsychism, from being a really bizarre hypothesis, is now being actively considered as a solution to the so-called "hard problem" of how phenomenal, subjective qualities are connected to merely material quantities. Even electrons have an inner life already.

> Our mechanistic model of the universe still, of course, recognizes forces that are invisible to the human eye, and that regulate the operations of the world around us. We do not name such forces spirits, and do not credit them with moralities and with intelligences, but we know them just as our forebears knew spirits.[25]

But perhaps we *should* consider that they are really spirits, that they have a genuine point of view.

Our original position, as social and reasoning beings, requires us to acknowledge both our own responsibility as reasoning beings and the real presence of other creatures, human and non-human, in the world we inhabit and enjoy. In positing as the underlying reality a merely "material" nature—having no qualities of the sort we ourselves immediately experience, and so without any sensibility, ethical norms or purposes—we create a grave epistemological and ontological problem. How should such a nature be expected to engender the worlds of our own immediate experience? Why should we trouble to discover it, supposing that we could? How, in brief, could "matter"—so envisaged—ever engender "mind"? And what reason could there be to posit such a nature as a real explanation when it cannot actually *explain* the very experience whose existence we need to understand? Plotinus grasped the question, in his dispute with Stoics and Epicureans alike:

> The most extraordinary of all is that, though they are assured of the existence of each and every thing by sense-perception, they posit as real being what cannot

---

25 Caciola, "The Science of Knowing Spirits," 301.

be apprehended by sense.... But if they say they grasp it by intellect, it is an odd sort of intellect which ranks matter before itself and attributes real being to matter but not to itself.[26]

I propose that the methodological and theological reasons advanced in the early modern period, in imitation of earlier Christian iconoclasm, for abstracting a merely "material" and "unmeaning" nature from our lived experience do not support fashionable ontological or metaphysical conclusions (that, for example, we are latecomers in cosmic history and exist on the margins of an alien cosmos). On the contrary, as Plotinus argued, our very existence as social and reasoning beings, with some reasonable hope of discovering real patterns and real causes, as well as a real duty to respect both reason and the truth, demands that we accept his conclusion that it is "soul" which animates and creates all things. The real world is not the abstracted "material" world, but the lived reality of our shared experience. Any world "before" or "apart from" sentient experience was not, and is not, "large" or "long." Indeed, without "soul" there could be no unitary entities, or a unified cosmos, at all—granted that "materiality" is essentially defined by the difference of each part (each instant, each location) from all others.[27] On Plotinus's account there is a reason (*logos*) that makes things at once the same and different: "Some gods, some spirits (a nature of the second rank), then men and animals after them in order, not out of grudging meanness (*phthonos*) but by reason of containing all the rich variety of the intelligible world."[28]

And if that is so, we can consider fairies, *daimones*, yet again: everything we encounter has its own inner being and is busy about its own affairs. Our thoughts are real and are often something more than simply *our own* thoughts: they come upon us from outside, as it were, with different emotional valencies at different times and places. We may choose to filter those thoughts and sudden impressions, for personal as well as ideological reasons, but it is as well, at least occasionally, to acknowledge them—and also to

---

26   Plotinus, *Ennead*, VI.1 [42].28, 3–22.
27   Plotinus, *Ennead*, V.1 [10].2, 33–35; IV.1 [21].2, 5–7; see also ibid., III.6 [26].6, 57–58: "When every kind of earthy body is cut, each part stays separate forever."
28   Ibid., III.2 [47].11, 7–9; see also ibid., III.2 [47].15, 31–33.

acknowledge the sudden shifts of seeming associated with fairies. Is the midwife misled in seeing a gorgeous palace, or in seeing a decaying hut? Maybe both are "real."

Like other products of evolutionary change, we only notice, as a rule, what is likely to matter to us: we experience only a fragment of what is happening in the world. And what is out of our sight and sense is also, mostly, out of mind. Our conscious experience and intention run alongside the supposed material happenings in our brains and bodies. Similarly, the presence of "fairies" is not ruled out merely because what happens "naturally" also involves the motion of material parts. Nor is it ruled out by the fact that there are very general "laws" to describe what happens: the laws of nature that we discover are not explanations but very general descriptions—and real explanations, if there are any, may lie in the conscious intention of spirits with their own agendas and inclinations. As Buber remarked: "The tree is no impression, no play of my imagination, no aspect of a mood; it confronts me bodily and has to deal with me as I must deal with it—only differently."[29]

And that is what encountering "the soul of a tree or a dryad" is like. By removing the mere *fantasy* of a humanoid dryad mysteriously attached to a tree, we may actually encounter *the tree*. Something is really *there*, and we describe it in the terms with which we are most familiar, while also knowing that those familiar terms are strictly inapplicable. Or rather, in applying them to trees or rocks or stars, we may suddenly find that they are unfamiliar terms, and that we hardly know even what other *human* creatures are. We may find that we are in Fairyland already—a discovery that is true to the "Magian" background even of our contemporary "Western" views: "The world of Magian mankind is filled with a fairy-tale feeling!"[30]

Neanderthals and the rest of our now-vanished cousins may already have run together in our ancestors' imaginations with the presences they felt in woods and streams and starlight. Neanderthals and the rest are gone away, and we have tried very hard to extinguish fairies and false chimeras. Some such fairies are present still in human thought: they disguise themselves and their more nihilistic threat by letting us see only the domestic and national

---

29 Buber, *I and Thou*, 58–59.
30 Spengler, *Decline*, vol. 2, 237: Spengler's insights are to be valued despite his manifold errors and exaggerations.

fantasies. But maybe presences of the older sort can now be properly acknowledged. Fairy tale monsters, of course, were often as frightening as any of Lovecraft's cosmic horrors. But, like those horrors, they can also be conceived or experienced as something beautiful in their own right. Just so the childish fascination with dinosaurs is a way of confronting, even partly taming, bogeys: dinosaurs inhabit Fairyland as well as approved Fact and should not be emptied of significance even when we realize that they are more than phantoms. Unlike Lovecraft, fairy tales give us some hope of victory, even if it comes by meteor strike! The world is not to be understood in merely domestic categories, as though nothing existed that lay beyond "the fields we know." Nor is it an unmeaning chaos from which (to preserve our sanity) we need to avert our eyes. Fairyland is many things, or one thing under many different descriptions. It is the hint of a wilder and wider world than the domestic, from which the bolder of us might bring treasures if they can avoid its perils; a reminder of a world unconstrained by any of our familiar values and threatening therefore to alienate us from our own; the dream of a world where everything can speak, and everything contribute its own beauty to the growing whole.

MANY WAYS OF
BEING TOGETHER

SO TO SUMMARIZE MY INITIAL ACCOUNT OF
the Plotinian world, as it was experienced and rationalized by
Plotinus and his successors: it is a world in which our own *human*
intelligence, even if it permits a wider view of experienced reality
than (perhaps) other earthly creatures can enjoy, has its roots in
that same multifaceted wider world. We are not alone: the whole
world expresses an intelligible order through its manifold connections, facets, faces—an order which is at once mysterious and
open to be loved. We are not only or essentially human—or at any
rate "we humans" are surrounded, infiltrated, supported by many
sorts of being and can learn to see the divine origin of all things
in all those manifold beings. We should not expect to surpass our
ancestors, nor expect a final resolution of all conflicts in the here-
and-now. But we should also not forget the real world that we can
now encounter only in fragmented images and partial memories.
We should also not forget that our own assumptions are not ones
shared by all our kind: we are the ones who are out of step.

> The Western conception of the person as a bounded,
> unique, more or less integrated motivational and cog-
> nitive universe; a dynamic center of awareness, emotion,
> judgment, and action organized into a distinctive whole
> and set contrastively both against other such wholes
> and against a social and natural background is, however
> incorrigible it may seem to us, a rather peculiar idea
> within the context of the world's cultures.[1]

How then can we hope to organize our lives together in the
here-and-now? What different ways of living together can we
expect to manage, or learn from our maybe-enlightened ancestors?

---

1   Clifford Geertz, "From the Native's point of view: on the nature of anthropological understanding," *Bulletin of the American Academy of Arts and Sciences* 28,
no. 1 (1974): 31: cited by Henrich, *Weirdest People in the World*, 21.

To live is always to live together: there are no merely solitary and self-enclosed living creatures. Certainly, there are no merely solitary and self-enclosed people. Political fantasies that imagine that our ancestors at least were once born "free" and "independent" are plainly false: we are born dependent beings, subject to others' commands and care, and almost all of us are bound to continue so. Our own problem, or opportunity, or fate, as self-consciously human beings, is that we must sometimes *invent* how best to live together (or at least must be persuaded that we have had a choice). As humans we have an opportunity, but we are not *essentially* human. In this following section I shall seek to offer some different models of community (roughly: *polis,* empire, borderless community, eremites and friendship groups) that were present in Plotinus's day (and later), drawing both on his own passing judgements and on the long tradition of (broadly) Platonic thought.

5
Platonopolis

CITIZENS OF THE LARGER WORLD

The world of our everyday experience, when honestly reported, is never wholly rationalized or even rationalizable. There are no clear and stable boundaries between kinds or even between individuals. Nor can we quite escape from contradiction: on the one hand, everything we think and do seems to be what the world as a whole requires; on the other, we have to believe that we ourselves can be "free," or at least unimpeded, that we might be co-workers with the gods. "There is no contradiction," Plotinus says, "between necessity and free-will (since necessity contains the free-will),"[1] but it feels as if there is. We struggle to remember both the "blooming, buzzing confusion" of the life within and around us and the recurrent patterns that suggest there is, overall, some (relatively) simple plan or even purpose. We live amongst pressing memories, figments of the imagination, riddling ambiguities, and wish at once to see things "straight" without forgetting their moral and spiritual weight. One response to all this is sometimes, not without excuse, attributed to Plotinus. We need, somehow, to escape, "alone to the Alone."[2]

> Let us fly to our dear country. What then is our way of escape, and how are we to find it? We shall put out to sea, as Odysseus did, from the witch Circe or Calypso—as the poet says (I think with a hidden meaning)—and was not content to stay though he had delights of the eyes and lived among much beauty of sense. Our country from which we came is There, our Father is There. How shall we travel to it, where is our way of escape? We cannot get there on foot; for our feet only carry us everywhere in this world, from one country to another. You must not get ready a carriage, either, or a boat. Let all these things go, and do

---

1   Plotinus, *Ennead*, IV.8 [6].5, 1–3.
2   Ibid., VI.9 [9].11, 51. This translation is by now canonical, and is itself difficult to escape: it is, as I shall argue later, misleading. The point is not to abjure company: quite otherwise.

not look. Shut your eyes, and change to and wake another
way of seeing, which everyone has but few use.[3]

But the "escape" that he envisages is, explicitly and precisely, *not*
a journey to some clearly other world or age. It depends, he says,
on seeing all things otherwise.[4] Gregory of Nyssa used the same
image, as it were in reverse: "Blessed is he that cometh in the name
of the Lord. How does He come? He crosses over into human life,
not by boat or by chariot, but through the incorruption of a Virgin."[5]
On the Christian account we have no need to go ourselves, since
He (the Word of God) has come to us (as Plotinus said the gods
should do): and this too involves a change of heart and way of
seeing, not simply or "literally" a change of place.[6] This was also
a familiar Hebrew and Christian reading of Israel's exodus from
Egypt, considered as the creation of a new form of life, divorced
from merely physical concerns, "the fleshpots of Egypt."[7]

---

3   Ibid., I.6 [1].8, 16–28.
4   See J. N. Deck, *Nature, Contemplation, and the One* (New York: Larson, 1991),
110: "Plotinus does not have two worlds, but only one. His world of true
being is not, except metaphorically, a world above the everyday world. It is
the everyday world, not as experienced by sense, by opinion, or by discursive
reasoning, but as known by intellect, the *Nous*, the Knower." See also Armstrong,
Enneads, vol. 7, 79: "In the end we are left with the very strong impression
that for Plotinus there are not two worlds but one real world apprehended
in different ways on different levels." But it is worth insisting that the world
as it is known by *Nous* is indeed the *real* world, and very unlike the world we
imagine ourselves to inhabit.
5   Gregory of Nyssa, "Homily on the Nativity of Christ" (*Patrologia Græca*,
XLVI, 1128A–1149C), citing *Psalm* 117:26.
6   Cf. Porphyry, *Life*, 10.34–40: Plotinus declined Amelius's invitation to tour
the local temples, saying simply that "they ought to come to me, not I to
them." In my judgement this was an expression of Plotinus's humility, not his
arrogance, but opinions, understandably, differ. Zosimus of Panopolis advised
Theosebeia in the same terms: "Do not roam about searching for God; but
sit calmly at home, and God, who is everywhere and not confined in the
smallest place like the daemons, will come to you" (Fowden, *Egyptian Hermes*,
122). Armstrong's suggestion (Plotinus, *Enneads*, vol. 1, 34–35), that Plotinus
probably had malevolent *daimones* in mind, at first makes little sense: why
would Plotinus think that such entities should or even must come to him?
But Zosimus too suspected that *daimones* were confined in particular spaces,
and that these might therefore be encountered in some temples. The gods to
be trusted were the ones already present to our hearts and minds.
7   Exodus 16.3; see for example, Philo of Alexandria, "*De Migratione Abrahami*
[20.160]," in *Complete Works*, vol. 4, trans. F. H. Colson and G. H. Whitaker (Boston:
Harvard University Press, Loeb Classical Library, 1929–1962), 225. Sarah J. K.

We are fortunate, perhaps, if we can see things new, whether by opening an inner eye or by the condescension of the Word—a distinction of less importance than some have supposed. Plotinus too could hope for divine intervention: "If someone is able to turn around, either by himself or having the good luck to have his hair pulled by Athena herself, he will see God and himself and the All.... He will stop marking himself off from all being and will come to all the All without going out anywhere."[8] Most of us, however, may have to depend instead on the good fortune of our birth within a long tradition stemming from Gayomard or Manu, Minos or Moses, or any other of the "wise men of old."[9] Or else, perhaps, we may imagine a new beginning, a new city founded to reflect the recurrent message.

Could that new city simply be the cosmos, or at least the part that we inhabit? This has often been the implicit message of some philosophers, that they are citizens, along with the gods, of a single, universal "city," even a single household. "We distinguish nations and tribes: to God the whole world is a single household."[10] Indeed, the relation is even closer: "This universe is all bound together in shared experience and is like one living creature," of which we are all parts.[11] When Anaxagoras was asked whether he did not care about his fatherland, he gestured at the sky and said

Pearce, *Land of the Body: Studies in Philo's Representation of Egypt* (Tubingen: Mohr Siebeck, 2007), 127: "Philo consistently reads the migrations of the ancestors to and from Egypt in terms of the moral and spiritual progress of the soul in relation to the corporeal." Philo also, like many other non-Egyptian commentators, believed that the use of animal images in worship was the worst form of idolatry (thereby misunderstanding their import). Proclus, *Commentary on Timaeus*, 190 [I.96, 4–8] records a similar association but prefers himself to see Egypt allegorically as the invisible source of all things visible.

8   Plotinus, *Ennead*, VI.5 [23].7, 9–10. The reference is to Homer's *Iliad* (I.197f), where Athena (the goddess of good sense) recalls Achilles from a murderous rage.
9   Or in later years, Mohammad. See Crone, *Medieval*, 176: "Already Philo of Alexandria (d. after 41), a Hellenized Jew much read by Christians, had cast Moses as the philosopher king envisaged by Plato (see Runia, "God and Man in Philo," 54). Eusebius similarly presented Moses as a lawgiver (*nomothetes*) who gave the Jews a constitution (*politeia*), that is a religious law which kept their crude natures under control while at the same time pointing to the ultimate truth in symbolic form (Eusebius, *Praeparatio Evangelica*, ed. and trans. G. Schroeder and É des Places (La preparation évangélique, livre VII, Paris, 1975), 7.9.1; 324)."
10   Minucius Felix, *Octavius*, 417 [33.1].
11   Plotinus, *Ennead*, IV.4 [28].32, 14.

that was his fatherland.[12] Marcus Aurelius enquired, rhetorically: "The poet says, dear city of Cecrops, and will you not say, dear city of Zeus?"[13] The moral was that true philosophers should be obedient only to those laws that could be considered universal. So Aristippus the Cyrenaic, citizen of no one particular city, placed the virtue of philosophy in that the philosopher was at ease everywhere and would not alter his behavior even if the laws of the land were all repealed.[14] The image was not confined to antiquity: Berkeley, for example, used very much the same arguments as pagan philosophers to remind us of our membership of "that Great City, whose author and founder is God,"[15] and suggested that we should live in accordance with general laws like those by which God regulated the natural universe (these laws were not, perhaps, quite what Aristippus imagined).

Strictly, it could be said that Anaxagoras meant that the heavens "above" were his fatherland, not the sublunary world, and that he hoped, like later believers, to ascend. "I am a child of earth and starry heaven, but my race [*genos*] is of heaven alone," according to the Orphic Tablets.[16] That is a moral to which I shall return. But the more usual understanding of what it is to be "cosmopolitan," *cosmopolites*, is that we owe our lives and loves to the whole world around us, that *eikon aei eikonizomene*, that image of the eternal that is always being reimagined.[17] We cannot close ourselves off from that wide world, either as individuals or as communities, and we ought to acknowledge both its ever-renewed beauty and our own reliance on its continuing in good health without our constant assistance. Recent environmentalist rhetoric to the effect that we ought to consider ourselves "stewards" of the terrestrial biosphere exaggerates our importance to the whole. Let us simply

---

12   Diogenes Laertius, *Lives*, 2.7.

13   Marcus Aurelius, *Meditations*, 4.23.

14   Xenophon, *Memorabilia*, 2.1.13; Diogenes, *Lives*, 2.68.

15   Berkeley, "*Alciphron,*" in *Works*, vol. 3, 129.

16   Jane Harrison, *Prolegomena to the Study of Greek Religion*, 3rd ed. (New Jersey: Princeton University Press, 1991), 573, citing the *Petelia Tablet*. See further Edmonds, "Children of Earth," on the context and likely meaning of the claim as one that "rejects the hierarchy of status embedded in the local context, where different families boast of their heroic lineage, in favor of another genealogy, one in which all such claims are dwarfed by the central importance of humanity's relation to the divine family" (ibid., 113).

17   Plotinus, *Ennead*, II.3 [52].18, 17.

not be vandals. Philosophers have been too quick to suggest that only those who can *conceive* of the whole world around us (rather than the world simply as it affects our immediate interests) can be supposed to have, as it were, any voting rights in its management. Only gods and humans, they have supposed, are truly *citizens* of the cosmos, and all other creatures no more than necessary servants, hangers-on, foreigners in residence or even slaves. The likelier truth, however uncomfortable, is that it is the microbial population that has most influence on what goes on, together with other ecologically significant species which build upon that underlay.[18] We are better conceived as guests than as proprietors, even of the most smugly benevolent kind.

A "smug benevolence," indeed, may be the most obvious vice of the would-be cosmopolitan. Those who are convinced of their own significance, their indifference to merely local and parochial conventions, are very often merely applying their own local, parochial, conventions to the wider world.

> "We moderns [said Barker] believe in a great cosmopolitan civilization, one which shall include all the talents of all the absorbed peoples—." "The Señor will forgive me," said the President. "May I ask the Señor how, under ordinary circumstances, he catches a wild horse?" "I never catch a wild horse," replied Barker, with dignity. "Precisely," said the other; "and there ends your absorption of the talents. That is what I complain of your cosmopolitanism. When you say you want all peoples to unite, you really mean that you want all peoples to unite to learn the tricks of your people. If the Bedouin Arab does not know how to read, some English missionary or schoolmaster must be sent to teach him to read, but no one ever says, 'This schoolmaster does not know how to ride on a camel; let us pay a Bedouin to teach him.'"[19]

---

18 See Lynn Margulis and Dorion Sagan, *Microcosmos: Four Billion Years of Microbial Evolution* (New York: Summit Books, 1986).

19 Chesterton, *Napoleon of Notting Hill*, 25-26. The imagined conversation is between a British bureaucrat and a former, exiled, President of Nicaragua, in Chesterton's 1984. Solovyov's Politician (Vladimir Solovyov, *War, Progress and the End of History: three conversations including a short story of the Anti-Christ*, trans. Alexander Bakshy and Thomas R. Beyer, ed. Czeslaw Milosz and Stephan A. Hoeller [New York: Lindisfarne Press, 1990], 106-7, 132) more openly and honestly equates "civilization" with *European* civilization and expects to found universal peace on the spread of European power. Ironically, he also imagines,

Cosmopolitanism, in short, is sometimes merely a less immediately brutal form of imperialism, the imposition of one particular way of life and sight upon others considered heathen, barbarous or savage. Even a laudable concern for national parks and "wilderness areas" may conceal contempt for the actual human beings who live, or had lived, there until a more powerful authority evicted or imprisoned them. Imperial powers routinely relocate their subject populations, with whatever excuse is needed to conceal their crime or charm away opposition. The cosmopolitan pretext, even the environmentalist pretext, is no different in kind from the forced relocation of Cherokees, Creeks, Choctaws, Chickasaws and Seminoles in "the trail of tears" in the 1830s, for the imaginary "common good" and for the sake of gold.[20]

And yet there is still some virtue in the real ideal of Earth as one great city, the understanding that we, all of us, depend upon the wider world, and that this world is *composite*, a co-dependent assembly of all the creatures, lineages, symbioses that have survived disasters even greater than the ones by which we are all now threatened. Better, perhaps, consider ourselves *subjects* rather than, grandiloquently, "citizens," and to accept that we are all indeed subject to one law and one fortune. "Everything under the sun, says the sage, follows the same law and the same destiny."[21] How then shall the would-be philosopher respond to merely parochial rules and titles except like Rogatianus, "who advanced so far in renunciation of public life that he gave up all his property, dismissed all his servants, and resigned his rank."[22] If we can come to understand ourselves as elements, components, subjects within the wide world's rich embroidery, we may realize that we are all at play, "God's living toys."[23]

> Those who die in wars and battles anticipate only a little
> the death which comes in old age—they go away and come
> back quicker. But if their property is taken away while

---

in 1900 (ibid., 90–102) that there was no chance of renewed hostilities between the existing European nations. Solovyov was himself less sanguine.

20 See James Wilson, *The Earth Shall Weep: a history of Native America* (New York: Grove Press, 1998).

21 Michel de Montaigne, *Apology for Raymond Sebond*, trans. Roger Ariew and Marjorie Grene (Indianapolis: Hackett, 2003), 22, after Ecclesiastes 9.2.

22 Porphyry, *Life*, 7.32–36.

23 Plotinus, *Ennead*, III.2 [47].15, 32; ibid., 15, 57–59; cf. Plato, *Laws*, 7.803cd.

they are still alive, they may recognize that it was not theirs before either, and that its possession is a mockery to the robbers themselves when others take it away from them; for even to those who do not have it taken away, to have it is worse than being deprived of it.[24]

In other words, we have no absolute "rights" to life or property, as actors in the world-play, nor any "right" to a voice in how the play is played. Imagining that we *own* anything, even our own lives and bodies, is a strange delusion, given that we neither make them nor can even sustain them by our "independent" selves. "Which of you by taking thought can add one cubit unto his stature?"[25] The best we can ever manage is to play our parts or let the life of the world play on in us, as a dancer dances as his art moves him.[26]

The true "cosmopolitan," in brief, lives in obedience to the wider world, acknowledging no special merit in the status, rituals, rights or duties of any local enclaves. There are no truly independent individuals or clans or cities: nothing, that is, that can own or create or even sustain its own good without the quick cooperation of a wider world. From which it might seem to follow that Plotinus can have no personal interest in any *merely* "political" theory, since all such *poleis* and all cognate human societies are momentary associations which demand a loyalty they cannot earn. All merely local States demand an obedience and pretend to an authority that rests only on bribes and threats that cannot influence any real "philosopher," as if we had all been signed up to a club without being asked, and then instructed that we must obey club rules forever.

> Reason and experience alike tell us that the governments now existing in the world were established by bayonet-point, by force. None of the monarchies or governments that we see in the world are based on justice or on a correct foundation that is acceptable to reason. Their foundations are all rotten, being nothing but coercion and force.[27]

---

24 Plotinus, *Ennead*, III.2 [47].15, 38–45.

25 Matthew 6.27.

26 Plotinus, *Ennead*, III.2 [47].16, 24.

27 Ayatollah Ruhollah Khomeini, *Kashf al-Asrar* (1943), 221, quoted in F. Rajaee, *Islamic Value and World View* (Lanham: University Press of America, 1983), 76. This is perhaps a slight exaggeration—but only a slight one. The charge is an old and plausible one: cf. Minucius Felix, *Octavius*, 390 [25.8]: "All that the

THE ORGANIC POLIS

But the cosmos or even the terrestrial globe cannot be our only city, if only because few people are "philosophers" in the sense imagined here. And even those who might hope to be philosophers may still have ties to their immediate kin and context, from which—within the cosmos—they derive their lives, their language and their longings. Loyalty to "our own" precedes any loyalty to governments; governments indeed make a practice of stealing that former loyalty for their own ends.

> There are two communities—the one, which is great and truly common, embracing gods and men, in which we look neither to this corner nor to that, but measure the boundaries of our state (*civitas*) by the sun; the other, the one to which we have been assigned by the accident of our birth.[28]

I shall attempt in a later chapter to describe how Platonists might now see themselves as citizens or subjects of a cosmos within which there were no geographical or taxonomic boundaries nor established orders. But it is first important to see what a more ordinary Plotinian city might be like, and what Plotinus might have intended for Campania.[29] We do well to remember that we all start from our own mortal beginnings, even those who hope to discover a new life.

> It is clear to anybody that the imitative tribe will imitate most easily and most excellently the things that one's brought up with. For any group to give a good imitation of what is beyond their native experience is hard in deeds and harder still in words.[30]

And we also have duties to those from whom we took that start: parents, family, friends, teachers, farmers, physicians, cleaners and the rest—including domesticated non-humans, cattle, "pets." Even Pythagoras is said to have written to Anaximenes to say that "always to be watching the heavens is not good, and it is nobler to

---

Romans [and by extension other imperial powers] hold, occupy and possess is the spoil of outrage; their temples are all of loot, drawn from the ruin of cities, the plunder of gods and the slaughter of priests."

28 Seneca, *On Leisure*, 4.1: Long and Sedley, *Hellenistic Philosophers*, vol. 1, 431 [67K].

29 Porphyry, *Life*, 12: it may be, as I shall suggest below, that Porphyry misunderstood the project.

30 Plato, *Timaeus*, 19de.

care for one's *patris*"[31]—which is to say, in context, the Italian *polis* of Croton. Asked how someone could best educate his son, he replied, "by making him a citizen of some well-governed *polis*."[32] The true and consistent *sannyasin*, or renouncer, may manage to live as the lone wanderer I have just described—but even Plotinus still relied on Roman friends, on senatorial acquaintances and even, perhaps, an emperor. He had abandoned his old lives in Lycopolis, in Alexandria and in Gordian's army, and declined to talk about his childhood or his early years. But he did not live like Diogenes, still less like the stray dogs to which Diogenes and his disciples were compared. Citizenship was defined in those days by descent rather than residence,[33] so Plotinus remained a citizen of Lycopolis, and Porphyry of Tyre, despite being resident in Alexandria or Rome as "domiciled aliens." A rather different Plotinus might have stayed behind in Lycopolis and hoped to bring that city back to its ideal (not its historical) beginnings. Maybe, in accompanying (as seems likely) Philip the Arab, the next imperial claimant, back from Syria to Rome[34] he had hopes of reforming Rome itself. But neither option would have seemed very easy. Hadot's suggestion that he had no interest in "political life," since he praised Rogatianus for abandoning his senatorial role, and that it must therefore be surprising that he thought of founding a city, misses the mark.[35] Plotinus knew well that not everyone was fitted to live a "philosophic" life and that even those who were would still have need of the others. Even he might have had some hope of living as a citizen of a newly founded city. Even if all usual human life is no more than a game, it can still be properly played, without cheating as well as without complaining. Even if Rogatianus was right to reckon the senatorial life of his time was pointless or corrupt, good government might still be possible somewhere. Philosophers—and perhaps especially

---

31 Diogenes, *Lives*, 8.50.

32 Ibid., 8.16.

33 A. H. M. Jones, *The Later Roman Empire 284–602*, vol. 2 (Oxford: Blackwell, 1964), 712.

34 Porphyry, *Life*, 3.21–4: why else would Plotinus, disappointed in his hope (as Porphyry supposed) of encountering Persian or Indian philosophers, have gone instead to Rome when the emperor Gordian was murdered? Why else befriend Gallienus?

35 Pierre Hadot, *Plotinus, or the Simplicity of Vision*, trans. Michael Chase (Chicago: University of Chicago Press, 1993), 99.

those who had no current "official" standing—could often be asked to advise about the constitutions of old and of newly created cities.[36]

> [Their] teachings, like the revelations of the mysteries, claimed to transform the individual from within, to lift him to a higher state, to make of him a unique being, almost a god. When the city fell victim to disorder and pollution and turned to such a sage to ask the way out of its difficulties it did so precisely because he seemed a being apart and exceptional, a holy man isolated and removed to the fringes of the community by his whole manner of life.[37]

Do such holy men always wish to be isolated forever? Those of us who are not thus "true philosophers" and sages may be less confident that we can even rule our "own" lives, let alone all others, and ourselves hope to be found in some well-governed state, established without anyone's clear plan by the mere accumulation of past decisions, guided perhaps by gods. We may also wonder whether those who live only on the fringes of an actual community are best placed to understand their kindred's problems, and whether even they can be trusted with such power. Deioces, according to Herodotus, began by giving good advice to those who asked—but swiftly acted to seize all power and approbation when once offered the opportunity.[38]

> The Buddha, narrating [a similar tale about the costs of seeking another's judgement on a quarrel], adds his own conclusion: "in the same way, when a dispute arises between men, they have recourse to a judge, since he is their guide. And so their wealth diminishes, while the king's (store of) treasure grows."[39]

---

36   See Ousager, *Plotinus on Selfhood*, 233.

37   Jean-Pierre Vernant, *The Origins of Greek Thought* (London: Methuen, 1982), 58–59; see further Stephen R. L. Clark, "City of the Wise," *Apeiron* 20 (1987): 63–80.

38   Herodotus, *Histories*, 1.97–9: "He ordered them to build him houses worthy of his royal power, and strengthen him with a bodyguard. The Medes did so. They built him a big and strong house wherever in the land he indicated to them, and let him choose a bodyguard out of all the Medes. And having obtained power, he forced the Medes to build him one city and to fortify and care for this more strongly than all the rest. The Medes did this for him, too. So he built the big and strong walls, one standing inside the next in circles, which are now called Ecbatana."

39   Steven Collins, *Nirvana and the Other Buddhist Felicities* (Cambridge: Cambridge University Press, 1998), 455, citing *Dabbhapuppha-jataka*, no. 400.

But first, what is a "city," or a *polis*? Translators of the "political" writings of Plato, Aristotle and other ancient authors almost always speak of them as planning a new "State" and so swiftly treat their theories as ones that easily apply (or not) to modern "nation states" or other contemporary unions, including empires, federations, amphictyonies and tribes. This may sometimes be helpful: after all, most of us live within such "States," with negotiated borders and the recognition of other "States," and not in *poleis*, as that term was first intended. Maybe we can learn how we should organize a "State" by seeing how philosophers have hoped to organize a *polis*, whether by following their advice or consciously disregarding it. But it is wiser first to acknowledge that they were speaking of a different sort of social union than those we normally encounter now, just as it is wise to notice that "democracy" did not then mean what good moderns think it should, any more than "freedom" or "equality" (or rather their Greek and Latin cognates). Even our notion of an "individual human being," as I have already emphasized, is not entirely helpful in examining the ancients' thought. No one was even a human being, just by herself, any more than an isolated draughts-piece is genuinely a draughts-piece.[40] It is literally, obviously, true that "a *polis* is naturally prior to the household and to each of us, just as any organism is prior to its parts."[41] And like other such organisms, its many parts are united by a common goal—and probably animated by a single soul. Plotinus would not disagree with Aristotle in this:

> The city as a whole has a single end. Evidently, therefore, the system of education must also be one and the same for all, and the provision of this system must be a matter of public action. It cannot be left, as it is at present, to private enterprise, with each parent making provision privately for his own children and having them privately instructed as he himself thinks fit. Training for an end which is common should also itself be common. We must not regard a citizen as belonging just to himself: we must rather regard every citizen as belonging to the city, since each is a part of the city; and the provision made for each part will naturally be adjusted to the provision made for the whole.[42]

---

40 Aristotle, *Politics*, 1.1253a1-7.
41 Ibid., 1.1253a19-20.
42 Ibid., 8.1337a21-5.

But this need not imply that all citizens, let alone all residents, are the same: quite the reverse. The world we lost, and now barely understand, was one where everyone knew her place and her attendant duties.[43] Different castes and clans and classes, crafts, ages and genders had their own roles, responsibilities and rights. Most of us were born to them, inheriting a status (however high or low) that specified what we should do and what we should expect of others. We might more readily have thought of ourselves as elements in a lineage or line than simply as "independent selves." Even those crafts and new identities that some of us might sometimes choose, or had thrust upon us, had their own unchosen rules and rites. Maybe we could become a clerk, a smith, a squire, even though we hadn't been born into that caste or clan, but what we then became was just as much a fixed identity as any hereditary knight's or serf's, and we learnt our duties by imitation. And only the celibate classes were likely to recruit their members solely from those born into another class: the rest, even if they accepted some outsiders, could hope to raise their children in the craft.

> The virtuous city is then compared by al-Fārābi to a sound body, whose organs cooperate in ensuring the health of the animal, as well as its survival. Like the body, whose organs differ in rank or function, the parts of the city differ in rank and function, too. Hence, just as we find in the former a master organ, which is the heart, subserved by other, lower organs, we find in the latter a human master (*raʾīs*), served by subordinates, who carry out his orders. These subordinates are in turn served by other subordinates until we reach the lowest category of subordinates who are not served by anybody. The basic difference between the organs of the body and the parts of the city, al-Fārābi explains, is that the actions of the former are natural, whereas the actions of the latter are voluntary.[44]

In such a world it might still be true that everyone should do their duty, and everyone remember to respect the rights and duties of the other classes. But what those rights and duties, rites and

---

43   See Stephen R. L. Clark, "Deference, Degree and Selfhood," *Philosophy* 80 (2005): 249–60.
44   Majid Fakhry, *Al-Fārābi, Founder of Islamic Neoplatonism: his life, works and influence* (Oxford: Oneworld Publications, 2002), 102.

expectations were depended wholly on class, caste, profession, age and gender. In some tongues even the manner of speech must differ, and there is no single thing that *anyone* can call herself (as nowadays we say "I" or think of ourselves as "people"). Even those words that we now translate as "people" usually only meant "free, native-born and (probably) male"—and "free," in turn, meant only "propertied." The virtue of the freeman, *eleutheriotes*, is to make proper, *generous*, use of property,[45] and "generosity," in turn, is the virtue of those "with breeding." The excellence of women is not that of men.[46] The excellence of ordinary citizens is not that of the nobly born. Clerics and smiths and farmers and farmers' wives and servants all have their own responsibilities and need particular virtues or particular ways of expressing deeper virtues to complete them well, as do cattle, horses and dogs. Sometimes there are also statesmen, with the job of interweaving all the virtues of the different castes and crafts and ages to the best effect. More often, there is no need of such a weaver, because the job was done before, by Manu[47] or the invisible hand of evolutionary adjustment.

This was likely the rule in every human group—but *civilized* groups were the likeliest to insist on this diversity of role and rule. *Primitive* societies are, exactly, ones where there are rather fewer such distinctions. Almost any adult can do almost anything that any member of such a group can do. Only the bare divisions between male and female, initiate and child, insider and outsider remind the "uncivilized" of the rich array of roles and rules of which their neighbors—or sometimes their ancestors—might boast. And even those divisions are regularly subverted: there are often accepted roles, for example, for males who wish to live as women supposedly do, or females who wish to live as men—irrespective of their sexual preferences (neither "wimps" like myself nor "tomboys" need be "gay," nor do they need any surgical transformations[48]). Amusingly,

---

45   See Aristotle, *Nicomachean Ethics*, 4.1119b19ff.

46   Aristotle, *Rhetoric*, 1361a8-9; *Politics*, 1.1260a20-5; 3.1277b24-6.

47   That is, by some legendary lawgiver of the past. Manu's laws defined the Hindu castes, whereas those of Moses or Minos at least *hinted* at some more egalitarian possibility.

48   This is not to say that such surgery must always be forbidden: some, after all, have in the past made themselves eunuchs for the kingdom of heaven's sake, perhaps including Origen (see Matthew 19.12), or for the love of Cybele. But this is a larger topic than I can address here-now.

as Douglas has observed, it is the obviously *primitive* tribes whose form of life is most like that of would-be liberals in modern times.[49] *Civilized* peoples, until very recently, have boasted of their divisions. Each role has its own particular honor. According to the code, a master who is too familiar with his servants offers *them* an insult as severe as they would offer him if *they* were too familiar. The hierarchy within a servants' hall may be more careful than amongst the gentry. An insult anywhere is an assault and must be avenged. *Hubris*, in Greek circles, is more than violence: it is an attempt to demean and to humiliate and so exalt oneself through a contemptuous assault. Betrayal—perhaps of the code of hospitality—is more than an inconvenience. Justice, in such a system, lies in knowing one's place and claiming its due honor. Nor should we suppose that those who merely "serve" are therefore to be despised: on the contrary, they are the foundation of the whole enterprise. But not everyone has an honorable place. Slaves stand outside the sphere of justice and get no honor whatever it is they do. Slaves, as Orlando Patterson has suggested, are the world's first *individuals*, dishonored, alienated from all family connections.[50] Slaves have no one to count on but themselves alone and are past caring about further shame.

> There are, according to [Al-Farabi], four generic types of non-virtuous cities: the ignorant, the wayward (*dāllah*), the depraved (*fāsiqah*) and the renegade (*mubadillah*). To these four categories is added in the *Civil Polity* the class of parasites or outgrowths, who may be compared to weeds, since they grow on the periphery of political life and contribute little to it. This anti-social class is followed by a "beastly" class, which consists of people who resemble "human beasts" or wild animals. Some of them live in woods, in isolation or in groups, copulate like wild beasts and feed on raw meat and vegetables, or hunt for their prey like fierce animals. They might be found at the extremities of the inhabited world, either the extreme south or the extreme north. Such people, al-Fārābi observes, should be treated like wild animals. If they can be put to human use, they should be assimilated; if not, and they prove

---

49   Mary Douglas, *Natural Symbols*, 2nd ed. (Harmondsworth: Penguin, 1973), 57, 72.

50   "Slavery is the permanent, violent domination of natally alienated and generally dishonored persons": Orlando Patterson, *Slavery and Social Death* (Boston: Harvard University Press, 1982), 13.

to be useless or even dangerous, they should be treated like dangerous animals. The same applies to dealing with their offspring.[51]

So what, in this context, is a *polis*, if it is not really what we would call a "state" or even a "nation"? It is a self-governing, mostly self-sufficient body centered on civic buildings such as temples, libraries and gymnasia, and with what sea or countryside around can supply its major needs. Many such cities were founded long enough ago to seem a natural growth, from clusters of related villages (perhaps), but many around the classical Mediterranean were created in then living memory by colonists considered surplus to their mother-cities' needs. It would be true of them at least—or true of the principal citizens—that they had made a real contract or signed up to a known project. Colonies might continue to keep in touch with their mother-cities or might on the other hand adopt some wholly contrary ethos to distinguish them from the old. How members of the city were ranked, who had any sort of vote in an assembly, who might own what property, or how they reckoned themselves related to the heroes of old stories: all these things were settled somehow, though very rarely after clear debate. Sadly, the usual conclusion was that all cities are involved ceaselessly in a lifelong war against all others,[52] and any alliances they might make were always transient and pragmatic—except when all such cities might remember a common descent and language, and shared religious duties as well as ancestral rivalries.

Establishing the city needed more than simply a gang of people settling down on otherwise unclaimed land (or land claimed only by "savages"). The central places of the city, at least, must be marked out, in imitation of the heavens. Ecbatana, for example, had seven walls, each of a different color, apparently to evoke the seven planetary stars then known to ancient astronomers and still memorialized in the days of the modern week.[53] In laying out the plan for a new *polis*, the "great temple of the sky" was projected

51 Fakhry, *Al-Fārābī*, 107. A less anthropocentric reading would rather admit that those other "wild" tribes, whether human or non-human, are only going about their own business in the ways the world requires.
52 Plato, *Laws*, 1.625e.
53 So also in later Muslim city design, "which adopted the septenary division of Ptolemaic zonal geography": Aziz Al-Azmeh, *Muslim Kingship: Power and the Sacred in Muslim, Christian and Pagan Polities* (London: I. B. Tauris, 1996), 72.

onto the landscape to establish it as an authentic image of heaven.[54] Roman colonies were laid out in imitation of Rome herself, and Rome was first created by a line drawn round her sacred space, in imitation of the heavens. The analogy of cosmos and *polis* was not just a philosopher's fancy, but what defined the city, as an imitation or reflection of the larger world. What is true of the city's structure is a guide to the cosmic order, and vice versa.

> Plato explained the ideal city as divided into twelve sectors
> which allowed cosmic laws and proportion to penetrate the
> city and allow the inhabitants to live under cosmic laws....
> This cosmic pattern is especially clear in the royal circular
> cities of the ancient Orient. A number of Median, Parthian,
> Sassanian, and Abbasid cities might here be cited.[55]

The symbolic analogy is also a moral one.[56] As Plotinus argues: "The public executioner, who is a scoundrel, does not make his well-governed city worse," and so neither does he, or any other villain, make the cosmos worse.[57] Cosmos and city alike need many different sorts of human and non-human creatures to prosper, and the value of those wholes cannot be determined solely by the apparent virtue or value of their parts.[58] Neither proper cities nor the cosmos are made up from equals, any more than any ordinary drama, which needs its rogues and yokels just as much as heroes.[59]

The tradition, finding or devising the same form in body, city and cosmos, continued for centuries:

> For Calcidius [a fourth century philosopher, author of a
> commentary on Plato's *Timaeus*], not only is the city a small
> world—an ordered microcosm of the universe—it is also
> a body writ large—a macrocosm of the human being; all
> ordered and functioning according to the same principles
> and overall design, which in the city are present in its

---

54   See Rykwert, *The Idea of a Town*, 45-48.
55   H. P. L'Orange, "Expressions of Cosmic Kingship in the Ancient World," in *The Sacral Kingship/La Regalità Sacra: Contributions to the 8th International Congress for the History of Religions* (Rome, 1955): 481-512 (Leiden: Brill, 1959), 481-82.
56   See further Plato, *Timaeus*, 17c; Ousager, *Plotinus on Selfhood*, 250-51.
57   Plotinus, *Ennead*, III.2 [47].17, 87-90. So also Origen, *Contra Celsum*, 475 (8.31); Augustine, *On Order*, 2.12, discussed by Gillian Clark, "Desires of the Hangman: Augustine on Legitimized Violence," in *Violence in Late Antiquity: perceptions and practices*, ed. H. A. Drake (Aldershot: Ashgate, 2006), 140.
58   Plotinus, *Ennead*, II.9 [33].7, 5-8; III.2 [47].3, 9-13.
59   Plotinus, *Ennead*, III.2 [47].11, 12-17.

spatial form as well as in its social order. . . . The medieval city, it will be seen, acquired its cosmological symbolism both through its spatial forms, for example in the ordered geometries it shared with the cosmos, and in its functions, as a "body" made up of hierarchically arranged parts mirroring the moral topography of the Christian universe as a whole, all created to God's divine plan.[60]

MAGNESIA, UR-ATHENS AND ENFORCING VIRTUE

So any city, like the cosmos itself, is bound to contain many sorts of creature, including ones that, by themselves, seem dangerous, superfluous, sick or feeble. A well-ordered city, we may conclude, finds some proper place and occupation for all its members, as different faculties or elements of the soul should also find their proper places.

Whatever the precise form of government (monarchical, oligarchical, democratic), there will be fixed rules and rituals, as the course of the fixed stars indicates. There will also be more malleable, changeable regulations, mirroring the course of the wandering "planetary" bodies. Does this require authoritative action by its rulers, or will every component, given the opportunity, migrate to its proper place? Are there good reasons for authorities to intervene when things seemingly go astray? Plotinus might seem averse to intervention:

> If some boys, who have kept their bodies in good training, but are inferior in soul to their bodily condition because of lack of education, win a wrestle with others who are trained neither in body or soul and grab their food and their dainty clothes, would the affair be anything but a joke? Or would it not be right for even the lawgiver to allow them to suffer this as a penalty for their laziness and luxury?[61]

The bullies will in due course be punished "first by being wolves and ill-fated men," and in subsequent lives by being forced themselves to suffer what they did, as "this world-order is truly *Adrasteia*, the Inescapable."[62] The question of their (and our) future

60   Keith Lilley, *City and Cosmos: the medieval world in urban form* (London: Reaktion Books Ltd, 2009), 8, 12.
61   Plotinus, *Ennead*, III.2 [47].8, 16–21.
62   Plotinus, *Ennead*, III.2 [47].8, 27–28; III.2 [47].13, 4–18. Cf. Plato, *Laws*, 5.741b: "Necessity (as the proverb runs) not even God himself can compel" (after Simonides: see Plato, *Protagoras*, 345d5).

(and past) lives will concern me later: what matters here is the apparent moral, that there need be neither intervention nor judicial punishment for such assaults. This should not in fact be surprising: neither Greek nor Roman law, in general, took account of (as it were) *private* acts of violence. In most modern jurisdictions, murder, assault and theft are counted not only as offences against the actual victim, but against the State: even if the victim, or the victim's immediate family, choose not to seek revenge, the State will generally take action (though there may be problems with securing a conviction). In the ancient city aediles and other civic officers may have taken account of events that disturbed the public peace: riot, sacrilege and rebellion. In other cases, it would be up to particular citizens to take offenders to court (as Socrates' accusers did, and Euthyphro), or even take personal vengeance. How this shift in sentiment, giving "the State" an interest in all such lawless acts, has happened is itself of interest, but it is not surprising that Plotinus and other moralists seem to think only of the apparent "private" wrongs, and are ready to discount them. "And if you are wronged, what is there dreadful in that to an immortal?"[63] Maybe he might himself think a little differently about injuries sustained by those who are not, in his sense, "philosophers," as he did about the property of orphans in his care?[64] But even then it might depend on whether he would himself have any standing in the case: in Platonopolis, assuming that he might have been on its council,[65] he might have been more proactive, but more probably he would have expected the occasion not to arise.

What then is the role of the "lawgiver," if that government is best that governs least (and best of all is one that governs not at all)?[66] A similar thought has often been extorted from Daoist writings, anthologized many centuries after the purported date of Lao Tzu.[67] The best city, like the cosmos, emerges without any

---

63   Plotinus, *Ennead*, II.9 [33].9, 15–16.
64   Porphyry, *Life*, 9.14.
65   As Euree Song is prepared to envisage in "The Ethics of Descent in Plotinus," *Hermathena* 187 (2009): 27–48.
66   Henry David Thoreau, *Walden and Civil Disobedience* (Wordsworth, 2006), 132.
67   See Russell Kirkland, *Taoism: the enduring tradition* (London: Routledge, 2004), 33–39, 52–65. Kirkland makes it clear that the idea of *wu-wei* ("non-action"), identified first in the writings of the Legalist Shen Pu-hai (d. 337 BC) in his advice against micro-management, actually includes the shrewd manipulation of one's circumstances, personally and politically: ibid., 26.

prior planning, but in such form as *would* be chosen by the best possible planner.[68]

> If anyone were to ask nature why [she] makes, if [she] cared to hear and answer the questioner [she] would say: "You ought not to ask, but to understand in silence, just as I am silent and not in the habit of talking. Understand what, then? That what comes into being is what I see in my silence, an object of contemplation."[69]

This is, at least at first sight, very unlike the deliberately centralized and authoritarian rule imagined in Plato's *Laws*, which was perhaps to be Plotinus's partial model for his projected Platonopolis, at least if we interpret the plan that the settlers in Platonopolis should live "according to the laws of Plato" as a reference to his *Laws*.[70] But even in Magnesia it is not clear that the rulers will always intervene in private "quarrels."

Might Platonopolis resemble Ecbatana, a walled city established to support and dignify the King, just as the phenomenal cosmos is an image or echo of the eternal, and that in turn an "image" of the unimaginable One? There seem echoes of that idea in Plotinus's use of the monarchical metaphor, which I shall address below. But perhaps there is some scope for a divergent thesis, especially as Magnesia, the city described in the *Laws*, is *not* to be walled: "A wall is by no means an advantage to a city as regards health, and, moreover, it usually causes a soft habit of soul in the inhabitants, by inviting them to seek refuge within it instead of repelling the enemy."[71] The very attempt to "wall off" the city (or oneself) runs counter to our actual dependence, always, on the wider world. Another *walled* city described by Plato is the metropolis of Atlantis,[72] encircled by many moats and walls of white, black and red. Athens, at that distant (imaginary) time, had only a small acropolis (in a land more fertile than the erosion of many centuries had left for Plato's contemporaries), and lacked the multiple barriers that

---

68 Plotinus, *Ennead*, III.2 [47].14, 1–7.

69 Ibid., III.8 [30].4, 1–7, replacing Armstrong's "it" by the gender appropriate to "*phusis*."

70 Porphyry, *Life*, 12.3–10.

71 Plato, *Laws*, 6.778e.

72 Plato, *Critias*, 115a–118a. For the afterlife of this clearly fictitious land, see Pierre Vidal-Naquet, *The Atlantis Story: A Short History of Plato's Myth*, trans. Janet Lloyd (Liverpool: Liverpool University Press, 2007).

sustained the Atlantean kings. Plotinus himself makes no direct mention of the story of Atlantis, though one of his followers, Zoticus, wrote an epic poem on the subject,[73] and both Amelius (probably his oldest friend and follower) and Porphyry sought to understand the story as a cosmological allegory.[74] Amelius thought that the island of Atlantis, like Ecbatana, was divided into seven circles (without clear warrant in *Critias*). Others saw the war as one between fallen *daimones* and other, healthier souls:

> Just as the ancient theologians refer this to Osiris and Typhon or to Dionysus and the Titans, Plato attributes it to Athenians and Atlantines out of reverence. For he hands down the tradition that, before they come into three-dimensional bodies, there is rivalry between souls and the enmattered *daimones* that he assigned to the west; for the west, as the Egyptians say, is the region of harmful souls. The philosopher Porphyry is of this view, and one would be surprised if he is saying anything different from the view authorized by Numenius.[75]

Proclus himself, though he insisted that "these things have happened in every sense,"[76] took the main point of the story to describe the acting out on the historical and phenomenal plane of a perennial, foundational contest, couched in terms of the One versus the Indefinite Dyad.

> If we focus on the unification and the plurality of things within the cosmos, we shall say that the constitution summarized by Socrates is the image of its unification, establishing as its goal the all-pervasive communion of things, while the war between Atlantis and Athens narrated by Critias is the image of their division, particularly of the opposition implied by the two columns. Whereas if

---

73 Porphyry, *Life*, 7.12–16. Presumably he was inspired by the suggestion that Solon should have written the epic, had he not been distracted by immediate political concerns: Plato, *Timaeus*, 21c.

74 Proclus, *Commentary on Timaeus*, 169 [I.76, 26–30]; Porphyry, *in Tim.* 20d8–9 Fr. 10; see also Porphyry, *De Antro Nympharum*, 13, and *On Abstinence*, 2.41, 16–20 for the association of such dangerous *daimones*, including Naiads, with the West. See K. Nilüfer Akçay, *Porphyry's On the Cave of the Nymphs in its Intellectual Context* (Leiden: Brill, 2019), 93–108.

75 Proclus, *Commentary on Timaeus*, 170 [I.77, 15–25], after Porphyry, *in Tim.*, fr. X; see also Porphyry, *On Abstinence*, 70–71 [II.38–39].

76 Proclus, *Commentary on Timaeus*, 171 [I.77, 27–28].

[we go] by the distinction between heavenly and sublunary realms, we shall claim that the constitution is assimilated to the heavenly arrangement (for Socrates too says that its paradigm is founded in the heavens), while the Atlantine war is likened to generation, which subsists through opposition and change.[77]

I shall not address the supposed cosmological significance of the story,[78] save to acknowledge again that city and cosmos are intended to reflect each other. Nor on the other hand am I concerned with the supposed historical verisimilitude of the story, beyond the obvious truth that cities and lands have often been destroyed by flood, or fire.[79] Proclus, though he occasionally seems to endorse the historicity of the story, himself offers a reason for Plato to choose this sort of story rather than the more overtly mythological to represent his meaning:

> He took his subject matter from history to avoid setting in the divine realm his account of mutual hostilities. Rather, by introducing events in the human realm, through the cautious use of analogy he tries to bring it to bear upon the gods as well.[80]

---

77 Ibid., 95 [I.4, 14–25].

78 See José Maria Zamora Calvo, "Proclus on the Atlantis Story," *Rupkatha Journal on Interdisciplinary Studies in Humanities* 10.3 (2018): 1–9.

79 See Harold Tarrant, "Atlantis: Myths, Ancient and Modern," *The European Legacy* 12, no. 2 (2007): 159–72 for criticism of the notion that the historicity of the story was debated from the beginning. Plato could hardly have devised a more obviously unreliable narrator and provenance! See also Christopher Gill, "Plato's Atlantis Story and the Birth of Fiction," *Philosophy and Literature* 3, no. 1 (1979), 64–78: "Plato's narrative is not actual historiography but rather a pastiche of historiography, almost a parody." How Atlantis—the villain in Plato's story—has come to stand in popular fantasy for an Enlightenment utopia is a further puzzle.

80 Proclus, *Commentary on Timaeus*, 172 [I.79, 30–80, 3]; 297 [I.197, 18–21]. See also ibid., 277 [I.177, 22–27]: "But, even if...some such island did arise, it is still possible to take the story about it both as history and as an image of something that arises naturally within the whole universe, both explaining this [island] in terms of what it resembles, and gradually accustoming those who hear of such spectacles to the whole study of encosmic things." See also ibid., 272 [I.172, 24–8]: "Through the parallel between humans and things divine, he teaches us even of this war before the origin of the cosmos, adopting the Athenians to represent Athena and the Olympian gods and the people of Atlantis to represent the Titans and Giants, for it is possible to study the same things in images as one can in universals."

A further possible twist might be that Atlantis owes something to the Homeric Phaeacia, which Proclus mentions in passing, as a case where the story itself explains the absence of present evidence of its truth.[81] Both lie beyond the lands we know, Atlantis indeed explicitly in the "real ocean."[82] They both came to suffer the anger of the gods and were blockaded from the normal world thereafter:[83] they chose, it could be said, their eventual isolation. Atlantis and Phaeacia alike are Fairyland, luxurious beyond belief, where once the gods walked freely.[84] The Phaeacians, it was rumored, were born, like Aphrodite, from the blood of the castrated Ouranos;[85] the nobler Atlanteans at least had their descent from Poseidon. But what is the precise *political* moral? How do the ideal Athens, Ur-Athens, of so many thousand years earlier and the slowly declining Atlantean model differ? And a subsidiary question also arises: why were Proclus and the other commentators so adamant in *ignoring* the obvious political context of the story?

The Egyptian priests of Sais, it was said, told Solon (or so Plato said Critias said was a private family tradition) that their records told of a time before the cataclysms that had overthrown most of the Mediterranean cities.

> It is related in our records how once upon a time your *polis* stayed the course of a mighty host, which, starting from a distant point in the Atlantic Ocean, was insolently advancing to attack the whole of Europe, and Asia to boot. For the ocean there was at that time navigable; for in front of the mouth which you Greeks call, as you say, "the pillars of Heracles," there lay an island which was larger

---

81 Proclus, *Commentary*, 289 [I.190, 7]; Strabo, 2.3.6, 13.1.36 (after Aristotle).
82 Plato, *Timaeus*, 25a. See also *Phaedo*, 109b: "We who dwell between the pillars of Heracles and the river Phasis live in a small part of it about the sea, like ants or frogs about a pond, and many other people live in many other such regions."
83 Compare especially *Timaeus*, 25cd and Homer, *Odyssey*, 13.161–4 (see also 8.565–9): in both cases the land is now blockaded, by mud or immovable stone.
84 The identification of Scheria, Phaeacia, with Fairyland, and the suspicion that Plato drew on the Homeric description to develop his Atlantis, were more popular in the past: see A. Shewan, "The Scheria of the Odyssey," *The Classical Quarterly* 13, no. 1 (1919): 4–11 for a robust but inconclusive rebuttal of at least the former idea. The latter was apparently suggested by Walter Leaf, *Homer and History* (London: MacMillan, 1915).
85 See Edmonds, "Children of Earth," 104, citing *Scholion for Apollonius Rhodius*, 982–92a.

than Libya and Asia together; and it was possible for the travelers of that time to cross from it to the other islands, and from the islands to the whole of the continent over against them which encompasses that veritable ocean. For all that we have here, lying within the mouth of which we speak, is evidently a haven having a narrow entrance; but that yonder is a real ocean, and the land surrounding it may most rightly be called, in the fullest and truest sense, a continent. Now in this island of Atlantis there existed a confederation of kings, of great and marvelous power, which held sway over all the island, and over many other islands also and parts of the continent; and, moreover, of the lands here within the Straits they ruled over Libya as far as Egypt, and over Europe as far as Tuscany.[86]

The contest was between lands originally allocated to Athena (and Hephaistos) and to Poseidon respectively, but whereas—it was said—the old Athenians had maintained their god-given constitution and ideals, the Atlanteans, despite their superior location far from the mists and sediments of the Mediterranean puddle, drifted away from virtue and sought to dominate our own familiar lands:

When the portion of divinity within them [the Atlanteans] was now becoming faint and weak through being ofttimes blended with a large measure of mortality, whereas the human temper was becoming dominant, then at length they lost their comeliness, through being unable to bear the burden of their possessions, and became ugly to look upon, in the eyes of him who has the gift of sight; for they had lost the fairest of their goods from the most precious of their parts; but in the eyes of those who have no gift of perceiving what is the truly happy life, it was then above all that they appeared to be superlatively fair and blessed, filled as they were with lawless ambition and power.[87]

They became, in brief, an aggressive empire, very like late-fifth-century Athens—and the Roman Empire. Ur-Athens, it was said, saved all the Mediterranean peoples from their domination.

The manhood of [Ur-Athens] showed itself conspicuous for valor and might in the sight of all the world. For it stood pre-eminent above all in gallantry and all warlike

---

86 Plato, *Timaeus*, 24e–25b.
87 Plato, *Critias*, 121ab.

arts, and acting partly as leader of the Greeks, and partly standing alone by itself when deserted by all others, after encountering the deadliest perils, it defeated the invaders and reared a trophy; whereby it saved from slavery such as were not as yet enslaved, and all the rest of us who dwell within the bounds of Heracles it ungrudgingly set free.[88]

Both Ur-Athens and Atlantis were subsequently drowned, all Greek memory of the event was lost, and the way back to Atlantis barred forever.[89]

Plato's intent in telling the story may simply have been to find or invent an older tradition for the Athenian constitution than the contemporary appeal to Cleisthenes or even Solon himself as having established the proper form of democracy, and to suggest, covertly, that a truly egalitarian democracy was something that only the gods or godlike men could handle.[90] But the actual accounts of the Old Athenian order, and the Atlantean, suggest a slightly different moral. "Plato designs [Atlantis] as a Utopia, a maritime empire of vast dimensions ruled by a federation of kings, to confront it with a Utopia of quite another stripe: Ur-Athens, which in the end saved Europe and Africa from the imperial yoke."[91] Atlantis was, in effect, a feudal society, supplying its warriors from each subordinate grouping, with kings and princes descended, as they supposed, from Poseidon and a mortal woman. Ur-Athens and its land were cultivated and supplied by the main body of the people, with both the priestly and the warrior class divided from them and living according to the rules imagined in Plato's *Republic*.[92] Neither civilization was democratic, and still less egalitarian, but in Ur-Athens the aim, at

---

88   Plato, *Timaeus*, 25bc.

89   Ibid., 25d.

90   Plato, *Laws*, 5.739d: "In such a *polis*, be it gods or sons of gods that dwell in it, they dwell pleasantly, living such a life as this." See Casey Stegman, "Plato's *Timaeus-Critias*, the Ancestral Constitution, and the Democracy of the Gods," *Political Theory* 45 (2017): 240–60; Yves Charbit, "The Platonic City: History and Utopia," *Population* (English edition) 57, no. 2 (2002): 207–35 for further discussion of the differences between the utopian projects of *Republic*, *Laws* and *Timaeus-Critias* (and especially the number 5040, with its 60 divisors, including itself and 1).

91   T. G. Rosenmeyer, "Plato's Atlantis Myth: 'Timaeus' or 'Critias?'" *Phoenix* 10, no. 4 (1956): 166.

92   Though the conversation mentioned at the opening of the *Timaeus* cannot have been the one recorded or imagined in the *Republic*: only Socrates was present for both events (cf. *Republic*, 1.327-8; *Timaeus*, 17-19).

least, was to preserve the warrior and priestly classes immaculate—
saved, supposedly, from temptation by being barred from personal
property or private family life,[93] and taught that a ruler's primary
duty must always be to sustain the welfare of the ruled. In the ideal
city, so Plato supposed, "All that is called 'private' is everywhere and
by every means rooted out of our life."[94] The Atlantean failure was
to forget that lines do not reliably breed true, and that all mortal
souls are corruptible.[95] The original well-ordered city, in Plato's
imagination, was self-sufficient and easily satisfied: "a city of pigs,"
in the eyes of the oversophisticated. Its ruin, and need for a cure,
would be caused by desire for luxury and concomitant fear of rivals.[96]
Ur-Athens surpassed Atlantis because, it was said, it remembered its
own true good and kept its most powerful classes pure. In Atlantis
the "higher" were served by the "lower": in Ur-Athens, the higher
are to serve the lower. The Atlantean capital is a fortress city like
Ecbatana: Ur-Athens lies open to the world.

The purity rule, enforcing a division of labor, seems to be
imagined even more strictly than it was in the *Republic*:

> You see, first, how the priestly class is separated off from
> the rest; next, the class of craftsmen, of which each sort
> works by itself without mixing with any other; then the
> classes of shepherds, hunters, and farmers, each distinct
> and separate. Moreover, the military class here [that is, in
> Egypt], as no doubt you have noticed, is kept apart from
> all the other classes, being enjoined by the law to devote
> itself solely to the work of training for war.[97]

---

93 Ibn Rushd (Averroes, d. 1198) is one of the very few philosophers to
accept this argument whole-heartedly: "It was against this dissolution of the
sphere of collective interest by private households that he endorsed Plato's
abolition of the household for the guardians of the city (i.e., rulers and soldiers). People with access to public power should not have private property
or wives and children of their own; rather, their lives should be collectivized:
they should live together, eat together, and share their women and children,
on a highly regimented basis (for eugenic purposes). This would promote love
among them and ensure that their only interest would be the furtherance of
the public good" (Crone, *Medieval*, 190). We may suspect that both Plato and
Ibn Rushd were wrong.

94 Plato, *Laws*, 5.739c.

95 See Ousager, *Plotinus on Selfhood*, 264.

96 Plato, *Republic*, 2.369a; see Clark, "Herds of Free Bipeds," on the significance of pigs.

97 Plato, *Timaeus*, 24ab.

So it seems that Plato is here preferring a strictly *caste* society to a feudal, one with a more limited ambition to one with an imperial reach. Is it reasonable to wonder whether Plotinus had the same opinion? And what would that mean in practice, for Platonopolis? May we guess that his model was not simply the imagined city of Magnesia, but Ur-Athens, a deliberate image of the perennial cosmological conflict and a reminder of what a proper *polis* must defend against? Perhaps it was not the courtiers' mere spite that prevented Plotinus's plans: the plan was perhaps too clearly a rebuke to Imperial, would-be Atlantean, Rome. The king of kings does not rule over different, alien peoples and so is not an imperial power.[98] "Officially," as Ousager remarks, "Rome was a law-abiding republic or monarchy. In reality it had become a capricious military dictatorship"[99] in which even the dictator was a slave to his own armed forces and liable to swift assassination.

But even if, as seems likely, the idea of Ur-Athens, victorious against Atlantis, was a factor in Plotinus's dream, the practicalities of founding a new *polis* would be against any exact embodiment of that ideal. In Ur-Athens all things were held in common: even the lower classes of the city followed the same rules as the rulers of Plato's Republic, and there were no natural families, except for resident aliens. Ur-Athens maintained an armed class of twenty thousand (both men and women), against Magnesia's limit of 5040 armed (male) citizens and households.[100] Aristotle rounded that latter number down to 5000 in commenting on Plato's notion, adding that "a territory as large as that of Babylon will be needed for so many inhabitants, or some other country of unlimited extent, to support five thousand men in idleness and another swarm of women and servants around them many times as numerous. It is proper no doubt to assume ideal conditions, but not to go beyond all bounds of possibility!"[101] It is unlikely that Campania could

---

98   Plotinus, *Ennead*, V.5 [32].3, 16–18: see Ousager, *Plotinus on Selfhood*, 259–60.
99   Ousager, *Plotinus on Selfhood*, 265.
100   Plato, *Critias*, 112d; *Laws*, 5.738a. The number allows multiple ways of dividing the total into different but equal sectors, clans or professions. Iamblichus seems to have had more hopes than Plotinus of grounding his political philosophy in mathematics: see O'Meara, "Aspects of Political Philosophy in Iamblichus."
101   Aristotle, *Politics*, 2.1265a. Plotinus could have opted for a smaller *polis* if that proved necessary. If the number of citizens and households were reduced to 2520 this number too could be sorted into almost as many equal divisions.

support even so many, or Gallienus accept the existence of a rival army (or would he have considered it a more securely loyal company than the overmighty legions?). The analogue for the military caste in Campania might simply be the principal citizens, with the right and responsibility to ensure the rules of the city were kept fresh and properly enforced. In Imperial colonies—and Platonopolis would presumably have been counted so—citizens were relieved of any duty to provide new soldiers for the empire. And even when such a duty was imposed, most *poleis* preferred to pay a tax for mercenaries to be hired from within or outside the borders.

Founding a new city was a commoner event in the eastern than the western empire[102] and usually involved enlarging and reconstructing some existing village or administrative region. Sometimes those new cities might be fortified. By Porphyry's account, there was said already to have been "a city of philosophers" in Campania (maybe meaning no more than that there were once several citizens with philosophical interests or ambitions), and it was this that Gallienus agreed to revive on Plotinus's plan. Maybe there were still residents, enough to make a village or a neglected district. It seems hard to believe otherwise that Plotinus could have expected to recruit the full account of 5040 (male) citizens merely from among his acquaintance, or even the wider world. Nor is it clear that would-be philosophers, by themselves, would easily manage a new city and the attendant farmland! In villages, responsibility for managing public goods might rest with a mass assembly; in a city, a council co-opted from the more secure residents would elect the necessary civic officials from its ranks each year.

> The people played a humble but essential role in the administration of the city by providing its night-watchmen, fire brigade, street and sewer cleaners, and craftsmen and laborers for the repair and erection of public works; it also, through the civic authorities, supplied workers to the imperial government for the public post and other services.... The selection of citizens for the various duties was in the West entrusted to the craft guilds into which the urban population was organized. In Egypt a different system was employed.[103]

---

102 Jones, *Later Roman Empire*, vol. 2, 719.
103 Ibid., 724.

I shall return to considering those craft guilds below. In the Egyptian system, with which Plotinus would have been more familiar, a city was divided into separate tribes or wards, which supplied the necessary workers in rotation. This echoes the Magnesian system: the city was to be divided between twelve wards or tribes, each with their tutelary deity, "when he has first set apart a sacred glebe for Hestia, Zeus and Athena, to which he shall give the name 'acropolis' and circle it round with a ring-wall."[104]

The most interesting feature of Magnesia, distinct from the supposedly ideal Republic, was its author's emphasis on religious ritual and obedience.[105]

> No man of sense, whether he be framing a new State or reforming an old one that has been corrupted, will attempt to alter the advice from Delphi or Dodona or Ammon, or that of ancient sayings, whatever form they take—whether derived from visions or from some reported inspiration from heaven.[106]

Platonopolis is to be run as a sacred trust, careful both of the earth, our mother, and the local gods and *daimones*.[107] The doctrine would have been especially appropriate in that most Mediterranean cities were essentially rural, drawing most of their wealth from farming their territory.[108] Magnesian citizens had two allotments of land within their ward, one urban and one rural, and their principal duty was to look after the land, helped by their obedient household.

> Within the order and relative safety of the living conditions guaranteed by their master's authority, women, children, slaves, and flocks all found the means to contribute to the common prosperity by fulfilling their respective roles. Virgil, better than anyone, sketched in the ideal picture of this agricultural Arcadia, in which a diligent laborer, through wise management of his dependents,

---

104 Plato, *Laws*, 5.745: that is, the city's sacred spaces are marked off, not the whole city.
105 See O'Meara, *Platonopolis*, 116–31, drawing chiefly on Plato's *Laws*, the Emperor Julian's program, and Iamblichus.
106 Plato, *Laws*, 5.738bc.
107 Ibid., 5.740a.
108 Jones, *Later Roman Empire*, vol. 2, 714.

"provides sustenance for his country and his little grandson and . . . for his herds of kine and faithful bullocks."[109]

But the duty was more than agricultural.

> First of all, we say, if—after the honors paid to the Olympians and the gods who keep the *polis*—we should assign the Even and the Left as their honors to the gods of the under-world, we would be aiming most straight at the mark of piety—as also in assigning to the former gods the things superior, the opposites of these. Next after these gods the wise man will offer worship to the *daimones*, and after the *daimones* to the heroes. After these will come private shrines legally dedicated to ancestral deities; and next, honors paid to living parents.[110]

Plotinus himself mentions the honors to be paid to the dead, and the oracular shrines established by some formerly human souls, as evidence of the soul's continued being:[111] we can presume that these would be active, and authorized, in Platonopolis. Not only space but time as well is to be marked out with an eye to the divine. "In the *Laws*," according to Catherine Pickstock's reading, "it is the divine gift of the liturgical cycle with all the concomitant sustenance which the deities bring to these festivals, which distinguishes human beings from the wild animals which have no such gifts of order, rhythm or harmony."[112] But in Magnesia *unauthorized* rituals and shrines, however private, were, precisely because they would be *private*, banned.[113] No alien

---

109   Descola, *Beyond Nature and Culture*, 327-28, citing Virgil, *Georgics*, 2.514-5. It is probably merely coincidental that both Virgil and Plotinus had Campania in mind.

110   Plato, *Laws*, 4.717ab.

111   Plotinus, *Ennead*, IV.7 [2].15.

112   Plato, *Laws*, 2.653dff according to Catherine Pickstock, *After Writing: On the liturgical consummation of philosophy* (Oxford: Blackwell, 1998), 40. Graeber and Wengrow, *Dawn of Everything*, 111-12, emphasize the significance of such regular, seasonal, alterations of social structure, as showing people that things can always, if we choose, be different. Wild animals, obviously, do in fact follow similar seasonal patterns.

113   Plato, *Laws*, 10.910cd. Though elsewhere "private," or at least "family," associations seem to be accepted as part of the diverse polity. In Egypt, at least, "associations were more or less complex organizations, formed by people who gathered together for a series of purposes, with some sense of durability and communal self-identity. In principle, their formation and membership were voluntary, although peer-pressure, professional obligations, hereditary attitudes,

loyalty or deviant piety could be permitted. The Emperor Julian agreed: ancient traditions could be respected, even if—like the Hebrew religion—they made exclusive demands for worship, but the Christian cult could not, being both novel and revolutionary in its implications.

> I am overwhelmed with shame, I affirm it by the gods, O men of Alexandria [he says], to think that even a single Alexandrian can admit that he is a Galilaean. The forefathers of the genuine Hebrews were the slaves of the Egyptians long ago, but in these days, men of Alexandria, you who conquered the Egyptians—for your founder was the conqueror of Egypt—submit yourselves, despite your sacred traditions, in willing slavery to men who have set at naught the teachings of their ancestors. You have then no recollection of those happy days of old when all Egypt held communion with the gods and we enjoyed many benefits therefrom. But those who have but yesterday introduced among you this new doctrine, tell me of what benefit have they been to the city?[114]

The respect its citizens should pay to the past also requires a duty to the future: all its citizens should procreate, despite the problem of finding any role for surplus sons (as the citizen's allotments were entailed in perpetuity, never to be divided or allowed to lapse).[115] There are severe penalties for males that refuse or fail to marry,[116] and even for any failure actually to procreate: surplus

---

and other more or less external impositions may have played a role in membership of associations. They could be—and usually were—very much active in the public life of their communities. Despite this, they remained private: *associations were not formally controlled by the state with its officials and were not formal parts of the constitutional setup of civic communities.* As institutions, they were bodies created by men, and sometimes women, for social interaction and possible economic advantage. They had not only informal customs and codes of conduct, but often also codified rules and regulations in the form of charters, by-laws, or 'contracts,' adopted and chosen by the members themselves": Mario C. D. Paganini, "Private Associations and Village Life in Early Roman Egypt," in Micaela Langellotti and D.W. Rathbone, *Village Institutions in Egypt in the Roman to Early Arab Periods* (Oxford: Oxford University Press, 2020), 41 (my italics).

114 Julian, *Works*, vol. 3, epistle 47, 433ac, p. 145; see O'Meara, *Platonopolis*, 121 (citing a different edition of Julian's works).

115 Cf. Leviticus 25.8–13; II Chronicles 36.21.

116 The Hermetic Corpus records an even harsher penalty: the childless suffer at the hands of *daimones* and are reborn neither as male nor female (Copenhaver, *Hermetica*, 12 [2.17]).

sons can perhaps be donated to childless couples.[117] Children are the main path to immortality for the individual, for the *polis* and for humanity.[118] "The bride and bridegroom must set their minds to produce for the *polis* children of the greatest possible goodness and beauty."[119] The Stranger suggests that further regulation and oversight of the growing family would also be very good—except that such an attempt would likely have the unwelcome "consequence of our incurring ridicule in abundance, in addition to meeting with a blank refusal to obey on the part of the nurses, with their womanish and servile minds" (or, of course, their enduring common sense and practical experience).[120] Aristotle proposed a more brutal form of control:

> The question arises whether children should always be reared or may sometimes be exposed to die. There should certainly be a law to prevent the rearing of deformed children. On the other hand, if the established social customs forbid the exposure of infants simply to keep down the number of children, a limit must be placed on the number who are born. If a child is then conceived in excess of the limit so fixed, a miscarriage should be induced before sense and life have begun.... It remains to determine the length of time for which [men and women] should render public service by bringing children into the world. The offspring of elderly men, like that of very young men, tends to be physically and mentally imperfect; and the children of old age are weakly. We may therefore fix the length of time for which procreation lasts by reference to the mental prime. This comes for most men—as some of the poets, who measure life in seven-year periods, have suggested—about the age of 50.[121]

Whether Plotinus would have been so certain that we could reliably identify "deformities" and "excess" births so long before

---

117   Plato, *Laws*, 5.740c.
118   Cf. Bill Gammage, *The Biggest Estate on Earth: how Aborigines made Australia* (Sydney: Allen & Unwin, 2011), 127: "If the soul leaves, the body dies and loses shape, but the soul remains in living offspring. In this way it continues forever, taking shape in later generations as in earlier, though since time is irrelevant not necessarily in that order."
119   Plato, *Laws*, 6.783d.
120   Ibid., 7.790a.
121   Aristotle, *Politics*, 7.1335b19–25.

maturity may be moot. That he would have had some interest in ensuring the worth of new generations, and their not overwhelming the city's resources, seems more plausible. In sum: Plotinus's notorious indifference (as it seems) to the plight of children bullied by their peers has a somewhat different moral than it seems. The legislator's job would be to ensure that all children are confident enough and well-equipped to *prevent* their being bullied. For a *polis* to be well-ordered, its members must themselves be reared, coaxed, trained in necessary virtues, even if those virtues are less than philosophical.

> Man, as we affirm, is a tame creature: none the less, while he is wont to become an animal most godlike and tame when he happens to possess a happy nature combined with right education, if his training be deficient or bad, he turns out the wildest of all earth's creatures. Wherefore the lawgiver must not permit them to treat the education of children as a matter of secondary or casual importance.[122]

> What is it that renders this world habitable, but the prevailing notions of order, virtue, duty, and Providence?[123]

> As for unbounded liberty, I leave it to savages, among whom alone I believe it is to be found.[124]

Such moral education must continue into adolescence (at least). "Shall we not plainly wish that the kind of love which belongs to virtue and desires the young to be as good as possible should exist within our *polis*?"[125] Plato's Stranger recommends that young men and women should indeed get to know each other, and even watch each other's naked choral dancing, but they must be deterred by shame and respect from having sex together until their authorized

---

122 Plato, *Laws*, 6.766a; see also 7.808d: "Just as no sheep or other grazing beast ought to exist without a herdsman, so children cannot live without a tutor, nor slaves without a master. And, of all wild creatures, the child is the most intractable; for in so far as it, above all others, possesses a fount of reason that is as yet uncurbed, it is a treacherous, sly and most insolent creature. Wherefore the child must be strapped up, as it were, with many bridles—first, when he leaves the care of nurse and mother, with tutors, to guide his childish ignorance, and after that with teachers of all sorts of subjects and lessons, treating him as becomes a freeborn child."
123 Berkeley, "Discourse to Magistrates [1738]," in *Works*, vol. 6, 202.
124 Berkeley, *Alciphron*, in *Works*, vol. 3, 215 (Crito speaks). He was, of course, mistaken about the lack of "savage" discipline.
125 Plato, *Laws*, 8.837d.

marriage.[126] Plotinus agreed: "If they remain chaste (*sophron*) there is no error in their intimacy with the beauty here below, but it is an error to fall away into sexual intercourse."[127]

> He that counts bodily desire as but secondary and puts longing looks [*horon*] in place of love [*horon mallon e eron*], with soul lusting really for soul, regards the bodily satisfaction of the body as an outrage, and, reverently worshipping temperance, courage, nobility and wisdom [*to sophron kai andreion kai megaloprepes kai to phronimon*], will desire to live always chastely in company with the chaste object of his love.[128]

To show how to achieve this goal of disciplining adolescent and even adult desires, Plato's Stranger points to the general loathing of incestuous relations, produced by universal condemnation from early infancy.

> Is it not true, as I said just now, that when a lawgiver wishes to subdue one of those lusts which especially subdue men, it is easy for him at least to learn the method of mastering them—that it is by consecrating this public opinion in the eyes of all alike—bond and free, women and children, and the whole State—that he will effect the firmest security for this law. [Megillus asks how this would ever be possible, and the Stranger answers:] A very proper observation. That was precisely the reason why I stated that in reference to this law I know of a device for making a natural use of reproductive intercourse, on the one hand, by abstaining from the male and not slaying of set purpose the human stock, nor sowing seed on rocks and stones where it can never take root and have fruitful increase; and, on the other hand, by abstaining from every female field in which you would not desire the seed to spring up. This law, when it has become permanent and prevails, if it has rightly become dominant in other cases, just as it prevails now regarding intercourse with parents is the cause of countless blessings.[129]

---

126 Ibid., 6.772.
127 Plotinus, *Ennead*, III.5 [50].1, 38–39.
128 Plato, *Laws*, 8.837c.
129 Plato, *Laws*, 8.838d–839a. See Henrich, *Weirdest People*, 74–75: "By harnessing our disgust reaction at the idea of sex with siblings or parents, cultural evolution need only 'figure out' ways to (1) stretch this feeling out to other individuals and (2) deploy it in judging others."

Sexual intercourse is to be licensed and approved only with a view to procreation, so putting same-sex intimacies as well as rash heterosexual intercourse in the same class as incest. Sadly, this Platonic judgment is also reinforced by contempt for any male who would willingly take a "female" part.[130]

There is, as Samaras has observed,[131] a considerable inconsistency in the Magnesian rules for women. "On the one hand, [the Stranger affirms] that the practice which at present prevails in our districts is a most irrational one—namely, that men and women should not all follow the same pursuits with one accord and with all their might. For thus from the same taxation and trouble there arises and exists half a *polis* only instead of a whole one, in nearly every instance; yet surely this would be a surprising blunder for a lawgiver to commit."[132] On the other, Magnesian women seem to have no property rights, nor even any say in whom they are to marry, and there are many occasions, both in *Laws* and in *Timaeus*, where contempt seems evident. By Timaeus's account women only exist because some of the Firstborn humans were too cowardly to sustain a proper male life: wimps are reborn as women.[133] Even the claim that the law should be even-handed and that women should join in the proper civil pursuits is partly based on fear of what women would do otherwise:

> The lawgiver ought to be whole-hearted, not half-hearted—letting the female sex indulge in luxury and expense and disorderly ways of life, while supervising the male sex; for thus he is actually bequeathing to the *polis* the half only, instead of the whole, of a life of complete prosperity.[134]

---

130 Plato, *Laws*, 8.836e. Plotinus, *Ennead*, IV.4 [28].31, 54–55 speaks with similar disdain of those who are "effeminate, womanish in their doings and feelings and committing indecencies." Despite common modern belief it was not only the Christian Church that condemned same-sex liaisons, or even "wimpishness." Julian disparaged Gallienus for having "the dress and languishing gait of a woman" (*Works*, vol. 2, 361 ["The Caesars" 313b]), partly—it is reasonable to suspect—because Gallienus was insufficiently opposed to Christians: Plotinus, presumably, had a higher opinion of him. See Lukas de Blois, *The Policy of the Emperor Gallienus* (Leiden: E. J. Brill, 1976), 175–94.

131 Samaras, "Family and the Question of Women."

132 Plato, *Laws*, 7.805a; see also Aristotle, *Rhetoric*, 1.1361a8–9.

133 Plato, *Timaeus*, 91a.

134 Plato, *Laws*, 7.806c; see also Aristotle, *Politics*, 2.1269b12, where the cowardly behavior of Spartan women at the time of the Theban invasion in 369 BC is given as evidence of a systematic failure to ensure their proper virtue.

His admirers, including myself, can hope that Plotinus himself was not so contemptuous, and more consistent: it seems, at least, that he respected the women in whose household he found a home, and he found fault with the notion that mothers provided nothing more than matter for the fathers' form.[135] Roman customs would probably count against Magnesian conventions, both about naked dancing and the absence of property rights for women. But the overall thesis remains: everyone in Platonopolis is to be held to a strict moral standard by raising them to *feel*, not merely to believe, that pleasure is not to be pursued at any cost, and that the common good of the *polis* requires these strict divisions of child from adult, slave from free, manual from intellectual and men from women. And yet: "The prudent lawgiver admonishes the older folk to reverence the young, and above all to beware lest any of them be ever seen or heard by any of the young either doing or saying anything shameful; for where the old are shameless, there inevitably will also the young be very impudent."[136] If the old are to revere the young and offer them the best example of courtesy and self-possession, perhaps they may also extend that courtesy to their supposed inferiors (remembering, as we shall see, that they might themselves be one day in that role).

In a merely economic alliance, as Aristotle said, the partners have no strong interest in each other's *virtue*: it is enough to insist that proper contracts be enforced, and that no one side aggress against the other.[137] Such a merely libertarian alliance, however, must in the end be unstable. We cannot forever be indifferent to the virtue even of merely economic partners (nor easily trade with principled cannibals, pedophiles or torturers), or expect even a minimal regard for contracts and for a non-aggression pact from those reared without any regard for personal or public virtue. We cannot bind ourselves to tolerate forever what we perceive as obvious evil.

---

135   Plotinus, *Ennead*, III.6 [26].19, 19–26; see also ibid., II.4 [12].16; Aristotle, *De Generatione Animalium*, 1.729a10–15.

136   Plato, *Laws*, 5.729b. Juvenal's tag is to the same effect, and a warning both to parents and lawgivers: "maxima debetur puero reverentia; si quid turpe paras, nec tu pueri contempseris annos, sed peccaturo obstet tibi filius infans" (*Satires*, 14.47–9).

137   Aristotle, *Politics*, 3.1280b5–8: "Any *polis* that is truly so called and is not a *polis* merely in name must pay attention to virtue; for otherwise the community becomes merely an alliance, differing only in locality from the other alliances, those of allies that live apart."

"No faith with heretics" is not an ecclesiastical rule; it is a natural and inevitable human emotion. To make a frontier agreement with a nation of cannibals cannot really forbid an intention to interfere with the cannibals as soon as or as much as is convenient; we cannot seriously be expected to let the cannibals against all basis of good go on eating their aged parents. It is inhuman, and with the inhuman there can be no treaty.[138]

Similarly, there can be no lasting treaty between *dar al-Islam* and the fully infidel, *dar al-harb,* the world at war.[139] The international or global implications of the problem will concern me later. A *polis*, at any rate, and other cognate human associations, depends on a shared morale, a conviction that there is indeed a proper way to live: ideally, one that allows each individual, each household, phratry, club to live together in friendship—and the same ideal must govern each distinct *polis* too. "A *polis* is the partnership of clans and villages in a full and independent life."[140] The good life is the same for *polis* and for the individual.[141] Atlantis, populated by self-seekers forgetful of their origin, is itself self-seeking. The Ur-Athenians better understood their limits, and the proper goal of their lives together, and were therefore, in the story, the rock against which imperial aggression foundered, even if they did not entirely manage to banish all the "private" from their lives together.

OCCUPATIONS, CASTE AND SLAVERY

In thinking of Platonopolis, or of the general situation in the third-century empire, it is as well to remember that infant and maternal mortality rates were high. The probable life expectancy at birth was between 30 and 40 years, and nearly half of all infants may have died before they were five years old. Even those who survived infant disease and accident, plague, imperial command

---

138 Charles Williams, *The Descent of the Dove* (London: Collins, 1963), 163–64.
139 See Moussa Abou Ramadan, "Muslim Jurists' Criteria for the Division of the World into Dar al-Harb and Dar al-Islam," in *International Law and Religion: Historical and Contemporary Perspectives,* ed. Martti Koskenniemi, et al. (Oxford: Oxford University Press, 2017) for a summary account of the shifting definitions and implications of these concepts for many Muslim traditions. I should emphasize that majority Muslim opinion is not in favor of anything but *defensive* war, not unilateral aggression.
140 Aristotle, *Politics*, 3.1280b30.
141 Aristotle, *Nicomachean Ethics*, 1.1094b7–10; *Politics*, 7.1324a5–7.

or murderous riot could not expect very helpful health care: life was always precarious, and the chance of escaping one's particular niche was also low. Since this condition was then normal, maybe nobody paid attention to the general situation, though personal losses were as agonizing as our own—except that there were clear injunctions at least in Hebrew tradition to care for widows and orphans, and the poor in general.

> Behold, this was the iniquity of thy sister Sodom: pride, fullness of bread, and abundance of idleness was in her and in her daughters, neither did she strengthen the hand of the poor and needy.[142]

A descent into abject illness, destitution, loss of civil status through debt or kidnap was always possible, even for the imperial court, even for the most prosperous of cities. Care for the poor and needy, and for the morals of the tribe, was not a luxury, but the most obvious of insurance policies. No one, in short, could really afford to neglect the civil context of their lives, or expect to live entirely by their own unguided, unassisted efforts. Plotinus's projected legislator must have regard to the virtues and consequently the upbringing of the city's residents. They must also care for strangers.

> In his relations to strangers, a man should consider that a contract is a most holy thing, and that all concerns and wrongs of strangers are more directly dependent on the protection of God, than wrongs done to citizens; for the stranger, having no kindred and friends, is more to be pitied by Gods and men.[143]

But this is clearly not to say that they will all be reared as "philosophers," or even as equals, any more than the parts or organs of any animal or plant organism are all the same. Nor will strangers have any authority to change the city's ways, any more than the "lower" classes. Platonopolis will be composed of many sorts of person, however they may be identified. Some occupations are apparently allowed only to resident aliens, slaves, or transients: anything, indeed, which seems to require too much dealing with foreign powers and sensibilities, or the accumulation of capital. But the rule is even

---

142   Ezekiel 16.49.
143   Plato, *Laws*, 5.729.

stricter: nothing that requires long practice and close attention can be allowed to interfere with a citizen's main duty, and his eye to the eternal. It is the "duller children...who are incapable of learning and contemplative studies [who] turn to crafts and manual work."[144] Division of labor rules, and suspicion of manual crafts:

> No resident citizen shall be numbered among those who engage in technical crafts, nor any servant of a resident. For a citizen possesses a sufficient craft, and one that needs long practice and many studies, in the keeping and conserving of the public system of the State, a task which demands his full attention: and there hardly exists a human being with sufficient capacity to carry on two pursuits or two crafts thoroughly, nor yet to practice one himself and supervise another in practicing a second. So we must first of all lay down this as a fundamental rule in the State: no man who is a smith shall act as a joiner, nor shall a joiner supervise others at smith-work, instead of his own craft, under the pretext that, in thus supervising many servants working for him, he naturally supervises them more carefully because he gains more profit from that source than from his own craft; but each several craftsman in the State shall have one single craft, and gain from it his living. This law the city-stewards shall labor to guard, and they shall punish the resident citizen, if he turn aside to any craft rather than to the pursuit of virtue, with reproofs and degradation, until they restore him to his own proper course; and if a foreigner pursue two crafts, they shall punish him by imprisonment, money-fines, and expulsion from the State, and so compel him to act as one man and not many.[145]

---

144 Plotinus, *Ennead*, III.8 [30].4, 45–48. This unfortunate judgement is still, of course, widely believed, that "intellectual" pursuits are vastly superior to "manual" (though, as I shall observe a little later, we mistake the nature of Plotinian "intellect" in thinking of "intellectuals"). Plotinus, a little later in the same treatise, acknowledges that it is the *bad* workman who makes "ugly (*aischra*) forms," and the good, by implication, assists the gods and the world soul in making, as Euthyphro and Socrates recommend (Plato, *Euthyphro*, 13b–14b), many and beautiful things for the delight and health of others, even if these are "dim and weak imitations, toys not worth much" (Plotinus, *Ennead*, IV.3 [27].10, 17–20). Intellectuals should hope to do as well: see Matthew Crawford, *The Case for Working with your Hands: Or why office work is bad for us and fixing things feels good* (London: Penguin, 2010), for a recent robust defense of "manual" crafts. The Desert Fathers (as I shall observe below) identified such work as a partial remedy for accidie.
145 Plato, *Laws*, 8.846d–847a.

This indeed seems to be the most obvious difference between Magnesia and the standard Mediterranean city—though perhaps most merchants indeed, whether by sea or land, would not expect to be *citizens* of the cities they traded with. The same argument should also debar most scientists and academics—whose crafts also require a long apprenticeship and nearly-obsessive concentration—from any "political" role! And of course Plotinus himself was not a citizen of Rome, any more than Aristotle of Athens.

> The lawgiver of our State is rid, for the most part, of shipping and merchandise and peddling and inn-keeping and customs and mines and loans and usury, and countless matters of a like kind; he can say good-bye to all such and legislate for farmers and shepherds and bee-keepers, and concerning the preservation and supervision of the instruments employed in these occupations. This he will do, now that he has already enacted the most important laws, which deal with marriage, and with the birth and nurture and education of the children, and with the appointment of magistrates in the State.[146]

Ur-Athens was perhaps not quite so narrow in its account of what a citizen might do, and maybe Platonopolis would not be. But even those occupations, rather more extensive than simply "farmers and shepherds and bee-keepers," allowed to permanent, free residents, are carefully constrained. Magnesia and Ur-Athens alike are strictly class societies; more strictly so, indeed, than Socrates's Republic:

> The fact that all this arrangement is somehow more particular than Socrates' constitution, and more divided than that one through its imitation of the intermediate creation, may be learned from the number and character of the classes in the city. For there had been three classes there, guardians, auxiliaries, and laborers—for the triad belongs closely to the creative monad—while here there are double that number, hieratic, military, manufacturing, cultivating, pasturing, and hunting.[147]

---

146 Plato, *Laws*, 8.842de. Aristotle agreed that "the citizens must not live a mechanic (*banauson*) or a mercantile (*agoraion*) life (for such a life is ignoble [*agennes*] and inimical to virtue), nor yet must those who are to be citizens in the best state be tillers of the soil (*georgoi*)": Aristotle, *Politics*, 7.1328b33–5; see also *Politics*, 8.1337b. We might reasonably add computer nerds, scientists and bureaucrats to the list of "banausic" persons.

147 Proclus, *Commentary on Timaeus*, 150–51 [I.150, 20–28].

In fact Proclus himself underestimated the number of distinct classes in Ur-Athens: "manufacturing" covers a wide range of crafts, each with their appropriate style and virtue: "*Each sort* [of craftsmen, *demiourgoi] works by itself without mixing with any other*; then the classes of shepherds, hunters, and farmers, each distinct and separate."[148]

This feature is compared by Solon's priestly informant to Egyptian caste divisions, and sometimes allegorized as follows:

> The priests correspond to the archangels in the heaven which are turned towards the gods whose messengers they are. The military correspond to the *daimones* who come down into bodies. The pastors correspond to those stationed over the flocks of "animals," which they secretly explain as being souls that have missed out on human intelligence and have a condition similar to animals—for of humans too there is a particular "protector" of their flock and certain particular [powers] some of whom watch over tribes, some cities, and some individual persons. The hunters correspond to those that hunt down souls and confine them in the body—for there are some who also enjoy the pursuit of animals, the type that they suppose both Artemis to be and another host of hunt-oriented *daimones* with her. The cultivators correspond to those stationed over fruits. The whole of this constitutional scheme of sublunary *daimones*, distributed into many groups, was said to be "manufacturing" by Plato because he was concentrating on a finished product that was either in existence already or being generated.[149]

Once again, the well-ordered human society is meant to mirror the cosmological. We can suspect that this mirroring was to be reflected in the actual rituals and customs of each separate occupational class, with whatever compromise with the rituals of the twelve distinct *phyla* of Magnesia. Whether this imagined—and partly realized—order was meant to be as severe as more familiar caste societies, like the Hindu, we may doubt. Al-Farabi (870–950) and the Brethren of Purity (a society of Muslim philosophers in 8th- or 10th-century Iraq) perhaps offer a more agreeable witness to the sort of

---

148 Plato, *Timaeus*, 24a.
149 Porphyry, in *Tim.*, fr. 17: Proclus, *Commentary*, 249–50 [I.152, 13–30]; Proclus describes this particular allegory as "foreign humbug." See Akçay, *Porphyry's On the Cave of the Nymphs*, 93–95.

society required by "division of labor," with proper acknowledgment of the merits, and necessities, of the "manual crafts":

> The division of labor and the consequent division of society into occupational groups are, according to al-Farabi, dictated by nature; but they have to be organized by the legislator. "Everyone in the ideal city must have assigned to him a single art with which he busies himself solely."[150]

> The argument that human beings depend on the division of labor and a variety of crafts was a special favorite of the Brethren. They had a pro-artisan mentality: in shaping matter into form, the craftsman mirrors the Creator's work; the humblest occupations, such as refuse collection, are innately noble. In fact, craftsmen could rise to the top of the Ismàʿílí hierarchy. All the crafts (the Brethren went on) were legislated for by the Prophets and sages. And, in order to assign them to their proper rank, the Legislator must know each of the faithful's occupation and conduct.[151]

Different tasks do not necessarily result in different values, even if some tasks are supposed to "militate against virtue." At the least the members of "higher" classes need always to remember that they themselves depend on the good will and poorly rewarded labor of those considered "lower."[152] Al-Farabi was more humane, while still agreeing with philosophical tradition that "philosophers" should rule:

> He "insists that the best state can only be preserved from destruction if philosophy somehow wins a share in its government" (Walzer, *Al-Farabi,* 450). Similar to its predecessors, *The Virtuous City* also discusses social classes. Farabi's virtuous state has five ministries—education, culture, administration, economy, and defense; and consequently, the citizens of the virtuous state are classified into five groups, among which philosophers are of the highest rank. The "orators," the "poets," the "masters of the spoken word," "the upholders of religion," and "the

---

150   Al-Farabi, *Aphorisms of the Statesman (Fusul al-madani)*, ed. and trans. D. M. Dunlop (London: I. B. Tauris, 1996), 55.

151   Black, *History of Islamic Political Thought,* 73.

152   See Anastassios D. Karayiannis, "The Platonic Ethico-Economic Structure of Society," *Quaderni Di Storia Dell'Economia Politica* 8, no. 1 (1990): 3–5, for a detailed account of Plato's economic notions, which turn chiefly on the division of labor, and the importance of preserving the life of the whole *polis.*

administrative officials" form the second class of society (Walzer, *Al-Farabi*, 438). The people who are concerned with mathematics and its applications are of the third rank. The fourth place is for the guardians and soldiers. Finally, the people engaged in economic activities and who provide the wealth of the state such as farmers, traders, and the like are in the fifth class, which "is no longer held in contempt as in the century of Plato and Aristotle," and, along with the people of the fourth class, "are supposed to be full citizens of the virtuous state" (Walzer, *Al-Farabi*, 437). There is no discrimination between different classes. The virtuous state, as explained above, is the state administered by the best and most talented ruler, who aims at prosperity and happiness for all. If its constitution fails to provide the people with prosperity, and the rulers do not possess the qualities of virtuous rulers, then the state ceases to be virtuous and becomes a vicious state.[153]

We can hope that Plotinus would, eventually, have believed the same. But class may easily mutate to "caste," and notions about the relative "purity" of different occupations may create an even less egalitarian order.

> Meanwhile, however, the duties and obligations of the life into which one was born are those that are to be clung to.... Even a person born into an unclean caste (a sweeper, an undertaker, for example) should hold to the inherited career. By performing the work as well as possible, in the ordained way, he becomes a perfect, virtuous member of society; breaking loose and intruding upon other people's duties, on the other hand, he would become guilty of disturbing the sacred order.[154]

And by proper obedience he may win a "better" life next time, like those souls consigned to "animal" existence. So also, we may suppose, such domesticated non-humans as share the city.[155]

---

153 Alireza Omid Bakhsh, "The Virtuous City: the Iranian and Islamic heritage of Utopianism," *Utopian Studies* 24, no. 1 (2013): 47.

154 Heinrich Zimmer, *Philosophies of India*, ed. Joseph Campbell (London: Routledge & Kegan Paul, 1967), 388.

155 In passing: Plotinus himself would not have eaten any such cattle (Porphyry, *Life*, 2.5-6), and the normal diet of Platonopolis would be vegetarian (Plato, *Republic*, 2.372)—a diet not all that far from the Mediterranean norm.

The English term "caste" covers two different sorts of grouping in Hindu society.[156] The original division of society dictated in the Laws of Manu is into four *varnas*, "colors": *Brahmins, Kshatriya, Vaishya* (these three being "twice born" through birth and later initiation), and *Sudra:*

> In order to protect this universe He, the most resplendent one, assigned separate (duties and) occupations to those who sprang from his mouth, arms, thighs, and feet. To Brahmanas he assigned teaching and studying (the Veda), sacrificing for their own benefit and for others, giving and accepting (of alms). The Kshatriya he commanded to protect the people, to bestow gifts, to offer sacrifices, to study (the Veda), and to abstain from attaching himself to sensual pleasures. The Vaisya to tend cattle, to bestow gifts, to offer sacrifices, to study (the Veda), to trade, to lend money, and to cultivate land. One occupation only the lord prescribed to the Sudra, to serve meekly even these (other) three castes.[157]

The theme, though less insistently, is repeated in Zoroastrian thought.[158] The "colors" in question, it should be noted, are more likely those symbolizing the three *gunas*, humors (*sattva, rajas* and *tamas:* peace, energy and inertia) than skin-colors. Even Gandhi offered the convenient rationalization that the *varnas* merely distinguish different sorts of person, different goals and motivations—very much as Mediterranean theorists distinguished them. Some people wish to discover a transcendent truth; others seek honor in political or military success; others seek prosperity or

---

156 See Stephen R. L. Clark, "Ethical Thought in India," *Routledge Companion to Ethics*, ed. John Skorupski (London: Routledge, 2010); Roy W. Perrett, *Hindu Ethics: A Philosophical Study* (Honolulu: University of Hawaii Press, 1998); Louis Dumont, *Homo Hierarchicus: the Caste System and its Implications* (Chicago: University of Chicago Press, 1980).

157 George Bühler, trans., *Manu Samhita: the Laws of Manu* (Delhi: Motilal Banarsidass, 1964), 1.87–91.

158 "The main source for the Zoroastrian doctrine of sacral kingship is the *Denkard* (Acts of the Religion), an encyclopedia of Zoroastrian knowledge, which greatly emphasizes the importance of this doctrine. This text also emphasizes the role of the Sasanian monarch as the supreme representative of Ahura Mazda on earth . . . four classes of the religion by which the world is arranged, which are the priesthood, the warrior class, the herdsman class and the artisan class": http://balkhandshambhala.blogspot.com/2013/02/shambhala-sacral-kingship.html (accessed 11 May 2020).

are able simply to serve as laborers (these divisions, perhaps, were not at first hereditary). The different motives are all to be found in each human soul, but it is supposed that one predominates in each and thereby justifies the social division.

So also Sallustius, in Julian's day:

> The forms of polities are produced according to the triple division of the soul; for the rulers are assimilated to reason [which does not mean simple intelligence], the soldiers to anger, and the common people to desire. Hence, when all things are administered according to reason, and he who is the best of all men possesses dominion, then a kingdom is produced: but when, from reason and anger in conjunction, more than one hold the reins of government, an aristocracy is produced: but where government is carried on through desire, and honors subsist with a view to possessions, such a polity is called a timocracy; and that polity which takes place in opposition to a kingdom is called a tyranny; for the former administers everything, but the latter nothing, according to reason. But an oligarchy, or the dominion of the few, is contrary to an aristocracy; because in the former, not the best, but a few only, and those the worst, govern the city. And lastly, a democracy is opposed to a timocracy; because in the former, not such as abound in riches, but the multitude alone, is the ruler of all things.[159]

There is some evidence that the tripartite division of society (with additions) goes back in time to Indo-Aryan roots: in India *Brahmin, Kshatriya, Vaisya;* in Ireland, druid, lord and freeman.[160] Other analyses, like that of Louis Dumont, *Homo hierarchicus,* identify the notion of "purity" as the system's source. "Untouchables" are outside the system, yet support it, being at the opposite end of a spectrum leading down from Brahminical "purity." Without their practical and symbolic association with *impurity* there could

---

159 Sallustius, *Concerning the gods and the universe,* chap. 11. Plotinus seems to make no great use of these divisions, which aren't clearly endorsed in Plato, *Laws.*
160 Alwyn D. Rees and Brinley Rees, *Celtic Heritage,* 111–15; Georges Dumézil, *Mitra-Varuna: Essay on Two Indo-European Representations of Sovereignty,* trans. Derek Coltman (New York: Zone Books, 1988), 22–24. Dumézil's theories about the past have sometimes been adopted as recommendations for the future, especially by those opposed to liberal ideals: he himself rejected the association. See Bruce Lincoln, *Theorizing Myth: narrative, ideology, and scholarship* (Chicago: University of Chicago Press, 1999), 123–27.

be no "pure." The issue is not only ritual: it is hardly surprising that people condemned to handle human excrement and dead bodies are barred from the society of "cleaner" castes (a problem Gandhi sought to alleviate by encouraging even Brahmins to deal with their own shit, or else by praising the dedication and high virtue of "the ideal *bhangi* [Dalits assigned, by birth, to these excrementalist duties]"[161]). The Mediterranean version of these divisions does not seem to have found a formal rank for such "impure" occupations, though "purity" of a more "spiritual" sort is a key term in Platonic ethics. The usual Roman arrangement was for the two annually appointed *aediles* to manage such matters

---

161 Understandably many actual Dalits resent this apparent attempt to solidify and excuse a highly oppressive system, as described by Gandhi. See Thenmozhi Soundararajan, "Why It is Time to Dump Gandhi," *Medium* (June 14, 2017): "The ideal *bhangi* of my conception would be a Brahmin par-excellence, possibly even excel him. It is possible to envisage—the existence of a Bhangi without a Brahmin. But without the former the latter could not be. It is the Bhangi who enables society to live. A Bhangi does for society what a mother does for her baby. A mother washes her baby of the dirt and insures his health. Even so the Bhangi protects and safeguards the health of that entire community by maintaining sanitation for it. The Brahmin's duty is to look after the sanitation of the soul, the Bhangi's that of the body of society. But there is a difference in practice; the Brahmin generally does not live up to his duty, the *bhangi* does willy-nilly no doubt.... But that is not all. My ideal *bhangi* would know the quality of night-soil and urine. He would keep a close watch on these and give a timely warning to the individual concerned. Thus, he will give a timely notice of the results of his examination of the excreta. That presupposes a scientific knowledge of the requirements of his profession. He would likewise be an authority on the subject of disposal of night-soil in small villages as well as big cities and his advice and guidance in the matter would be sought for and freely given to society. It goes without saying that he would have the usual learning necessary for reaching the standard here laid down for his profession. Such an ideal *bhangi* while deriving his livelihood from his occupation, would approach it only as a sacred duty. In other words, he would not dream of amassing wealth out of it. He would consider himself responsible for the proper removal and disposal of all the dirt and night-soil within the area which he serves and regard the maintenance of healthy and sanitary condition within the same as the *summum bonum* of his existence" (Mohandas Karamchand Gandhi, "The Ideal *Banghi*," in *Collected Works of Mahatma Gandhi*, vol. 70 [New Delhi: Publications Division Government of India, 1999], 126–28 [*Harijan*, 28th November 1936]). This can be read as a defense of the very system that, superficially, he was deploring, but at least Gandhi's declared aim was "to remove the invidious distinction between Brahmin and Bhangi" and acknowledge the importance of the latter's role: "The profession, far from being a dirty one, is a purifying, life-protecting one. Only we have debased it": Gandhi, *Collected Works*, vol. 70, 145 (1st December 1936).

as sewage, water, firefighting, and the markets. Were there guilds of street cleaners or excrementalists, as there were of butchers? Urine was valuable, for fullers, and taxed by Vespasian.[162] "Night soil" was collected, probably by gangs of public or privately owned slaves, for use in local market gardens or else dumped outside the city. It seems likely that there were people who made the management of the gangs their trade.[163]

Must we suppose that there will be slaves in Platonopolis, as in every actual Mediterranean city, and in Magnesia? Unfortunately (for many reasons), yes. It is worth remarking, of course, that enslavement then had no necessary ethnic or racial element: any-one could be enslaved, and any slave could be freed (with residual duties to their former owner). Plotinus had no general complaint against the place and rank that fortune assigns to anyone. Being enslaved is an injury neither to those who are naturally slavish (that is, incapable of managing their own desires and fears), nor to those who aren't, though particular wrongs may be done to slaves—and such bad masters may expect to be enslaved them-selves in their next incarnation, like other evil doers.[164] It is of course a philosophical truism that we ourselves are slaves—to greed, fear, falsehood and the like.[165] De St. Croix makes a good point in observing that "such austere philosophical notions are of greater assistance in the endurance of liberty, riches and peace than of slavery, poverty and war."[166] And the truism may have helped anesthetize philosophers against too great an empathy for those whom they could not free. But it is difficult, after all, to see what other option there was: any city that emancipated its slaves

---

162 Suetonius, *The Twelve Caesars*, trans. Robert Graves, ed. James Rives (London: Penguin, 2007), 287 [Vespasian, 23]. Notoriously, *pecunia non olet*.

163 O. F. Robinson, *Ancient Rome: City Planning and Administration* (London: Routledge, 2003), 106. Robinson adds that Roman diet was grain-based, and the night soil might therefore have turned to a manageable crumble faster than excrement from the standard modern diet. The practice would still have helped spread disease.

164 Plotinus, *Ennead*, III.2 [47].13, 4–7; see further on what carries each soul to its appropriate place of punishment, Plotinus, *Ennead*, IV.3 [27].24.

165 See Thomas Wiedemann, *Greek and Roman Slavery* (London: Routledge, 1988), 235.

166 Geoffrey de St. Croix, "Slavery and Other Forms of Unfree Labor," in *Slavery and Other Forms of Unfree Labor*, ed. L. J. Archer (London: Routledge, 1988), 29.

would be plausibly suspected by all its neighbors of fomenting slave rebellion. Plato's Stranger sadly declares:

> The slave is no easy chattel. For actual experience shows how many evils result from slavery—as in the frequent revolts in Messenia, and in the *poleis* where there are many servants kept who speak the same tongue, not to speak of the crimes of all sorts committed by the "Corsairs," as they are called, who haunt the coasts of Italy, and the reprisals therefor. In view of all these facts, it is really a puzzle to know how to deal with all such matters. Two means only are left for us to try—the one is, not to allow the slaves, if they are to tolerate slavery quietly, to be all of the same nation, but, so far as possible, to have them of different races—and the other is to accord them proper treatment, and that not only for their sakes, but still more for the sake of ourselves. Proper treatment of servants consists in using no violence towards them, and in hurting them even less, if possible, than our own equals. For it is his way of dealing with men whom it is easy for him to wrong that shows most clearly whether a man is genuine or hypocritical in his reverence for justice and hatred of injustice. He, therefore, that in dealing with slaves proves himself, in his character and action, undefiled by what is unholy or unjust will best be able to sow a crop of goodness—and this we may say, and justly say, of every master, or king, and of everyone who possesses any kind of absolute power over a person weaker than himself.[167]

Slaves, that is, are not to be allowed their own tribes and guilds, whatever their expertise and virtue, but must rely on their masters' "justice." "Slavery is the permanent, violent domination of natally alienated and generally dishonored persons":[168] they have no standing. Many in the Roman Mediterranean would have been bred and reared on an estate, but they might also—especially eunuchs—be the product of piracy, kidnapping and war.[169] Until Justinian declared all foundlings free they might even have been simply abandoned infants.[170] In Platonopolis, as Plotinus presumably intended it, slaves would mostly be home-bred, or acquired

---

167   Plato, *Laws*, 6.777be. Those who mistreat "animals," we may fairly add, are also proving their malice.

168   Patterson, *Slavery and Social Death*, 13.

169   Jones, *Later Roman Empire*, vol. 2, 851-2.

170   Ibid., 853.

by accident: certainly they would not be captives, nor purchased locally, as Platonopolis would not itself go to war, nor permit merchants in its borders for anything but essentials. And certainly there would be no usurers—a trade from which Plotinus sought to divert his student Serapion of Alexandria (or so Porphyry says),[171] and therefore no debt-slaves. But there is little doubt that there would still be slaves, for household and agricultural use.

> Sensible serfs [perhaps better, simply hired laborers] with one part of themselves serve their master, but with another belong to themselves, and therefore receive more reasonably limited orders from their master *since they are not slaves and do not totally belong to another.*[172]

Slaves apparently do belong entirely to another. Roman custom might allow them to seek asylum against an especially vile master (though there was no guarantee that the asylum would be granted or would last) or even save enough from the cash allowed them eventually to buy their partial freedom (with residual duties to their former master). Even Indian Untouchables might have a better life, at least amongst their kind, and their own professional guilds. For the "castes" which have more definite and daily reality in Hindu India are not the four (or five) *varnas*, but the many thousand *jātis*, which are both kinship and professional groupings, to be found amongst Indian Muslims, Christians and Untouchables as well as amongst Hindus. On the one hand, membership of such a *jāti* will make it difficult to marry outside it, or to take on work belonging to a different *jāti*. On the other, it provides support to individuals, even when far from home. Such groups may move up and down the social and economic scale, and even—over many generations—between *varnas*. Those who have suffered oppression or contempt for their membership of a low-ranking *jati* may understandably and justly be enraged,[173] but at least the groupings provide some sense of fellowship and purpose that may be lacking in a more individualistic society, and certainly lacking for slaves until the

---

171   Plato, *Republic*, 555e–556b; *Laws*, 742c; see *Life*, 7.47–50.
172   Plotinus, *Ennead*, IV.4 [28].34, 4–6 (my emphasis); see also IV.4 [28].35, 34–38: *serfs* have the same ultimate goal as their master, distinct from his immediate orders.
173   See Kancha Ilaiah, *Why I am not a Hindu: a Sudra Critique of Hindutva Philosophy, Culture and Political Economy* (Calcutta: Bhatkal & Sen, 2001).

spread of a religion *fit* for slaves. Recognizing that people are indeed born into familial and professional groupings may sometimes have some merits: any more *egalitarian* society may, in practical fact, be imposing the values and inhibitions of one historically dominant group on all. In Britain, for example, it has been said that "middle class values" (of educational attainment, deferred gratification, individual choice) may not be shared at all by the poorer classes (who have good reason to doubt that "education" does them any good or that there is a point in putting off presently attainable enjoyments, and value family solidarity far more than personal achievement).[174] Filial obedience is one example of the notion that we are *born* into our obligations and should not expect to remake our lives at will. "Friends," in "educated Western" society, are the family one makes for oneself, and those loyalties, perhaps, should trump any original duties.[175] It might seem that Plotinus would have agreed: he left his home-city and refused "to talk about his race or his parents or his native country"[176]—except to offer the strange story that he went on breast-feeding till he was eight and only desisted when he was told he was being a pest.[177] Whether his chosen life was one he would have recommended to everyone remains obscure. Whether a society can survive that is based *entirely* on such *voluntary,* easily unmade associations is doubtful: certainly it would seem absurd to most non-Western societies—and most Western classes.

Jati, in effect, are not confined to India. Plato apparently agreed with Manu: "everyone must practice one of the occupations in the city for which he is naturally best suited,"[178] as it is "far better to carry out one's own Law (*svadharma*) imperfectly than that of someone else's perfectly, for a man who lives according to someone

---

174 See Pierre Bourdieu and Jean-Claude Passeron, *Reproduction in Education, Society and Culture*, trans. Richard Nice (London: Sage Publications, 1990).

175 It is worth acknowledging that small foraging societies—and even modern "liberal" societies—may be the more stable precisely because people can easily leave them to find more congenial company. "Many humans just don't like their families very much. And this appears to be just as true of present-day hunter-gatherers as anybody else. Many seem to find the prospect of living their entire lives surrounded by close relatives so unpleasant that they will travel very long distances just to get away from them" (Graeber & Wengrow, *Dawn of Everything*, 279–80)!

176 Porphyry, *Life*, 1.2–5.

177 Ibid., 3.3–7.

178 Plato, *Republic*, 4.433a5–6.

else's Law falls immediately from his caste."[179] This might, in principle, allow each individual's own skills and temperament to determine the appropriate occupation. But in any traditional society children are likely to learn their trade from parents or older family, and those trades are learned by imitation and apprenticeship rather than by book learning as potential equals in a separate college. And when those trades are considered vital for the prosperity of the whole community, legislators may seek to protect the continued flow of recruits. By the late fourth century at least (and possibly well before) bakers, for example, inherited their lot in life (by birth, by marriage or even by legacy) and were not permitted to give up their duty or even to buy themselves out.[180] Similar rules applied to mutton, beef and pork butchers, as well as lime-burners and carters, brewers, oil sellers, honey dealers, fishmongers and coppersmiths. Guild members, *collegiati*, were prevented from escaping to the country.[181] The same, of course, might apply to the governing body of the city, whose members inherited and could not, unlike Rogatianus, disavow their duties—but theirs were not the only "indispensable" occupations.[182]

So slavery, compulsory guild-membership and radical caste-division are likely to be features of Platonopolis. Nor will there be, in Plato's account, an entirely clear distinction between the "free" and the "slave."

> The main principle is this—that nobody, male or female, should ever be left without control, nor should anyone, whether at work or in play, grow habituated in mind to acting alone and on his own initiative, but he should live always, both in war and peace, with his eyes fixed constantly on his commander and following his lead; and he should be guided by him even in the smallest detail of his actions—for example, to stand at the word of command, and to march, and to exercise, to wash and eat, to wake up at night for sentry-duty and dispatch-carrying, and in moments of danger to wait for the commander's signal

179 John Bussanich, "Ethics in Ancient India," in *Ancient Ethics*, ed. J. Hardy and G. Rudebusch (Göttingen: Vandenhoek & Ruprecht, 2014), 43, citing *Manava Dharmasastra* 10.97.
180 Jones, *Later Roman Empire*, vol. 2, 699–700.
181 Ibid., 858–61.
182 Ibid., 724–28, 738–39.

before either pursuing or retreating before an enemy; and, in a word, he must instruct his soul by habituation to avoid all thought or idea of doing anything at all apart from the rest of his company, so that the life of all shall be lived *en masse* and in common; for there is not, nor ever will be, any rule superior to this or better and more effective in ensuring safety and victory in war. This task of ruling, and being ruled by, others must be practiced in peace from earliest childhood; but anarchy must be utterly removed from the lives of all mankind, and of the beasts also that are subject to man.[183]

Plotinus is perhaps not quite so sure: there is a distinction to be drawn between being a slave and being a hired laborer, even of the lowest sort. Slaves, remember, are chattels,[184] and how we ourselves are to escape the totalitarian vision requires another chapter to explore. But before insisting that our forebears were simply stupid, ignorant or wicked, it is worth remembering that, as I urged earlier, species are not natural kinds. There is nothing in principle against the claim that there are people born within our species who do not share the mainstream "human" grasp of acting for good reason, doing what is right—if only in the agent's own opinion. Those who are "natural slaves" are moved only by immediate desire and fear and therefore *will* be slaves in any social order, since they are so easily controlled by bribes and threats: "savages," "barbarians," "heathens" (just like most of us). Only those who can transcend their own emotions so as actually to *act* (that is, to do things for a good purpose) can reasonably be trusted to make decisions either for their own futures or for the *polis* of which they are a part. "Natural slaves," in short, are very like domestic animals, for whom we may feel affection but never seek to obey.[185] If our forebears were wrong about the actual slaves among them, perhaps we too are wrong about our "pets" and "cattle." Our descendants may be as baffled by our casual treatment of "domestic animals," in households, farms, circuses, laboratories and zoos, as we are by our ancestors' acceptance of chattel slavery.

---

183 Plato, *Laws*, 12.942ad.
184 Plotinus, *Ennead*, IV.4 [28].34, 4–6.
185 See Stephen R. L. Clark, "Slaves and Citizens," *Philosophy* 60 (1985): 27–46; Stephen R. L. Clark, "Slaves, Servility and Noble Deeds," *Philosophical Inquiry* (Thessaloniki) 25, no. 3 (2003): 165–76.

6

The King is the Only Maker

TOWARDS A WORLD MORALE

Platonopolis, if it is to be based on Plato's *Laws*, turns out to be very much like an ordinary *polis* under the *Pax Romana*. On the one hand, it is therefore possible that Plotinus and Gallienus did indeed plan such a venture. On the other, it is unclear why either would have bothered—except perhaps as a showcase for a more general recommendation to existing *poleis*: that their councilors should be chosen (if only from established families) for their honesty and good sense (at least) rather than simply for their wealth or social contacts. Platonopolis, in any case, could only exist within the *Pax Romana*, and the maintenance of that peace must, realistically, have been of more importance to Gallienus than the management of any particular *polis*. The Empire of his time was perpetually at war, with rivals abroad and disaffected parties within. How could its unity and being be preserved?

By Porphyry's account one of the works of Origen, a student of Ammonius Saccas alongside Plotinus himself, was entitled *That the King is the Only Maker.*[1] It is barely possible that some compliment to Gallienus was intended,[2] but far more likely that the reference of "King" is rather to *Nous* itself (or himself): *Nous* is King (alongside the One), "but we too are kings (*basileuomen*), when we are in accord with [him]; we can be in accord with [him] in two ways, either by having something like [his] writing written in us like laws, or by being as if filled with [him] and able to see [him] and be aware of [him] as present."[3] If we or Platonopolis are to be well-governed, it

---

1   Porphyry, *Life*, 3.33; see Armstrong, *Enneads*, vol. 1, 10-11. Whether this Origen, a member of Ammonius's inner circle, is or is not identical with the Christian theologian is a contested issue: both Origens (if there were two) were acquainted with Ammonius, and both shared a Neo-Platonic sensibility and doctrine. If there was only one, he wrote for distinct schools. See Ilaria L. E. Ramelli, "Origen and the Platonic Tradition," *Religions* 8 (2017): 21-41 for a defense of the unitary hypothesis.

2   Ousager, *Plotinus on Selfhood*, 217.

3   Plotinus, *Ennead*, V.3 [49].4.1-4 (replacing Armstrong's "it" by a pronoun more in keeping with the gender of the term: whether this always indicates

must be by *Nous,* whether this means only that we and the city keep the established laws or (better) that we see their value for ourselves.

That we might ourselves, as individuals, be "kings" is an attractive notion. If this were so we could manage without external government and be at peace. Everyone, we might hope, should be a law unto himself—and all those laws would be compatible. As Crone summarizes one strand in later Islamic thought, "Every Muslim who polished the mirror of his soul could hope to become a philosopher king unto himself, or even something resembling a prophet."[4] That we should all instead discover or revere a single "philosopher king" to regulate our unruly natures is perhaps no more realistic. But perhaps it will be safer, for the moment, to put aside our own easy assumption that we are all already polished enough to be either kings or prophets, and that everyone should therefore act only according to his or her own conscience, or their own muddled conception of what their conscience says. Self-deception is especially the vice of Very Clever People, but not unknown elsewhere—on which matter I shall say more below.

As far as Plotinus's projected city goes, *Nous* will be, we may hope, embodied in the conscripted council (though there may, on Roman precedent, be an imperial governor to oversee its workings). The less realistic hope encountered in Plato's writings is that the *polis* should be monarchical.

> This is what the lawgiver will say [when asked what he really wants]: "Give me the *polis* under a monarchy; and let the monarch be young, and possessed by nature of a good memory, quick intelligence, courage and nobility of manner; and let that quality, which we formerly mentioned as the necessary accompaniment of all the parts of virtue, attend now also on our monarch's soul, if the rest of his qualities are to be of any value."[5]

Plotinus may have hoped as much from Gallienus.[6] For there was a larger problem for well-ordered life than merely the life

---

a more "personal" view of *Nous* is debatable); see Ousager, *Plotinus on Selfhood,* 214–15 for some Platonic background for the metaphor.

4   Crone, *Medieval,* 196.

5   Plato, *Laws,* 4.709e; see also *Republic,* 5.473ce.

6   Ousager, *Plotinus on Selfhood,* 258–59: "Gallienus was remarkably more philhellenic than his predecessors" and was initiated at Eleusis when he became sole Emperor in 260.

of one *polis*. "You cannot manage civic affairs successfully without some knowledge of the wider world-society of men."[7] Rome's empire encompassed the shores and immediate hinterland of all the Mediterranean (and there were other tribes and empires beyond its borders). Cities could no longer be imagined as always at war with all others, as the Athenian Stranger's Spartan and Cretan friends imagine Lycurgus knew:

> He condemned the stupidity of the mass of men in failing to perceive that all are involved ceaselessly in a lifelong war against all *poleis*. If, then, these practices are necessary in war—namely, messing in common for safety's sake, and the appointment of relays of officers and privates to act as guards—they must be carried out equally in time of peace. For (as he would say) "peace," as the term is commonly employed, is nothing more than a name, the truth being that every *polis* is, by a law of nature, engaged perpetually in an informal war with every other *polis*.[8]

That goal was always a false one: war can only, sanely, be for the sake of peace, not otherwise, and the "war of each against all" is always a losing contest.[9] No one city can be lastingly at peace even with itself until the whole inhabited world is at lasting peace.

> The city in which people cooperate to attain happiness is the virtuous city, and the society in which there is cooperation to acquire happiness is the virtuous society; and the nation in which all of its cities cooperate toward happiness is the virtuous nation. In the same way, the virtuous universal state will arise only when all nations cooperate for the purpose of reaching happiness.[10]

But how is such global peace, such universal happiness, to be obtained, if we must look beyond the bounds of the city? "What kind of politics can you have without the *polis*?"[11] A *polis*, remember, is a self-governing, largely self-sufficient social unit, whose citizens discuss, debate and disagree, but share a language, heritage and

---

7 Minucius Felix, *Octavius*, 357 [17.2].
8 Plato, *Laws*, 1.625e–626a.
9 Aristotle, *Politics*, 7.1325a5–7; Plato, *Laws*, 1.628c: "The highest good is neither war nor civil strife—which things we should pray rather to be saved from—but peace one with another and friendly feeling."
10 Bakhsh, "The Virtuous City," 45; citing Walzer, *Al-Farabi*, 231.
11 Black, *History*, 77.

(broadly) ethical values. An empire cannot be run—and certainly the Roman Empire was not run—even by a pan-imperial council, let alone an assembly, even a virtual assembly, of all its citizens. One route to global peace is through a network of alliances and treaties, both political and economic: in such a system there may be a well-trusted way of visiting other cities, making bargains with the help of diplomats and merchants, and occasionally mounting common festivals and games, under the aegis of familiar gods. That perhaps describes the happier phases of pre-imperial Greek society but is subverted (was indeed subverted) by the greed and pride of individual cities. Trading arrangements tend to favor the wealthier partners, and the absence of any independent, uncorrupted, universally acknowledged judge, or even any universally accepted rules, leaves cities always on the brink of war, and therefore vulnerable to assault from outside the system, whether by existing empires, tribes or—in the modern era—by churches and transnational corporations.

Maybe the casually federal system, sustained by trade and opportunistic treaties, could have lasted, or could help us now. Maybe the actual issue turned on unpredictable, individual actions. Arnold Toynbee, aiming to suggest that individual action has played a real part in history (contrary to what some had inferred from his most general theories, and more obviously Spengler's, about the fate of various "civilizations") pictured what might have happened if Philip of Macedon and Artaxerxes III of Persia, on the one hand, or Alexander of Macedon, on the other, had lived long enough to achieve rather more of what they wished.[12] If Philip and Artaxerxes had survived, so Toynbee imagined, we would by now be living in a world composed and controlled by many little city-states with varying local and more distant treaties and mercantile understandings, all worshipping the "local god of Jerusalem" and employing Aramaic as a lingua franca. If Alexander, on the other hand, had survived long enough to encounter and demolish Ch'in, we would instead have inherited a global imperial order, with the heirs of Alexander as symbols of global unity. In that latter case, Toynbee proposed, it would be Buddhism, together with Stoic

12   Arnold Toynbee, *Some Problems in Greek History* (London: Oxford University Press, 1969), 421–86; see further Stephen R. L. Clark, "Citizens of the World and their Religion," *Philosophical Papers* 48, no. 1 (2019): 103–22.

and Epicurean variations on that theme, which fulfilled the role of an acknowledged World Religion or Morale. The stories are, as Toynbee knew, absurd: if history depends on individual actions, and can be shifted to quite other paths, by some easy alteration, then we cannot possibly know what *would* have happened in those alternate timelines, inhabited by very different people. But the global options are still relevant: a federation of *poleis* might emerge, or a simpler imperial order. Can we detect what might have been more likely or agreeable to Neo-Platonic, Plotinian sensibilities?

> Al-Fārābi proceeds to discuss the principles of political association in the *Virtuous City* and the *Civil Polity*. In both treatises, he starts from the premise that humans cannot attain the perfection they are destined to attain, outside the framework of political association. For, they are constantly in need of the assistance of their fellows in the provision of their basic needs and their very survival. Thus arise the three types of association: the large, identified with the world at large (*ma'mūrah, oikoumene*), the intermediate, identified with the nation (*ummah*), and the small, identified with the city-state (*madīnah, polis*).[13]

This is more than a merely scholarly inquiry. Our own situation is so much more perilous than Plotinus's that we desperately need some sort of global agreement, sustained by shared sensibilities and (at least) almost consistent priorities. One outcome would be to be ruled by absolute, imperial fiat: a single source of authority with the power to compel obedience, an option I identified in an earlier work as GEA (the Global Ecological Authority[14]). But that would as likely encourage thoughts of rebellion, as well as preventing free enquiry and adventitious progress. As Hocking declared many years ago, "precisely because we do *not* want a world state, we do require a world morale," which is to say a world religion.[15] And if we do stumble into the undesired world state we shall still need some sort of world religion to support and partly excuse it. If we are standing on the threshold of a new thing, civilization in

---

13   Fakhry, *Al-Fārābi*, 101.
14   Stephen R. L. Clark, *How to Think about the Earth: models of environmental theology* (London: Mowbray, 1993), 49–54, 108–9.
15   W. E. Hocking, *Living Religions and a World Faith* (London: Allen & Unwin, 1940), 264. Religions, in the sense intended here, need not be "supernaturalist"—but that issue is, for the moment, another story.

the singular, spun by us all together, what could it be like? It will matter very much what that world religion is. There seem to be many possibilities—and perhaps too many ever to achieve a real peace. This was Chesterton's answer to H. G. Wells's conviction that peace can be achieved by a "cosmopolitan civilization": on the contrary, "If there were no longer our modern strife between nations, there would only be a strife between Utopias," between entirely different models of the cosmos and of happiness.[16] Consider the Nazi attempt to create and sustain a new religion of blood and soil. Or the Marxist attempt to regulate the means of production by party dictatorship. Or Hindu *Homo hierarchicus*, Islamic *Shari'a* (in many different forms), post-Christian humanism or romantic "naturism" (which last is a label for a form of thought and action that looks back to Native American, African or Celtic traditions for its—largely fictional—inspiration). Consider even the effects of a more sophisticated—and complacent—version of a supposedly open-hearted Western aesthetic: when the Taliban destroyed the Buddhist statues of Bamyan they maybe did so not only because they rejected *Buddhism* (so after all did almost all their critics), nor even from ethnic hatred of Bamyan civilization, but because they despised—so to call it—Western aestheticism.[17] Would we all really be happy to be ruled entirely by those who valued *art* or *traditional culture* more than human (and other) life? Consider other half-forgotten ways, and the possibility of their return: science fiction writers regularly conceive some version of Pharaonism

16   Chesterton, *Heretics*, 80. Samuel P. Huntington, *The Clash of Civilizations: and the remaking of world order* (London: Simon & Schuster, 1996), has been widely criticized both for exaggerating the supposed moral and political differences between (for example) "Western," Confucian and especially Muslim societies, and their internal consistency, and for providing excuses for economic and military violence by existing political units (both Western powers and extreme "Islamist" groups). Those criticisms may be just, and still miss the point: people do disagree, at some fundamental level, about their own place in the world and our duties to each other. Such disagreements occur even within state boundaries, and certainly in the inhabited world at large, and "if Satan is divided against himself, how can his kingdom stand?" (Luke 11.18).

17   *The New York Times* reported (19th March 2001) that the Taliban envoy to the US had said "that the Islamic government made its decision in a rage after a foreign delegation offered money to preserve the ancient works while a million Afghans faced starvation. 'When your children are dying in front of you, then you don't care about a piece of art'": https://www.nytimes.com/2001/03/19/world/taliban-explains-buddha-demolition.html (accessed 26th August 2021).

as our future. A world state not animated by any corresponding religion—not even by the supposedly "secular" dream of respect for all the diversity of human custom and opinion—could only rule by the sword. "For how can there be an international law or order or working league or federation of states until there is an accepted level of moral understanding among men to give vitality to its legal code?"[18] But that religion cannot simply be imposed, but must arise from or at least be congruent with the desires and affections of us all—a "catholic" rather than sectarian morale. Those who do not notice the disagreements and imagine that their own assumptions are obviously both universal and veridical, may be as dangerous as those who identify dissent as (obviously) Satanic.

What then would the Neo-Platonic vision be? There is a simple answer: it is a vision of the past.

> Long before the cities whose formation we described earlier, there is said to have come into being a certain very happy rule and arrangement under Kronos. The best of arrangements at the present time is in fact an imitation of this ... Kronos understood that, as we have explained, human nature is not at all capable of regulating the human things, when it possesses autocratic authority over everything, without becoming swollen with hubris and injustice. So, reflecting on these things, he set up at that time kings and rulers within our cities—not humans, but *daimones*, members of a more divine and better species. He did just what we do now with sheep and the other tame herd animals. We don't make cattle themselves rulers of cattle, or goats rulers of goats; instead, we exercise despotic dominion over them, because our species is better than theirs. The same is done by the god, who was a friend of humanity: he set over us the better species of spirits, who supervised us in a way that provided much ease both for them and for us. They provided peace and awe and good laws and justice without stint. Thus they made it so that the races of men were without civil strife, and happy. What this account is saying, making use of the truth, is that there can be no rest from evils and toils for those cities in which some mortal rules rather than a god. It holds

---

18 Hocking, *Living Religions*, 19. See also Morgenthau, *Politics among Nations: the struggle for power and peace* (New York: Alfred A. Knopf, 1956), 481: "There can be no world state without a world community willing and able to support it."

that we should imitate by every device the way of life that is said to have existed under Kronos; in public life and in private—in the arrangement of our households and our cities—we should obey whatever within us partakes of immortality, giving the name "law" to the distribution of reason (*tên tou nou dianomên eponomazontas nomon*).[19]

We may hope to be ruled by *daimones*, under the rule of Kronos, as Plato also imagined in his *Statesman*.[20] That rule is to be channeled through distinctive spirits: each *polis*, tribe or amphictyony obedient to its own eternal pattern, and all obedient to the one God overall. The world is not to be simply uniform.

One ought to try to become as good as possible oneself, but not to think that only oneself can become perfectly good—for if one thinks this one is not yet perfectly good. One must rather think that there are other perfectly good men, and good spirits as well, and, still more, the gods who are in this world and look to the other, and, most of all, the ruler of this universe, the most blessed Soul. Then at this point one should go on to praise the intelligible gods, and then, above all, the great king of that other world, most especially by displaying his greatness in the multitude of the gods. It is not contracting the divine into one but showing it in that multiplicity in which God himself has shown it, which is proper to those who

19   Plato, *Laws*, 4.713a. See also Dillon, "Plutarch, Plotinus and the Zoroastrian Concept of the *Fravashi*," on the Zoroastrian concept of a helpful *daimon* that may also, in the end, be our own higher self. Julian drew the same conclusion, that "Reason" ought to rule: Julian, "Letter to Themistius [258–59]," in *Works*, vol. 2, 213–15: "The lesson is that we ought by every means in our power to imitate that life which is said to have existed in the days of Kronos: and in so far as the principle of immortality is in us we ought to be guided by it in our management of public and private affairs, of our houses and cities, calling the distribution of mind [*ten tou nou dianomen*] 'law.'" That *nous* is, in principle, itself a *daimon*, or better still a god.

20   So also the Hermetic Corpus: gods are to take care of humans, and humans of other, non-rational, creatures: Copenhaver, *Hermetica*, 35 [10.22]. C. S. Lewis constructed his Malacandra on these lines, so that the three imagined sorts of "rational animal" in that world (aka Mars) were governed by celestial spirits (*eldili*): see C. S. Lewis, *Out of the Silent Planet* (London: Harper Collins, 2005). One consequence of the Incarnation, he imagined in a later volume (C. S. Lewis, *Perelandra* [London: Harper Collins, 2005]), was that *human* beings should instead begin to rule themselves as well as their non-rational kin. One may reasonably suspect, of course, that goats and other "non-rational" creatures can actually manage their own affairs quite well.

know the power of God, inasmuch as, abiding who he is, he makes many gods, all depending upon himself and existing through him and from him.[21]

All the differing styles and expressions of creative life are to be accepted within the manifold, on the clear condition that they never think themselves uniquely correct, uniquely privileged. Even though there is to be a single universal authority there are also to be many lesser, and yet still partly autonomous, authorities. Minucius Felix records the judgment that this was the real secret of the Romans' imperial success:

> Thus it is that their power and authority has embraced the circuit of the whole world, and has advanced the bounds of empire beyond the paths of the sun, and the confines of ocean; while they practice in the field god-fearing valor, make strong their city with awe of sacred rites, with chaste virgins, with many a priestly dignity and title; besieged and imprisoned within the limits of the Capitol, they still reverenced the gods, whom others might have spurned as [enraged], and through the ranks of Gauls amazed at their undaunted superstition [the audacity of their superstition] passed on armed not with weapons but with godly reverence and fear; in captured fortresses, even in the first flush of victory, they reverence the conquered deities; everywhere they entertain the gods and adopt them as their own; while they raise altars even to the unknown deities, and to the spirits of the dead. Thus is it that they adopt the sacred rites of all nations, and withal have earned dominion.[22]

It should be remembered that it was not only the Hebrews who resented this assimilation, and subordination, of their own gods and rituals,[23] but the *principle* was perhaps a sound one. Plotinus's

---

21 Plotinus, *Ennead*, II.9 [33].9, 28–40; see also Origen, *Principles*, vol. 1, 93 (1.5.2), citing Deuteronomy 32.9: "When the Most High divided the nations, and scattered the sons of Adam, He fixed the boundaries of the nations according to the number of the angels of God."

22 Minucius Felix, *Octavius*, 329 [6.2–3].

23 See Béatrice Caseau, "Sacred Landscapes," in *Late Antiquity: a guide to the post-classical world*, ed. G. W. Bowersock, et al. (Cambridge, Mass: Harvard University Press, 1999), 21: the citizens of Gholaia in Libya, as soon as the Roman legionnaires had withdrawn in 270, "carefully desecrated the religious spaces within the Roman camp and destroyed the cult statues."

tripartite vision of the divine, mythologized as Ouranos, Kronos, Zeus (the One, the Intellect and the Soul), demands a multiple expression. *Nous,* the Intellect, is indeed always already multiple: "Intellect is not simple but many; it manifests a composition, of course an intelligible one, and already sees many things. It is, certainly, also itself an intelligible, but it thinks as well: so it is already two."[24] But its multiplicity is not at odds with itself. The fall into a *material* world of division, distance and darkness begins in self-isolation, in the rejection of all other forms of being:

> [Individual souls] are free from sorrow if they remain with universal soul in the intelligible, but in heaven with the universal soul they can share in its government, like those who live with a universal monarch and share in the government of his empire; these also do not come down from the abode of royalty: for they are then all together in the same [place]. But they change from the whole to being a part and belonging to themselves, and, as if they were tired of being together, they each go to their own.[25]

The story also allows for the existence of malicious *daimones*[26] and malicious humans, so that the age of innocence, the undisputed rule of Kronos, passes by: in this age of the world, we may need a painful discipline to keep us safe, but this can only be endurable because there are such things as Health, Peace and Prosperity, which we imitate here below. The imagined World Morale consists in the conviction that all the differing gods and spirits of the cities, nations and tribes have their origin, and lasting home, in the eternal, where even seemingly antagonistic powers are reconciled.

> Common humanity as a basis for moral values, and there-fore for political association, was discussed by a Christian *faylasuf,* Yahya Ibn Adi (893–974: pupil of al-Farabi and a translator of Aristotle). One ought to develop friendship

---

24 Plotinus, *Ennead,* V.4 [7].2, 9–11.

25 Plotinus, *Ennead,* IV.8 [6].6, 7–14.

26 See Minucius Felix, *Octavius,* 399–400 [26.8–9]: "There exist unclean and wandering spirits, whose heavenly vigor has been overlaid by earthly soils and lusts. These spirits, burdened and steeped in vices, have lost the simplicity of their original substance; as some consolation for their own calamity, these lost spirits cease not to conspire for others' loss, to deprave them with their own depravity, and under the alienation of depraved and heathen superstitions to separate them from God."

(*mahabba*), he said, towards all human beings because "men are one tribe [*qabil*] ... joined together by humanity. And the adornment of the divine power is in all and in each ... of them, it being a rational soul.... All men are really a single entity in many individuals."[27]

Better, perhaps, to remember that the non-human also are a part of the one tribe, and that this is consistent with great differences between the multiple embodiments.

Neo-Platonic cosmology reflects—or is reflected by—late Roman imperial organization. But Chlup, who makes this suggestion, is—or so I suggest—mistaken in supposing that "the systems of the Neoplatonists [unlike the Middle Platonists] resemble the hierarchic multilevel administration of the late Empire, when 'soft' government was replaced by a 'hard' one, and imperial supervision increasingly tended to stretch down to local particularities."[28] On the one hand, this greatly exaggerates the role of the Imperial bureaucracy in local and regional affairs; on the other, it neglects Plotinus's own insistence that particular agents like ourselves have their own lives. If that were not so, "providence" would not exist, as there would be nothing for it to provide for![29] Some later Muslim Platonists might more consistently affirm the king's (the caliph's) absolute and universal authority, as image and representative of the One Itself,[30] but a properly *Plotinian* metaphysics allows, by analogy, a more distributed and flexible authority.

This is not to say that we are to expect that life here-now will be peaceful, nor even that at least the Empire will always be at peace: competition and even mortal combat may still be part of life:

> This All is visibly not only one living creature, but many; so that in so far as it is one, each individual part is preserved by the whole, but in so far as it is many, when the many encounter each other they often injure each other because they are different; and one injures another to supply its own need, and even makes a meal of another

---

27 Black, *History of Islamic Political Thought*, 58, citing Kraemer, *Humanism in the Renaissance of Islam*, 115.

28 Radek Chlup, *Proclus: an introduction* (Cambridge: Cambridge University Press, 2012), 16.

29 Plotinus, *Ennead*, III.2 [47].9, 1–3.

30 See Al-Azmeh, *Muslim Kingship*, 121: "Many Muslim authors postulated the dilution of absolutism as the primary cause for the decline of the state."

which is at the same time related to and different from it; and each one, naturally striving to do the best for itself, takes to itself that part of the other which is akin to it, and makes away with all that is alien to itself because of its self-love. Each as it does its own work benefits that which can profit in any way from its workings but makes away with or injures that which cannot endure the impact of its activity, like the things which are withered when fire comes near them, or the smaller animals which are swept aside or even trampled underfoot by the rush of larger ones. The coming into being and destruction and alteration for worse or better of all these individual things brings to its fullness the unhindered life according to nature of that one [universal] living creature; since it was not possible for all the individual things to be as if they were alone nor for the final purpose to be directed and look towards them when they are [only] parts, but it must be directed to that of which they are parts, and since they are different, they cannot all have their own forever in a single life; it was not possible for anything to persist altogether the same, if the All was going to persist, which has its persistence in its movement.[31]

Neo-Platonic Religion, that is to say, accepts that it is only in the Original Intellect that all things are clearly one: here-now it is enough that all things get their turn—which is also one understanding of the Book of Job. The Creator plays fair by all His creatures and "gives to [them] His boundary so that each may become fully itself," whether it be Satan, or Leviathan, or Job.[32] God's power, according to Rabbinic thought, "is revealed in His ability to restrain himself from destroying the wicked."[33] He will disentangle "good" from "evil" only at the end of time,[34] if there is any such end. Then it will be true that "mercy and truth are met together; righteousness and peace have kissed each other"[35]—or rather, by Plotinus's account, they *are* meeting together "there." He has no expectation, it seems, that this world here, however

---

3 1   Plotinus, *Ennead*, IV.4 [28].32, 32–53.

3 2   N. N. Glatzer, ed., *The Dimensions of Job* (New York: Schocken Books, 1969), 63.

3 3   Hannah K. Harrington, *Holiness: Rabbinic Judaism and the Graeco-Roman World* (London: Routledge, 2001), 25.

3 4   See Matthew 13:24–30.

3 5   Psalm 85.10.

fine, will ever fully accommodate an eternal peace, nor that it will be conclusively remade. We can expect no better image of the Eternal than the one we have already, the changeful and contested landscape of our lives.[36] "All things must exist forever in ordered dependence upon each other."[37]

GODS, DAIMONES AND THE SOULS OF CITIES

So how are the spirits to rule us (granted that we cannot all encounter them, as it were, in the flesh)? For us they exist as objects of proper worship, manifest in established laws and ancient customs, and also in festivals, architecture and art. The city—to return for a moment to Platonopolis—honors Hestia, Zeus and Athena in the acropolis and divides the rest of the city, and the surrounding country, into twelve wards.

> First of all, we say, if—after the honors paid to the Olympians and the gods who keep the State—we should assign the Even and the Left as their honors to the gods of the under-world, we would be aiming most straight at the mark of piety—as also in assigning to the former gods the things superior, the opposites of these. Next after these gods the wise man will offer worship to the *daimones*, and after the *daimones* to the heroes. After these will come private shrines legally dedicated to ancestral deities; and next, honors paid to living parents.[38]

In working the land they must honor Earth their mother, as well as local gods and *daimones*, spirits of wood and stream.[39] They must also honor their own souls.[40] The Athenian proceeds on the further assumption that he and his interlocutors all believe that the sun, moon, stars and earth are "gods and divine beings" (*theous kai theia onta*).[41] We pray, Plotinus agrees, to the sun, and

---

36 Plotinus, *Ennead*, II.9 [33].4, 26–27.
37 Ibid., II.9 [33].3, 12.
38 Plato, *Laws*, 4.717ab; see Robert Mayhew, "The Theology of the Laws," in *Plato's Laws: a Critical Guide*, ed. Christopher Bobonich (Cambridge: Cambridge University Press, 2010).
39 Plato, *Laws*, 5.740ab.
40 Ibid., 5.726a; "psychotherapy," it is worth noting, is not originally aimed at *healing* but *serving* the soul, that is, our higher self: see Stephen R. L. Clark, "Therapy and Theoria Reconstructed," *Philosophy as Therapy*, ed. Clare Carlisle and Jonardon Ganeri (Cambridge: Cambridge University Press, 2010).
41 Plato, *Laws*, 10.886d.

other men to the stars.[42] The city and the cosmos alike are full
of spirits whom we should not easily dismiss as fictions or merely
ceremonial objects: they are at least to be present to the residents'
thoughts and imagination. "The wise men of old ... made temples
and statues in the wish that the gods should be present to them":[43]
the temples and statues that they made, as I remarked earlier, were
richly imagined ones. They "came alive" in the vivid imagination of
their spectators and may even have been *seen* to move or to have
moved, without any need to have them automated, whether by
steam or clockwork. And maybe there are indeed, or were indeed,
real "animals" of another, airy sort whom we have now forgotten
or dismissed! "There is nothing absurd in spirits and souls in the
air using voices: for they are living creatures of a particular kind."[44]
Some of those spirits were human. A citizen's duty is to "leave one
son, whomever he pleases, as the inheritor of his dwelling, to be
his successor in the tendance of the deified ancestors."[45] The city,
that is, is a living whole, compounded of the living and the dead,
the merely mortal and immortal spirits. "Supposing the city had
a soul and included other beings with souls, the soul of the city
would be more complete and powerful, but there would certainly
be nothing to prevent the others being the same kind of thing."[46]
And perhaps it does indeed have a soul, and an immortal patron
or presiding genius,[47] somehow embodied or represented in a
reigning king or emperor. Gallienus, for example, sought to present
himself—partly through his coinage—as Hercules, Mercury, the

---

42   Plotinus, *Ennead*, IV.4 [28].30, 4–5. Proclus prayed to the sun thrice daily
(Marinus, *Life of Proclus*: Mark Edwards, trans., *Neoplatonic Saints: the lives of
Plotinus and Proclus by their students* [Liverpool: Liverpool University Press, 2000];
see Fowden, *Egyptian Hermes*, 127), and the Hermetic Corpus identified the
sun as the greatest god in heaven (Copenhaver, *Hermetica*, 18 [5.3]). Plotinus
thinks indeed that the stars should be respected but does not expect clear
guidance or instruction from them. Successive emperors, from Elagabalus to
Aurelian, attempted to promote Sun-worship as a way of unifying the empire:
see Clark, *Plotinus*, 214–6.

43   Plotinus, *Ennead*, IV.3 [27].11.

44   Ibid., IV.3 [27].11, 25–26.

45   Plato, *Laws*, 5.740bc. Surplus sons may be passed on to childless couples
or, in extremis, sent away as colonists. Neither the size nor the structure of
Magnesia is to be changed by demographics.

46   Plotinus, *Ennead*, IV.8 [6].3, 16–19.

47   See Birte Poulsen, "City Personifications in Late Antiquity," in *Using
Images in Late Antiquity*, ed. Stine Birk, et al. (Oxford: Oxbow Books, 2014).

Genius Populi Romani, Kore, Zeus, Sol Invictus and Minerva.[48] What patron might Plotinus have chosen for his city? Hestia might certainly be an option, and one interestingly conjoined to Hermes,[49] but perhaps any distinct deity or divinely inspired image must be put aside. Or perhaps not.

It is possible—though this is to go far beyond any contemporary evidence—that Platonopolis was to be more than a simple, well-organized *polis*. Perhaps Gallienus at least may have dreamed that it would be a genuine *metropolis,* at once a new home for a truly "godly" emperor, and the center from which imperial power would radiate.[50] When Constantine, half a century later, transformed Byzantium into Constantinople it was not merely an administrative convenience, but a declaration that the empire would be reborn, transformed, owing less to merely military force and more to spiritual attraction. Somehow the sprawling empire must have a focal point, and that point must itself be worth our admiration. The city itself must also have a focal point—a place where the merely earthly reveals the heavenly. The Egyptians built their temples to be worthy residences for the god or gods of their devotion,[51] and later generations have identified such architecture as openings to an unearthly realm: so, centuries later, the envoys of Vladimir of Kiev, visiting the great church of Hagia Sophia in Constantinople, reported: "We were led into a place where they serve their God, and we did not know where we were, on heaven or on earth; and do not know how to tell about this. All we know is that God lives there with people and their service is better than in any other country. We cannot forget that beauty."[52] And in Western Christendom Abbot Suger, architect and builder of the abbey church of St. Denis, said that when in the church he saw himself "dwelling in some strange region of the universe which neither exists entirely in the slime of earth nor entirely in the purity of heaven, and that by the grace of God, [he could] be

---

48   Blois, *Policy of Gallienus*, 211.

49   See Jean-Pierre Vernant, "Hestia-Hermès: Sur l'expression religieuse de l'espace et du movement chez les Grecs," *L'Homme* 3 (1963): 12–50; Clark, *Plotinus*, 222–24.

50   See Al-Azmeh, *Muslim Kingship*, 72–73.

51   Hornung, *Conceptions of God*, 229.

52   See Bruce V. Foltz, *The Noetics of Nature: Environmental Philosophy and the Holy Beauty of the Visible* (New York: Fordham University Press, 2013), 78, 126.

transported from this inferior to that higher world in an anagogical manner."[53] Whether Plotinus (or Gallienus) had such ambitions is impossible to tell. Later Platonists clearly did.

It is likely—it is almost certain—that an imperial city, the center of imperial power, must attract attention, devotion, even worship, whether or not that is for its architectural splendors. So must the figure of the emperor himself. Whatever exists at all, Plotinus said, exists by virtue of the One:[54] as an opening gambit this is indeed a truism. Whatever exists must somehow be *one* thing, whether it is a single animal, a chorus, or the cosmos. Plotinus offers an account of how this unity is to be achieved. It is not by mere material continuity: materiality depends, exactly, on each bit's *not* being any other. Nor is it simply united by the presence in it of a single soul as its efficient cause, for soul itself needs something to make it single. Nor yet by the presence of a single form, for form, of its nature, is a complex structure, in which cognition and the thing cognized are to be at one. What is left is the *final* cause of a thing's being, what it aims at and is invested in.[55] Its form and its animating principle are born in concentration on the final goal. A city, like a chorus, becomes a single agent and observer, in its devotion to what surpasses it. Insofar as it is thus united, it is an animate being, adjusting its parts to the music as well as any dancer.[56]

> It is like a choral dance: in the order of its singing the choir keeps round its *koruphaios* [that is, the musician sitting, like Apollo, in the center of the dance] but may sometimes turn away so that he is out of their sight, but

---

53 Panofsky, *Abbot Suger*, 21, 65.
54 Plotinus, *Ennead*, VI.9 [9].1.
55 See Stephen R. L. Clark, *Commentary on Ennead VI.9* (Las Vegas: Parmenides Publishing, 2020), 88–89. Augustine agreed, proposing that a people or republic had its being from its goal: "But if we discard this definition of a people [an assemblage associated by a common acknowledgment of right, and by a community of interests] and, assuming another, say that a people is an assemblage of reasonable beings bound together by a common agreement as to the objects of their love, then, in order to discover the character of any people, we have only to observe what they love. Yet whatever it loves, if only it is an assemblage of reasonable beings and not of beasts, and is bound together by an agreement as to the objects of love, it is reasonably called a people; and it will be a superior people in proportion as it is bound together by higher interests, inferior in proportion as it is bound together by lower" (Augustine, *City of God*, 19.24).
56 See Plotinus, *Ennead*, III.2 [47].16, 23–27; IV.4 [28].33, 12–219.

when it turns back to him it sings beautifully and is
truly with him; so we are always around him—and if we
were not, we should be totally dissolved and no longer
exist—but not always turned towards him; but when we
do look to him, then we are at our goal and at rest and do
not sing out of [time] as we truly dance our god-inspired
dance around him.[57]

In this Plotinus echoes Aristotle: a human being's identity is
based in her *prohairesis*, her fundamental choice.[58] And a city's
identity likewise turns on its constitution:[59] not the formal rules
laid down for its everyday working, but its goal, its very reason
and standard for well-being. So also the Empire. Platonopolis, like
Magnesia, was to be guided by *Nous,* and *Nous* exists by its concentration on the One—which is to say, the Good. That *Nous* may
be represented mythologically by Kronos,[60] but ritually, perhaps,
by only an empty shrine—the unimaginable and unimagined God,
encountered (in a way) only by the high priest going up to the
Holy of Holies, having shed his garments entirely.[61]

Without religion there would be no polity and no salvation
for the masses. But religion only offered a relative truth,
and it was only by means of philosophy that one could
escape from relativism.[62]

---

57   Ibid., VI.9 [9].8, 38–41. Armstrong (*Enneads,* vol. 7, 333) makes, in my judgment, two errors in his version of the passage: first, by translating *"koruphaios"*
as "conductor," and second by speaking of the chorus being out of *tune,* rather
than as not keeping time (*apadein*). See Clark, *Plotinus,* 118–19.
58   Aristotle, *Nicomachean Ethics,* 6.1139b4; 3.1112a1; see Clark, *Aristotle's Man,*
100–3.
59   Aristotle, *Politics,* 3.1276b10–12.
60   See Plato, *Laws,* 4.713a: "The best of arrangements at the present time is
in fact an imitation of [the ancient age]. Kronos understood that, as we have
explained, human nature is not at all capable of regulating the human things,
when it possesses autocratic authority over everything, without becoming
swollen with hubris and injustice. So, reflecting on these things, he set up at
that time kings and rulers within our cities—not humans, but spirits, members
of a more divine and better species. He did just what we do now with sheep
and the other tame herd animals."
61   Plotinus, *Ennead,* I.6 [1].7, 4–9; VI.9 [9].11, 21–22. See Clark, *Plotinus: myth,
metaphor and philosophical practice,* 45–63 for a fuller examination of the metaphor.
62   Crone, *Medieval,* 174, after al-Farabi. The philosophy al-Farabi had in
mind was not, of course, simply the disciplines now commonly studied in
most University departments.

It is as well to remember that very image. It is all too easy, when hearing that the city is to be ruled by *Nous*, to interpret that as "Reason," which—in our modern assumptions—usually amounts to the careful calculation of the easiest means to easily accepted ends. One of the strangest features of American science fiction in the 1950s, during a time when "Communism" was the bogey, is the suggestion that we would all be gladly ruled by computers programmed to serve the common (unquestioned) good, as though that good was obvious and the means to it entirely clear and ethically acceptable. Conversely, there is a long history of religious zealots, set to found their New Jerusalem according to their own reading of the scriptures, stepping away from any established order, any consensus reading, and openly despising the results of merely human "reason." Neither version of Plato's city seems likely to appeal to a Plotinian sense. And yet both share with Plato's city a contempt and fear, almost a hatred, of here-tics: in the "rational" city, rogues who prefer their own account of Good are readily sequestered, re-educated or killed; in the "religious" city, they must be traduced, exiled—or killed. And in Magnesia the "Nocturnal Council" does the same to all who are reckoned dangerously "atheistical," disloyal to the abiding gods of the city. Even those atheists "who, though they utterly disbelieve in the existence of the gods, possess by nature a just character, both hate the evil and, because of their dislike of injustice, are incapable of being induced to commit unjust actions, and flee from unjust men and love the just,"[63] are nonetheless dangerous, for the support they lend, unwillingly or unknowingly, to those who reckon that there can be no proper universal justice. Can this inquisition and condemnation be what Plotinus would have wished, or Gallienus endorsed? It does not seem, at least, that Plotinus chose to dominate discussion in his seminars; on the contrary, "Since he encouraged his students to ask questions, the course was lacking in order and there was a great deal of pointless chatter!"[64] And Gallienus was both praised and abused in later years for his liberal attitude towards *Christians*, who firmly denied the divinity of stars and of all the civic gods. Gallienus differed in this from both Valerian, his father, and his pre-Constantinian

---

63 Plato, *Laws*, 10.908bc.
64 Porphyry, *Life*, 3.36–8.

successors, like Aurelian.[65] May this be another reason the plan
to create Platonopolis was not pursued? If it is to survive as Plato
wished it must demand an absolute loyalty from all its residents,
directed to a specific version of the Good. But such loyalty to one
flawed image is itself inconsistent with the Platonic and Plotinian
vision. True piety is to prefer the truth, even to the views and
good opinion of our dearest friends, and even to our own.[66] The
Brethren of Purity "thought that all prophets, despite differences
in the laws they gave, shared the same basic opinions. Indeed, they
argued that religious differences, far from being harmful, served
a purpose by promoting discussion and knowledge."[67] We must
all be ready to be proved wrong.

> Refutation is the greatest and chiefest of purifications,
> and he who has not been refuted, though he be the Great
> King himself, is in an awful state of impurity; he is unin-
> structed and deformed in those things in which he who
> would be truly blessed ought to be fairest and purest.[68]

There might be a good reason to expect that Platonopolis should
have a single philosopher-king, if only to represent the proper
focus of all our loyalty. That notion will concern me on a later
page. But there is better reason, in practice, to trust the rule of
the city to a council, whose various distinct errors and confusions
can be absorbed and answered.[69] Such a council is recommended
for Magnesia and expected in most usual *poleis*. This is not to say

---

65 According to the *Historia Augusta*, vol. 3, 43–45 (13.1–5), Zenobia of Palmyra "ruled for a long time, not in feminine fashion or with the ways of a
woman, but surpassing in courage and skill not merely Gallienus, than whom
any girl could have ruled more successfully, but also many an emperor": cited
by Olivier Hekster, *Rome and its Empire, AD 193–284* (Edinburgh: Edinburgh
University Press, 2008), 98. Eusebius, on the other hand, praised him as one
who ended Valerian's persecution of Christians: Eusebius, *History of the Church*,
trans. G. A. Williamson, ed. Andrew Louth (London: Penguin, 1989), 231–32,
238 (7.13; 7.23). See Blois, *Policy of Gallienus*; Clark, *Plotinus: myth, metaphor and
philosophical practice*, 140, 167, 177.
66 Plato, *Republic*, 10.595c; Aristotle, *Nicomachean Ethics*, 1.1096a16–7.
67 Black, *History of Islamic Political Thought*, 59, citing Marquet, *La Philosophie
des Ihwan al-Safa*, 429–30, 448.
68 Plato, *Sophist*, 227c.
69 Plotinus, *Ennead*, VI.5 [23].10; Aristotle, *Politics*, 3.1281a42–b2. See James
Surowiecki, *The Wisdom of Crowds: why the many are smarter than the few* (New York:
Random House, 2004) for some evidence of the superior accuracy of many voices,
so long as they aren't coerced or cajoled by group-think or a charismatic voice.

that the city will be "democratic" in any familiar sense: the council will also be needed to educate and discipline a larger assembly of discordant voices,[70] just as we need a legacy of wise rules and images to control our own internal monsters.

The danger of debate and disagreement is that too many of us are enamored of our own opinions, and swiftly conclude that our opponents, being in obvious error, must be either fools or knaves to maintain their opposition. All sides swiftly forget their unifying aim, their concentration on the god among them.

> Where offices of rule are open to contest, the victors in the contest monopolize power in the *polis* so completely that they offer not the smallest share in office to the vanquished party or their descendants; and each party keeps a watchful eye on the other, lest anyone should come into office and, in revenge for the former troubles, cause a rising against them. Such polities we, of course, deny to be polities, just as we deny that laws are true laws unless they are enacted in the interest of the common weal of the whole *polis*. But where the laws are enacted in the interest of a section, we call them feudalities rather than polities; and the "justice" they ascribe to such laws is, we say, an empty name.[71]

Cities rot, like fishes, from the head (an epigram attributed to the Sufi poet, Rumi), and when an animal, and an ensouled city, dies, others spring up from it, with their own souls and brief identities:[72] these may be factions, sects or individual persons destined to be lost in the general sea of souls—or yet more likely, buried in the earth. Those who are utterly persuaded of their own virtue and wisdom make very dangerous masters, even if it is also fair to agree that those who deny the very possibility of an eternal moral order make very dangerous partners.[73] Our

---

70 Plotinus, *Ennead*, IV.4 [28].17. On the management of those disorderly voices see also Plotinus, *Ennead*, VI.4 [22].15.18–40. Both passages are discussed by David G. Robertson in "Plotinus on Disorderly Men in Political Communities," *Politeia* 1, no. 4 (2019): 183–94.

71 Plato, *Laws*, 4.715ab.

72 Plotinus, *Ennead*, IV.3 [27].8, 48–51.

73 It is often the case nowadays that those who fiercely deny the existence of any gods still prefer to believe that there are real moral standards that must be recognized by any rational creature of whatever biological kind: it is not easy to see what sort of being those standards have, nor why we "ought" to

best response is to accept and be molded by the mobile, flexible, self-adjusting real, *eikon aei eikonizomene*. And in the absence of an actual Platonopolis, to build the city, Callipolis, in our own souls, so as bring all our interior gods and *daimones* together into one.[74] But that may require self-exile.

THE MAKING OF AN EMPEROR

A Neo-Platonic ritual and religion of the sort described might possibly serve the needs of a mere federation of mostly independent *poleis*, tribes and amphictyonies. But it would perhaps be better represented if there were a single focus for the whole: in brief, an imperial monarchy. "Because a plurality of heads corrupts government and produces division, it is necessary for a single man to rule, whether over a city, great cities, a country, great countries, or most of the world."[75] Plotinus himself would have been less confident: "'Know Yourself,'" after all, "is said to those who because of their selves' multiplicity have the business of counting themselves up and learning that they do not know all the numbers and kinds of things they are, or do not know any one of them, nor what their ruling principle is, or by what they are themselves."[76] But the apparent unity of a single person may still seem more secure than the unity of an obvious coalition, even to Christians influenced more by Stoic than Platonic thought, such as Minucius Felix (d. 250).

> When has joint monarchy ever started in good faith, or ended without bloodshed? I need not refer to Persians, choosing their ruler by omen of a horse's neigh, nor to the dead and buried legend of the Theban brothers. Who does not know the story of the twins fighting for kingship over a few shepherds and a hut? Wars waged between son-in-law and father-in-law spread over the whole world, and the fortunes of a world empire could not find room for

follow them: see Stephen R. L. Clark, *Can We Believe in People? Human Significance in an interconnected cosmos* (Brooklyn: Angelico Press, 2020), 41–70.

74   Plato, *Republic*, 9.592b.

75   The argument of a letter (probably) from Themistius in response to Julian's more cautious epistle—*Risāla* 13, 98.3–11, cited in John W. Watt, "Julian's *Letter to Themistius*—and Themistius' Response?" in *Emperor and Author: the writings of Julian the Apostate*, ed. Nicholas Baker-Brian and Shaun Tougher (Swansea: Classical Press of Wales, 2012), 99.

76   Plotinus, *Ennead*, VI.7 [38].41, 22–26. See also Plato, *Phaedrus*, 229b4–30a6.

two. Look where you will: bees have but one king, flocks one leader, cattle one monarch of the herd.[77]

Because, it is supposed, all empires, flocks and hives must have a single ruler, it is absurd to think that the cosmos should have more than one. It is an unconvincing argument, in the light of a long tradition that there is indeed war in heaven, and ample reason to believe (even if incorrectly) that there is no single, undisputed plan in action. Experience might easily suggest that all things end in bloodshed, or else don't end at all.

> Even if we retain any sense of a divine presence in the world, we have to admit that it manifests itself in innumerably various, apparently clashing, often inscrutably odd and terrifying ways. Divine unity, not divine plurality, requires an effort of reflection and faith to attain it; and when attained, it does not necessarily exclude plurality.[78]

The converse argument is that because there is after all—or so we must believe—a single consistent order in the world and a single source, there should also be a single rule and ruler, a final court of appeal, a unique source of authority, in any empire, flock or herd.[79] Anything else permits an appeal from one leader to another, with no way of settling the dispute but bloodshed—as was indeed the case when Licinius disputed Constantine's approval for the Christian sect. According to the historian Eusebius,

> As [Licinius] was about to begin the war [with his fellow and rival emperor Constantine], he called together the select members of his bodyguard and valued friends to one of the places which they consider sacred. It was a grove, well-watered and thickly growing, and all sorts of images of those he thought were gods were erected in it carved in stone. He lit candles to them, and made the usual sacrifices, and is said to have delivered such a speech as this: "Friends and comrades, these are our ancestral gods, which we honor because we have received them for worship from

---

77 Minucius Felix, *Octavius*, 363 [18.6–7]. These stock historical or mythological references are to the trick that gave Darius the Persian throne; the dispute of Eteocles and Polynices, sons of Oedipus of Thebes; Romulus's murder of Remus; and the dispute between Julius Caesar and Pompey.

78 A. J. Armstrong, "Some advantages of polytheism," *Dionysius* 5 (1981): 184.

79 See also Al-Azmeh, *Muslim Kingship*, 73: "To the unicity of God corresponds the unicity of the king."

our earliest forefathers. The commander of those arrayed against us has broken faith with the ancestral code and adopted godless belief, mistakenly acknowledging some foreign god from somewhere or other, and he even shames his own army with this god's disgraceful emblem."[80]

What was so difficult for pagans like Licinius to assimilate? Mediterranean religion, even Roman religion, was mostly syncretic and inclusive. Even such rites as struck most ordinary Romans as indecent might still have their respect: the rites of Cybele, for example, which sometimes included ecstatic self-castration, were nonetheless parts of Roman official religion, as linking them to their purported Trojan ancestors.[81] Conversely, child-sacrifice was an evil mostly because it was practiced by the Carthaginians! Homeland and ancestry, in short, were crucial. Better maintain the religions handed down to us, even or especially if we have no proof that Nature is really providential, or really "on our side."[82] So perhaps Minucius's argument does after all have some pragmatic force: if there is to be a single imperial ruler there had better also be *supposed* to be a single cosmic ruler. If tradition tells us that there are many gods, owing no strict allegiance to any superior power, then the way is always open for one imperial faction to appeal against another: both will have their patrons, and there will be no other solution than the war of rival utopias that Chesterton imagined.

The Emperor Julian attempted to deal with the problem by ensuring that he, as Pontifex Maximus, was the one to appoint provincial high priests (who would in turn appoint the lesser clergy). As O'Meara remarks, this is to evoke "a Neoplatonic metaphysics of emanation in which all good, power, and knowledge are transmitted vertically, through intermediaries, from higher to lower levels."[83] Over a thousand years later the Mughal emperor Akbar (r. 1556–1605) similarly presented himself as the sacred focus of

---

80   Eusebius, *Life of Constantine*, ed. Averil Cameron and Stuart G. Hall (Oxford: Clarendon Press, 1999), 97 [2.5].

81   Mary Beard, "The Roman and the Foreign: the cult of the 'Great Mother' in Imperial Rome," in *Shamanism, History and the State*, ed. Nicholas Thomas and Caroline Humphrey (Ann Arbor: Michigan University Press, 1996).

82   Minucius Felix, *Octavius*, 327 [6.1–2].

83   O'Meara, *Platonopolis*, 122. It does not follow that those lesser authorities could simply and uncontroversially apply the imperial rules: there must always be room for flexible interpretation and re-prioritization of those rules (see Aristotle, *Nicomachean Ethics*, 5.1137b30–1).

all the different creeds and traditions in his realm—drawing on a similar metaphysics.[84]

Priests, so Julian insisted, were to be both pious and philanthropic, and so emulate the divine generosity that creates and sustains the world.

> It is disgraceful that, when no Jew ever has to beg, and the impious Galilaeans support not only their own poor but ours as well, all men see that our people lack aid from us. Teach those of the Hellenic faith to contribute to public service of this sort, and the Hellenic villages to offer their first fruits to the gods; and accustom those who love the Hellenic religion to these good works by teaching them that this was our practice of old. At any rate Homer makes Eumaeus say: "Stranger, it is not lawful for me, not even though a baser man than you should come, to dishonor a stranger. For from Zeus come all strangers and beggars. And a gift, though small, is precious" (*Odyssey* 14.56). Then let us not, by allowing others to outdo us in good works, disgrace by such remissness, or rather, utterly abandon, the reverence due to the gods. If I hear that you are carrying out these orders I shall be filled with joy.[85]

That generosity, unfortunately, did not—for Julian—extend to the animals he insisted on sacrificing to show his allegiance to all gods and *daimones* (though perhaps he thereby intended that the human poor of each city should be fed[86]). Porphyry thought that it was only maleficent *daimones* who "rejoice[d] in the 'drink offerings and smoking meat' on which their pneumatic part grows fat."[87] In this he followed "the theologian" (most probably Pythagoras), who says that "not a single animate creature should be sacrificed, but offerings should not go beyond barley-grains and honey and the fruits of the earth, including flowers."[88] We may guess that Plotinus agreed,[89] and that Julian's belief that *killing* creatures

---

84 See A. Azfar Moin, *The Millennial Sovereign: Sacred Kingship and Sainthood in Islam* (New York: Columbia University Press, 2012), 2–4; see also Al-Azmeh, *Muslim Kingship*.

85 Julian, *Works*, vol. 3, Epistle 22, 430d, p. 71.

86 Julian, *Misopogon*, in ibid., vol. 2, 487–89.

87 Porphyry, *On Abstinence*, 73 [II.42, 2], quoting Homer, *Iliad*, 9.500.

88 Porphyry, *On Abstinence*, 70 [II.36, 4].

89 "Even his pagan admirer Ammianus expressed some reserve at [Julian's] ritual excesses (Ammianus XXII.12, 6–7)": Clarke, *De Mysteriis*, 51.

would be pleasing to the gods played also a part in his acceptance (at least) of military violence against the Empire's neighbors: they too would be sacrificed to the gods of Rome (though perhaps not as literally as in the Roman past).[90]

Even if an empire is more peaceable than Julian's (or Constantine's), well-structured and unanimous, of course, there may always be the threat of an alien, rival empire, just as persuaded of its divine authority; so Roman and Persian empires battled it out for centuries, until each empire was in turn transmogrified, and the battle continued between Christian and Muslim empires. Chesterton's point applies: war between single nations or single *poleis* is replaced by a war between would-be utopias, alternative visions of the common good, alternative divinities.[91] Even if the World Morale I sketched before is the common context, there may be good reason to desire a *single* final authority—emperor or senate or even public assembly—to organize and discipline all local customs and religions, on some better basis than Licinius's blank appeal to his, and by implication others', ancestral traditions. How then shall we, or Neo-Platonists, find an Emperor?

> Plato, [al-Farabi] says, "showed that the philosopher and king are one, that both are perfected by a single craft and faculty" (*Aphorisms*, 17). Without the perfect ruler the perfect city "will undoubtedly perish."[92]
>
> Al-Fārābi proceeds next to characterize the chief ruler of the city, who corresponds to the heart, or master organ of the body, as the supreme manager of the affairs of the city, or its head. This ruler may be compared to the First Cause, who presides over immaterial entities, beneath which lie the heavenly bodies, followed by material entities. All inferior entities follow and imitate the higher, culminating in the highest, who is the First

---

90 Cf. Psalm 50, 9-13: "I will not take a bull from your house, nor goats out of your folds. For every beast of the forest is Mine, and the cattle on a thousand hills. I know all the birds of the mountains, and the wild beasts of the field are Mine. If I were hungry, I would not tell you; for the world is Mine, and all its fullness. Will I eat the flesh of bulls, or drink the blood of goats? Offer to God thanksgiving and pay your vows to the Most High." See also Isaiah 1.15: "When you spread out your hands, I will hide My eyes from you; Even though you make many prayers, I will not hear. Your hands are full of blood."

91 Chesterton, *Heretics*, 80.

92 Black, *History*, 66.

Cause. The two essential qualifications of the chief ruler are the natural disposition or aptitude to rule, coupled with voluntary traits or habits suited for that purpose. Like the First Cause, the chief ruler of the virtuous city is then characterized as one who possesses full intellectual perfection, as both subject and object of thought (*'āqil, ma'qūl*). In addition, he is one in whom the imaginative faculty has reached the highest pitch, whereby he is able to receive from the Active Intellect the knowledge of particulars, in either themselves or their likenesses, as well as that of intelligible forms. At that point, the ruler is able to achieve the condition known as the acquired intellect (*'aql mustafād*), which is the highest intellectual stage attainable by humankind. This condition is labelled by al-Fārābi proximity (*muqārabah*) to the Active Intellect, called elsewhere conjunction (*ittisāl*).[93]

It may be that mere chance, or Providence, may bring such a person to the imperial throne. Plotinus, as I remarked, may have hoped for as much in Gallienus, as Plato did (apparently) in Dionysius II of Syracuse, Longinus in Zenobia of Palmyra.[94] Julian might have been expected to think so of himself, but actually rejected the suggestion, saying that he was neither competent nor willing.[95] In an established dynasty, perhaps, there may be scope to encourage the appropriate virtues and understanding in a princely heir. In the Persian court, so Plato seems to have thought, the wisest of the four tutors assigned to the fourteen-year-old prince "teaches him the Magian lore of Zoroaster, son of Horomazes [which is to say, of God]; and that is the worship of the gods: he teaches him also what pertains to a king."[96]

---

93 Fakhry, *Al-Fārābi*, 102–3.

94 Once Aurelian had defeated the small kingdom of Palmyra in 272, Longinus was executed as her advisor in "treason" (*Historia Augusta*, 30.3; Zosimus, *New History* I.56, 2–3): Ousager, *Plotinus on Selfhood*, 260–61. It is perhaps of set purpose that Porphyry insists that Plotinus and Longinus were not themselves associates: Porphyry, *Life*, 14, 17–21.

95 Julian, "Letter to Themistius [266cd]," in *Works*, vol. 2, 235. See Watt, "Julian's Letter to Themistius."

96 Plato, *I Alcibiades*, 122a. The authorship of the dialogue has been disputed, though not for wholly persuasive reasons, but it was taken to be Plato's work during Plotinus's era, and indeed preferred as an introductory text for students: see Nicholas Denyer, *Plato: Alcibiades* (Cambridge: Cambridge University Press, 2001), 11–26.

The Zoroastrian teaching is confirmed in the Denkard (from a later century, but with the blessing of tradition):

> Be it known that the best king is he who is noble in glory, who creates divine faith among the people, who keeps the state ever prosperous, who sympathizing with the afflictions of others makes the world happy and looks to the welfare of all, who is the source of delight to others, who bestows freedom upon man and shines far and wide by his philanthropy. The worst ruler is he who has an evil appearance, who loves evil and defends the ways of the evil doers, who encourages the godless, who keeps the world in distress, who debases his subject by his rule, who is the source of all evil and injury, who oppresses others as well as aids those who oppress the world, who weakens his subjects but gives strength to his enemies, and who renders the world helpless through his meanness.[97]

And again:

> Be it known that those are the rulers of people who have the goodwill of God and the strength coming from wisdom.... Just as God is the protector and by his good deeds the adorner of all men, so also is the earthly king of all mortals. And every man can be the lord of his race. The reason of giving a man ruling power over his race is that by ruling over his fellow creatures in a just manner he may lead them wisely, and may prevent them from going wrong by training them up to resist evil temptations; so that everyone may be able to participate in the happy Frashegird (i.e., final reform) and may be governed in this world in the happy manner which is to come at the time of the filial [sic] Doom. Owing to which the earthly king may become such a beneficent ruler over men's houses, villages, cities, and the whole world in the capacity of the omniscient, all-powerful, all-protecting God's representative, as He Himself is the benignant Lord of all his creation. It is the duty of the king to look well after the good of his subjects, and this duty is very virtuous as that of Jamshid the good monarch of this world. But if the king be a great evil-doer, he has the name of a bad monarch like Zohak.[98]

---

97 Sanjana, *Denkard*, 283 [3.283].

98 Ibid., 289 [3.289]. Jamshid was the supposed fourth ruler of the world in the 9th century Persian epic, *Shahnameh*, until he began to boast of his own attainments. Zohak (or Zahhak), in the same works, was an Arabian prince

The World Empire is to have a World Emperor, with whatever subordinate rulers, appointed from above, the many tribes and cities may require. "The supreme ruler without qualification is he who does not need anyone to rule him in anything whatever, but has actually acquired the sciences and every kind of knowledge....The men who are governed by the rule of this ruler are the virtuous, good and happy men. If they form a nation then that is the virtuous nation."[99] Or perhaps we may be content instead to have a ruler who can more easily acknowledge that others may have some expertise to offer which he does not have himself, and that he too is only a servant of the Divine.

Plotinus does not himself offer Julian's solution—that the Emperor shall appoint the high priests of the Empire's many cults as well as governors for the Empire's many provinces and *poleis*. But the hierarchical motif is still employed: cosmology is exhibited in the varied ranks of courtiers:

> There must be an inconceivable beauty going out before [the First], as in the procession before a great king the lesser ranks go first, and then in succession the greater and after them the yet more majestic and the court which has still more of royal dignity, and then those who are honored next after the king; and after all these the great king himself is suddenly revealed, and the people pray and prostrate themselves before him—those at least who have not gone away beforehand, satisfied with what they saw before the coming of the king. Now in our example the king is a different person from those who go before him; but the king there in the higher world does not rule over different, alien people, but has the most just, the natural sovereignty and the true kingdom; for he [that is, Kronos] is king of truth and natural lord of all his own offspring and divine company, king of the king

---

seduced by Ahriman or Eblis who usurped the thrones of Arabia and Persia (Abolqasem Ferdowsi, *Shahnameh: the Persian Book of Kings*, trans. Dick Davis [New York: Penguin, 2006], 6–27). Jamshid divided the people into the familiar four classes: priests, warriors, farmers and artisans, "so that each man knew his appropriate duties, and knew his own worth and rank" (Ferdowsi, *Shahnameh*, 6). Farmers, Ferdowsi adds, "receive no man's thanks, although no one reproaches them when it is time to eat." The manual workers, he says, "are contumacious people, and their hearts are always filled with anxiety."

99 Al-Farabi, *Governance*, 36–7, quoted in Black, *History*, 64. See also Copenhaver, *Hermetica*, 66 [18.15].

and of the kings, and more rightly than Zeus called the father of the gods.[100]

These hierarchies have an echo in the later Byzantine court, which also served to elevate the Emperor,[101] and in the Muslim Caliphate.[102] As a description of the Roman court in Plotinus's own lifetime they seem less familiar. The third-century emperors were promoted by the army and served at the army's pleasure. There is no hint that they were surrounded by such hierarchical splendors, nor would the title "great king" have been widely accepted. The more obvious contemporary reference was the *Persian* Emperor. Shapur I, then dominant in the East, having thrown back Gordian's army, accepted Philip the Arab's indemnity and peace in 244, captured another emperor (Valerian, father of Gallienus) in 260 and defeated Odaenathus of Palmyra (an aspiring local lord, soon succeeded by Zenobia) a few years later in 264: "King of Kings," by his own preferred title.[103] Echoes of Zoroastrian thought, or at least of interest in that thought, in Plotinus's circle, and his own supposed interest in Persian philosophers, all serve to suggest that Plotinus was more interested in the rival Empire, and maybe more admiring, than other high-ranking Romans perhaps approved.[104] Later Persian philosophers returned the compliment, though they were far more emphatic than Plotinus that it was the *male* human being that better embodied "reason":

> What the philosophers called "political science" formed part of practical philosophy, traditionally divided into

---

100   Plotinus, *Ennead*, V.5 [32].3, 8–22.

101   See Constantine, et al., *The Book of Ceremonies: With the Greek Edition of the Corpus Scriptorum Historiae Byzantinae (Bonn 1829)*, ed. Johann Jacob Reiske, trans. Ann Moffatt and Maxeme Tall (Canberra: Australian Association for Byzantine Studies, 2012), 18; Herrin, *Margins and Metropolis*.

102   Al-Azmeh, *Muslim Kingship*, 141–48: the caliph himself, indeed, is almost as invisible behind the layers of the court as the One Itself.

103   Shapur died in 270, in the same year as Plotinus and two short-lived Roman emperors (Claudius and Quintillus), and perhaps of the same plague.

104   Three hundred years later, in 569, Damascius and other members of the Athenian school supposed that Persia (under Chosroes) would be a friendlier environment, and emigrated there (returning a few years later in some disillusionment): see O'Meara, *Platonopolis*, 23; Aleksey Kamenskikh, "The Dialectic of the Other: Political Philosophy and Practice in the Late Neoplatonist Communities," *Deformations and Crises of Ancient Civil Communities*, ed. Valerij Gouschin and P. J. Rhodes (Stuttgart: Franz Steiner Verlag, 2015), 191–92.

ethics, household management and politics. All three
branches concerned themselves with the male aspiring to
be in control, of himself in the first case, of his women,
children and slaves in the second case, and of his co-
religionists in the third. In the third case, however, the
control was envisaged as intellectual. "Political science"
did not have much to do with what we know by that
name today. Rather, its focus was on what Pico della
Mirandola (d. 1494), the Florentine Neoplatonist, called
the "dignity of man" (and to most *falasifa*, this really did
mean the male half of the species): man rising above
the limitations imposed by his self and others, trying
to elevate himself to the rank of the angels. Altogether,
it is Renaissance Platonism that the reader should have
in mind as the comparable phenomenon in Europe, not
the medieval Latin political thought inspired by Aristotle's *Politics*.[105]

An interesting suggestion, in passing, has been made that "an
individual *genius* also attached itself to every man between birth and
death (and a *juno* to every woman), acting as a divine counterpart
and guardian. This made it a natural duty for all inhabitants of
the empire to honor and encourage the guardian spirit (in this
case usually called the *numen*) of the reigning emperor, both to
care for him and to enable him to rule well. An especially good
ruler was revered upon death by the belief that he had become
one with his *numen* and could now be granted the honors of a
divinity (a distinction also accorded to a few empresses)."[106] But
this may be to read too much into veneration of the Emperor,
and to rationalize it too much. At any rate, there seems to be
no clear statement of this particular suggestion in the ancient
literature. It may nonetheless be a possible way of understanding
theiosis, and the way that a Plotinian soul may be taken up into a
higher form of being.

The Emperor, at least in hopeful fantasy, was to be the Ideal
Man, in whom all lesser powers and *daimones* are to be united.
"Such a ruler needs no Pheidias nor Polycleitus nor Myron to
model him, but by his virtue he forms himself in the likeness

---

105 Crone, *Medieval Islamic Political Thought*, 169.
106 Ronald Hutton, *Pagan Britain* (New Haven: Yale University Press, 2013),
335. A closer parallel must be with the Egyptian Pharaoh, united with Osiris
in his afterlife.

of God and thus creates a statue most delightful of all to behold and most worthy of divinity."[107] Some scholars have proposed that Plutarch developed the idea still further, to the point where the ideal ruler was an incarnate *Logos*, as being guided not by any external, written law but by the law that animated him. That is not a thought supported by the text, but the ruler is at least symbolically like the sun, spreading his beneficence around the land.[108] The ruler may be, in a way, a sun. It does not follow that he would be the Son.[109]

One further gloss, drawing on the ancient distinction between Brahmin and Kshatriya, priest and noble: it may be better to rely on a unifying *moral* authority which has itself no military power of the sort attributed to emperors or other State rulers. This was indeed the expectation of the medieval Western church, that the power of the sword was reserved to the "secular" ruler, while moral and religious judgment was to be passed by those isolated from ordinary domestic and political concerns. Maybe Chesterton was right in his sardonic defense of the Papacy:

> Suppose somebody were to advance the old idea as if it were a new idea; suppose he were to say; "I propose that there be erected in some central city in the more civilized part of our civilization the seat of a permanent official to represent peace and the basis of agreement among all the surrounding nations; let him be by the nature of his post set apart from them all and yet sworn to consider the rights and wrongs of all; let him be put there as a judge to expound an ethical law and system of social relations; let him be of a certain type and training different from that which encourages the ordinary ambitions of military glory or even the ordinary attachments of tribal tradition; let him be protected by a special sentiment from

---

107 Plutarch, "Discourse to an Unlearned Prince," in *Moralia*, vol. 10, 59 [780].
108 E. R. Goodenough, "The Political Philosophy of Hellenistic Kingship," *Yale Classical Studies* 1 (1928): 94–96, paraphrasing Plutarch "Discourse" 65 [781–82]; see also Scott, "Plutarch and the Ruler Cult."
109 An Ismà'ílí sect, the Druze, much influenced by Neo-Platonic thought, have chosen to consider their founding prophets, Hamza and al-Hàkim, not merely symbolically but "literally" as the embodied Logos and—still more oddly—the One Itself: Obeyesekere, *Imagining Karma*, 309. Identification as the (or at least as "an") Incarnate Word might make sense in a Plotinian cosmology, but not any special identity with the One beyond all Being.

the pressure of kings and princes; let him be sworn in a special manner to the consideration of men as men."[110]

He was of course right to suspect that most of his readers would be hesitant to grant such authority to any individual, however well bred, trained, educated and motivated. Better, they might say, a properly constituted council whose power lies only in the agreement of the people—a notion also adumbrated in John C. Wright's ambiguous utopia.[111] Chesterton's response was to observe that "it is not the people who would be the heirs of a dethroned Pope; it is some synod or bench of bishops. It is not an alternative between monarchy and democracy, but an alternative between monarchy and oligarchy."[112] And the power of fashion, group think and propaganda may too easily subvert what seems the more "liberal" institution (as it does in Wright's imagined world). Oligarchs can also hide behind each other's views, explaining (afterwards) that the decision was not really theirs: monarchs must take responsibility, even if they also appeal to a body of advisors.

One final gloss—and perhaps the most persuasive—would be to emphasize that the emperor is indeed a *symbol* of the One and acts only through his ministers. The monarch is still human and as such is likely often to be flawed and foolish, without much damage to the crown.

> As for what is called absolute monarchy, that is to say, when a king governs all other men according to his own will, some people think that it is not in accordance with the nature of things for one man to have absolute authority over all the citizens; since those who are by nature equal must necessarily have the same rights.[113]

Such a *constitutional* monarch, and the dynasty of which he/she is part, may be the focus of a loyalty and affection that transcends

---

110 Chesterton, *The Thing: why I am a Catholic* (London: Sheed & Ward, 1929), 162–63.

111 John C. Wright, *Golden Age Trilogy: The Golden Age; The Phoenix Exultant; The Golden Transcendence* (New York: TOR Books, 2002–2003): Wright imagines a far-future, high-tech society in which formal laws only demand that contracts be kept, but it is possible to refuse any dealings with those who too far offend against wide-spread moral feeling.

112 G. K. Chesterton, *The Thing*, 163.

113 Julian, "Letter to Themistius [261b]," in *Works*, vol. 2, 221, quoting Aristotle, *Politics*, 3.1287a.

all merely factional commitments. "The monarchy is not a political office like that held by a president or prime minister who has achieved power as the result of a contested popular election. Still less is it a celebrity status created by the fickle mass media and powerful commercial interests. It is rather the shared symbol of the sacred authority that stands above politics, money and sectional interest, a tangible pointer to the ultimate rule of God rather than of man or Mammon."[114]

WAR, PREDATION AND THE RULES OF WAR

"The highest good is neither war nor civil strife—which things we should pray rather to be saved from—but peace one with another and friendly feeling."[115] A proper *polis* is not organized exclusively for war, and we reasonably hope that a world order—whether this be federal or imperial—would manage without all military violence. "No one is so foolish as to prefer war to peace: in peace children bury their fathers, while in war fathers bury their children."[116] But war may still, unfortunately, be an endemic feature, not only of human life but of all the physical world. The Pindaric fragment, that *nomos* is king, may echo Heraclitus's claim that it was *war* that was king.[117]

> What is the necessity of the undeclared war among animals and among men? It is necessary that animals should eat each other; these eatings are transformations into each other of animals which could not stay as they are forever, even if no one killed them, and if, at the time when they had to depart, they had to depart in such a way that they were useful to others, why do we have to make a grievance out of their usefulness?[118]

---

114 Ian Bradley, *God Save the Queen: the spiritual heart of the monarchy* (London: Continuum, 2012), xxvi.
115 Plato, *Laws*, 1.628c.
116 Herodotus, *Histories*, 1.87, 4.
117 Heraclitus, in Waterfield, *First Philosophers*, 40 [22B53DK]; see Sally Humphreys, "Law, Custom and Culture in Herodotus," *Arethusa* 20, nos. 1–2 (1987): 213.
118 Plotinus, *Ennead*, III.2 [47].15, 15–21. It is not an uncommon rationalization of what is supposed a necessary but worrying practice: "When the prey delivers itself up to the one who will consume it, it is always out of a feeling of generosity. The animal is moved by the compassion that it feels for the sufferings of humans, creatures that are vulnerable to famine, who depend upon itself for their survival": Descola, *Beyond Nature and Culture*, 16 (speaking

Unlike many other moralists, it is fair to add, Plotinus did not infer from this continuing "war" that he too should eat animals: "He refused also to take medicines containing the flesh of wild beasts, giving as his reason that he did not approve of eating the flesh even of domestic animals."[119] His reason for this abstention may have had more to do with a wish not to be enticed by merely physical pleasures or take on (by absorption) the qualities even of tame beasts, than any overt concern for the injuries involved in farming or trapping them. Porphyry allowed both sorts of reason—the hygienic and the empathic—against denying animals justice.[120] The extent to which Plotinus wished or hoped to withdraw from the physical world is a later topic, but he chose not wholly to denounce the present state of things, but rather supposed that a physical, linear world could be no better than it currently is. We can expect no better image of the Eternal than the one we have already, the changeful and contested landscape of our lives.[121] Reconciling ourselves to that necessity seems the only alternative to the merely Manichaean belief that this world here is evil. Even the supposition that there are malicious *daimones*, spirits of the air, is consistent with an overall acceptance of necessity (as well as with the contrary conclusion that we are all in the grip of evil). That latter option leads only to ethical and epistemic disaster: even heroic empathy, parental affection, careful dialectic would only be tools of the devil, and we would have no available escape or answer. It is correspondingly better to have at least a Plotinian faith, and to assimilate the inevitable *human* warfare to the ongoing war of worlds, without which there would be only a desert:

> A manifold life exists in the All and makes all things, and
> in its living embroiders a rich variety and does not rest

mainly of Amerindian hunters' beliefs in North and South America). The worry may remain: "A niggling doubt always lingers: beneath the body of the animal or plant that I am eating, what remains of its human subjectivity? What guarantee is there that I am not munching (or worse) on a subject just like me?": Descola, *Beyond Nature and Culture*, 285.

119 Porphyry, *Life*, 2, 4–6.

120 Porphyry, *On Abstinence*; see Stephen R. L. Clark, "Vegetarianism and the Ethics of Virtue," in *Food for Thought: the debate over eating meat*, ed. Steve F. Sapontzis (New York: Prometheus Books, 2004).

121 Plotinus, *Ennead*, II.9 [33].4, 26–7.

from ceaselessly making beautiful and shapely living toys. And when men, mortal as they are, direct their weapons against each other, fighting in orderly ranks, doing what they do in sport in their war-dances, their battles show that all human concerns are children's games, and tell us that deaths are nothing terrible, and that those who die in wars and battles anticipate only a little the death which comes in old age—they go away and come back quicker.[122] But if their property is taken away while they are still alive, they may recognize that it was not theirs before either, and that its possession is a mockery to the robbers themselves when others take it away from them.[123]

Cities are not best organized purely for war, but their citizens had better be equipped to cope with it when it comes, and not complain—any more than the ill-conditioned boys who find themselves bullied by their wolfish peers have any claim to overmuch compassion: "Would it not be right for the lawgiver to allow them to suffer this as a penalty for their laziness and luxury?"[124] One response might be that rulers also have a duty to their subjects: that is why they are acknowledged rulers, so that the peace can be kept, and ordinary folk go about their business safely. But that peace—especially in Plotinus's day—must still depend on a general willingness, and power, to maintain it. Relying wholly on others to keep the peace for us is to allow those others to become our masters. "The wicked rule by the cowardice of the ruled; for this is just, and the opposite is not."[125]

So how are we to be better raised, so as to be neither wolves nor sheep? One answer is to rely on punishment, whether physical

---

122 W. B. Yeats, "Under Ben Bulben" [1938], in *Collected Poems*, ed. Richard J. Finneran (London: Walter Scott Publishing, 1890), 301, apparently agreed: "Whether man die in his bed/ Or the rifle knocks him dead,/ A brief parting from those dear/ Is the worst man has to fear."

123 Plotinus, *Ennead* III.2 [47].15, 40f; see also III.2 [47].5, 15: "Some troubles are profitable to the sufferers themselves, poverty and sickness for example." This may well be true, but it is probably not much comfort. As Bertie Wooster remarks in P. G. Wodehouse, *The Mating Season* (London: Everyman, 2001 [1949]), 87: "I doubt, as a matter of fact, if Marcus Aurelius's material [about the great web, ordained for you from the beginning] is ever the stuff to give the troops at a moment when they have just stubbed their toe on the brick of Fate. You want to wait till the agony has abated."

124 Plotinus, *Ennead*, III.2 [47].8, 16–21.

125 Ibid., III.2 [47].8, 51–52.

or mental; shame, remember, is to restrain the adolescents from unseemly sexual adventures. But mere shame and fear are hardly good grounds for genuinely virtuous characters. *Sophrosune*, for example, as seen by those who gaze on the divine beauty, is "not the kind which men have here below, when they do have it (for this is some sort of imitation of that other)."[126] Porphyry, and other later Platonists, preferred to use the title "virtue" in a more general sense, and distinguished civic, purificatory, theoretic and paradigmatic "virtues."[127] The merely civic virtues are accommodations to the world of our present reality, and those thus virtuous may often be merely lucky in their circumstances: they have never been tried or tempted past their power, and their motives are often, at least, confused. Even if they behave with civic decency, this may be only an effect of their several conflicting vices! They may even still be adolescent in their motivations: chiefly shame and envy.[128] The ordinarily virtuous, so Plotinus may suggest, are courageous, self-possessed, fair-minded and the rest in ways that mimic the attitude and behavior of those purified of all physical entanglements. Their motive—and it is the motive which modern moralists will mostly recognize—is to avoid disasters of one sort or another, including public shame. Chesterton thought poorly of this:

> [Warnings about the perils of this or that activity] only affect that small minority which will accept any virtue as long as we do not ask them for the virtue of courage. Most healthy people dismiss these moral dangers as they dismiss the possibility of bombs or microbes.[129]

After all, we do not think altogether ill of those who risk death or damage—both to themselves and others—by playing games or going on adventures; why despise those who run similar risks in pursuit of less respectable pleasures? Those who can be shamed

---

126 Ibid., V.8 [31].10, 14ff.
127 See Julia Annas, *Platonic Ethics: old and new* (Ithaca: Cornell UP, 1999), 66–67; Sebastian Gertz, *Death and Immortality in Late Neoplatonism* (Leiden: Brill, 2011), 51–58, discussing Porphyry, *Sententiae*, 32: Richard Sorabji, ed., *Philosophy of the Commentators*, vol. 1, *Psychology* (London: Duckworth, 2004), 341 [17(a)10].
128 See Aristotle, *Rhetoric*, 2.1388a30ff on *zelos* (envy, emulation) and *aidos* (shame, embarrassment) as pre-virtues; "they are bashful, for as yet they fail to conceive of other things that are noble, but have been educated solely by convention" (*Rhetoric*, 2.1389a10).
129 Chesterton, *Heretics*, 26, 30.

into good behavior, can also be shamed into bad. Nor will it be easier to deter young men, especially, from volunteering to fight if we simply ignore the delight they may have in fighting. Ares, even if he is the most hated of all the gods,[130] is still in his way divine.

> And life is colour and warmth and light,
> And a striving ever more for these;
> And he is dead who will not fight;
> And who dies fighting has increase.
> The fighting man shall from the sun
> Take warmth, and life from glowing earth;
> Speed with the light-foot winds to run
> And with the trees to newer birth.[131]

"And when the pains concern others?"[132] Decent people nowadays care about others' pains. It is therefore a shock to learn that Plotinus, like the Stoics, thought "we should be spectators of murders, and all deaths, and takings and sacking of cities, as if they were on the stages of theatres."[133] Such things are no more than children's games: "One must not take weeping and lamenting as evidence of the presence of evils, for children, too, weep and wail over things that are not evils."[134] It is a thought with a long history:

> It becomes us with thankfulness to use the good things we receive from the hand of God, and patiently to abide the evil, which when thoroughly considered and understood may perhaps appear to be good, it being no sure sign that a thing is good, because we desire, or evil, because we are displeased with it.[135]

On the one hand, the genuinely virtuous can neither be bribed nor bullied, and only they are genuinely "free." On the other, such

---

130 Homer, *Iliad*, 5.890–891.
131 Julian Grenfell, "Into Battle (1915)," in G. H. Clarke, *A Treasury of War Poetry* (Plano, TX: Last Post Press, 2015), 178–80. Grenfell died a few days later. See Stephen R. L. Clark, *The Mysteries of Religion: an introduction to philosophy through religion* (Eugene, OR: Wipf & Stock, 2017), 158: "Really to preach against fornication is to try and tame an Olympian. Really to preach against war is no less a tour-de-force." Readers please note that I am only *reporting* this, not approving worship of Ares (whose form down here is demonic), nor yet of Aphrodite.
132 Plotinus, *Ennead*, I.4 [46].8, 13f.
133 Ibid., III.2 [47].15, 44f.
134 Ibid., III.2 [47].15, 61.
135 Berkeley, "Sermon on the Will of God," in *Works*, vol. 7, 134.

virtuous persons may not always intervene to stop the bullies. I remarked earlier that it was surely "obvious" that a good man's *eudaimonia* could not be taken away merely because he is aware that not all people prosper.[136] If it could, then no one can be *eudaimon* until God makes all things new, except by hiding from the present truth (which would itself be unvirtuous). As a would-be Bodhisattva recognizes, no one can escape from *dukkha* until all escape. No one is free until all are. Our own lives could not be worth living if we always recognized and were deeply affected by the evils that others must endure. "There is evidence for this in the fact that we think it something gained if we do not know about other people's sufferings, and even regard it as a good thing if we die first."[137] That at least *is* weakness, and one best avoided by facing up to what "ordinary nature normally finds terrible," as nothing worse than children's bogeys.[138] It is an opinion not reserved for pagan philosophers:

> We should not therefore repine at the divine laws, or show a frowardness or impatience of those transient sufferings they accidentally expose us to, which, however grating to flesh and blood, will yet seem of small moment, if we compare the littleness and fleetingness of this present world with the glory and eternity of the next.[139]

It does not, of course, follow that the good man is indifferent to the apparent evils others endure. But how might those evils be alleviated, or made to seem less harsh, except by urging that they do not matter much? "Therefore we do not lose heart, but though our outer man is decaying, yet our inner man is being renewed day by day. For momentary, light affliction is producing for us an eternal weight of glory far beyond all comparison, while we look not at the things which are seen, but at the things which are not seen; for the things which are seen are temporal, but the things which are not seen are eternal."[140] "For I reckon that the sufferings of this present time are not worthy to be compared with the glory which shall be revealed in us."[141] Generosity for those in need is still required.[142]

---

136 Plotinus, *Ennead*, I.4 [46].11, 12–14.
137 Ibid., I.4 [46].8, 14–20.
138 Ibid., I.4 [46].8, 23–7.
139 Berkeley, "Passive Obedience," in *Works*, vol. 6, 40.
140 2 Corinthians 4:16–18.
141 Romans 8:18.
142 1 Corinthians 8:1–15.

We ought to share our money with all men, but more gen-
erously with the good, and with the helpless and poor so
as to suffice for their need. And I will assert, even though
it be paradoxical to say so, that it would be a pious act to
share our clothes and food even with the wicked. For it
is to the humanity in a man that we give, and not to his
moral character. Hence I think that even those who are
shut up in prison have a right to the same sort of care;
since this kind of philanthropy will not hinder justice.[143]

So mere physical perils are not necessarily enough to hold us
back from danger, or even from war. Indeed, the very demand that
we should care for all the daughters of our Father may require
an armed intervention, at the judgment of whatever authority is
in place. Some fates are worse than war, including an oppressive
"peace" (though it is dangerous to be sure, too soon, that the peace
we enjoy is flawed because we find it offensive).

Certainly death is better for them than to stay living
in a way in which the universal laws do not want them
to live; so that if the opposite happened, and peace was
preserved in every sort of folly and vice, providence would
be neglecting its duty in allowing the worse really to get
the upper hand.[144]

Just as the ill-conditioned boys should have been reared and
trained to resist the wolfish boys, so may citizens determine not to
put up with tyrants, and the rule of those not of their kind, even
if this means war. "Thoughts and prayers" are rarely comforting
to the victims of tyranny, any more than of natural disasters.[145]

The law says that those who fight bravely, not those who
pray, are to come safe out of wars; for, in just the same
way, it is not those who pray but those who look after
their land who are to get in a harvest, and those who

---

143   Julian, *Letter to a Priest*, 290d–291a, in *Works*, vol. 2, 303, echoing Aristotle's
retort on being once reproached for giving alms to a bad man, "It was the man
and not his character that I pitied *(ou ton tropon alla ton anthropon)*"; Diogenes
Laertius, *Lives*, vol. 1, 461 (5.1, 16); cf. ibid., 465 (5.1, 21): "It was not the man
(anthropos)," said he, "that I assisted, but humanity *(to anthropinon)*."
144   Plotinus, *Ennead*, III.2 [47].8, 47–52; Ousager, *Plotinus on Selfhood*, 239–40.
145   James 2:15–16: "Suppose a brother or sister is in rags with not enough
food for the day, and one of you says, 'Good luck to you, keep yourselves
warm, and have plenty to eat,' but does nothing to supply their bodily needs,
what is the good of that?"

do not look after their health are not to be healthy; and we are not to be vexed if the bad get larger harvests, or if their farming generally goes better.[146]

It is still true that war, in any viable civilization, should be for the sake of a just peace, and still true that war is horrible, though not everyone has agreed. It is not only States and Empires that go to war. In Papua New Guinea neighboring villages were at war, or feud, forever, and it was a mark of manhood to have killed some easy prey.[147] In many ages of the world the main virtue has been the warrior's, and for a man to die in bed considered a disgrace. "Souls slain in war are more pure than those which die through illness."[148] Aztecs went to war to acquire new victims for their sacrifice (and the loathing this inspired in all their neighbors helped to bring them down).[149] Other empires have gone to war to find an excuse for empire, and this may indeed be very close to what the Roman Empire did. "The army was by far the largest organization of the Romans state, dwarfing its civil administration and any other corporate body before the advent of the Christian church."[150] And its Emperor, its Commander-in-Chief, earned his position by winning battles (or at least by appeasing his soldiers). The world in which Plotinus worked was one at ceaseless war, internal and external, and the Empire was tied into a vicious cycle: needing its armies to seize land and goods to pay the costs of the armies. We can construct what arguments he might have used to divert imperial and soldierly interest, but it does not seem that he had any hope of imposing "rules of war."

> What distinguishes the [predatory city] is that the sole aim of its inhabitants is conquest for its own sake and the pleasures attendant upon conquest. This goal, al-Fārābi explains, is common to the inhabitants of all the "ignorant"

---

146   Plotinus, *Ennead*, III.2 [47].8, 38–44.
147   See Robert Gardner and Karl G. Heider, *Gardens of War: Life and Death in the New Guinea Stone Age* (New York: Random House, 1968); Paula Brown, "Conflict in the New Guinea Highlands," *Journal of Conflict Resolution* 26 (1982): 525–46.
148   Heraclitus in Waterfield, *First Philosophers*, 45 [22B136DK]. What he meant by this, I don't know!
149   See J. P. Aho, *Religious Mythology and the Art of War* (London: Aldwych Press, 1981), on various attempts to rationalize such violence and inspire the troops; see also Clark, *Mysteries of Religion*, 144–61.
150   Shaw, "War and Violence," 141.

cities. Some seek conquest for the sake of the money, blood or liberty of the conquered. The means used in the process may be treachery or open warfare. However, some conquerors will refuse to seize the property of the enemy when they are asleep or otherwise occupied. They vie with each other in the number of conquests, the instruments used or the endurance shown in warfare. As a result, they become so hardened and cruel that they are marked by "quickness of anger, love of luxury, gluttony in the consumption of food and drink, sexual excess and competition for all other worldly goods."[151]

One origin of this perversion, so Al-Farabi proposes, is an ignorant inference from the "war" between animals and ourselves:

> Having observed that the law of the universe is one of conflict and opposition and that animals and humans prey on each other, sometimes for no avail, they have concluded that the conqueror always seeks to destroy or enslave the vanquished because he is convinced that the very existence of the vanquished is inimical to his own. Moreover, since there is no order or justice in the world, war or conquest is perfectly justified according to them. For in the end the mightiest is the happiest, since there is no bond of friendship or social affinity between people, whether by will or by nature. If people must get together and work together, it can only be for a while or as long as need or necessity justifies it. For the "solitary" (*mutwahhid*) cannot attend to their needs without the assistance of others, and this is how social association (*ijtimā*) is justified. To this pragmatic view of political association is opposed a genetic view, according to which the social bond is rooted in kinship or marital relations. Or it may be rooted in the recognition that submission to the will of the chief ruler, who provides for the needs of his subjects and safeguards their security against invasion, is the wise thing to do. A further view regards the social bond as the by-product of community of character, national traits or language, holding the nation (*ummah*) together. Still others regard it as the by-product of neighborly contiguity or community of interest in matters of food, drink, trade or pleasurable pursuits, as in certain forms of geographic or economic association.[152]

---

151   Fakhry, *Al-Farabi*, 109.
152   Ibid., 114.

Chesterton noted the same fallacious inference from Darwinian theory:

> Among the innumerable muddles, which mere materialistic fashion made out of the famous theory, there was in many quarters a queer idea that the Struggle for Existence was of necessity an actual struggle between the candidates for survival; literally a cut-throat competition. There was a vague idea that the strongest creature violently crushed the others. And the notion that this was the one method of improvement came everywhere as good news to bad men; to bad rulers, to bad employers, to swindlers and sweaters and the rest. The brisk owner of a bucket-shop compared himself modestly to a mammoth, trampling down other mammoths in the primeval jungle. The business man destroyed other business men, under the extraordinary delusion that the eohippic horse had devoured other eohippic horses. The rich man suddenly discovered that it was not only convenient but cosmic to starve or pillage the poor, because pterodactyls may have used their little hands to tear each other's eyes. Science, that nameless being, declared that the weakest must go to the wall; especially in Wall Street. There was a rapid decline and degradation in the sense of responsibility in the rich, from the merely rationalistic eighteenth century to the purely scientific nineteenth. The great Jefferson, when he reluctantly legalized slavery, said he trembled for his country, knowing that God is just. The profiteer of later times, when he legalized usury or financial trickery, was satisfied with himself, knowing that Nature is unjust.[153]

Civilizations with global ambitions and a global reach must desire a "just" peace, not a constant state of war (though their rulers may still get some benefit from maintaining a war-footing, a readiness for war in their various populations, by providing a common cause). The problem remains that there are differing criteria for what counts as a "just peace," different reasons to take offence at what is reckoned oppression, and no reason for one Court to trust another. In the "world at war," *dar al-harb*, winner

---

153   G. K. Chesterton, "The Return to Religion," in *The Well and the Shallows* (London: Darwen Finlayson, 1962). The "great Jefferson," as Chesterton neglected to notice, was himself a slave-owner, and the father of slaves. If he feared God's justice it seems not to have much affected him.

takes all and will not be dislodged by anything but violence. This again seems more or less the condition of both Roman and Sassanid Empires in Plotinus's day and later: the only restraints imposed on military violence were financial or geographic—with perhaps occasional pauses, truces, which depended on personal or tribal loyalties across the borders. The gods (on both sides) might disapprove of openly aggressive war, the desecration of temples and the denial of mercy to harmless suppliants—but victorious armies need pay but little attention to their disapproval. Within *dar al-Islam* it is *Shari'a*, the body of law built up from the *Koran* and the Hadith by generations of scholar-judges that determines justice (and even this is not unambiguous: different versions of *Shari'a* dictate different rules). The Christian West has in the past been guided, or at least has hoped to be guided, by some version of "Just War Theory," created by theologians and theorists as far as *"ius ad bellum"* is concerned,[154] and by mercenary and national soldiers as for *"ius in bello."*[155] It is now engaged in constructing "International Law," partly on that basis, through a complex of particular treaties and the founding statements of the United Nations, but those latter statements are usually either ignored or so construed as to have no real bearing.[156] To outsiders, Western cant about international law and a just peace is simply rhetoric, having no ethical basis or any real effect. What *reason* have modern Westerners, after all, to keep their word or acknowledge any rights of property, let alone any sense of the sacred? Even those who acknowledge that other people feel deeply about their sacred

---

154 Some clear injustice must be remedied, and all other methods have failed, before aggressive violence can be considered. Even then there must be questions: can the attempt succeed, and at some appropriate cost?

155 Some ways of killing are to be excluded, prisoners are to be treated decently (not tortured, killed or enslaved), and non-combatants are not to be harmed. These rules seem not to prevent rape or looting in a conquered city, but some commanders at least have punished offenders harshly. Nuclear exchanges, it must be obvious, are to be absolutely condemned.

156 The rules of the United Nations organization declare that signatories must intervene to prevent genocide, for example, but it is always possible to declare that even mass murder in the name of "ethnic cleansing" isn't really *genocide* (and notice also that masterly excuse for perpetual inaction, that we should not intervene *anywhere* if we can't intervene *everywhere*). See Stephen R. L. Clark, "Genocide, War and Consistency," in *Human Rights and Military Intervention*, ed. Richard Normal and Alex Moseley (Aldershot: Ashgate, 2002).

sites, or their sacred beasts, will suppose that these are only the sentiments of a few, to be weighed against more familiar feelings. How often have Westerners openly broken their word, and why should they not? It's difficult enough for any political unit to keep a treaty when it isn't to its taste or in what it takes to be its interests; in days gone by we might have done so for fear of the god who held our oath, but if there is no such god, or none with any *political* existence, our only reason for faithfulness is our own temporal self-interest (whatever that may be), including our doubtful self-respect. Outsiders, knowing this, would be fools to take our word! And we would be fools, correspondingly, to take theirs, since they cannot mean it sincerely.

Plotinus's only (covert) answer to the problem seems to be (again) to encourage a proper education at least in *civic* virtue, and to hope that actual leaders will indeed take "Reason as their Caliph": the firm intuition, that is, that we are all, both human and non-human, one universal tribe, all daughters of the Father. *Poleis* may represent this thesis most of all, and would-be global empires with a proper monarch, but even open and unnecessary war may sometimes demonstrate the primacy of "Reason": "Vice works something useful to the whole by becoming an example of just punishment."[157]

---

157 Plotinus, *Ennead*, III.2 [47].5, 16–18.

7
Living beyond Boundaries

GIVING TO ALL THEIR DUE

A proper *polis* allows all residents their place, some as citizens and householders, others as craftsmen, laborers or even slaves and other domestic beasts. Merchants, passing between such *poleis,* are to be protected in their trade, though denied any personal say in the order of the *poleis.* A proper "empire" would be an association of *poleis,* tribes and amphictyonies which could endure to share at least the elements of religion and be guided by the intuition that we are all daughters of One Father.

> If all that there is in the Universe is pervaded by God, that is to say, if the Brahmin and the *Bhangi,* the learned man and the scavenger, the *Ezhava* [currently classified as a "backward caste," in Kerala] and the Pariah, no matter what caste they belong to—if all these are pervaded by Lord God, in the light of this mantra [*Isha Upanishad,* 1], there is none that is low, all are absolutely equal, equal because all are the creatures of that Creator. And this is not a philosophical thing to be dished out to Brahmins or Kshatriyas, but it enunciates an eternal truth which admits of no reduction, no dilution.[1]

A focus for their unity would be a person equipped to be an emperor, and the city in which he had his home. Unfortunately, actual empires may depend too much on oppressive rule of their subjects and aggressive war against all rival powers. All these human enterprises occur within the context of a natural physical world whose elements are also at war with each other. Might there be a still wider sense of community, one that sought to embrace all available living creatures, even without any concrete or official structure to enforce that sense? Or must any such

---

1   Gandhi, "*Harijan,* 30 January 1937," in *Collected Works,* vol. 70, 304. The first verse of the *Isha Upanishad* is variously translated: for example, "The Lord is enshrined in the hearts of all. The Lord is the supreme Reality. Rejoice in him through renunciation. Covet nothing. All belongs to the Lord." Plotinus would agree.

attempt founder on the psychological difficulty of remembering and valuing all members of the whole natural order? Can we live without constructing barriers between Us and Them? Can we live as if we were all, equally, members of the living cosmos?

Too clear a concentration on the manifest evils that surround us may or must breed anger or depression. We may perhaps avoid the worse effects by holding firm to the conception of an eternal world without these flaws and chances. Or else we may find some consolation, exactly, in the thought of change.

> How, then, is it possible rightly to disapprove of a city which gives each man his deserts? In this city [of the world] virtue is honored and vice has its appropriate dishonor, and not merely the images of gods but gods themselves look down upon us from above, who, as the saying goes, will easily acquit themselves of men's blame, leading all things in order from beginning to end, giving to each his fitting portion in changes of lives as a consequence of the deeds he did in previous existences; he who ignores this is one of the rasher sort of humans who deals boorishly with divine things.[2]

We are to console ourselves, that is, with the thought that all wrongdoing is avenged and that everyone is where she ought or needs to be.

> There is no accident in a man's becoming a slave, nor is he taken prisoner in war by chance, nor is outrage done on his body without due cause, but he was once the doer of that which he now suffers; and a man who made away with his mother will be made away with by a son when he has become a woman, and one who has raped a woman will be a woman in order to be raped.[3]

The story would perhaps be easier to accept if all of us—not simply the favored few like Hermotimus (who "remembered" being Euphorbus, a hero of the Trojan War, and was later to be Pythagoras)[4] or Empedocles—could *remember* our earlier lives. But the story about our life hereafter actually emphasizes that hardly anyone will remember, and that this is as it should be:

---

2 Plotinus, *Ennead*, II.9 [33].9, 19–27. The gods looking down from above are what we call stars.

3 Ibid., III.2 [47].13, 11–15.

4 Diogenes, *Lives*, vol. 2, 185.

Euphorbus, Hermotimus and Pythagoras are different lives, with different duties. Each life we live has its own time and reason, even if those lives do, somehow, share "a soul." And even if we do not share the doctrine, there are good reasons to take it as a serious story, with various implications.[5]

One unfortunate inference is that those who are thus enslaved, or killed, or raped must really deserve this to happen—though their assailants in turn must suffer for what they do. There seems then to be no end to bloodshed: "An eye for an eye makes the whole world blind." But "although all karma must bear fruit, not all fruit has been produced by karma,"[6] and so we cannot honestly assume that anyone "deserves" their fortune. Even when, in some sense, perhaps they do, it is not up to us to enforce their fate. According to the Laws of Manu, even animal sacrifice has its costs: "Let him never seek to destroy an animal without a (lawful) reason. As many hairs as the slain beast has, so often indeed will he who killed it without a (lawful) reason suffer a violent death in future births."[7] According to those laws—and perhaps in agreement with Plotinus's view of predation as an inescapable element of the physical world—it is permissible to *sacrifice* animals at proper times and places (and then eat their flesh). The victims themselves may profit from the event.

> Svayambhu (the Self-existent) himself created animals for the sake of sacrifices; sacrifices (have been instituted) for the good of this whole (world); hence the slaughtering (of beasts) for sacrifices is not slaughtering (in the ordinary sense of the word). Herbs, trees, cattle, birds, and (other) animals that have been destroyed for sacrifices, receive (being reborn) higher existences. On offering the honey-mixture (to a guest), at a sacrifice and at the rites in honor of the manes, *but on these occasions only*, may an animal be slain; that (rule) Manu proclaimed.[8]

---

5   The frequent claim that Pythagoras, Plato, Plotinus could not "really" have believed in reincarnation, that their stories must have been meant "symbolically," seems to rest only on the assumption that they were "really clever," and must therefore have believed only what seems sensible to the (obviously clever) claimant.

6   Obeyesekere, *Imagining Karma*, 132.

7   Bühler, *Manu-Samhita*, 5.37–38.

8   Ibid., 5.39–41, 45. The text goes on to say: "He who injures innoxious beings from a wish to (give) himself pleasure, never finds happiness, neither living nor dead. He who does not seek to cause the sufferings of bonds and

Jain anecdotes, on the other hand, warn sacrificing priests that they will themselves endure multiple deaths as an effect of having killed animals in sacrifice until the karmic effects of their misdoings have been exhausted.[9]

From which we may conclude both that we may expect to endure the effects of our own violence, in a later life, and that "those who have killed unjustly [will be] killed in their turn, unjustly as far as the doer of the deed is concerned but justly as far as concerns the victim."[10] The killer in these cases has the role, we may say, of that aforementioned "public executioner, who is a scoundrel"[11]—and can, perhaps, choose *not* to kill, leaving the case to Providence. None of us, perhaps, *deserve* any better life or fate; it is our task to make what we can of it. And those who insist that animals were *made* for sacrifice may begin to wonder whether they were too. A story is told of the Rabbi Judah that when he heard a calf complaining on the way to slaughter, he rebuked him, saying that it was for this that the calf had been created. For this insensitivity he had

death to living creatures, (but) desires the good of all (beings), obtains endless bliss. He who does not injure any (creature), attains without an effort what he thinks of, what he undertakes, and what he fixes his mind on. Meat can never be obtained without injury to living creatures, and injury to sentient beings is detrimental to (the attainment of) heavenly bliss; let him therefore shun (the use of) meat. Having well considered the (disgusting) origin of flesh and the (cruelty of) fettering and slaying corporeal beings, let him entirely abstain from eating flesh. He who, disregarding the rule (given above), does not eat meat like a Pisaka, becomes dear to men, and will not be tormented by diseases. He who permits (the slaughter of an animal), he who cuts it up, he who kills it, he who buys or sells (meat), he who cooks it, he who serves it up, and he who eats it, (must all be considered as) the slayers (of the animal). There is no greater sinner than that (man) who, though not worshipping the gods or the manes, seeks to increase (the bulk of) his own flesh by the flesh of other (beings)": ibid., 45–52. *Only* the appointed sacrifices can be a proper source of meat: anything beyond that is excess. Which is why Paul's report that some were troubled by the prospect of eating meat from animals sacrificed to idols (1 Corinthians 8:1–12) had a wider implication than is now commonly remembered (see also Acts 15:29; Romans 14:14–23; Revelation 2:20). Paul allows the practice on the grounds that there really are no demons: others had more doubts—and all the more plausibly in the light of the current callous and unnecessary slaughter of far too many animals for meat that is not needed.

9   Appleton, *Narrating Karma*, 67–68; Phyllis Granoff, *The Forest of Thieves and the Magic Garden: an anthology of medieval Jain stories* (London: Penguin, 2006), 78–79.
10   Plotinus, *Ennead*, III.2 [47].13, 8–9.
11   Ibid., III.2 [47].17, 64–67.

toothache for thirteen years until one day he saved a weasel's life and was pardoned.[12]

If each soul has existed forever and been shuffled up and down the continuum from stars to immobile plants, we may consider that we have all been many things, both saints and sinners, honest citizens and slugs, innumerable times. "In the beginningless cycle of time," everyone or everything that you meet will sometime have been your mother[13]—or your victim. This may even, though probably not for Plotinus himself, be divine policy!

> The Druses believe that perfect justice requires man to undergo a succession of lives in different situations in order to perfect himself.... Everyone should know wealth and poverty, health and sickness ... so that in each life he or she may strive a little more toward the perfection of character that God wishes each person to attain.[14]

Those who are now being violated, tortured, robbed and killed do not deserve their fate any more than those who, at this moment, aren't.[15] Nor is there any duty to overlook their pains: on the contrary, it is always right to show concern for the daughters of our Father and not to draw unnecessary distinctions. The Lord makes his rain to fall on the just and the unjust,[16] the wicked as well as the virtuous draw water from the river.[17] This does not omit the need for a proper rebuke, even a proper punishment, for those who break the laws, whether that comes of itself or by the legislator's fiat. It may even be compatible with the requirement

---

12   Schwartz, *Judaism and Vegetarianism*, 29, citing Baba Metzia 85a, Midrash Genesis Rabbah 33.3.

13   Appleton, *Narrating Karma*, 176-7, citing *Samyutta Nikaya* 15, 14-19: Bhikku Bodhi, trans., *Connected Discourses of the Buddha: a translation of the Samyuuta Nikaya* (Boston: Wisdom Publications, 2000), 659. Ian Harris, "A Vast Unsupervised Recycling Plant: Animals and the Buddhist Cosmos," ed. Paul Waldau and Kimberley C. Patton (New York: Columbia University Press, 2006), 208-9, describes the universe as "a vast unsupervised recycling plant"!

14   Ian Stevenson, *Twelve Cases in Lebanon and Turkey: Cases of the Reincarnation Type*, vol. 3 (Charlottesville: University Press of Virginia, 1980), 6: cited by Obeyesekere, *Imagining Karma*, 313.

15   Cf. Luke 13.1-5: "Those eighteen who died when the tower in Siloam fell on them—do you think they were more guilty than all the others living in Jerusalem? I tell you, no! But unless you repent, you too will all perish."

16   Matthew 5.45.

17   Plotinus, *Ennead*, IV.4 [28].42, 15-16; see IV.3 [27].16.

that we now play our parts as best we can, in the hope, mentioned earlier, of having a better part next time—as actors hope for a more significant role once they have shown their talents.[18] But such occasional penalties must not undermine the truth: that we belong together.

> So, then, there are good men and wicked men, like the opposed movements of a dancer inspired by one and the same art; and we shall call one part of his performance "good" and another "wicked," and in this way it is a good performance (*kalōs echei*). But, then [so some will say], the wicked are no longer wicked. No, their being wicked is not done away with, only their being like that does not originate with themselves....There is a place for every man, one to fit the good and one to fit the bad.[19]

Nor are they "essentially" or forever "wicked." On Plotinus's account, at any rate, there is an unfallen part or element of each soul, forever joined to the holy ones.[20] Each incarnating soul is bound to experience all things from within—there may even be some question as to whether there are *many* souls at all (as Plotinus supposes) or really only one (the singular god in all of us).

HOW WE RISE AND FALL

From this perspective neither the *polis* nor the would-be global empire is the proper context of our lives together. The assembly of all living creatures, even if there is no official, legal, administrative reality, is what we should be considering: Aurelius's "city of Zeus," but one without any unique center.[21] Aurelius may have supposed that only "philosophers," only "the wise," would be proper citizens of that city, but the real cosmos is more extensive

---

18   Ibid., III.2 [47].17, 45–53. See also Bühler, *Manu Samhita*, 9.335: "(A Sudra who is) pure, the servant of his betters, gentle in his speech, and free from pride, and always seeks a refuge with Brahmanas, attains (in his next life) a higher caste."

19   Plotinus, *Ennead*, III.2 [47].17, 9–14, 22–24.

20   Plotinus, *Ennead*, IV.2 [4].12–17; IV.8 [6].8, 1–4. Cf. Kant, who reports— attempting to suggest some intercourse between Tibetan Buddhism and the Hellenic Mysteries—that Tibetan lamas told Francesco Orazio della Penna (1680–1745), that "God is the community of all the holy ones": Immanuel Kant, "Perpetual Peace," in *Kant's Political Writings*, trans. H. B. Nishet, ed. Hans Reiss (Cambridge: Cambridge University Press, 1970), 107.

21   Marcus Aurelius, *Meditations*, 4.23.

and more egalitarian. We are all, so Plotinus says, "naturally and spontaneously moved to speak of the god who is in each one of us one and the same."[22] Or as another teacher insisted: "The King will answer and say to them, 'Assuredly, I say to you, inasmuch as you did it to one of the least of these My brethren, you did it to Me.'"[23] And nothing in the record requires us to suppose that only our conspecifics are included in the class of "these My brethren."

Is that latter claim too far from the tradition? Aristotle borrowed from Plato's cosmological myth about the origin of all non-human (indeed all non-male) creatures in the gradual decline of the souls that came from the hands of the Maker.[24] In his account, all other creatures are in a literal sense *descended* from the archetypal form, the most perfect of all animals, who alone "stands upright . . . because his nature and essence is divine."[25] "Compared with man, all the other animals are dwarf-like," including birds and fishes.[26] "This is why all animals are less intelligent than man."[27] The decline continues, even past those creatures that have blood, and even past the animal kingdom entirely:

> The animals' bodies wane, and they will be many-footed; and finally they lose their feet altogether and lie full length on the ground. Proceeding a little further in this way, they actually have their principal part down below, and finally the part which answers to a head comes to have neither motion nor sensation; at this stage the creature becomes a plant and has its upper parts below and its nether parts aloft; for in plants the roots have the character and value of mouth and head.[28]

That this was indeed a literal, chronological hypothesis is difficult to establish; perhaps it was only a manner of speaking, a way of representing all the different creatures *as if* they were deformations of the most familiar kind, ourselves. It seems just as

22 Plotinus, *Ennead*, VI.5 [23].1, 3–4.
23 See Matthew 25:40. It has been suggested that the original reference of the saying is only to the members of Christ's church, rather than just any neglected creature of whatever kind or creed. I do not myself think this a plausible reading, nor does it match the usual patristic interpretation of our duties.
24 Plato, *Timaeus*, 91; see Clark, *Aristotle's Man*, 28–31.
25 Aristotle, *De Partibus Animalium*, 4.686a28–9.
26 Ibid., 4.686b4–5; Aristotle, *De Generatione Animalium*, 2.736b26–7.
27 Aristotle, *De Partibus Animalium*, 4.686b21–4.
28 Ibid., 4.686b30–6.

likely that Aristotle—persuaded that the generations of human-kind were infinite, that there was no absolute beginning but that the world underwent continual catastrophe—was ready to believe, as I proposed in an earlier chapter, that all the other creatures constantly re-evolved from the remnants of humankind. In either case, the natural order is a continuum:

> Nature stretches without a break from lifeless objects to animals through things that are animated but not animals, so that there seems to be very little difference between one thing and the next, they are so close together.[29]

Plotinus shared the picture, even agreeing that *plants* were the most "self-willed" of all souls, finally burying their heads in earth to avoid all knowledge of the wider world;[30] he was, as we now realize, entirely mistaken in this! Trees at least communicate through the fungal network, whether or not they are "conscious."[31] Most moderns would now prefer to believe that human beings are not the *origin* but the present crown of life: lately evolved from very much "simpler" beginnings. Despite many disclaimers by Darwin and by others, we far too often retain the notion that there is a single order of creation: humans are at the top, with apes and Old-World monkeys very much below them, followed in turn by New-World monkeys, other mammals and birds (excepting "vermin"), reptiles, amphibians, fish and then below them still the vaster hordes of invertebrate, vegetable and prokaryotic life. We (supposedly) have "reason," other animals have varying degrees of "sense" (somehow forgetting that their senses are often far more acute and wide-ranging than ours), and oysters and such like are as insentient as "plants." The truth is far more complicated than we like to think. And Plotinus at least would disagree about our status and about the simple linearity of the biological order. Even Aristotle was at pains to remark that human beings were *not* the best things in the world,[32] and that other creatures might often

---

29 Ibid., 4.681a12–15.

30 Plotinus, *Ennead*, V.2 [11].2.

31 See Peter Wohlleben, *The Secret Network of Nature: the delicate balance of all living things* (London: Bodley Head, 2018).

32 See Aristotle, *Nicomachean Ethics*, 6.1141a20–22. Later Scholastic thought has usually ignored the concession, insisting rather that we human beings are God's only love. The Catholic Catechism oddly insists, on the word of

have a share in reason, and even political sense. Plotinus's hierar-chical order encompassed gods and the star-gods, including the Earth herself, *daimones*, humankind and all sublunary life, so that "the soul is many things, and all things, both the things above and the things below down to the limits of all life."[33] But it isn't a simple line of descent: it is a bush rather than a pine tree, with its real roots in heaven.

> The gathering together of all things into one is the prin-ciple, in which all are together and all make a whole. And individual things proceed from this principle while it remains within; they come from it as from a single root which remains static in itself, but they flower out into a divided multiplicity, each one bearing an image of that higher reality, but when they reach this lower world one comes to be in one place and one in another, and some are close to the root and others advance farther and split up to the point of becoming, so to speak, branches and twigs and fruits and leaves; and those that are closer to the root remain forever, and the others come into being forever, the fruits and the leaves; and those which come into being forever have in them the rational forming principles of those above them, as if they wanted to be little trees; and if they produce before they pass away, they only produce what is near to them. And what are like empty spaces between the branches are filled with shoots which also grow from the root, these, too, in a different way; and the twigs on the branches are also affected by these, so that they think the effect on them is only produced by what is close to them; but in fact the acting and being acted upon are in the principle, and the principle itself, too, is dependent. The principles which act on each other are different because they come from a far-off origin, but in the beginning they come from the same source, as if brothers were to do something to each other who are alike because they originate from the same parents.[34]

John Chrysostom, that man is "more precious in the eyes of God than all other creatures! For him the heavens and the earth, the sea and all the rest of creation exist": *Catechism of the Catholic Church* (London: Burns & Oates, 2004), 358, citing John Chrysostom, *In Gen. sermo* 2, 1: *Patrologia Graeca* 54, 587D–588A.

33 Plotinus, *Ennead*, III.4 [15].3, 21–22.

34 Ibid., III.3 [48].7, 9–28.

So the soul's descent, or her multiple refraction and reflection, comes "down" through many fractal lines, as she emerges from the first companionship of heaven. That descent, or flowering, or generous expansion, has many stages, and Plotinus would not agree, does not agree, with "Gnostics" (if that is a genuine class) or Manichaeans who suppose that this multiplicity of creation is altogether a Bad Thing.

> There must not be just one alone—for then all things would have been hidden, shapeless within that one, and not a single real being would have existed if that one had stayed still in itself, nor would there have been the multiplicity of these real beings which are generated from the One, if the things after them had not taken their way out which have received the rank of souls.[35]

Such sterile meanness cannot be attributed to the primary Good of all things, whose *generosity* is (almost) its defining nature (not that the One has a nature beyond its own will). All things are contained "at first" within the eternal intellect, but Soul may step a little away from the complete, unchanging perfection so as to *experience* the world successively, and from multiple "points of view."

> Around Soul things come one after another: now Socrates, now a horse, always some one particular thing; but Intellect is all things. It has therefore everything at rest in the same place, and it only is and its "is" is forever.[36]

Soul, mythologically identified as Zeus, is the one of Kronos's children who thus stepped aside, leaving (perhaps) many other ways of seeing and of being still enclosed in the eternal intellect.[37] So far no *error* has been made, nor is it made as the World Soul orders the physical cosmos to her taste, nor when seemingly other versions of Soul-as-Such, ourselves, emerge from contemplation to take our part in making and experiencing many and beautiful things.

---

35 Ibid., IV.8 [6].6, 1–6. So also Descola, *Beyond Nature and Culture*, 203: "In Plotinus, for example, the generative world soul that, through its emanations, creates the chain of being has one essential property, that of creating otherness; for if the universe is at peace with itself, even if its parts are often in conflict, it is because this conforms with reason, and the unity of reason stems from the contraries that it encompasses. Reason makes things different from one another, in fact as different as possible."

36 Plotinus, *Ennead*, V.1 [10].4, 20–2.

37 Ibid., V.8 [31].12–13.

We must take our understanding of Zeus from Plato, from the *Phaedrus* [246e4] where he says that this god is a "great leader," but elsewhere he says, I think, that Zeus is the third [*Letter 2*, 312e4]: but he is clearer in the *Philebus* [30d1], when he says that there is in Zeus "a royal soul and a royal intellect."[38]

Where then is the error, the self-will (*tolma*) that needs remediation? "The beginning of evil for them was audacity (*tolma*)":[39] better, perhaps, "self-will" than mere "audacity," the desire to have things our own way, being tired of "being together," like lieutenants of a supreme King who decide to carve out their own little fiefdom from the imperial whole.[40] We began, that is, to despise the company of our equals and the constraint of the Great King, to be laws unto ourselves. "We all, like sheep, have gone astray; everyone to his own way."[41] This enterprise is of its nature fissiparous: mistaken as Plotinus was about the nature of plants and of most non-human animals, he was right to observe the long downward descent of denial. Being "autonomous," as we now suppose we should be, is a mistake.

In each stage of the prolonged descent we may find various resting points and even, sometimes, reversals:

> Those who guarded the man in them become men again. Those who lived by sense alone become animals; but if their sense-perceptions have been accompanied by passionate temper they become wild animals.... But if they did not even live by sense along with their desires but coupled them with dullness of perception, they even turn into plants; for it was this, the growth-principle which worked in them, alone or predominantly, and they were taking care to turn themselves into trees. Those who

---

38 Ibid., III.5 [50].8, 7-11.
39 Ibid., V.1 [10].1, 4. So also Solovyov: "This abnormal attitude toward everything else—this exclusive self-assertion, or egoism, all powerful in our practical life even we deny it in theory, this opposition of the self to all other selves and the practical negation of the other selves—constitutes the radical *evil* of our nature." Vladimir Solovyov, *Lectures on Divine Humanity*, trans. Peter Zouboff, ed. Boris Jakim (New York: Lindisfarne Press, 1995), 123. Solovyov, like Plotinus, identifies this self-assertion as the origin of our fall; unlike Plotinus, he concludes that this world here is indeed a *flawed* creation, "something that ought not to be" (ibid., 121).
40 Plotinus, *Ennead*, IV.8 [6].4, 7-12.
41 Isaiah 53:6.

loved music but were in other ways respectable turn into song-birds; kings who ruled stupidly into eagles, if they had no other vices; astronomers who were always raising themselves to the sky without philosophic reflection turn into birds which fly high. The man who practiced community virtue (*arete politike*) becomes a man again; but one who has a lesser share of it a creature that lives in community (*politikon zoon*), a bee or something of the sort.[42]

So what is the *political* or social moral here? Men of very great civic virtue are, traditionally, "godlike,"[43] but the title is more complimentary than real. Aristotle ranks genuine godlikeness as far beyond "virtue" as beastliness is below it.[44] A merely "political" life of the sort I have described may turn out to be more suitable for such "eusocial" creatures as bees or ants or termites:[45] human beings have the opportunity, at least, to reinvent themselves as something greater. And yet such virtues are at least a step on the road. "The civic virtues do genuinely set us in order and make us better by giving limit and measure to our desires."[46] As citizens we are saved, perhaps, from the merely bestial life, the likely fate of one who is *apolis*.[47]

One who has been set free from a beast-like life and purified, as much as possible, of the immoderation of the passions and thus becomes instead of a beast, as it were, a man, is promised in [Hierocles'] later verses to be made a god instead of a man, to the extent that man can become god.[48]

That is the final point of the laws.

---

42 Plotinus, *Ennead*, III.4 [15].2, 16–31. Plotinus does not seem to expect the age-long punishments or rewards for discarnate souls of the sort imagined by Plato himself (Plato, *Republic*, 10.614–21), and by many others (including Jains, Buddhists, Christians and Muslims); see Appleton, *Narrating Karma*, 43–50.
43 Plotinus, *Ennead*, I.2 [19].1, 23–27.
44 Aristotle, *Nicomachean Ethics*, 7.1145a15–30.
45 A familiar trope in modern speculative fiction at least since H. G. Wells, *First Men in the Moon* (Oxford: Oxford University Press, 2017 [1901]), is the imagining of a thoroughly biological caste system as a seemingly effective alternative to the muddled lives of would-be independent humans. See Stephen R. L. Clark, "God, Reason and Extraterrestrials," in *God, Mind and Knowledge*, ed. Andrew Moore (London: Ashgate, 2014).
46 Plotinus, *Ennead*, I.2 [19].2, 14–16.
47 Aristotle, *Politics*, 1.1253a1–4, "like an isolated piece in draughts."
48 Schibli, *Hierocles of Alexandria*, 273.

The Cretan laws [so Plato's Athenian Stranger says] are
with reason famous among the Hellenes; for they fulfil
the object of laws, which is to make those who use them
happy; and they confer every sort of good. Now goods
are of two kinds: there are human and there are divine
goods, and the human hang upon the divine; and the
state which attains the greater, at the same time acquires
the less, or, not having the greater, has neither. Of the
lesser goods the first is health, the second beauty, the
third strength, including swiftness in running and bodily
agility generally, and the fourth is wealth, not the blind
god [Plutus], but one who is keen of sight, if only he has
wisdom for his companion. For wisdom is chief and leader
of the divine class of goods, and next follows temperance
[better, "self-possession"]; and from the union of these
two with courage springs justice, and fourth in the scale
of virtue is courage. All these naturally take precedence
of the other goods, and this is the order in which the
legislator must place them, and after them he will enjoin
the rest of his ordinances on the citizens with a view to
these, the human looking to the divine, and the divine
looking to their leader, *nous*.[49]

Ethical and political virtues, so he says, are *divine* goods, and
especially the four which came to be called "cardinal": in Jowett's
translation, wisdom, temperance, justice, courage. Their value is
not merely consequential: they are shadows or images of the
real excellences that true gods enjoy. They are not to be taken as
essential: to think that the gods are "virtuous" merely in that civic
sense is a vulgar error, as Aristotle insisted.[50] Plotinus picked up
the point. If the best life lay in exercising courage (for example),
we should need wars to give us an opportunity—but the truly
"virtuous" would not want the opportunity to arise, any more than
a good physician *wants* there to be sicknesses to heal or wounds to
bind.[51] The better life is symbolized rather in the single Kingdom
from which we have descended, rather than the *polis* that must
often, perforce, be wary of war with its neighbors. "The higher
justice in the soul is its activity towards intellect; its self-control

---

49   Plato, *Laws*, 1.631b.
50   Aristotle, *Nicomachean Ethics*, 10.1178b7–18.
51   Plotinus, *Ennead*, VI.8 [39].5, 13–21. See John M. Rist, *The Road to Reality*
(Cambridge: Cambridge University Press, 1967), 32–33.

[better, 'its self-possession'] is its inward turning to intellect; its courage is its freedom from affections [better, 'passions']."[52]

> The virtuous city, over which the chief ruler or Imām should preside, is represented by al-Fārābi as the political framework for the attainment of humankind's ultimate goal of happiness. Its inhabitants are held together by a community of purpose, both theoretical and practical. Accordingly, they should seek in the first place the knowledge of the First Cause and all its attributes, and in the second place that of the immaterial forms (or intelligibles), as well as that of the "spiritual" entities (or intellects), their properties, their actions and their ranks, ending in descending order with the Active Intellect. Next, the inhabitants of the virtuous city should seek the knowledge of the heavenly bodies and their properties, followed by the physical bodies, how they come into being and pass away and how whatever happens in the world of generation and corruption happens according to the principles of masterly production (ihkām), justice and wisdom, wherein there is no imperfection or injustice. Next, they should seek the knowledge of humans, how they are generated and how their faculties develop and are finally illuminated by that light which emanates from the Active Intellect and is the warrant of their apprehending the first principles on which all knowledge depends.[53]

Climbing back from our descent, from our wishing to have things "our way," we may learn to look only towards the Divine, not simply as a scholastic effort but to be once more "at one." And in achieving this much we pass beyond the need of any particular city.

But does any of this make sense? Some critics will be sure that it cannot: surely, they will say, I am myself identifiable as a particular physical organism, with an agreed birth date and a prospective death day. It is perhaps conceivable that an organism visibly indistinguishable from myself (or myself at some age or other) should come to exist in the future, with appropriate "memories" of my life here-now. But what could be meant by claiming that some entirely other creature could in the future be "me,"

---

52 Plotinus, *Ennead*, I.2 [19].6, 23–26.
53 Fakhry, *Al-Farabi*, 105–6.

without even any (misleading) "memories" of life here-now, and without even any special physical connection between this body and theirs? We can conceive of course that an all-powerful creator could summon my bodily fragments (including our manifold symbiotes) from their various places, or simply copy them into a new design. Science Fiction writers have often played with the notion that even less powerful creators could manage almost as much. Maybe the complete design for "me" could be transmitted over light years and many centuries to serve as the template for a newly created creature who would, momentarily and in some confusion, think that he was me, marvelously relocated.[54] Those who accept the diagnosis will usually add that the relation is no weaker than the ordinary case, that "personal identity" is really no more than a figment, a socially managed way of connecting one moment to another. Truly, as Nagasena told King Milinda, there is no abiding self at all. "Nagasena" itself is "but a way of counting, term, appellation, convenient designation, mere name for the hair of the head, hair of the body...brain of the head, form, sensation, perception, the predispositions and consciousness. But in the absolute sense there is no ego to be found."[55] So also Epicurean theorists: the many atomies that make me up will be dispersed throughout the infinite array and may coincide again, or an indistinguishable organism form elsewhere. Some of those atomies are intrinsically "psychic." Anger, fear and indolence are mingled with soul-particles in the composite living being: "So heat and air and the invisible power of breath, mixed up, create one nature, together with that mobile force which causes them to move and so give sensitive movement to the whole body."[56] But neither of these options will appeal to any Platonist: there must be real identities, real selves, to choose and to take responsibility for

---

54 Amongst many other authors see especially, Algis Budrys's *Rogue Moon* (London: Gateway, 2012 [1960]), Greg Egan's *Incandescence* (London: Gollancz, 2011), Frederik Pohl & Jack Williamson's *Farthest Star* (London: Macmillan, 1976), and Tony Daniel's *Warpath* (London: Gollancz, 1994).

55 S. Radhakrishnan and Charles Moore, eds., *Sourcebook of Indian Philosophy* (New Jersey: Princeton University Press, 1957), 281–84; see also Thomas William Rhys-Davids, *The Milinda Panha: the Questions of King Milinda* (Loschberg: Jazzybee Verlag, 2017), 16–17. Milinda was King Menander of the Hellenistic kingdom of Bactria.

56 Lucretius, *On the Nature of Things*, 3.268ff. For Buddhists it is the triad of anger, greed and ignorance that moves the Wheel.

what they choose. How then can such selves be found identically in wholly different creatures?

The first thing to notice is that there is a distinction between the embodied soul here-now and the eternal soul—a distinction that can be found in Egyptian theory long before Plotinus.[57] On the one hand, there is a psycho-physical unity, whose mere shadow remains in the afterlife; on the other, there is the real self, *nous* or *ba*, that is native to the stars and need not remember (perhaps should not remember) its merely earthly history. It is possible, or so Platonists believed, that we could awaken, even in this life, to our real identity, as Plotinus, he said, occasionally did, and then wondered how he had ever "come down" again.[58] But there is a sense in which what wakens is not (for example) just *Plotinus,* a particular third-century Egyptian. It is worth noticing that caterpillars, in one ancient and respectable account, are not *turned into* butterflies, but only lay the eggs (the chrysalides) from which the butterflies will hatch![59] Plotinus even identifies our present corporeal selves, exactly, as *grubs* in the tree of nature.[60] And "*psyche*" means both soul and butterfly. The ancient Egyptian story suggested that "one aspect of the god's nature, his *ba*, is in heaven; another one, his body, rests in the realm of the dead."[61] Even the human dead may have at least two modes of "survival": the *ka* is given form through the body's mummification, the array of funeral goods, and seems to persist simply as an echo of the once living being; the *ba*, represented as a bird with a human head, can be expected to join the Sun in his progress across the heavens, maybe as a star, probably in the constellation Orion (the sidereal home of Osiris).[62] In the Homeric version of the story,

---

57   See further Stephen R. L. Clark, "Souls, Stars and Shadows," in *Differences in Identity in Philosophy and Religion: A Cross-Cultural Approach*, ed. Lydia Azadpour, et al. (London: Bloomsbury, 2020), and Stephen R. L. Clark, "Heracles, Hylas and the Uses of Reflection," in *Plotinus and the Moving Image*, ed. Thorsten Botz-Bornstein and Giannis Stamatellos (Leiden: Brill, 2017).

58   Plotinus, *Ennead*, IV.8 [6].1, 1–11.

59   Aristotle, *De Generatione Animalium*, 2.733b11–17.

60   Plotinus, *Ennead*, IV.3 [27].4, 26–30.

61   Siegfried Morenz, *Egyptian Religion*, trans. Ann E. Keep (New York: Cornell University Press, 1973), 151, after the Leiden Hymns (13th century BC).

62   R. Drew Griffith, "Sailing to Elysium: Menelaus' Afterlife (*Odyssey* 4.561–569) and Egyptian Religion," *Phoenix* 55 (2001): 215, after Pyramid Text utterances (24th century BCE).

all that can be found in the Unseen, in Hades, are memories and images of "the departed," perhaps to be given momentary life by the blood of sacrifice, but best walled off from the life of the survivors.[63] If there is any conscious experience there at all it is a life of regretful memory—a notion that in later years amounts to eternal damnation, whether or not particular punishments are imagined.[64] The eternal self, on the other hand, does not remember, either in its subsequent embodied lives or even, it seems, in heaven.

So what identifies one soul as having animated Hermotimus and another as having "been Socrates"? Plotinus reckoned that we could simply *recognize* our friends, as Pythagoras recognized his friend, in the sound of a beaten dog.[65] "For here below, too, we can know many things by the look in people's eyes when they are silent; but there all their body is clear and pure and each is like an eye, and nothing is hidden or feigned, but before one speaks to another that other has seen and understood."[66] "There," that is, we apparently have recognizable, and naked, bodies—or at least we have some public presence, even if that presence is not so easily locatable, nor yet as divisible, as our present corporeal being. And of course we shall have better things to talk about than current gossip! But precisely because these souls—or better, perhaps, these *daimones* or *spirits*—are not identical with any one of their earthly lives—we cannot expect to recognize (say) the soul that once was Socrates merely from the *look* of things: his spirit is not snub-nosed, even symbolically. But if there were no individualized public presence we might have to expect that there is just *one* spirit for all of us, wholly indistinguishable and therefore wholly identical. That indeed seems, sometimes, to be the implication of the philosophers' account: "Mind is the god in us—whether it was Hermotimus or Anaxagoras who said so—and mortal life contains a portion of some god."[67] And maybe this is common

---

63 See John Heath, "Blood for the Dead: Homeric Ghosts Speak Up," *Hermes* 133, no. 4 (2005): 389–400.

64 See James Hillman, *The Dream and the Underworld* (New York: Harper, 1979), 56.

65 According to Xenophanes of Colophon, DK21B7 in Diogenes Laertius, *Lives*, 8.36.

66 Plotinus, *Ennead*, IV.3 [27].18, 19–24.

67 Aristotle, *Protrepticus* in Ross, *Works of Aristotle*, 42 [fr. 10c]; see Gábor Betegh, *The Derveni Papyrus: Cosmology, Theology and Interpretation* (Cambridge: Cambridge University Press, 2004), 284.

knowledge: "All men are naturally and spontaneously moved to speak of the god who is in each one of us one and the same."[68] But though there may be only one absolute *Nous* (at once Mind and Being), each living spirit is a distinct face of *Nous*, a really distinct individual not identical with any ordinarily earthly being.

> If one likens it [that is, Reality] to a living richly varied sphere, or imagines it as a thing all faces, shining with living faces, or as all the pure souls running together into the same place, with no deficiencies but having all that is their own, and universal Intellect seated on their summits so that the region is illuminated by intellectual light—if one imagined it like this one would be seeing it somehow as one sees another from outside; but one must become that, and make oneself the contemplation.[69]

So really individuated souls emerge, in this account, as echoes of one facet or another of the eternal *Nous,* and busy themselves— at first—in assisting their great sister-soul, the World Soul, in its perpetual making and remaking of the passing world. Their error—that is, *our* error—is to forget our beginning and value instead the reflections of eternal beauty and delight. It is worth recalling that two thousand years ago and more, mirrors were mostly bowls of water, or else polished obsidian and silver.[70] Our ancestors mostly looked *down* into them (that is why a mirror is *katoptron*[71]) and might imagine themselves pulled down into the watery realm, literally *nympholeptoi*, nymph-caught, frenzied, besot- ted, like Heracles's ward Hylas, who was pulled into the water by nymphs, and left only an echo for Heracles as he tried to find his ward.[72] Or, like Aesop's dog, we might be misled by the sight

---

68   Plotinus, *Ennead*, VI.5 [23].1.

69   Ibid., VI.7 [38].15, 25–16, 3. Cf. Ezekiel 1:2–11.

70   Clark, *Plotinus*, 83–90. Ayfre, "Le corps miroir de l'ame," in *Un Cinéma Spiritualiste*, ed. René Prédal (Paris: Éditions du Cerf, 2004), 87, acknowledges the point about ancient mirrors, "with a tain that is always a little fluid," cited by Susan Cooper, *The Soul of Film Theory* (Basingstoke: Palgrave MacMillan, 2013), 80.

71   Plato, *Cratylus*, 414c suggests that *"katoptron"* has an intrusive *rho*: the word, he says, should be *katopton*, with its suggestion that we look *downwards* into the reflective surface.

72   See Plotinus, *Ennead*, I.6 [1].8, 9: we might thereby sink down into Hades and consort with shadows; see also III.6 [26].7, 41–2 on "falling into falsity, like things in a dream or water or a mirror." On Hylas see Apollonius Rhodius, *Argonautica*, 1.1172–1272; Theocritus, *Idyll*, 13; Virgil, *Eclogues*, 6.41–2; Propertius, *Elegies*, 1.20.

of a supposedly *other* dog with *another* and *better* bone.[73] The story that we now more commonly remember concerns the sad fate of Narcissus, who was punished for despising the nymph Echo by being trapped in admiration of his own reflection in a pool.[74] And according to the *Hermetic Corpus* the eternal Mind sees his own image reflected in the Earth, and falls in love (and so into the physical world).[75] But this was not because they knowingly admired *themselves*. Narcissus was not a narcissist! All these unfortunates mistook reflections for the reality that loomed over their shoulders and they need now to remember![76]

The *political* moral of this account is to acknowledge that our real selves are not exhaustively determined by our caste, our class, our gender, our nation or our species. The very claim—no doubt designed to reconcile the oppressed to their condition—that they may have a "better life" next time requires that they are something in addition to the soul-body composite which labors (or does not labor) here. And if that is true, how seriously can we take even the *natural* divisions, let alone the social, that require or seem to require such different lives? Maybe indeed, being here, we have to manage as best we can to do what *polis*, nation and the living world require, but we do so knowing that it is indeed a game, a drama, even a children's play. Once upon a time, perhaps we knew it was a game.

> If human beings, through most of our history, have moved back and forth fluidly between different social arrangements, assembling and dismantling hierarchies on a regular basis, maybe the real question should be "how did we get stuck?" How did we end up in one single mode? How did we lose that political self-consciousness, once so typical of our species? How did we come to treat eminence and subservience not as temporary expedients, or even the pomp and circumstance of some kind of grand seasonal theatre, but as inescapable elements of the human condition? If we started out just playing games, at what point did we forget that we were playing?[77]

73 Aesop, *The Complete Fables*, trans. Olivia and Robert Temple (New York: Penguin, 1998), 137.
74 Ovid, *Metamorphoses*, 3.339–510.
75 *Poimandres*, 1.14: Copenhaver, *Hermetica*, 3.
76 Plotinus, *Ennead*, V.1 [10].1.
77 Graeber and Wengrow, *The Dawn of Everything*, 115.

PRE-POLITICAL WORLDS

And how now shall we escape, or rather release our real and abiding selves from the illusion?

> We cannot get there on foot; for our feet only carry us everywhere in this world, from one country to another. You must not get ready a carriage, either, or a boat. Let all these things go, and do not look. Shut your eyes, and change to and wake another way of seeing, which everyone has but few use.[78]

Remember our real location—or at least imagine the wider world even of our present theories and realize what that implies for all our present feeling. We may not now remember any detail of other lives, may not be able, as it were, to sense them "from within," and yet be able to intuit that there are other lives to live, and that they too contribute to the larger life. Becoming aware of history, and pre-historical fact, is itself an illumination, and more than an abstract conclusion. A character in one of Wilson's fictions recalls the moment when he became, in prospect, a dedicated historian:

> Just inside the farmyard there was a large pool of grey water, rather muddy. As I was taking the clothes from the line, my mind still in Nineveh, I happened to notice this pool, and forgot for a moment where I was or what I was doing there. As I looked at it, the puddle lost all familiarity and became as alien as a sea on Mars. I stood staring at it, and the first drops of rain fell from the sky, and wrinkled its surface. At that moment I experienced a sensation of happiness and insight such as I had never known before. Nineveh and all history suddenly became as real and as alien as that pool. History became such a *reality* that I felt a kind of contempt for my own existence, standing there with my arms full of clothes.[79]

Wilson may perhaps have drawn this case not merely from his own experience, but from the writings of Arnold Toynbee, who recounted similar episodes in his own growth as a fully engaged historian.[80] This is perhaps, as Spengler suggested, a feeling pecu-

---

78 Plotinus, *Ennead*, I.6 [1].8, 16–28.
79 Colin Wilson, *Mind Parasites* (London: Barker, 1967), 18.
80 Colin Wilson, *Religion and the Rebel* (London: Gollancz, 1957), 125–26, quoting Arnold Toynbee, *A Study of History*, vol. 1, 130–31, 139.

liar to "Western" or "Faustian" Civilization, and almost unknown to our "Classical" forebears. Plotinus at any rate does not seem to be so affected by any sense of *past* immensities, but may be similarly engaged by a sudden realization of *astronomical* distance and duration; that is, they suddenly feel *real*, even as we also understand that distance and duration are only relative features.

> Astronomy is peculiarly adapted to remedy a little and narrow spirit....There is something in the immensity [of astronomical distances] that shocks and overwhelms the imagination; it is too big for the grasp of a human intellect: estates, provinces and kingdoms vanish in its presence.[81]

Though really, as Berkeley knew, those distant times and places are no further away than Now.[82] Really our own present place and moment is no *more* real than those.

> It seems to me also that the discourse (*logos*) of the Pythagoreans, which prepares souls to recollect their former lives as well, imitates this historical study of the Egyptians. For just as in the case of one man—or one soul rather—duty requires that he grasp his different lives, so too in the case of one race it requires that they grasp their different cycles. So as among the former the recollection of their previous existences is perfective of their souls, so too among the latter the historical study of earlier cycles contributes very greatly to their perfection in wisdom.[83]

Scholars, scientists and visionaries have a place in a well-ordered *polis*, or an empire, or the wide world itself, since it is they who may uncover or illuminate these wider worlds and longer histories. They may serve, perhaps, as a Brahminical class, distinct from those who exercise *authority*. Like the Egyptian priests who tell Solon about the manifold catastrophes that are always setting us back to our beginnings, they exist to put our usual lives in context, and remind us of inevitable decay, in this world here, from even the best

---

81 Berkeley, "Guardian Essay on Minute Philosophers," in *Works*, vol. 7, 207-8.
82 We might reasonably ask a Berkeleian why the little lights we see in the sky must be taken to have real physical counterparts. Might not astronomy be merely a record of mammalian sensibilia, as Frank Ramsey suggested (*Foundations of Mathematics* [London: Routledge, 1931], 35-37)? But perhaps the evocation of immense distances and histories is the real point.
83 Proclus, *Commentary on Timaeus*, 219 [I.124, 5-13].

ideals. This is not to claim—and I doubt that Plotinus would have claimed—the excellence that later theorists imputed to the sage, but he would have shared their assessment of this "corporeal" world:

> In [Yahya al-Suhrawardi's] work the corporeal world in which we live our everyday lives is reduced to a mere stage-set, a cardboard front ceded without further ado to the kings and sultans of this world, mere wielders of brute force (who made use of that attribute to execute him). All the real action is in the world of images or archetypes, an invisible realm between this one and the next reminiscent of the Zoroastrian *menok*, a spiritual image of the world known as *alam al-mithal*. The true rulers are those who have freed themselves from the shackles of their bodies in the here and now and who inform mankind of sacred knowledge: prophets, kings, philosophers, sages, pillars of the universe. Their powers over the natural world in al-Suhrawardi's vision far exceeded that popularly ascribed to ordinary kings: they could raise earthquakes and tempests, ruin entire nations, cure the sick, sate the hungry, make wild beasts obey; some could ascend to the light and appear in any form they liked, or, with further light bestowed on them, walk on the water, fly in the sky, and traverse the earth. Even clear revelation might be given to them (as to Muhammad and, some said, to al-Suhrawardi himself).[84]

It is perhaps as well that we have no such great powers at hand, and that scholars and scientists are therefore not easily tempted to use them (unless, perhaps, such powers are indeed in the hands of scientists and technicians).

But there is one more possible transformation of our lives and sensibilities. In thinking of the local and global catastrophes that punctuate human and pre-human life, our usual concentration is on the repeated rise of some new civil order, some new civilization. What comes between is dismissed as the Dark Ages, bereft of social stability, cultural memory and the hope of human dominion. If we remember them at all, we rather focus on whatever social form preserved past glories and discoveries until the next "renaissance." In the most recent Dark Age of West European history it was the Church, its monks and priests, as well as Jewish and Muslim

---

84 Crone, *Medieval*, 192.

scholars, especially in Spain, who kept tradition alive. As Chesterton remarked of that time, it was only dark in patches, lit by long, narrow rays like searchlights.

> And just as any man, however much in darkness, if he looks right down the searchlight, looks into a furnace of white-hot radiance, so any medieval man, who had the luck to hear the right lectures or look at the right manuscript, did not merely "follow a gleam," a grey glimmer in a mystical forest; but looked straight down the ages into the radiant mind of Aristotle.... Such light as they had came, not only from the broad daylight, but from the brilliant daylight; it was the buried sunlight of the Mediterranean.[85]

The people of other supposed Dark Ages—"dark," that is, because we have no detailed reliable record of those days—could also retain past glories and discoveries through oral epics and deductions from the remaining ruins of great cities. But we can also turn the story round: as the Egyptian priests told Solon, the remnants who survived catastrophe remembered stories and garbled proverbs. But the real point is that it was *they* who survived: people, that is, who were not the social elite of the cities, but who were already well-used to doing without the luxuries, even the imagined necessities, of usual civilized life. The poor survive catastrophe rather better than the rich, and "primitives" survive still better because they are living already as well as "animals." Their world may be full of memories: stories embedded in landmarks, ghosts and bogeys, and the movement of stars above, but all this imagined excess is of a piece with the natural landscape, rather than being a cultural artefact encountered mainly in books or other written works.

Had Plotinus any occasion to consider the life of "primitives"? And if he had, what would he think of them? What counts towards a properly "successful" life, remember, is not wealth, nor rank, nor even health, but rather the enjoyment of abiding beauty, whether in art or nature. Even its creation, or a part in its creation, is of less value than the enjoyment of it.[86] "Enjoyment," I suggest, may

---

85   G. K. Chesterton, *Chaucer* (London: Faber, 1932), 126. There were also other lights: King Alfred of Wessex translated Boethius's *Consolation of Philosophy*, John Scotus Eriugena translated Ps-Dionysius. Scholarship, and civility, survived.
86   See Aristotle, *Prior Analytics*, 69a39–45; *Nicomachean Ethics*, 8.1159a27–36.

be a better translation of "*theoria*" than simple "contemplation": to contemplate, in current idiom, is to consider something without emotional distortion, with a view to grasping it from multiple points of view, or from an "objective" stance, as something—exactly— distinct from how we feel or think about it. This may well be a good goal, but it lacks the immediacy, the single-pointedness, that Plotinus requires of *theoria,* in which the knower and the known are unified. Still less does "theorizing" capture the nature of the goal, as though we ought to be thinking only "abstractly" of the world, with a view to working out an agreeable algorithm for some future action. *Theoria* is rather to lie open to the real, to be absorbed in enjoyment of something worth enjoying, which is no longer *separate* from the perceiving mind. "He is the true possessor of a thing who enjoys it, and not he that owns it without the enjoyment of it."[87] Berkeley had the beauties of sense chiefly in mind here, and offers a similar analysis of his hoped-for eternal felicity:

> Eternal happiness [will be] a happyness large as our desires, & those desires not stinted to ye few objects we at present receive from some dull inlets of perception, but propor- tionate to wt our faculties shall be wn God has given the finishing stroke to our nature & made us fit inhabitants for heaven, a happiness which we narrow-sighted mortals wretchedly point out to our selves by green meadows, fragrant groves, refreshing shades, crystal streams & wt other pleasant ideas our fancys can glean up in this Vale of misery.[88]

Plotinus did not disparage even such seemingly transient beauties, though preferring those of justice and self-possession: "Neither the evening nor the morning star are as fair."[89] Such enjoyments, clearly, are as open to "primitives" as to the most sophisticated of city-dwellers—more so, indeed, because there are fewer distractions. Which opens in turn the possibility that there may be those who positively wish to be "primitive," and so to escape the tyranny of "the State" and the whole apparatus of hierarchical division and ultimately pointless labor.

---

87 Berkeley, "Guardian Essay on Pleasure," *Works*, vol. 7, 195.
88 Berkeley, "Sermon on Immortality," *Works*, vol. 7, 12.
89 Plotinus, *Ennead*, I.6 [1].4, 11–13, after Aristotle, *Nicomachean Ethics*, 5.1129b28–9; see also Plotinus, *Ennead*, VI.6 [34].6, 39.

[In the age of Kronos] there were no states or families, but they had fruits in plenty from the trees and other plants, which the earth furnished them of its own accord, without help from agriculture. And they lived for the most part in the open air, without clothing or bedding; for the climate was tempered for their comfort, and the abundant grass that grew up out of the earth furnished them soft couches.... If the foster children of Cronus, having all this leisure and the ability to converse not only with human beings but also with beasts, made full use of all these opportunities with a view to philosophy, talking with the animals and with one another and learning from every creature that, through possession of some peculiar power he may have had in any respect beyond his fellows perceptions tending towards an increase of wisdom, it would be easy to decide that the people of those old times were immeasurably happier than those of our epoch. Or if they merely ate and drank till they were full and gossiped with each other and the animals, telling such stories as are even now told about them, in that case, too, it would, in my opinion, be very easy to reach a decision.[90]

The Age of Kronos may be over, and be now remembered, if at all, as only a dream of Cockaigne or the Big Rock Candy Mountain, but Plato was perhaps more serious in his intention than is usually allowed. There were no hierarchies then, nor boundaries, nor even the crass divide between humans and other animals. We may even allow that there is some truth in the notion that before we began to cultivate the land, domesticate the beasts and divide up the earth, our ancestors' lives were more leisurely.[91] Contemporary "primitives," no doubt, have more trouble, but that is mostly because we "civilized" peoples have driven them out of their best lands and continue to ignore their talents and their affections. It is widely supposed that "uncontacted primitives" ought now

---

90   Plato, *Statesman*, 272abc.
91   See Marshall Sahlins, *Stone Age Economics* (London: Routledge, 2017 [1972]) for arguments that "primitive" life was more leisurely than the agricultural life, let alone the modern "industrial" economy. Graeber & Wengrow offer sound rebukes to what they call the Garden of Eden story, as tending to suggest that agricultural and even industrial life had inevitable hierarchical consequences, as if "humans haplessly stumbled their way into a Faustian pact with wheat": Graeber & Wengrow, *Dawn of Everything*, 232.

to be contacted "for their own sake," despite the evidence that such contacts will be genocidal, by disease, the appropriation of the land they helped create and lived on and the destruction of their morale. If any are to survive the next turn of the Wheel it will be the uncontacted—and the lives they live may well be as enjoyable as ours.

By Plato's account, Kronos once ruled the world, and maybe still rules where Zeus does not.

> Tradition tells us how blissful was the life of men in that age, furnished with everything in abundance, and of spontaneous growth. And the cause thereof is said to have been this: Kronos was aware of the fact that no human being (as we have explained) is capable of having irresponsible control of all human affairs without becoming filled with pride and injustice; so, pondering this fact, he then appointed as kings and rulers for our cities, not men, but beings of a race that was nobler and more divine, namely, daemons. He acted just as we now do in the case of sheep and herds of tame animals: we do not set oxen as rulers over oxen, or goats over goats, but we, who are of a nobler race, ourselves rule over them. In like manner the God, in his love for humanity, set over us at that time the nobler race of daemons who, with much comfort to themselves and much to us, took charge of us and furnished peace and modesty and orderliness and justice without stint, and thus made the tribes of men free from feud and happy.[92]

This story at least avoids the folly into which later Europeans fell, of supposing that "savages" know no governor but their own changing wishes. Samuel Johnson may stand for many here: "A savage man and a savage woman meet by chance, and when the man sees a woman who pleases him better he will leave the first."[93] A similar folly lies behind the notion that such "primitives" live upon the land without affecting or engineering it—and so, as Locke supposed, have no natural right to the land they live on: since they have not properly cultivated it, it remains the common property of

---

92 Plato, *Laws*, 4.713cde.
93 James Boswell, *Life of Johnson*, ed. R. W. Chapman (Oxford: Oxford University Press 2008 [1791]), 348 [28 March 1772], quoting Johnson, who also supposed that "pity is not natural to man. Children are always cruel. Savages are always cruel" (ibid., 231 [20 July 1763]).

humankind, to be appropriated by those colonials who can make something of it. As Mark Goldie puts it in an editorial comment, "I have property in the fish I catch, but the ocean remains a great common," until it is carved up—by those with the power and will— and managed.[94] Native Americans were sometimes unwise enough to agree that they did not "own" the land (intending something rather different), although they depended on it. More honest and perceptive scholarship has since uncovered the extent to which, even by Locke's own standards, the original inhabitants most certainly did "own" the land, since they had, even as hunter-gatherers, worked hard over many centuries, even many millennia, to make it so. European invaders, both in the Americas and in Australia, were apparently blind to the way the natives they were displacing had been active participants in the land (as also were other species), even ignoring the fact that many were already cultivators.[95] Amongst the weird contradictions of colonial ideology was that "natives" were simultaneously derided as "uncivilized" and praised as "noble savages," exempt from the foolish rules of European society. Or perhaps not a contradiction: "natives" were treated as "children," both "innocent" and without authority. Or as something less than children, as destined by God or Nature to be displaced and exterminated, failed experiments. So Benjamin Franklin: "If it be the design of Providence to extirpate these savages in order to make room for cultivators of the earth, it seems not improbable that rum may be the appointed means. It has already annihilated all the tribes who formerly inhabited the sea-coast."[96]

---

94 John Locke, *Second Treatise on Government*, ed. Mark Goldie (Oxford: Oxford University Press, 2016), xix, 14–26 [ch. 5 *On Property*].

95 Gammage, *Biggest Estate on Earth*, emphasizes the way that Australian hunter-gatherers managed their territories before the European invasion; Bruce Pascoe, *Dark Emu: Aboriginal Australia and the Birth of Agriculture* (London: Scribe, 2018), points out that the first Australians were also actively farming land and water, and that the "hunter-gatherer" tag was "a convenient lie to justify dispossession" (within the Lockean narrative). See also Charles C. Mann, *1493: How Europe's Discovery of the Americas Revolutionized Trade, Ecology and Life on Earth* (New York: Knopf, 2011) on native Americans' arboriculture.

96 Benjamin Franklin, *Autobiography*, ed. Charles W. Elliot (New York: P. F. Collier, 1909), 121; see Patrick Brantlinger, *Dark Vanishings: Discourse on the Extinction of Primitive Races, 1800–1930* (Ithaca, NY: Cornell University Press, 2003), 46–8; Graeber and Wengrow, *Dawn of Everything*, for a more detailed, plausible and generous account of "pre-civilized" humanity.

Greek colonists were similarly sometimes inclined to deny justice to the peoples whose land they occupied, on the familiar ground that such "savages" could not make or be expected to keep contracts (and so the colonists needn't).[97] North European "savages" and Asiatic "barbarians" were alike considered to be "natural slaves," as being unable either to discipline their own desires, or to rebel against their despots. The colonists' treacheries, no doubt, were noticed—and perhaps provided evidence in turn that it was *they* who were indifferent to justice, and to the very notion of a universal code. There can in the end be little compromise between the "world at war" (*dar al-harb*) and the obedient world (*dar al-islam*)—but which is which?

We can describe the situation rather differently: in those days, or amongst those peoples, *daimones* rule. The primary constraint on personal autonomy (that is, a general refusal to take orders from anyone too much like ourselves) was the sense of something "sacred," manifested in particular places, objects, artefacts or practices.[98] People feel themselves to be governed or at least a little limited by principles more than human, which require that they keep their place. Such a belief is helpful at least—and may even be essential—to create more extensive bonds than those binding immediate kin.[99] The world of the first Australians' experience

97 My thanks to Alexei Zadorozhny of Liverpool University for help with trying to identify remarks—vaguely remembered from much earlier reading—to this effect by Plutarch, so far unsuccessfully! The closest so far is an anecdote concerning Caesar's dealings with the Germans, which also makes it clear that at least some statesmen sometimes objected to this excuse: "Concerning the battle which was fought with them Caesar says in his 'Commentaries' that the Barbarians, while treating with him under a truce, attacked on their march and therefore routed his five thousand cavalry with their eight hundred, since his men were taken off their guard; that they then sent other envoys to him who tried to deceive him again, but he held them fast and led his army against the Barbarians, considering that good faith towards such faithless breakers of truces was folly. But Tanusius says that when the senate voted sacrifices of rejoicing over the victory, Cato pronounced the opinion that they ought to deliver up Caesar to the Barbarians, thus purging away the violation of the truce in behalf of the city, and turning the curse therefore on the guilty man": Plutarch, "Caesar," chap. 22 of *Lives*, vol. 7, *Demosthenes and Cicero, Alexander and Caesar*, trans. Bernadotte Perrin (Cambridge, Mass: Harvard University Press, Loeb Classical Library, 1919), 497.

98 See Graeber and Wengrow, *Dawn of Everything*, 158–60, suggesting that such "sacred" things are the beginnings of the notion of "property."

99 See (for example) Henrich, *Weirdest People*, 89–90.

was established by the powers of the Dreaming, whose track across the world as they sang it into existence can be traced from one landmark to the next.[100] Those powers are both God's agents in the making of the world and the particular totems of the humans on the land. "The Dreaming conceives an unchangeable universe, hence free of time. This can be so because the universe is not natural: it was made from darkness by God." The story is remarkably Plotinian!

> Across Australia the creation story is essentially the same: God made light, brought into being spirits and creator ancestors, and set down eternal Law for all creation. The creator ancestors accepted the Law or suffered if they didn't, and made epic journeys across a formless space, giving land and sea substance and shape before settling to rest in a place important to them. They are there still, and where they went still bears marks of their trials and adventures. All things derive from their presence or deeds and are ruled by the Law they passed on. Since universe and Law never change, time is irrelevant, as in a dream. Change and time exist only as cycles: birth and death, the passage of stars and seasons, journeys, encounters, and after 1788 [the year of the first European invasion] the appearance of plants and animals seeming new but always there. Cycles are eddies, ending where they begin or eclipsed by larger cycles: travel by death for example, or seasons by life spans. Eddies exist not on a river of life, for a river has a beginning and end, but on bigger eddies, in a boundless pool. Time is an eddy; the pool is timeless. Pool, eddies and Law are the Dreaming.[101]

What are such supposedly "primitive" societies like in practice? On the one hand, it is *civilized* societies that have most careful differences and roles (as I observed on an earlier page, after Mary Douglas); on the other, "primitive" societies may still enforce what differences they have more fiercely. In such "primitive" societies, Men and Women have entirely different ceremonial parts to play, which they take on after initiation (though there may also be acknowledged "in-betweeners"). Children indeed may have no

---

100   See Ronald M. Berndt and Catherine H. Berndt, *The World of the First Australians: aboriginal traditional life, past and present* (Canberra: Aboriginal Studies Press, 1988), 227–92; Gammage, *Biggest Estate on Earth*, 125–26, 135–36.
101   Gammage, *Biggest Estate on Earth*, 123.

proper social existence till they are initiated, sometimes in deliberately painful and invasive ways which serve both to mark the end of childhood and bind the initiates together in a "democracy of pain."[102] Platonists may have no problem with the pain: in a violent age, without adequate analgesics, it is even a parent's duty to show children how to manage pain. The complaint against the Spartan regime was that they didn't show children how to manage pleasure![103] Initiations that involved genital mutilation of an even more brutal sort than male circumcision would not have been so welcome: that Egyptians and Hebrews practiced circumcision marked them as really weird in the eyes of most Europeans.[104] Subincision for boys, and cutting and deflowering rituals for girls, would be more than most Europeans, then and now, could contemplate or agree to.

While most "primitive" adults will be able to craft whatever tools they need, and find their way around their tribal lands, there may already be some with special skills, of smithying or medicine or communicating with the ruling powers. Such "primitives" may be both more open than we are to the wider world, the animals and plants around them, and also more confined by "peace and modesty and orderliness." The penalty of expulsion may be lethal— or else begin to involve disputes between clans and moieties that themselves are lethal. Or maybe such expulsions and emigrations merely facilitate the continued being of a web or network of friendships across the world. In this context we could say, again with Plato, that "each of us living creatures is an ingenious puppet of the gods, whether contrived by way of a toy of theirs or for some serious purpose,"[105] and that it is those who seek to cut the strings who are at fault. In the old days, under the rule of Kronos, we may accept to be pulled this way and that, in an unceasing dance. Our fall comes, again, when too many of us decide to try to go our *own* way (without then being expelled or emigrating),

---

102   Berndt, *World of the First Australians*, 150–87; see also Pierre Clastres, *Society against the State: essays in political anthropology*, trans. Robert Hurley and Abe Stein (Brooklyn: Urzone Inc., 1987), 177–88, speaking principally of the Tupi-Guarani, and their rebellion against the hierarchical order of a former centralized State; Henrich, *Weirdest People*, 91.

103   Plato, *Laws*, 1.633b–644b.

104   Herodotus, *Histories*, 2.37; Genesis, 17.11–14, 23–27; cf. 1 Maccabees, 1.48–64.

105   Plato, *Laws*, 1.644e.

and so are driven to construct the rule of human law to save us from the worst results of individual passions. Plato's "city of pigs" grows bloated and diseased by the desire for things beyond their immediate reach[106] and must endure a radical correction so as to imitate the old ways, with bred and disciplined "guardians" to imitate the *daimones,* the ever-present principles, who once ruled.

So amongst the options open to a Platonist is the nostalgic dream of a "pre-political" order, still partly realized among those we reckon "primitives": a universal "city" whose citizens are not just "the wise." Such primitives find nothing odd in conversation with animals or plants, nor in acknowledging the continued presence of spirits who speak in ceremonials. They are engaged, alongside other species, in constructing and sustaining the land and waters around them.

Most of the entities that people the world are interconnected in a vast continuum inspired by unitary principles and governed by an identical regime of sociability. Relations between humans and nonhumans in fact appear to be no different from the relations that obtain between one human community and another.[107]

And they may also be at ease across whole continents, identifying with one or other *daimon.* In North America, for example:

> It was possible for a traveler hailing from a Bear, or Wolf or Hawk clan in what's now Georgia to travel all the way to Ontario or Arizona and find someone obliged to host them at almost any point in between. This seems all the more remarkable when one considers that literally hundreds of different languages were spoken in North America, belonging to half a dozen completely unrelated language families.[108]

They do not expect any radical alteration in their ways and the world, except, perhaps, that the powers embedded or symbolized in the landscape may occasionally stir to life. "The Dreaming has

---

106 Plato, *Republic,* 2.372d–373b.
107 Descola, *Beyond Nature and Culture,* 9. Descola describes a world-wide non-binary attitude, for which animals and plants alike are recognized as agents within a social web.
108 Graeber and Wengrow, *Dawn of Everything,* 456. Such clans are not mere kinship groups. "They are more like ritual societies, each dedicated to maintaining a spiritual relation with a different totem animal which is usually only figuratively their 'ancestor'" (ibid., 456).

two rules: obey the Law and leave the world as you found it—not better or worse, for God judges that, but the same."[109] We here-now, the citizens of some great city or the subjects of a would-be global empire, are unlikely ever to revisit those imagined days, until some great catastrophe compels us. If and when it does, we may be grateful for the help of any surviving primitives. Whether they in their turn may be grateful for the aphorisms and distorted stories of times past we bring with us will be another matter.

---

109   Gammage, *Biggest Estate on Earth*, 124. This conservationist ideal, of course, may often require some active management, and maybe regular prophetic intervention by the heirs of Gayomard.

8

The Eremitic Option

ALONE TO THE ALONE?

"The wise man...will abstain from command, office and any worldly kingship no matter how superior to Xerxes' this kingship would be."[1] So Plotinus, probably, would not himself have been the governor of Platonopolis, any more than Rogatianus. This is not to say that no one should have been its governor: there is a place even for emperors, as well as conscientious officials of a lower rank. But there is a more radical option even than the Brahminical: rather than seeking even to be admired as civic sages, one aiming to return to heaven may choose instead to leave, in spirit if not in body.

> A man has not failed if he fails to win beauty of colors or bodies, or power or office or kingship even, but if he fails to win this and only this. For this he should give up the attainment of kingship and of rule over all earth and sea and sky, if only by leaving and overlooking them he can turn to [beauty itself] and see.[2]

This was the choice presented to Siddhartha Gautama Sakyamuni: whether to be World Ruler (even a wise and compassionate one),

---

1   Ousager, *Plotinus*, 247: citing I.4 [46].14; I.4 [46].16; I.6 [1].7, 34–39; VI.7 [38].34, 32–38.

2   Plotinus, *Ennead*, I.6 [1].7, 35–40. See Glenn W. Most, "Plotinus' Last Words," *Classical Quarterly* 53, no. 2 (2003): 587: "Reading between the lines of Porphyry's hagiographical account, we can suspect that much in Plotinus's life in fact went very wrong. His disciples abandoned him; a fellow-student, Olympius, tried to use magic to make the stars harm him (Porphyry, *Life*, 10.1–13); contemporary Greek philosophers accused him of plagiarism (Porphyry, *Life*, 17.1–2); he followed Gordian III towards India but after the emperor's murder he barely managed to return from Mesopotamia to Rome (Porphyry, *Life*, 3.17–22); his grand plans for a philosophical community came to nothing (Porphyry, *Life*, 12.9–12); he found no one better to become his philosophical heir and literary executor than the low-wattage, neurotic Porphyry" (which is a little unfair to Porphyry). The astrologer Firmicus Maternus gloated that he fell into a cold torpor, and his entrails slowly dissolved (*Mathesis* 1.20; Mark Edwards, trans., *Neoplatonic Saints: the lives of Plotinus and Proclus by their students* [Liverpool: Liverpool University Press, 2000], 3n16)! But he was not a failure.

or else an Enlightened Savior.[3] World Rulers, Cakravartins, later theorists suggested, could only rule effectively in the golden age, rather as Plato described the age when Kronos ruled.[4] In these darker days, the choice may have been obvious. As the emperor Julian remarked:

> Who, I ask, ever found salvation through the conquests of Alexander? What city was ever more wisely governed because of them, what individual improved? Many indeed you might find whom those conquests enriched, but not one whom they made wiser or more temperate than he was by nature, if indeed they have not made him more insolent and arrogant. Whereas all who now find their salvation in philosophy owe it to Socrates.[5]

It may even seem that the choice requires a complete secession from society, as some have supposed Plotinus must really have preferred. Some souls, he says, who have "peeped out of the intelligible world go first to heaven, and when they have put on a body there go on by its means to earthier bodies, to the limit to which they extend themselves in length."[6] Our first instantiation here is as a star, to which we may hope to return if all goes well. "When the souls are set free they come to the star which is in harmony with the character and power which lived and worked in them; and each will have a god of this kind as its guardian spirit, either the star itself or the god set above this power."[7]

But for the moment, we here-now have come much lower.

> And some of [us] have altogether become subject to the destiny of this world, but others are sometimes subject to it and sometimes belong to themselves; others again accept all that it is necessary to endure but are able to be self-possessed in all that is their own work, living according to another code of laws, that which governs the whole of reality, and submitting themselves to [this] other ordinance.[8]

---

3 See Peter Harvey, "Buddha and Cakravartins," in *Encyclopedia of Buddhism*, ed. Damien Keown and Charles S. Prebish (London: Routledge, 2013), 153.
4 Plato, *Statesman*, 268d–272e; see also Plato, *Laws*, 3.713–4.
5 Julian, "Letter to Themistius [264d]," in *Works*, vol. 2, 231.
6 Plotinus, *Ennead*, IV.3 [27].15, 1–4.
7 Ibid., III.4 [15].6, 27–30.
8 Ibid., IV.3 [27].15, 11–15.

"Self-possession" is the real *Sophrosune*, and those who are thus *sophrones, spoudaioi*, are free. This might serve to explain one of Plotinus's oddest remarks, that the *spoudaios* "would not have been *spoudaios* if he had had the guardian spirit (*daimon*) as a partner in his own activity."[9] Why should it be wrong for the spirit assigned or chosen to guide him, according to Plato's myth of Er,[10] actually to do so? Is the point, perhaps, that *spoudaioi* transcend the destiny identified as a *daimon*: they are *themselves* already *daimones*, and their guardian is a god?[11] Or is it only that no one deserves credit, or displays her own abiding character, if her acts are rather to her *daimon's* credit? The passage is obscure, and the moral (for me) quite out of reach! But Most is probably correct, at least in broad outline.

> As the philosopher dies, he rectifies the disciple's love for his person and redirects it as a whole beyond himself to an object which, unlike him, is immortal. To love him truly is to love him as a philosopher; if we will be true to him, we must not betray his teachings. So Socrates, with Crito; and so Plotinus, with Eustochius.[12]

Most's argument is that Plotinus, in saying to Eustochius, "I am still waiting for you" (*"se eti perimeno"*), meant not the banality that he had been waiting on his death-bed for Eustochius to visit, but that he was *still* waiting for Eustochius properly to philosophize and realize that Plotinus, the real Plotinus, was not the dead or dying body, nor that particular body-soul composite.[13] "Imagination," said Blake, is "the real and Eternal World of which this Vegetable Universe is but a faint shadow, and in which we shall live in our Eternal or Imaginative Bodies, when these Vegetable Mortal Bodies are no more."[14] Blake himself believed, with Plotinus, that

9   Ibid., III.4 [15].6, 2–3.
10   Plato, *Republic*, 10.620de; see also *Timaeus*, 90a. Obeyesekere points out that Plotinus seems to have decided against Plato's suggestions that there is a period between successive earthly incarnations, and that the discarnate souls "choose" their future lives, hinting instead that souls are immediately re-embodied as justice requires (Obeyesekere, *Imagining Karma*, 296–97).
11   Plotinus, *Ennead*, III.4 [15].6, 3–4: note, *pace* Armstrong, "a god," not "God," "either the star itself [to which they at last ascend] or the god set above this power" (Plotinus, *Ennead*, III.4 [15].6, 27–30).
12   Most, "Plotinus' Last Words," 587.
13   See also Plato, *Phaedo*, 115a5–e8.
14   Blake, "*Jerusalem*, plate 77," in *Works*, 717.

the real world was not only *our* imagination, and wrote in 1827 that "in The Real Man The Imagination which Liveth for Ever" he was "stronger and stronger as [his] Foolish Body decay[ed]."[15] The advice Plotinus went on to give, "to bring the god in you back to the god in the all," was not directed merely at Eustochius, but at all his friends and followers. And to this I shall return.

Plotinus's goal, it is too often supposed, was merely for his *own* escape from Here; the words with which Porphyry chose to end his edition of the Collected Works are a description of the "life of gods and of the godlike and *eudaimones*" as one that is "deliverance from the things of this world, a life which takes no delight in the things of this world, a flight of the alone to the Alone (*phuge monou pros monon*)."[16] That last phrase has become canonical, at least since John Smith's account,[17] and is used to intimate that Plotinus, rather as Cardinal Newman said of himself, was isolated from the objects that surrounded him, confirmed in his mistrust of the reality of physical phenomena and resting in the thought of two and only two absolute and luminously self-evident beings—himself and his Creator.[18] The command, indeed, to go up "naked" into the shrine, might require just that: our heavenly selves have no more need to remember earthly things, and are no longer moved by any old attachments, so as to see That alone with oneself alone (*autoi monoi auto monon*).[19] We cannot wholly hope to achieve that equanimity here-now, but we may still believe, with Plotinus, that our *real* self is already "There" (in the alongside, Real World) and exists in its felicity whatever happens here.[20] Even in the bull of Phalaris, even in the utmost agony, "There is another which, even while it is compelled to accompany that which suffers pain, remains in its own company and will not fall short of the vision of the universal good."[21]

---

15 Blake "To George Cumberland, 12th April 1827," in *Works*, 878.

16 Plotinus, *Ennead*, VI.9 [9].11, 48–51.

17 John Smith, "The Excellency and Nobleness of True Religion (1660)," in C. A. Patrides, *The Cambridge Platonists* (Cambridge: Cambridge University Press, 1969), 180.

18 After John Henry Newman, *Apologia pro Vita Sua* (Teddington, Middlesex: Echo Library, 2007), 28.

19 Plotinus, *Ennead*, II.6 [1].7, 5–12. See also VI.7 [38].34, 8. See Clark, *Plotinus*, 45–63.

20 Plotinus, *Ennead*, IV.8 [6].8.

21 Ibid., I.4 [46].13, 6ff. Phalaris, tyrant of Acragas (570–554 BC), served as a recurrent example of bestial and sadistic tyranny. His "bull" was designed by

So the message may seem to be that the aspirant to enlightenment should abandon all entanglements, and go out into the world "alone," in complete obedience. "If a man is able to follow the spirit which is above him, he comes to be himself above, living that spirit's life,"[22] and so (perhaps) no longer needing it as a partner. He becomes, one might say, a god, beyond all human and animal connections as only a god can be. "He who has thus given up (the performance of) all rites, who is solely intent on his own (particular) object, (and) free from desires, destroys his guilt by his renunciation and obtains the highest state."[23] The Hindu would-be *sannyasin* celebrates his own funeral and is thereafter dead to all earlier caste, civil and family restrictions—a renunciation even more complete than Rogatianus's refusal of official rank and duties. A closer and yet more alarming analogue would be the Cynic's life, deliberately and consciously *apolis*:

> The life-style that the Cynics were supposed to adopt was based on deliberate transgression of all interdictions, especially those of a dietary or sexual nature, upon which society is founded: hence the defense of raw versus cooked, of masturbation and incest versus a regulated sexuality, and in fact, of cannibalism.[24]

> The enemy of the Cynics was the civilizing hero of Aeschylus and of Protagoras, Prometheus. In short, to borrow from Plutarch, the intention was "to brutalize our lives" (*ton bion apotheriosai*): we should not be surprised, therefore, that the Cynics should have adopted as their own the slogan: "freedom as in the time of Cronos."[25]

Obviously, Plotinus's own life-choices were unlike that vision (which sounds much like the garbled account of supposedly "savage" life I have discussed before), but we need to understand more clearly *why* they were, and what might be amiss with the sheerly

---

an Athenian bronze-worker, so that the screams of the one roasted inside it should be transmuted, through a system of valves, to "music" of a sort. The bronze-worker himself was its first victim, and Phalaris (reputedly) its last (though the same technique is also reported later).

22 Ibid., III.4 [15].3, 18–19.
23 Bühler, *Manu Samhita*, 127 [6.96].
24 Pierre Vidal-Naquet, "Plato's Myth of the Statesman, the Ambiguities of the Golden Age and of History," *The Journal of Hellenic Studies* 98 (1978): 137.
25 Ibid., 135.

antinomian life. The "Guru Trap" is one that has corrupted many grand designs:[26] if we are so sure of ourselves, and of our own proclaimed "identity" or "intimacy" with the One, then everything we do and feel is somehow sacralized, despite the initial demand that we cut off all usual affections and desires. Those who most fondly proclaim their own pure motives and their disdain for ordinarily civil virtues are unfortunately liable to act out fantasies of control and self-assurance that humbler souls don't dare.[27] Plotinus's own vehement rejection of the suggestion that pupils have sex with their teachers on demand[28] is an indication of his own superior thought.

For the connotations of "*monos*" are not quite so clear. Earlier in the same treatise with which Porphyry closed the work, Plotinus speaks rather of gazing upon the One "the most pure with the pure intellect" (*katharoi toi noi to katharotaton theasthai*), and it is the *purity* of both parties rather than their supposed "solitude" that matters.[29] "Single-minded" is a better gloss than "alone." The point is not that either the attentive soul or intellect or the One itself have no company, that nothing and no one now matters to the aspirant, but that nothing additional is needed for the vision. So also Evagrius (345–399), a Christian monk much influenced by Origen:

> When you pray do not form images of the divine within yourself, nor allow your mind to be impressed with any form but approach the Immaterial immaterially (*aulos toi auloi prosithi*) and you will come to understanding.[30]

The Intellect, as Anaxagoras obscurely claimed, is "pure and unmixed," and the One is "separate,"[31] but neither is therefore "alone." On the contrary, the Intellect "encompasses in himself all

---

26   See John Wren-Lewis, "Death-knell of the Guru System?: Perfectionism Versus Enlightenment," *Journal of Humanistic Psychology* 34 (1994): 46–61 with particular reference to the life of Jiddu Krishnamurti.

27   See Clark, "Godlike Virtues," for further discussion of the apparent paradox that it is virtuous to wish to be godlike, though gods themselves aren't ordinarily virtuous. My view is that many scholars misunderstand Plotinus's supposed "intellectualism": for example, Bobonich, *Plato's Utopia Recast*, 202, citing Sedley "The Ideal of Godlikeness."

28   Porphyry, *Life*, 15, 7–17.

29   Plotinus, *Ennead*, VI.9 [9].3, 26–27.

30   Robert E. Sinkewicz, *On Prayer* 66, in *Evagrius of Pontus: the Greek ascetic corpus* (Oxford: Oxford University Press, 2003), 199.

31   Plotinus, *Ennead*, V.1 [10].9, 1–3.

things immortal, every intellect, every god, every soul, all forever unmoving."[32] And the One, the eternal focus of both Intellect and the Soul, "is all things and not a single one of them."[33] "Its superabundance makes something other than itself."[34] We are to avoid confusion, not to avoid company: on the contrary, it was avoiding company that ensured our fall.[35]

The metaphysical analysis of these claims has generated many volumes: in my present context, it is enough to say that going unburdened to the pure source and goal of all does not demand that we care less for what the One engenders. We are to be purged of error so as to meet, in silence, the reason for all existence and our own. "Nothing is separated or cut off from that which is before it."[36] We are united in ourselves and with all other daughters of the One by focusing upon the One, "bringing the god in us to meet the god in the All." So we may find ourselves within, as it were, Indra's Net of Jewels (first attested in the *Atharva Veda*, and amplified in the *Avatamsaka Sutra*), in which each jewel reflects the light in all the others.

> All things there are transparent, and there is nothing dark or opaque; everything and all things are clear to the inmost part to everything; for light is transparent to light. Each there has everything in itself and sees all things in every other, so that all are everywhere and each and every one is all and the glory is unbounded; for each of them is great, because even the small is great; the sun There is all the stars, and each star is the sun and all the others. A different kind of being stands out in each, but in each all are manifest.[37]

Once we have put aside delusion we have some chance of realizing that we are each a variant, a version, of the whole, and have our being in that choral dance.

---

3 2   Ibid., V.1 [10].4, 11–12.
3 3   Ibid., V.2 [11].1, 1–2.
3 4   Ibid., V.2 [11].1, 9–10.
3 5   Ibid., V.1 [10].1, 4.
3 6   Ibid., V.2 [11].1, 22–3.
3 7   Ibid., V.8 [31].4, 5–12. So also E. R. Dodds, "Numenius and Ammonius," in *Sources de Plotin* (Entretiens Hardt 5), 1–61 (Geneva: Fondation Hardt, 1960), 23; see Francis H. Cook, *Hua-Yen Buddhism: The Jewel Net of Indra* (Pennsylvania: Penn State Press, 1977); Thomas McEvilley, "Plotinus and Vijnanavada Buddhism," *Philosophy East and West* 30, no. 2 (1980): 181–93.

TAKING REFUGE IN THE SANGHA

One of the common features of the multifarious tradition generally known as "Buddhism"—a tradition as varied and sometimes acrimonious as its main rival, "Abrahamism"[38]—is that those embarking on the Buddhist project take refuge in "the Buddha, the Dharma and the Sangha." The Buddha is primarily, for all branches, the Nepalese prince and ascetic Gautama, and by imaginative extension all the enlightened Buddhas over uncounted ages. The Dharma comprises the Four Truths—that all is *dukkha,* that the origin and cause of *dukkha* is desire, that bringing an end to desire will therefore also end *dukkha,* and that the route to the end, the blowing out (*nirvana*) of desire, is the "noble eightfold path." *Dukkha* is, in Platonic terms, Becoming. The Sangha, finally, is the community, both locally and forever, of those who have "entered the stream," whether as monk or lay.[39] And it had earlier, more obviously political, associations.

> The word *sangha* was actually first used for the popular assemblies that governed many South Asian cities in the Buddha's lifetime—roughly the fifth century BC—and early Buddhist texts insist that the Buddha was himself inspired by the example of these republics, and in particular the importance they accorded to convening full and frequent public assemblies.[40]

Lay members share the goal but may hope only for a "better birth" next time, when they or their successor selves may be monks or nuns, and so hope a little more securely for an end of troubles in a few lives more. Monks bind themselves, or are bound, to refrain from killing, from theft, from sex, and from any boasting of their accomplishments.[41]

---

38   In taking "Abrahamism," comprising "religions of the book," as a religious taxon rival to "Buddhism" I do not imply that all Abrahamists necessarily share an essential doctrine unknown to other religious (though they do indeed share a great deal): the point is rather that they trace their historical origin to Abraham (whether he was a historical character or not), as members of a biological taxon have a common ancestor not shared with other taxa, "like saying that the clan of the Heraclids was a unity, not in the sense of a unity common to all its members, but because they all come from one ancestor" (*Ennead* VI.1 [42].3, 3–4).

39   See Richard F. Gombrich, *Theravada Buddhism: a social history from Ancient Benares to Modern Colombo* (London: Routledge, 2006), 89–118.

40   Graeber and Wengrow, *Dawn of Everything,* 319–20, citing Gombrich, *Theravada Buddhism,* 49–50.

41   Rupert Gethin, *The Foundations of Buddhism* (Oxford: Oxford University Press, 1998), 89.

> [One seeking ordination as a novice] recites the formula of
> going for refuge to the Buddha, Dharma, and Sangha, and
> takes the ten precepts or "rules of training" (1) to refrain
> from harming living creatures, (2) to refrain from taking
> what is not given, (3) to refrain from all sexual activity, (4)
> to refrain from false speech, (5) to refrain from intoxicants
> that cause heedlessness, (6) to refrain from eating after
> midday, (7) to refrain from attending entertainments, (8)
> to refrain from wearing jewelry or using perfumes, (9) to
> refrain from sleeping on luxurious beds, (10) to refrain
> from handling gold and silver.[42]

Full ordination may follow later, and the monk or nun is thereafter wholly dependent on the unforced gifts of others, having
neither household nor profession.

No doubt, since they are human, these restraints are often
endorsed in word more than in deed (and especially one last, to
refrain from boasting). The Guru Trap, as I acknowledged before,
is a risk especially for those who might otherwise be *good* Gurus.
Emphasis on the significance of the Sangha is an indication that
even for those branches of the tradition which have emphasized
"self-help" and admired the accomplished sage, the *arhat*, enlightenment and the path to it are not solitary endeavors. Even Gautama,
though in the end he was "enlightened" by himself, had worked
with others over many lives and at once sought out his most recent
companions to convey his gospel. Enlightenment itself precluded
any notion of saving oneself without considering "others." Later
Buddhist tradition made explicit the goal of the Bodhisattva—that
no one can be or should be "saved" till all souls are. Plotinus might
truly say that he is waiting still.

> I shall not come to my final passing away, Malignant One,
> until this holy life taught by me shall become successful,
> prosperous, far-renowned, popular and widespread, until
> it is well proclaimed among gods and men.[43]

---

42 Ibid., 87.

43 Sister Vajira and Francis Story, *Last Days of the Buddha (Mahà Parinibbana
Sutta)* (Kandy, Sri Lanka: Buddhist Publication Society, 1988), 43; Obeyesekere,
Imagining Karma, 115 (the Buddha is here addressing Màra, personification of all
the world's ills). Obeyesekere here prefers "Malignant One" to the translators'
"Evil One" (ibid., 379), doubting that Buddhism has any "theory of 'Evil' in
the monotheistic sense." Obeyesekere slightly misrepresents the passage: the
Buddha goes on to accept the Malignant One's suggestion that he can now

That there were Buddhist missionaries loose in the Mediterranean world by Plotinus's day seems certain: King Asoka of the Mauryan Empire (who reigned 268–232 BC), four centuries before, had sent such missions out to proclaim the Buddha's way.[44] The question might then arise, why were there no known Buddhist sects and coteries in Egypt and elsewhere? And the possible answer is that there was at least one such—moderately unorthodox—branch, which we call the Epicurean.[45] Would-be Epicureans also take refuge in three things: in the memory of their founder, the world-savior, Epicurus; in the fourfold remedy he announced to all, that "God presents no fears, death no worries, and while good is readily attainable, evil is readily endurable";[46] and finally, in the Society of Epicurean Friends. Epicurean doctrine, like the Buddhist, denied the existence of a distinct substantial self, preferring to notice transient thoughts and feelings, identifiable as soul-atoms which would disperse around the infinite expanse when their present framework fell apart.[47] Whether Epicureans committed to the notion that each agent must and should primarily seek her own pleasure can be as much concerned for the continuing welfare of their "friends" (as Cicero's Epicurean spokesman Torquatus claims) has been much discussed, without perhaps fully realizing the implications of a strong "no self" doctrine.[48] Whatever the meta-ethical or psychological theory here, it is, in practice, that society which offers a companionable model for a Plotinian order, one separate from all *poleis*, and all

die (as Gautama) since his disciples have properly internalized the *dharma*: Ananda is blamed for failing to ask the Buddha to live on till the end of the age before he agreed with the Malignant One (Mara).

44　Anandajoti Bhikkhu, trans., *Asoka and the Missions: from Extended Majavamsa V, XII–XV, XVIII–XX)*, ed. G. P. Malalasekera (Oxford: Pali Text Society, Oxford, 1988), 46, drawing from the *Edicts of Asoka*, inscribed on pillars throughout that King's domain: "The Seer Mahārakkhita went to the locality of the [Greeks] and preached the Kālakārāma Discourse in the midst of the people. One hundred and seventy thousand breathing beings attained Path and Fruit, and ten thousand went forth."

45　See Stephen R. L. Clark, *Ancient Mediterranean Philosophy* (London: Continuum, 2013), 151–56.

46　Philodemus, *Against the Sophists*, 4.9–14: Long and Sedley, *Hellenistic Philosophers*, vol. 1, 156 [25J].

47　Diogenes Laertius, *Lives*, 10.63–6.

48　See Cicero, *De Finibus* 1.67–8; see Matthew Evans, "Can Epicureans be Friends?" *Ancient Philosophy* 24 (2004): 407–24.

empires, but without the antinomian follies of some other sects.[49]

There was another possibility, of course, in the nascent Christian churches or assemblies, which were founded as explicitly as Plotinus would have wished on devotion to the Father, through the Incarnate Word—but those churches seem not to have attracted him. Ammonius Saccas, his teacher, may have been a Christian,[50] and there are points on which pagan and Christian thinkers could agree. But the treatise "Against the Gnostics" (as Porphyry labelled it) included harsh rebukes against those who thought themselves superior, even by adoption, to the stars, and presumed to "judge the angels" (as Paul of Tarsus expected[51]). Respectable pagans, for whom Minucius's Caecilius spoke, generally felt more strongly:

> Is it not deplorable that a gang—excuse my vehemence in using strong language for the cause I advocate—a gang, I say, of discredited and proscribed desperadoes band themselves against the gods? Fellows who gather together illiterates from the dregs of the populace and credulous women with the instability natural to their sex, and so organize a rabble of profane conspirators, leagued together by meetings at night and ritual fasts and unnatural repasts, not for any sacred service but for piacular rites, a secret tribe that shuns the light, silent in the open, but talkative in hid corners; they despise temples as if they were tombs; they spit upon the gods; they jeer at our sacred rites; pitiable themselves, they pity (save the mark) our priests; they despise titles and robes of honor, going themselves half-naked![52]

Plotinus would have been kinder but shared enough of pagan sensibility to find such gatherings disagreeable, despite also wishing to curb the influence of more malicious *daimones*. An Epicurean

---

49   Daniela Patrizia Taormina and Angela Longo, eds., *Plotinus and Epicurus: Matter, Perception, Pleasure* (Cambridge: Cambridge University Press, 2017), is concerned only with Plotinus's ongoing discussion of Epicurean metaphysics, but makes clear that Plotinus was well aware of the Epicurean alternative.
50   Eusebius, *History*, 158–60 [6.19, 5–10]. There is scope for confusion between Ammonius Saccas and Ammonius the Christian historian, as well as between the two putative Origens—one the friend of Plotinus, and another(?) the Christian theologian. See Mark Edwards, "Ammonius, Teacher of Origen," *The Journal of Ecclesiastical History* 44, no. 2 (1993): 169–81.
51   I Corinthians 6:3; see also Revelations 2:26.
52   Minucius Felix, *Octavius*, 335 [8.4–5] (Caecilius speaks).

fellowship displeased him for other reasons: he mocks materialists as being "flightless birds" and plainly would not agree to "pleasure" (ordinarily understood) as the true *summum bonum*.[53] But Epicurus himself would have been much more to his taste. And the example of either Christian or Epicurean companionships may still be helpful. The point in both cases is that they are companionships united by a faith, rather than by any ethnic, civic or professional identity, and their members have *determined* their own course (with whatever caveats about their genuine freedom). They have, both Christian and Epicurean, in some sense been "called out" from the prevailing culture, with no fear of civil or imperial commands, but also without a merely "cynical" rejection of all ancestral norms. If it seems strange to think of Epicureans so, it is because their doctrine has been diminished, by time and satire, into a merely hedonistic care for bodily pleasures such as food, drink and sex. Epicurus's own doctrine demanded that such demands be diminished till they can easily be satisfied without greed or scandal, and that friends should live together in amity.[54]

> This withdrawal into the Garden is a way of carving out
> a little plot of immanence, beyond the imperial powers,
> in which to cultivate healthy forms of life. As the old
> Athenian Agora was an immanent domain politically and
> socially structured very differently to the imperial states,
> the Epicurean Garden is a small plot of earth in which
> everyone can equally nurture his or her own pleasure

---

53 Plotinus, *Ennead*, IV.7 [2].2; V.9 [5].1.

54 Diogenes Laertius, *Lives*, 10.131–2: "When we say, then, that pleasure is the end and aim, we do not mean the pleasures of the prodigal or the pleasures of sensuality, as we are understood to do by some through ignorance, prejudice, or willful misrepresentation. By pleasure we mean the absence of pain in the body and of trouble in the soul. It is not an unbroken succession of drinking-bouts and of revelry, not sexual love, not the enjoyment of the fish and other delicacies of a luxurious table, which produce a pleasant life; it is sober reasoning, searching out the grounds of every choice and avoidance, and banishing those beliefs through which the greatest tumults take possession of the soul. Of all this the beginning and the greatest good is prudence. Wherefore prudence is a more precious thing even than philosophy; from it spring all the other virtues, for it teaches that we cannot [live pleasantly without also living wisely, well and justly: *tou phronimos kai kalos kai dikaios zen*]; nor [live wisely, well and justly without also living pleasantly]. For the virtues have grown into one with a pleasant life, and a pleasant life is inseparable from them." I have amended the Loeb translation to be a little closer to the Greek.

(*hedone*), in conjunction with the community, and beyond the touch of the Empire.[55]

A neglected feature of the Epicurean Garden is that Epicurus established cults in honor of his own family (in lieu of more conventional Olympian worship). He might have responded to questions about his own consistency in this (for his dead family was, he believed, dissolved and dispersed at random through the infinite array) as Matteo Ricci, the sixteenth-century Jesuit missionary, described the Chinese rituals that involved the presentation of food or drink "to their ancestral spirits":

> They [the Chinese] do not believe that the dead will come to eat or even need these things. They say that there is no other way to express their love and gratitude to the dead. Some told me that these rituals are set up for the living people, not the dead—that is, to teach the children and the ignorant to respect their parents that are still alive.... In any case, they do not think that the people who are gone are gods or spirits, thus they do not pray for anything. It has nothing to do with idolatry. Hence it seems not to be superstition.[56]

What rituals *Plotinus* would have preferred, beyond the continued celebration of the birth or death days of Socrates and Plato,[57] we can only guess. Hestia, Zeus and Athena would probably have featured there as well as in Platonopolis. Plotinus's patron Gallienus had revived Heracles as a focus for imperial loyalty and his own self-image (he also invoked Hermes, Demeter, Zeus and the Sun).[58] And Plotinus himself remarked that, while others worship the stars, "we worship the Sun."[59]

---

55   Ryan J. Johnson, "Ethics in the Garden of Epicurus," in Ryan J. Johnson, *The Deleuze-Lucretius Encounter* (Edinburgh: Edinburgh University Press, 2017), 214.

56   Matteo Ricci, *China in the Sixteenth Century: the journal of Matteo Ricci: 1583–1610*, trans. Louis J. Gallagher (New York: Random House, 1942), 96. I owe this reference to Yang Xiao of Kenyon College, Ohio.

57   Porphyry, *Life*, 2.39–44.

58   Blois, *Policy of Gallienus*, 150–59.

59   Plotinus, *Ennead*, IV.4 [28].30. Proclus also, nearly two centuries later, made "obeisance to the rising, midday and setting sun" (Marinus, *Life of Proclus*, 22: Edwards, *Neoplatonic Saints*, 93); see also Copenhaver, *Hermetica*, 53 [13.16]: whether Plotinus had a similar practice we cannot tell. See also M. Wakoff, "Awaiting the Sun: A Plotinian Form of Contemplative Prayer," in *Platonic Theories of Prayer*, ed. J. M. Dillon and A. Timotin (Leiden: Brill, 2016).

Were Plotinus's associates, as described by Porphyry, all of a similar mind? It is a mark of "real friends" that they have all things in common[60]—and that indeed is how Plotinus seems to have lived, whether with Gemina in Rome or in Zethus's Campanian villa. His friends, so Porphyry tells us, were almost all away in his last illness: "Porphyry was staying at Lilybaeum, Amelius was in Apamea in Syria, and Castricius was in Rome: only Eustochius was with him."[61] Of his other named friends, Gallienus, Zoticus and Zethus the Arab were dead, as well as his masseurs (Gallienus by assassination and the rest by plague), and the survivors, so Porphyry said, avoided him "because he had the habit of greeting everyone *apo stomatos*": a phrase which may either mean that he greeted them with a kiss (and so they kept away) or else that he would engage them in discussion, despite the damage to his throat (and so his friends were turned away).[62] He did not wish, we presume, to burden Gemina's household with his care (or was she dead too?). Edwards has proposed that Porphyry, in sketching Plotinus's life, was aiming to establish him as a sort of rival to Christ: deserted by his friends, and dying in some pain, but still with their welfare in mind.[63] But would Plotinus have thought of it as desertion? His last words may indicate otherwise: what happened to his body was of less concern, and "nothing is a long way off or far from anything else."[64] The companionship survives mere spatial distance, and all friends would be recognized hereafter.

The projected city in Campania may after all not have been intended as a Platonic *polis*, as Porphyry supposed, but simply—like Epicurus's garden[65]—as a home for Plotinus's group of friends, with

60 Epicurus disagreed: Diogenes Laertius, *Lives*, 10.11: "Such a practice in his opinion implied mistrust, and without confidence there is no friendship." Presumably friends would be expected to provide for others in their need, without disclaiming their personal rights of property.

61 Porphyry, *Life*, 2, 32–34.

62 See Lloyd P. Gerson, ed., *Plotinus: The Enneads*, trans. George Boys-Stones, et al. (Cambridge: Cambridge University Press, 2003), 18n3; Edwards, *Neoplatonic Saints*, 3.

63 Edwards, *Neoplatonic Saints*, xxxv–xxxvi; also Edwards, "Birth, Death and Divinity in Porphyry's *Life of Plotinus*," in *Biography and Panegyric in Late Antiquity*, ed. Tomas Hägg and Phillip Rousseau (Berkeley: University of California Press, 2000).

64 Plotinus, *Ennead*, IV.3 [27].11, 22–23.

65 Diogenes Laertius, *Lives*, 10.16–17: he bequeathed the garden for the common life of the fellowship, in perpetuity. See Diskin Clay, "The Athenian

a structure (if at all) determined solely by the needs of friendship.[66] "Friends," that is, of "the man within," not merely of the body-soul composite.[67] It may be that there were "Hermeticists" with a similar project, united by devotion to the teachings of Hermes Trismegistus, though there seems to be no clear evidence that their companionship was anything more than virtual. How practical could it be? How precisely would such a company be managed, and with what resources: who would be farming the land, weaving the clothes and clearing up after philosophers? Would these also be "friends," or novices awaiting initiation, or such slaves and servants as Gallienus or Castricius might have assigned the task? We may hope that they would be friends, and that all associates would take their turn at such necessary manual or menial occupations.[68] It would have been a would-be permanent home for what Sangharakshita recognizes as something very like an Indian *ashram*.[69]

But maybe there was, for Plotinus, a more familiar and acceptable model even than the ones I have described. Maybe the Egyptian priests achieved something like this life.

> In his account of the Egyptian priests, who, he says, were regarded in Egypt as being also philosophers, Chaeremon the Stoic [a first century Egyptian priest] tells how they chose the temples for places wherein to pursue wisdom.

Garden" for a sympathetic study of Epicurus's life and legacy (including the family cults that he established for his followers).

66 Sabo reaches a similar conclusion in "The Politics of the One." See also Mark Edwards, "Plotinus and the Emperors," *Symbolae Osloenses* 69 (1994): 137–47, and Kamenskikh, "The Dialectic of the Other," on later Neo-Platonic communities.

67 Plotinus, *Ennead*, I.1 [53].10, 14–15.

68 Georgette Heyer, *The Quiet Gentleman* (London: Arrow Books, 2005), 33, has a barbed and depressingly plausible comment on a similar project devised by Southey and Coleridge (see Samuel Taylor Coleridge, "Pantisocracy," in *The Complete Poems*, 57–58) in 1794, in which everyone would spend two hours each day (in a village to be established on the banks of the Susquehanna River) on necessary domestic duties: "Of course, Mama and Mrs [Robert] Southey readily perceived that although the gentlemen might adhere to the two-hour rule, it would be quite impossible for the ladies to do so. In fact, Mama was of the opinion that although the gentlemen might be induced, if strongly adjured, to draw water, and to chop the necessary wood, they would certainly have done no more. And no one ... could have placed the least reliance on their *continued* performance of such household tasks, for, you know, if they had been engaged in philosophical discussion they would have forgotten all about them."

69 Sangharakshita, *Sangha* (Kindle location 3085).

In view of their desire for contemplation, it was natural for them to pass their time in the temples, for there they found security on account of the reverence that men have for the divine—everyone honored the philosophers as if they were sacred animals. Besides, their living in the temples brought them peace, for they only mixed with other people during festivals and feasts....They divided the night for the observation of the heavens; sometimes also for the divine ritual; and the daytime for the adoration of the gods....The rest of their time they spent in the study of arithmetic and geometry, and they were constantly searching for and discovering something new—in short, their whole lives were dedicated to scholarly investigation.[70]

So also Philo's Therapeutai, as described in his *De Vita Contemplativa*, whether or not these were real communities or only utopian imaginings.[71] They even manage without slaves—and we might hope that Plotinus's friends would too (though Gemina's household had them).

But is there a problem with supposing that Plotinus's philosophy would encourage such friendly associations? Surely we already know that the death of friends and relations will not trouble one with a "perfect life," but only that part of him still lacking in "intelligence" (that is, *nous*)?[72] What sort of friendship can this be, if the death of friends doesn't bother him? Must not good friends mourn for each other? Perhaps, but not as "those who have no hope": distance, again, doesn't matter, and neither does departure. Perhaps he may suffer grief, as he may also suffer some sudden panic attack, but "the wise man [in him] will come and drive it

---

70 Porphyry, *On Abstinence*, IV.6, 8; see Fowden, *Egyptian Hermes*, 54–55.

71 "This kind exists in many places in the inhabited world, for perfect goodness must needs be shared both by Greeks and the world outside Greece, but it abounds in Egypt in each of the nomes as they are called and especially round Alexandria. But the best of these votaries journey from every side to settle in a certain very suitable place which they regard as their fatherland. This place is situated above the Mareotic Lake on a somewhat low-lying hill very happily placed both because of its security and the pleasantly tempered air": Philo, "On the Contemplative Life," in *Works*, 21–22; see further *Works*, vol. 9, 21–39, 64–90, 125–169; see Troels Engberg-Pedersen, "Philo's *De Vita Contemplativa* as a Philosopher's Dream," *Journal for the Study of Judaism* 30, no. 1 (1999): 40–64.

72 Plotinus, *Ennead*, I.4 [46].4, 32–37.

away and quiet the child in him." Our memories of friends and children and spouse will remain, but without the associated desires and pains of our worse parts, as we draw closer to that condition in which all good things are forever present.[73]

> A man of this sort will not be unfriendly or unsympathetic (not *aphilos* nor *agnomon*); he will be like this to himself and in dealing with his own affairs; but he will render to his friends all that he renders to himself, and so will be the best of friends as well as remaining intelligent [along with "having *nous*"].[74]

He will love others as himself and stay friends even with those whose opinions he thinks wrong-headed![75] His love, that is, is directed not to an image, the mere *appearance* of the one in question, but towards the real waking self, a companion in the chorus, whatever its current errors, mishaps or misleading looks. There is no trace, it seems, of the attitude to be found in some Jain literature, which positively requires that all family and friendly associations should be renounced if there is to be any hope of escaping the round of births.[76] Plotinus expects to know and to appreciate his friends forever.[77]

The community of friends, or of friends of this real sort, may be Plotinus's best image, in this world, of that sphere with many faces which is the eternal *Nous*,[78] as it is also Buddha's legacy to the world, the *Sangha*. "A community organizing its affairs by uncoerced vote rather than authoritarian fiat, and achieving (in aspiration, at least) a state of unanimous harmony, represents a powerful ideal," but perhaps not one that serves for everyone.[79] Such a congregation of the—relatively—like-minded is a social form different from either tribe or *polis*, and it may be that it can survive as such only if its members are as celibate as monks or nuns. Once there are children, and the responsibilities of

---

73 Ibid., IV.3 [27].32, 1–15; see also IV.4 [28].28 on the bodily passions that we must someday shed if we are to see things clearly.

74 Plotinus, *Ennead*, I.4 [46].15, 17–25: see above on the misleading equation of "having *nous*" with "being intelligent."

75 Ibid., II.9 [33].10, 3–6.

76 See Granoff, *Forest of Thieves*, for a collection of Jain fables.

77 See Plotinus, *Ennead*, IV.3 [27].18, 19–24.

78 Plotinus, *Ennead*, VI.7 [38].15, 25–28.

79 Collins, *Nirvana*, 447.

parenthood and teaching, it would seem hard to avoid the gradual emergence of households, villages and self-governing *poleis,* with manifold excuses to seek a little more, of land and inherited wealth. Such duties—of celibacy, poverty and even obedience—are best internalized through established codes and ceremonies, and it is does not seem likely that Plotinus himself encouraged such precise initiations: it seems that anyone who cared to come could join his discussion group. His successors might have found more formal rules (with an eye, perhaps, to the hierarchy of gods and demigods), or remained committed to his own more generous spirit.

DESERT DAYS

Once again, the instruction to all aspirant philosophers to fly "alone to the alone" did not mean that we should hope to progress "by ourselves," nor that we would then be isolated from all other lives, all by ourselves with "the One," as if that latter were a distinct entity, or as if we were ourselves wholly distinct individuals. Neither the body-soul composite that is now called "Stephen" nor whatever enduring soul has animated multiple "other" lives and will do so again can ever exist entirely by "herself." There are no such distinct and independent beings. Nor did Plotinus himself make any effort to live in solitude, even in the last days of his ongoing illness.

> Minds are essentially dialogical in that they are made to
> share in divine community and each other. This suggests,
> instead, an intimate, self-reflexive and dialogical model
> of mind, in which thought, at its best, is not really a
> function of one mind, but of all minds in God.[80]

And yet the ideal of earthly solitude deserves a little attention. Is that not, after all, how the Desert Fathers (and some Mothers) actually behaved? Did they not abandon their past lives and duties to live in isolation, in the Syrian or Egyptian deserts? "Holy Men" could be recognized by their dissociation from all social and natural goods. Was this, perhaps, what Plotinus *should* have meant, even though he didn't? And was he, unconsciously, deterred from the experiment because he preferred the "intellectual" to all merely "manual" crafts and so had to rely on menials? It seems that some

---

80   Kevin Corrigan, *Evagrius and Gregory: Mind, Soul and Body in the 4th Century* (London: Routledge, 2009), 42.

pagans at least accepted the vocation: "The Neoplatonist monk Serapion [sic: Sarapio] went into the desert in order to devote himself entirely to studying the hymns of Orpheus. Damascius, guided by a dream, withdrew into a noisome cave in order to pray continuously to Cybele."[81] Whether they managed their own necessary domestic tasks is unclear. The Desert Fathers at any rate were unmoved by ordinarily social hierarchies and willingly engaged in simple manual tasks (weaving rope or baskets), both to acquire what little cash they needed and (more importantly) to have some occupation for their hands! Abba Paul, far out in the Porphyrian desert and with no ready market for the baskets that he wove, continued to weave them, but burnt up the accumulation at each year's end,[82] so emphasizing that the point lay in the labor itself rather than the product: a form, perhaps, of deliberately transient artistry (for of course the baskets had to be well designed and woven).

> When the holy Abba Antony lived in the desert he was beset by accidie, and attacked by many sinful thoughts. He said to God, "Lord, I want to be saved, but these thoughts do not leave me alone; what shall I do in my afflictions? How can I be saved?" A short while afterwards, when he got up to go out, Antony saw a man like himself sitting at his work, getting up from his work to pray, then sitting down and plaiting a rope, then getting up again to pray. It was an angel of the Lord sent to correct and reassure him. He heard the angel saying to him, "Do this and you will be saved." At these words, Antony was filled with joy and courage. He did this, and he was saved.[83]

Accidie, acedia, is an all-too-familiar mood, mingling boredom, restlessness, despair. "When he reads," so Evagrius of Pontus said,

---

81   Spengler, *Decline*, vol. 2, 254, after Damascius, *Philosophical History*, ed. Polymnia Athanassiadi (Athens: Apamea, 1999), 267 [111]; see also ibid., 23-24. *Pace* Spengler, Damascius does not say that Sarapio went into the desert, but only that he stayed home, with no concern for comfort, and spoke only to the philosopher Isidore.

82   John Cassian, *Institutes*, in *Works*, trans. Edgar C. S. Gibson (New York: Veritatis Splendor, 2012), 210 [10.24].

83   Anthony of Sourozh, *Sayings of the Desert Fathers*, trans. Benedicta Ward (Collegeville, MN: Cistercian Publications, 1975), 1-2 [Apophthegmata Antonios 1]: Gabriel Bunge, *Despondency: the spiritual teaching of Evagrius Ponticus on Acedia*, trans. Anthony P. Gythiel (New York: Vladimir's Seminary Press, 2012), 18.

"the one afflicted with acedia yawns a lot and readily drifts off to sleep; he rubs his eyes and stretches his arms; turning his eyes away from the book, he stares at the wall and again goes back to reading for a while; leafing through the pages, he looks curiously for the end of texts, he counts the folios and calculates the number of gatherings. Later, he closes the book and puts it under his head and falls asleep, but not a very deep sleep, for hunger then rouses his soul and has him show concern for its needs."[84] Such a mood, or demon, may drive the monk from his cell, advancing specious reasons to go visiting, to see what his neighbors are doing, or to comfort a weary widow. Evagrius's own remedy is the simple demand: that the monk *not* leave his cell.

> You must not abandon your cell in the time of temptations, fashioning excuses seemingly reasonable. Rather, you must remain seated inside, exercise perseverance, and valiantly welcome all attackers, especially the demon of acedia, who is the most oppressive of all but leaves the soul proven to the highest degree. Fleeing and circumventing such struggles teaches the mind to be unskilled, cowardly, and evasive.[85]

The spiritual focus of the desert fathers may seem rather different from Plotinus's. Plotinus approves of prayer and hopes for divine guidance. He is conscious of the manifold temptations the physical world affords, and also disapproves of arrogance. But the desert fathers seem often to be competing, as Gleason remarks in her amusing and insightful essay on the gossiping, sometimes backbiting, community of the desert, in "one-downmanship."[86] They are forever, it seems, insisting on their own sins, and paying the price of offering good meals to visitors (as their duty dictates) by starving themselves thereafter. They are always conscious—as few can be who have not tried to notice and resist demonic promptings—of what might lead them to abandon their vocation. Of them it might more plausibly be said, what was not true of Plotinus, that they were following, at personal cost, a strictly

---

84 Evagrius, "Eight Thoughts [6.15]," in Sinkewicz, *Evagrius*, 84.

85 Evagrius, "*Praktikos* 27-8," in ibid., 102. Cf. Pascal, *Pensées*, 39 [139]: "All the unhappiness of men arises from one single fact, that they cannot stay quietly in their own chamber."

86 Maud Gleason, "Visiting and News: Gossip and Reputation-Management in the Desert," *Journal of Early Christian Studies* 6, no. 3 (1998): 507.

self-centered ethos. It is true that they offered hospitality, and sought to comfort their despairing peers, as well as revealing for what it was the casual contempt that was usually shown to slaves, or women or Ethiopians. But outsiders might reasonably wonder what more positive good they might have done if they were not self-isolating far from most usual civil communities. On the other hand, perhaps they knew better than most that all our wishes to "do good" may rest on dubious motives, and that we cannot reliably accomplish what we think we wish until those motives are uncovered, cleansed, dismantled.

> But [the soul of the Elect] takes thought, first, not to commit any evils, and secondly, not to do good things inconsiderately; and, after he has subdued wickednesses, he strives also to subject to himself his very virtues, lest they should be converted into the sin of pride, if they should get beyond the control of the mind. For since, as has before been said, evils frequently spring from good deeds, through the vice of negligence; he observes with watchful zeal how arrogance rises from learning, cruelty from justice, carelessness from tenderness, anger from zeal, sloth from gentleness.[87]

In his seminal early essay on late antique "holy men," Peter Brown thought them dedicated solely to a radical self-alienation from society:

> Altogether "my" holy man lived a lonely and abrupt existence. His asceticism had less to do with a notion of the relation of body and spirit within himself as it did to separating himself out, through a melodramatically afflicted body, from his fellows: such asceticism was "a long drawn out, solemn ritual of dissociation—a becoming the total stranger."[88]

In a retrospective essay Brown seriously questioned his own earlier judgement: the "holy men" of late antiquity were not in

---

87   Gregory the Great, *Morals on the Book of Job*, vol. 3, trans. James Bliss (Ex Fontibus Company, 2012), 31 (44).86. See Plotinus, *Ennead*, II.3 [52].11 on the decay of virtues!

88   Peter Brown, "The Rise and Function of the Holy Man in Late Antiquity, 1971–1997," in *Journal of Early Christian Studies* 6.3 (1998): 368, citing Peter Brown, "The Rise and Function of the Holy Man in Late Antiquity," in *Society and the Holy in Late Antiquity* (Berkeley: University of California Press, 1982), 131.

fact so strange, either to the pagan past or to contemporary civil life. Even the most ascetic "holy men," perhaps especially the most ascetic, had their own supportive, critical community of their fellow ascetics (male and female both), and were acknowledged and consulted also by the communities from which they were only a little separate. "Spiritual life in the desert was...a collective project in which even the lowliest had their say,"[89] as Gleason remarks. Even if solitude was what they wanted, they did not achieve it, nor do they seem to have minded very much: their desire, as it was also Plotinus's, was rather to *return* to the one abiding community, the "holy and adorable Trinity."

Can we conceive a yet more radical detachment? Those who sought out solitude may still have found themselves dependent on the community, even the dispersed community, of monks. They may still have found themselves available for consultation or subjected to the fact-finding missions of those who questioned their "holiness." But maybe solitude was still what they desired—or at least the end of conversation. True "solitude," after all, must do without the natural world entirely, the company of plants and beasts, the continuing supply of air and water: we cannot even imagine, realistically, what life would be like "alone." True solitude is simply the end of life: is it then a life cut off from everything, even in death, that anyone could desire? "I could be bounded in a nutshell, and count myself a king of infinite space, were it not that I have bad dreams"[90]—and maybe thinking oneself such a singular king, as one of Charles Williams's characters supposes, is itself one of the bad dreams.[91] Williams's story, it should be said, is an evocative account of a *descent*, precisely, into solitude, into a condition where there is no Other, and no meaning anymore. We may hope that even there, in Hell, there will someday be a helper. Plotinus, at any rate, is unlikely to have been there.

---

89 Gleason, "Visiting and News," 521.
90 Shakespeare, *Hamlet*, Act 2, scene 2.
91 Charles Williams, *Descent into Hell* (London: Faber, 1937), 206.

THE SHAPE OF
THINGS TO COME

POSTHUMAN FORMS

Platonism, or Neo-Platonism, it has been my central thesis, is not a dead, text-bound philosophy. If it is to be taken seriously it must also apply both to our present experience and to our possible futures. How might Plotinus address the coming age?

Amongst the many topics I have addressed only tangentially is a question about "natural forms and limits." How many changes in our "natural form" can we endure and still be considered "human," and how much does it matter? Are there any "natural" or properly social limits on the changes we might approve? Are there real abiding Forms to serve as templates in beginningless and endless Becoming? Is there even such a thing as "Human Being," or as "Man," "Woman," "Child," any more than there is such a thing as "White Man" or "Black Man," "Asian" or "Aboriginal"? Might our future offer a seamless continuity, stretching like the soul from stars to microbes?[1] "For the soul is many things, and all things, both the things above and the things below down to the limits of all life."[2] Might each briefly and incompletely separate entity make its own choices from the infinite array, whether to model itself on one template or another, or add unusual powers and organs to its born-nature? And what is to count as such an incompletely separate entity? Chesterton's warning stands:

> The subconscious popular instinct against Darwinism was ... that when once one begins to think of man as a shifting and alterable thing, it is always easy for the strong and crafty to twist him into new shapes for all kinds of unnatural purposes. The popular instinct sees in such developments the possibility of backs bowed and hunch-backed for their burden, or limbs twisted for their

---

1   See Aristotle, *De Partibus Animalium*, 4.681a12–15.
2   Plotinus, *Ennead*, III.4 [15].3, 21–3.

task. It has a very well-grounded guess that whatever is
done swiftly and systematically will mostly be done by a
successful class and almost solely in their interests. It has
therefore a vision of unhuman hybrids and half-human
experiments much in the style of Mr. Wells's Island of
Dr. Moreau....The rich man may come to be breeding
a tribe of dwarfs to be his jockeys, and a tribe of giants
to be his hall-porters.[3]

Pure Matter is infinitely malleable, having no nature of its own,
and—in imagination—infinitely divisible. But of course such matter
is never perceptible, being bound in golden chains[4] to present the
vast array of transient material things, both stuffs and seemingly
distinct bodies. Any such material thing can be molded, melted,
amended into something else: chamber pots into heroic statues, tree-
trunks into idols.[5] Modern nano-technological proposals suggest
that engineers could, in principle, transform any material stuff into
new machines, new organisms, by simply re-ordering their atomic
structure. Genetic engineering would only be one, relatively minor,
use of the techniques. Any existing machine or stuff or organism
could be re-ordered as easily, in principle, as a Lego model, to
whatever extent the engineers propose. Nor should we expect our
experience of these changes to be unified or stable. What seems to us,
at present, to be a distinct individual, a distinct person, must itself
be malleable, divisible and without fixed boundaries. Fluidity rules
at both a material and mental level, nor can there be more than a
transient, illusory referent for self-identity: "I" can never last long
enough, nor be discrete enough, to be worth taking as a real con-
tributor to the beginningless and endless process of existence. Why

---

3   G. K. Chesterton, *What's Wrong with the World* (London: Cassell & Co., 1910),
259.
4   Plotinus, *Ennead*, I.8 [51].15.
5   Herodotus tells of Amasis, who made himself king of Egypt (*Histories*,
2.172). Finding that the Egyptians despised him for his common birth he had
a footbath (in which the courtiers had vomited and pissed, as well as wash-
ing their feet) made into a golden statue, to which they paid great reverence.
Pointing this out to them, he insisted that he too should now be reverenced:
what mattered was the function, not the stuff. The story reverses a Hebraic
argument, in which the prophet Isaiah (ca. 760–ca. 690 BC) mocked those
who cut down a tree and shape it for different aims: "some of it he takes and
warms himself; some he kindles and bakes bread on it; and some he makes
into a god and prostrates himself, shaping it into an idol and bowing down
before it" (Isaiah 44.15-16).

then should there be any rule of "personal autonomy," any "respect for persons"? "If a man chooses to treat himself as raw material, raw material he will be: not raw material to be manipulated, as he fondly imagined, by himself, but by mere appetite, that is, mere Nature, in the person of his de-humanized Conditioners."[6] It may be that those engineers themselves *imagine* that they are "in control," that they themselves transcend the process: obviously, they are mistaken—or rather, there is an illusion grounded in the mere material which dictates what happens both to the engineers and to their seeming subjects.

The problem that Lewis posed is simple: what will motivate the ongoing practice of manipulating, re-ordering, transforming both material and mental stuff? Will anything guide the process? We may imagine that our own fears, desires and ideologies will survive the solvent, and that we can expect to transform the given material in line with some ideal, whatever that ideal may be. But what ground have we for that expectation? If our emotions and our morals alike have in the past been "selected" from the random flux simply as having survived "Darwinnowing" so far, why should we expect that they will matter to our successors, or even that those successors will care whether they themselves have descendants? "Human behavior—like the deepest capacities for emotional response which drive and guide it—is the circuitous technique by which human genetic material has been and will be kept intact. Morality has no other demonstrable function"[7]—that is, or so E. O. Wilson declares, there is nothing else that it consistently does, and that explains the particular shape it takes (if it takes any). Neither claim—that it has this effect consistently and that there are no other possible explanations for its form—is beyond dispute. Even if they are true, it does not follow, of course (though Wilson, like Wells, almost seems to think it does) that we would therefore have good reason to *amend* our moral code to help preserve that material. Who are "we"? And what could count as "reason"? "When antient opinions and rules of life are taken away, the loss cannot possibly be estimated. From that moment we have no compass to govern us; nor can we know distinctly to what

---

6   C. S. Lewis, *The Abolition of Man: Reflections on education with special reference to the teaching of English in the upper forms of schools* (London: Geoffrey Bles, 1943), 50.
7   E. O. Wilson, *On Human Nature* (Cambridge, Mass: Harvard University Press, 1978), 167.

port we steer."[8] We may seek to suppress or to control an appetite for sugar, but only because we are not suppressing an appetite for a long and healthy life (with healthy teeth and a sound digestion). If neither appetite is grounded in anything but past reproductive success, neither has any definite priority.

When Lewis described the planetary angel Malacandra's conversation with the corrupt scientist Weston, in his interplanetary fantasy, he can hardly have imagined that anyone would so readily admit the charge:

> You do not love any one of your race.... You do not love the mind of your race, nor the body. Any kind of creature will please you if only it is begotten by your kind as they are now. It seems to me ... that what you really love is no completed creature but the very seed itself; for that is all that is left.

Weston retorts by appealing to "a man's [fundamental] loyalty to humanity," and the angel continues:

> I see now how the lord of the silent world has bent you. There are laws that all *hnau* know, of pity and straight dealing and shame and the like, and one of these is the love of kindred. He has taught you to break all of them except this one, which is not one of the greatest laws; this one he has bent till it becomes folly and has set it up, thus bent, to be a little, blind Oyarsa in your brain. And now you can do nothing but obey it, though if we ask you why it is a law you can give no other reason for it than for all the other and greater laws which it drives you to disobey.[9]

More consistent nihilists—such as those represented in the last volume of Lewis's interplanetary fantasy (*That Hideous Strength*)—feel no particular concern for humankind, nor even "their own selves" (in which they do not believe[10]). They merely "go with the flow"

---

8   Edmond Burke, *Reflections on the Revolution in France*, ed. Conor Cruise O'Brien (Harmondsworth: Penguin, 1968), 172.
9   Lewis, *Out of the Silent Planet*, 163. "*Hnau*" means "rational animal"; "*Oyarsa*" is the title of a planetary ruler in Lewis's mythology.
10   C. S. Lewis, *That Hideous Strength: a modern fairy-tale for grown-ups* (London: Harper Collins, 2005), 444: "For many years he had theoretically believed that all which appears in the mind as motive or intention is merely a by-product of what the body is doing.... Increasingly, his actions had been without motive. He did this and that, he said thus and thus, and did not know why. His mind

of whatever impulse is momentarily stronger. To a naïve young man's humanistic declaration, matching Weston's own residual concern for his species, the would-be Conditioner replies that this "pseudo-scientific language [does not modify] the essentially subjective and instinctive basis of the ethics [he is] describing."[11]

Two issues here coincide. On the one hand, what (if anything) maintains the unity—and so the being—of anything? On the other, what (if anything) might serve as a standard of value for that thing? Mere material continuity does not determine unity—either as one thing rather than many, or as one thing rather than another. There are no discontinuities in the merely material, nor anything that holds one bit uniquely to another. Nor does merely *psychological* identity offer a sufficient explanation—again, either of being *one* soul rather than many, or of being a *different* soul than another.

> "Know Yourself" is said to those who because of their selves' multiplicity have the business of counting themselves up and learning that they do not know all the numbers and kinds of things they are, or do not know any one of them, nor what their ruling principle is, or by what they are themselves.[12]

The next possibility may be that bodies and souls are made what they are by the presence in their stuff of some relevant Form: so far as anything, material or psychic, is at all it is so by participation in some Form—but Forms themselves are in their nature complex, and the question of their unity is still to be answered. Plotinus's own answer, especially in his "Treatise on the One or the Good" (*Ennead* VI.9 [9]), is that every thing—and also Everything—is made one by its orientation and organization towards its final cause, its goal. And finding what that goal is to be must itself be our continuing project. Where shall we find Apollo, the god "who sits in the center, on the navel of the earth, and is the interpreter of religion to all mankind"?[13]

---

was a mere spectator. He could not understand why that spectator should exist at all....There was no tolerating such an illusion! There were not, and must not be, such things as men."

11   Ibid., 317.

12   Plotinus, *Ennead*, VI.7 [38].41, 22–26. See also Plato, *Phaedrus*, 229b4–30a6, where Socrates asks whether he is himself "a more complex creature and more puffed up with pride than Typhon."

13   Plato, *Republic*, 4.427c.

LIFEKIND AND HOW TO CARE

"Before soul," Plotinus tells us, there was or would be nothing but "a dead body, earth and water, or rather the darkness of matter and non-existence, and 'what the gods hate,' as a poet says."[14] It is soul alone that makes all living things, "those that the earth feeds and those that are nourished by the sea, those in the air and the divine stars in the sky."[15] This is true in at least two ways. First, it is literally true that everything around us has been constructed, or at the least drastically remodeled, by the action of living things over many million years. Soil, oceans, air, sedimentary rocks and fossil fuels are all the product of life. It is no great leap to suspect or simply assume that the extra-terrestrial worlds are also the last effects of life, even if they themselves turn out, now, to be unliving. Unliving matter, rather than being the origin of all things (as we moderns mostly now assume), is simply the left-over from soul's action, as Plotinus said. We may speak as if Soul or some other Divine Craftsman molded "matter," as earthly craftsmen mold the bronze or stone or wood, but such primordial "matter" has no nature of its own which might constrain the craftsman. Even when Plotinus suggests that it is matter that is "the beginning of evil," this is not because there is an Absolute Matter, a spooky and disagreeable "stuff," that is intrinsically evil, but because materiality allows for accident and corruption, being the context in which the many different forms are reflected and compete. An Absolute Evil would not have even being:[16] that is, it doesn't and never did *exist* (though materiality does, and though it still makes sense to distinguish "form" and "matter" in every real existent). "Illness is defect and excess of material bodies which do not keep order and measure; ugliness is matter not mastered by form; poverty is lack and deprivation of things which we need because of the matter with which we are coupled, whose very nature is to be need."[17]

The actual phenomenal world is essentially alive: without such life, such Soul, there would be nothing at all to see. Its problems are caused by the seeming separation of bodies, one from another,[18]

---

14 Plotinus, *Ennead*, V.1 [10].2, 26–8, quoting Homer's account of Hades in Homer, *Iliad*, 20.65.
15 Plotinus, *Ennead*, V.1 [10].2, 1–4.
16 Ibid., I.8 [51].5, 8–11.
17 Ibid., I.8 [51].5, 22–26.
18 Ibid., V.1 [10].2, 32–35.

their competition for each little space and moment, and their swift falling apart. Each seemingly separate space and moment is a little echo or reflection or abstraction from the unchanging Real, as each of Indra's jewels also reflects the Whole. What that Reality is cannot be learnt simply from what appears to us here-now, nor even from a thorough compilation of all that appears to everyone in all times "past." The optimistic hope is that what appears now distorts the proper relations of the abiding Forms of life. There is no conflict or oppression "There," and the better ways of Becoming should reflect that hope, as "once upon a time," perhaps, they did.

The further reading of Plotinus's account is that there is nothing material "beyond experience": as I observed on an earlier page, the "merely material" world that some metaphysicians imagine, with no more than "primary" qualities, can neither be observed by itself nor serve to *explain* the existence of our actual phenomenal world, and is therefore a useless postulate. The real changing world, even if it lacks the firmly stable nature of the intelligible cosmos contained within the Intellect, is the world of our common experience—common, that is, not only to human beings but to all the creatures around us and within. Without soul there is no distance nor duration, nothing to distinguish "past" and "future," no definite identities, no cause, no primary scale. The very evolution of our present world did not occur within the cosmos as we now conceive or perceive it: "before" there were time-binding creatures there was no past or present; "before" there was anything to recognize or construct identities there were no singular things; "before" there were lives to be lost or injured nothing was either good or evil, beautiful or ugly, badly or well adapted. Or rather, if there "was," it was held, as now, within the eternal Intellect from which Soul takes her beginnings.[19]

Can we conceive at all, or even fondly imagine, what the Original World is like?

Once upon a time, Ferdowsi says in the *Shahnameh*, the first king of the world, Kayumars, had all the beasts and birds on his side when he went to war with Ahriman. His grandson separated animals into the tame and the wild (and killed some for their pelts),

---

19   See Stephen R. L. Clark, "Nothing without Mind," in *Consciousness Evolving: Advances in Consciousness Research*, vol. 34, ed. James H. Fetzer (Amsterdam: John Benjamins, 2002) and Stephen R. L. Clark, "History of Appearances."

and his son in his turn showed how to tame animals "by treating them well and speaking gently to them," claiming as so often that "God had given mankind sovereignty over the earth's animals." The Really Bad King, Zahhak was seduced by Eblis (disguised as a cook) into eating the tame creatures and ended by eating people. The earlier age, of bloodless sacrifice and friendship with all creatures, is remembered (or invented) in many cultures, with casual inconsistencies that suggest the story has not been well thought out! Abel, for example, sacrificed the firstborn of his flock (and was praised for it), though it was not until Noah's day that "animals" were given to us for food.[20] In place of the earlier friendships, "justice" came to be admired: the conscious recognition of what was due to each, that expressly excluded "animals" as having no "rights" in the matter. "The son of Cronos has ordained this law for men, that fishes and beasts and winged fowls should devour one another, for right [dike] is not in them; but to mankind he gave [dike] which proves far the best."[21] And so we can devour them too.

How then might we hope to rationalize and order the world-to-come? A complete return to Eden is not ours to secure: indeed, we hardly know what Eden would be like. This world here, as Plotinus testified, is founded in a sort of war, predation and consumption: everything that lives depends on eating others and is eaten in its turn: nothing can last forever. "I am food (object), I am food, I am food! I am the eater of food (subject), I am the eater of food, I am the eater of food! I am the poet (who joins the two together), I am the poet, I am the poet!"[22] And the King is the only Poet.

There are many more or less brutal ways of realizing something like this vision for the future. And all our prophecies or speculations must be unconscious of whatever bright New Idea animates our successors:

> All speculation on what new forms will govern the life
> of future mankind (or, for that matter, whether there
> will be any such new forms), all building of majestic

---

20 Genesis 4.4; 9.2–4. "This bond," it is worth mentioning, "doth give thee here no jot of blood": Shakespeare, *Merchant of Venice*, IV.1.

21 Hesiod, *Works and Days*, trans. Hugh G. Evelyn-White (London: Loeb Classical Library, Heinemann, 1914), 1.275–8.

22 "Taittiriya Upanishad 10.6," in Max Müller, trans., *Upanishads*, vol. 2 (Oxford: Clarendon Press, 1869), 69.

card-houses on the foundation of "it should be, it shall be" is mere trifling.[23]

And yet, such trifling may sometimes have some worth, if only for our own enlightenment.[24] On the one hand, our descendants might embrace "the wild": the present human population, it could be argued, displays the same inordinate and deadly growth as any other species freed from its proper limits. If Yellowstone, for example, has been restored to health by reintroducing *wolves*,[25] perhaps we too need predators to cull our many herds. Such predators might not be far removed from familiar predatory lines, nor even from *hominin* lines. We have often fantasized of a past where gods or demons, vampires and shape-changers, have stalked the merely human. Alternatively, we might expect that *microbial* predators—the physical manifestation, perhaps, of the World Soul herself—will be more efficient reminders of the need to avoid mass concentrations of any animal population, including our (human) own. On the other hand, we might prefer a tamer, more controlled solution, allowing GEA to ration births and redirect populations. This too has often featured in our fantasies. In either case it seems that our hopes might be placed in the emergence of a class or species of creature of another kind than the ordinarily human, a return to the days when *daimones* ruled, back in the reign of Kronos. This is especially so for GEA and its bureaucrats. Not that such bureaucratic guardians (celibate, and vowed to personal poverty, we trust) are morally, intellectually or spiritually superior, but only that they have no local or parochial affections or responsibilities to distract them. Maybe we might prefer the predatory form to GEA: predators can sometimes even befriend their prey and allow unexpected escapes or changes.

> For I will consider my Cat Jeoffry.
> For he is the servant of the Living God duly and daily
>   serving him....
> For having consider'd God and himself he will consider
>   his neighbour.

---

23 Spengler, *Decline*, vol. 2, 37.
24 Cf. Plotinus, *Ennead*, III.8 [3].1, 1–2.
25 Weiss et al. "Social and Ecological Benefits of Restored Wolf Populations," in *Transactions of the 72nd North American Wildlife and Natural Resources Conference* (Washington, D.C.: 2007), describing a beneficent "trophic cascade" consequent on the reintroduction of wolves.

For if he meets another cat he will kiss her in kindness.
For when he takes his prey he plays with it to give it a
  chance.
For one mouse in seven escapes by his dallying.[26]

But GEA may seem to be the solution to be favored by philosophers of Plotinus's tradition, if only we could be confident that we
might find or breed or create reliable ruling powers. The problem,
which is more than merely pragmatic, is that there will either
be clear laws and protocols to govern all their actions, or there
won't. If there are, how confident can we be that such laws will
not have hideous effects? Isaac Asimov's Three Laws, for example,
combined with fixed opinions about who counts as human, and
what counts as harm, may easily demand a genocidal war against
all rival species, and covert control even of our privileged kind.[27]
If there are not, how confident can we be in our guardians' good
judgement as times and global conditions change? Maybe we should
after all prefer the wilder, freer option, the ultimate democracy,
"the most gorgeous political system there is," whose beauty "comes
from the fact that it is adorned with every species of human trait,
as a cloak might be adorned with every species of flower.... A sort
of general store for political systems."[28] And one that includes
such predators as diseases, thieves, killers, pirates and Alexander.[29]

---

26   Christopher Smart, "Jubilate Agno B695-6, B713-16," in *The Poetical Works of
Christopher Smart, I: Jubilate Agno*, ed. Karina Williamson (Oxford: Clarendon, 1980).
27   The Three Laws that Asimov devised, to allay his readers' paranoid fear
of really intelligent automata (see Isaac Asimov, *I, Robot* [London: Harper Voyager, 2018]), require that robots do no harm to humans (nor by inaction allow
harm to come), to obey human commands (unless this conflicts with the First
Law), and to preserve their own existence (unless this conflicts with the First
or Second Laws). The casuistic detail that must accompany these Laws should
do little to console attentive readers (see Stephen R. L. Clark, "Robotic Morals,"
Cogito 2 [1988]: 20-22).
28   Plato, *Republic*, 8.557cd.
29   Augustine, *City of God*, 4.4: "Justice being taken away, then, what are
kingdoms but great robberies? For what are robberies themselves, but little
kingdoms? The band itself is made up of men; it is ruled by the authority
of a prince, it is knit together by the pact of the confederacy; the booty
is divided by the law agreed on. If, by the admittance of abandoned men,
this evil increases to such a degree that it holds places, fixes abodes, takes
possession of cities, and subdues peoples, it assumes the more plainly the name
of a kingdom, because the reality is now manifestly conferred on it, not by the
removal of covetousness, but by the addition of impunity. Indeed, that was an

Most of these fantasies have focused solely on the merely *human* condition: what futures open before us if we begin to take more seriously the thought that there are no natural kinds, that we are members not simply of our *species* but of Lifekind itself? Occasional hints that we might come to respect, to reverence, to mind about just any living cousin have surfaced in modern fantasies—along with occasional worries that this will be to surrender the hard-won notion that our mere humanity should save us from exploitation, without really improving the affairs of others. What is the scope for Kindness in a world where Lifekind rather than Humankind is our primary classification, and we stop admiring merely "human" powers more than any others? As Aristotle insisted, humans are not the best things in the world, and there is something to be admired, something divine and marvelous, in even the smallest and basest creature.[30] The outcome of Clifford Simak's *City* (a set of folk-stories told by dogs, featuring the then-extinct species of humankind) is a thoroughly utopian arrangement allowing all former carnivores a diet of artificial proteins![31] This is not indeed an altogether novel thought. "No creature is there crawling on the earth, no bird flying with its wings, but they are nations (*umman*) like unto yourselves."[32] Muslims may be permitted—as other creatures are allowed appropriate benefits—to harness and even eat our cousins. And humanity may, in some sense, be made "in the image of God." It does not follow that we, qua human, somehow *deserve* that status. Further away than the religions "of the Book," most tribal peoples, living alongside other creatures, acknowledge our commonality and our contingent fortunes.

> The Tlingit environment [for example] is a bountiful one,
> full of fish and sea mammals, as well as a variety of land
> mammals and birds that are used for consumption. Yet,
> as with other groups in this cultural and geographic area,

apt and true reply which was given to Alexander the Great by a pirate who had been seized. For when that king had asked the man what he *meant* by keeping hostile possession of the sea, he answered with bold pride, What do you mean by seizing the whole earth; but because I do it with a petty ship, I am called a robber, while you who do it with a great fleet are styled emperor."

30   See Aristotle, *Nicomachean Ethics*, 6.1141a20–22; *De Partibus Animalium*, 1.645a15–17.

31   Clifford D. Simak, *City* (Baltimore: Old Earth Books, 2004).

32   *Koran* 6.38 ("The Cattle").

animal and human lives are interwoven in an intricate web
of species sentience. Both humans and animals possess
souls, and there is no fine line between the two because
animals in their spirit homes look like people and live
like them; they can even hear what people say (in Tlingit).
Kindness to an animal may be miraculously rewarded by
the ancestral spirits.[33]

Each sort of creature may be assigned its own proper mode of
living, and human beings be therefore required or at least advised
to live *as human beings* rather than sheep or wolves. This is not to say
that either sheep or wolves have an inferior part—they may, indeed,
be more important for a particular locale than "we humans" are.
Beavers may act so as to prevent flooding.[34] Whales play a part in
keeping the climate stable.[35] And the microbial population is, as I
remarked earlier, the principal embodiment of Plotinus's World Soul,
who prepared the way for eukaryotic life and still sustains the world.

As I have observed in many earlier works, the common demand
that creatures must be able to *speak* to us to earn themselves any
consideration does not match even our present sensibilities. John
Paul II, in *Evangelium Vitae*, makes the point, in rebuking

> the mentality which tends to equate personal dignity with
> the capacity for verbal and explicit, or at least percepti-
> ble, communication. It is clear that on the basis of these
> presuppositions there is no place in the world for anyone
> who, like the unborn or the dying, is a weak element in
> the social structure, or for anyone who appears completely
> at the mercy of others and radically dependent on them
> and can only communicate through the silent language
> of a profound sharing of affection.[36]

But why did he exclude non-humans from this silent language?
Where did we get the idea that only those in *human* form have the
sort of souls that allow it? In the future perhaps we shall find it

---

33   Obeyesekere, *Imagining Karma*, 51.

34   See Ellen Wohl, *Saving the Dammed: Why We Need Beaver-Modified Ecosystems*
(New York: Oxford University Press, 2019).

35   See William C. G. Burns and D. James Baker, "From the Harpoons to the
Heat: Climate change and the international whaling commission in the 21st
century," *Journal of International Wildlife Law and Policy* 3.1 (2000): 50–72.

36   *Evangelium Vitae*, 25th March 1995: http://www.vatican.va/holy_father/john_
paul_ii/encyclicals/documents/hf_jp-ii_enc_25031995_evangelium-vitae-en.html.

easier, and maybe even essential, to acknowledge the sort of direct communication that does not need to be verbalized.

This is perhaps essential for another reason. Species boundaries, which were always less precise and impermeable than is popularly supposed, are on the brink of final dissolution.

> Now, after some three billion years, the Darwinian era is over. The epoch of species competition came to an end about 10 thousand years ago when a single species, *Homo sapiens*, began to dominate and reorganize the biosphere. Since that time, cultural evolution has replaced biological evolution as the driving force of change. Cultural evolution is not Darwinian. Cultures spread by horizontal transfer of ideas more than by genetic inheritance. Cultural evolution is running a thousand times faster than Darwinian evolution, taking us into a new era of cultural interdependence that we call globalization. And now, in the last 30 years, *Homo sapiens* has revived the ancient pre-Darwinian practice of horizontal gene transfer, moving genes easily from microbes to plants and animals, blurring the boundaries between species. We are moving rapidly into the post-Darwinian era, when species will no longer exist, and the evolution of life will again be communal.[37]

If this is a post-Darwinian future, is it also post-Platonic? Are not the Forms of things the true reality? The answer is that things here-now have always been "rolling between being and non-being,"[38] and never entirely and permanently manifest any particular Form. The post-Darwinian future merely makes this more evident. The phenomenal world, the world experienced, is always a shifting, constantly re-invented image of the eternal Forms of Being as they are conceived in the eternal Intellect. Every living thing here-now, we can also say, is a daughter of the Father, a particular mode of experience that we might also share. There may be no better image of the Eternal than this actual, transient domain, as Plotinus said:[39] it does not follow that we should conceive it to be without its pains, or without anything that needs healing.

---

3 7   Freeman Dyson, "The Darwinian Interlude," *Technology Review* (16 February 2006).

3 8   Plato, *Republic*, 5.479d.

3 9   Plotinus, *Ennead*, II.9 [33].4, 26–32.

And is there something still to fear in the collapse of boundaries? Our present prevailing sensibility demands that we treat *human* beings better than we treat "animals," and our hope may be that we at least consider treating "animals" a little better than we do at present. But there is an obvious alternative: that we treat human beings no better than the animals in our care, or under our dominion. The dream of life in the age of Kronos was always somewhat ambiguous:

> The custom of men sacrificing one another is, in fact, one that survives even now among many peoples; whereas amongst others we hear of how the opposite custom existed, when they were forbidden so much as to eat an ox, and their offerings to the gods consisted, not of animals, but of cakes of meal and grain steeped in honey, and other such bloodless sacrifices, and from flesh they abstained as though it were unholy to eat it or to stain with blood the altars of the gods; instead of that, those of us men who then existed lived what is called an "Orphic life," keeping wholly to inanimate [that is, non-animal] food and, contrariwise, abstaining wholly from things animate.[40]

Something like Aristotle's charge against Plato may also apply: if all creatures are to be our "friends," maybe we shall not be "friends" at all, any more than all men can be "brothers" without their "brotherliness" being moot. Enemies, or at least "un-friends," may be necessary too, and some gradation even of a catholic affection.

Some recent SF writers have supposed that it will be the very collapse of life in the Sixth Extinction that will transform our sensibility, so as to revere and care for anything that has survived the cull. In such imagined futures, the opposite, all too familiar, mind-set is attributed to merely mechanical creatures: a lack of empathy is a sign that an otherwise indiscernible "android," a "replicant," is not really human, or alive, in Dick's vision; a failure to understand the inwardness of biological life, or what it is for it to be, is a mark of the mechanical in Benford's *Galactic Centre Saga*.[41] The stories have at least this moral: that what most matters in life is not verbal prowess (which can increasingly be replicated by computer systems)

---

40 Plato, *Laws*, 8.782cd.
41 See Philip K. Dick, *Do Androids Dream of Electric Sheep?* (New York: Doubleday, 1968)—filmed as *Blade Runner* [1982, 1992, 2007]; also Gregory Benford, *In the Ocean of Night* (New York: Delacorte Press, 1977), and its sequels.

but the possibility of affection. Only those appreciate Lifekind who feel kindness for our kin. It is Soul that deserves our affection and esteem, more than its transient shapes and shadows.

One further, epistemological gloss: in conceiving other creatures, and the whole of creaturely existence, as *alive*, we are doing more than recognizing a merely "objective" truth. We are to feel along with them, to appreciate their motives and their meanings, to *realize* their actual being by participating, so far as we can, in the lives they lead. "The whole world ought to be regarded as some immense and enormous animal, which is held together by the Power and Reason of God as by one soul."[42] Only so can we achieve the supposedly human goal of transcending our own parochial and personal natures. It is sometimes wise, of course, to back away from too easy sympathies, in order to acknowledge that their ways are, precisely, not quite ours, but this must be only a momentary discipline, allowing us to find and feel the apparently alien ways.

GODS AND ANTI-GODS IN THE FUTURE COSMOS

Plotinus, like most other Mediterranean philosophers, supposed that the phenomenal world has been forever, and will never come to any final end, despite repeated global and local catastrophes. That there are real conceptual and experimental problems with this notion seems clear, but it remains a deeply attractive vision: witness the efforts of modern cosmologists to treat the beginning of our cosmos, the "Big Bang," as merely an episode within a still larger world. Either the world undergoes repeated expansions and contractions, or else there are indefinitely (infinitely?) many local "Bangs" which create local "bubbles" to grow and dissipate. That this world here could be a singular, finite event, that has been going on for only a definite number of imagined years, and has only a definite number yet to come, is an alternative vision owing much to Persian and Hebrew speculation. Almost all other human societies which have considered the question at all prefer to suppose an *infinite* past and future, marked by repeated catastrophes. In such a world-expanse, as Fred Hoyle observed in passing, there need have been no first beginning of his imagined sentient, star-travelling clouds, nor of life and mind at all:[43] things have

---

42 Origen, *Principles*, vol. 1, 149 (2.1.3); see also Plato, *Timaeus*, 30b.
43 Hoyle attributed the remark to his invented intelligent "cloud" which

always looked very much as they do now, from whatever locus in the grand array. Our own terrestrial life, if this be so, is simply a contagion from the larger world, as Hoyle suspected in later years.[44] The same story may also suggest that there will never be a universal and final cosmic communion of the sort that Stapledon envisaged: if there were ever going to be, it would have happened already over the infinite ages.[45] The best that could be said is that there is indeed such a communion already (indeed, always already) but it is not now and probably never has been universal: we at least are outside it still and may not live to join it.

As to the supposedly beginningless and endless nature of physical existence, Plotinus—and perhaps other metaphysicians in Hindu and Buddhist tradition—do seem to have a problem with three seemingly inconsistent theses. Firstly, the number of souls, though immensely large, is not strictly infinite. Secondly, some souls may eventually "return" to their eternal being and will not thereafter be condemned again to physical existence. Thirdly, the whole world is without end or any beginning. But if any souls, however small a proportion, are always being released from Nature, there must be a gradual attrition: over infinitely extended time the supply of souls must always already have been exhausted, and all of us are alive only in the Eternal. Only if the number of souls is truly infinite (that is, there is no actual fixed *number* of them at all, whether because infinitely many souls are always already actual or because new souls are always emerging into actual being, constituting a merely *potential* infinite) can any soul escape without eventually (already)

---

passes through our solar system on its own affairs, pausing only to convey some unexpectable truths to us: Fred Hoyle, *The Black Cloud* (New York: Harper, 1957), 162. "There's one in the eye for the exploding universe boys." Hoyle himself (1915–2001) was usually blamed for the misleading tag "Big Bang" for the alternative picture of at least a *local* beginning to the world. See Helge Kragh, "Big Bang: the etymology of a name," *Astronomy & Geophysics* 54, no. 2 (2013): 2.28–2.30, for a more detailed account of the naming.

44 See Fred Hoyle and Chandra Wickramasinghe, *Evolution from Space* (New York: Simon & Schuster, 1981).

45 The issue is discussed by Milan M. Ćirković, *The Astrobiological Landscape: philosophical foundations of the study of cosmic life* (New York: Cambridge University Press, 2012), 12–14: "Why, if the Universe is infinitely old . . . [is it] not inhabited by technological communities of unlimited age." If such an outcome is ever possible it must have happened always already. As it has not, the infinitely old totality must be continually reset.

bringing an end to incarnation. And if such an end is really to be expected, we must conclude that the world also had a beginning, that the cosmos is a finite whole in time as well as space, however vast that whole. But that is, for the moment, another story.

The other, and currently more popular, cosmological theory imagines that there have been or are indefinitely (infinitely?) many bubble cosmoi, each with their own chance ratios of fundamental forces. Only some of these arrangements allow for sentient life (and therefore only some of them are ever to be observed). What is strangely neglected by most of those (literal) metaphysicians as postulate such an array of bubbles, whether they are spread out in a hyper-cosmic space or succeed each other over aeons, is that some of the bubbles will be yet more amenable to life and mind than ours, and their powers yet more accessible.[46] Somewhere in the array there will be intelligences that have lived since their bubble's beginning and have the whole of their bubble cosmos at their disposal: Epicurean gods, inhabiting very distant worlds in peace. And perhaps they are not quite Epicurean: such powers far exceed our own, nor can we place limits on what they would or could accomplish. In effect, the story allows for cosmic engineers who can create and modify what bubbles so ever they wish. Once again, there may already (always already) be a cosmic communion from which we are, so far, excluded, stemming from Omega Worlds whose inmates must either achieve peace or be embroiled in wars beyond our imagination.

A further gloss for these fantasies is Platonic: all such bubbles, as well as the alternate version that Hoyle favored—a continual emergence of new particles (and new souls?) from supposedly "empty" space vacated by the expanding cosmos—receive their bare possibility from the unchanging patterns that we feebly grasp in mathematics. The mathematical universe "precedes" and explains all the variants of temporal being, which can themselves be conceived as mathematical figures endowed with appropriate liberties and lives. The many (infinitely many?) worlds and ages are little, slanted images of the Eternal, and whatever vast intelligences inhabit Omega Worlds have better access to the Eternal than do we—and yet are simply daughters of that One as much as we. Some

---

46 See ibid. for an engaging study of the notion of "habitable" cosmoi, not all of which need replicate our own particularities.

of them at least will recognize that we are kin, however small and base our being. Can we be sure that some will not despise us?

These metaphysical speculations have this advantage, for us, over the myths that Plotinus and his peers could tell, that they are grounded, however loosely, in actual physical theories and the results of careful experiment.[47] They are therefore "credible," for us, in ways that the older stories aren't. Those older stories, of course, were often intended precisely to be *incredible*, as mere images of an unimagined truth which were not to be taken too literally, nor used as proper foundations for our lives here-now without very careful guidance. Whatever the powers of Omega Worlds decree or seem to decree we should not lose our grip on usual "humane" virtues, nor yet (conversely) be too confident that every such godling will aspire to justice. Maybe there really is War in Heaven. And maybe we are not wholly in the wrong to think that even the angels should revere the "Human" (which is to say the powerless), and the domestic virtues.

What might the War be like, and who or what are the "enemies"? The Olympian tradition from which Plotinus drew his examples includes a memory of wars, of Olympians against their forebears, of Gods against the Giants. Plotinus used the story of Ouranos, Kronos and Zeus only as an allegorical account of the relations between the One, *Nous* and Soul, wholly ignoring the patricidal hatreds that imbued the story as it was first told. Nor did he pick up Plato's reference to the war of gods and giants, preferring to mock materialists rather as "flightless birds" than rebellious giants under the sway of Gaia.[48] Other European and Asian traditions which imagine that there is or has been war in heaven also make it a war against the older ways. In Abrahamic terms the rebellion is rather a renewal: time does not, *pace* Lowell, "make ancient good uncouth,"[49] but rather ceaselessly reminds us of the world we've lost, and of a continuing war. Victory may be assured but it is not yet present, or not yet known to us, rather as the news of Babylon's fall took many days to spread across that city.[50]

47   See for example, Tegmark, *Our Mathematical Universe*; David Deutsch, *The Fabric of Reality: towards a theory of everything* (London: Allen Lane, 1997).
48   Plato, *Sophist*, 245e–249d; see Plotinus, *Ennead*, V.9 [5].1.
49   James Russell Lowell, "The Present Crisis" [1844], in *Poems*, vol. 2 (Boston: Ticknor, Reed & Fields, 1853), 53–62: 62.
50   Aristotle, *Politics*, 2.1276a27–30.

How might we imagine Plotinus, or a Plotinian, looking back from some immensely distant future?

> O snatch us hence, ye muses! to those days
> When, through the veil of dark antiquity,
> Our sons shall hear of us as things remote,
> That blossom'd in the morn of days, alas!
> How could I weep that we were born so soon,
> In the beginning of more happy times![51]

In fact, of course, they probably won't remember us at all. As the spirit of his ancestor warned Scipio Africanus, in a passage which influenced Boethius, and through him the whole of Western Christendom:

> Even if future generations should wish to hand down to those yet unborn the eulogies of every one of us which they received from their fathers, nevertheless the floods and conflagrations which necessarily happen on the earth at stated intervals would prevent us from gaining a glory which could even be long-enduring, much less eternal. But of what importance is it to you to be talked of by those who are born after you, when you were never mentioned by those who lived before you?[52]

But perhaps at least some vague tradition will remain. Perhaps indeed, as recent theorists have imagined, they will have reconstructed us—and we are living in some grand iteration of a mostly fictional past![53] How might we conceive, how might they wish us to conceive, our future?

The commonest suggestion from speculative cosmologists and science fiction writers is that there will someday be the sort of cosmic communion that Stapledon envisaged. The illusion of independent existence will at last be banished, and a single mind

---

51 Hugh Henry Breckenridge (1748-1816), "A poem, on the rising glory of America": http://www.poemhunter.com/poem/a-poem-on-the-rising-glory-of-america/ (accessed 8th June 2020); see Stephen R. L. Clark, "Imaginary Futures and Moral Possibilities: Blossoming in the Morn of Days," *International Social Science Journal* 62, nos. 205–6 (2013): 301–12.

52 Cicero, "Dream of Scipio," in *De Republica*, trans. Clinton W. Keyes (Cambridge, MA: Harvard University Press, Loeb Classical Library, 1928), 277 [Bk. 6. 21].

53 See Nick Bostrom, "Are You Living in a Computer Simulation?" *Philosophical Quarterly* 53 (2003): 243–55.

and sentience will know itself in uncountably many centers, and in all the moments of existence. We may already have an early model of that single mind—or at least a model of the World of Images known to Muslim philosophers as *alam al-mithal*—in the expanding and proliferating Internet: it is increasingly true that we can all share in the universal body of human artifice, both what is considered "knowledge" and what is considered art or fiction or philosophy. How will "individuals" have any clear identity if we all share that background, if we can all discover anything that anyone has thought or fancied? Merely personal memories will be overshadowed by the common memory; or else our "personal" covert memories will be vastly extended by this artifice—rather as a Roman senator mentioned by Seneca claimed an exact knowledge of Homer and other Greek poets because his gang of trained slaves could identify and cap any quotation.[54] But this little terrestrial Overmind (so to call it) is only a faint image of what will, perhaps, be possible, and one that is at the moment thoroughly contaminated by malicious or mischievous *daimones*, the "memes" or "mental microbes" that infect the credulous. Maybe it can be purified before it escapes the earth. If the speed of light is an absolute and universal limit then the "thoughts" of the cosmic mind must take millions of years to occur, and the bulk of its existence will be long after all the stars are dead, and maybe after all protons have dissolved. It will be sustained in being, we may suppose, by Hawking radiation from slowly dissolving black holes—or some yet more peculiar source unknown to us here-now.[55] A clearer analogue or image for Stapledon's—and maybe Plotinus's—vision would rather require the use of "hyperspace," an alongside set of connections where all points are effectively co-incident and communication is therefore instantaneous. It would then be clear that Plotinus was correct to say that nowhere is far off, and all things and events occur together. It would follow that the Cosmic Mind is already present in our own lives, without our realizing it—or rather, the Mind itself conceals itself from us. "Hyperspace" is a

---

54 "The same number of book-cases would have been cheaper, but Calvisius Sabinus's attitude was, that whatever anyone in his household knew, he knew" (Seneca, *Letters*, 27.5–6: Wiedemann, *Greek and Roman Slavery*, 126).

55 See Freeman Dyson, "Time without End: Physics and Biology in an Open Universe," *Reviews of Modern Physics* 51, no. 3 (1979): 447–60.

naturalized allegory for the sort of unity that idealists propose as an account of all our worlds. "We are the universe. The interlocking matrix of minds is coextensive with all of nature, which is our outward face, in every stone, in every blade of grass and grain of sand....The material cosmos is the outward manifestation of an infinitely complex mental inwardness, a sentient divine machine composed of minds within minds"[56]—or rather, those many minds are expressions of the one original.[57]

But this vision is not without its critics. Consider, for example, the version outlined in Clarke's *Childhood's End*: the alien Overlords—who turn out to resemble pantomime devils—briefly impose peace on the world (and a ban on bullfights) and humans bask in a passively pointless utopia. But the Overlords' goal was simply to preserve our species until a forced evolutionary change transforms the last generation of children into elements or cells within a terrestrial Overmind destined itself to merge with the Cosmic Mind, abandoning and obliterating everything terrestrial. This, or so Clarke's unreliable narrator proposes in his last moments, is the real goal of all religion. The Overlords themselves, we are led to suppose, have achieved an evolutionary dead-end, forever barred from the communion but dedicated to pushing other species into it, not knowing what the outcome really means. Other writers have suggested that this obliteration is exactly that: the end of any sort of personal existence, or creative action.[58] We are to resign ourselves, apparently, to being *merely* cells or elements within a vaster whole, whose goals and manners are not ours. Maybe the strange choice to depict the Overlords as pantomime devils is more ambiguous than at first it seems. In the story we are to suppose that humankind has had some premonition that such creatures will attend upon the last days of our species, and

---

56   George Zebrowski, *The Omega Trilogy* (Medford, OR: Armchair Fiction, 2015), 196: see Stephen R. L. Clark, *How to Live Forever: Science Fiction and Philosophy* (London: Routledge, 1995), 156.

57   Analogously, we multicellular creatures are not amalgams of independently existing eukaryotic cells (though we can conceive of such): *our* cells all have a common birth, each a variant of one original zygote—though we must also note that we depend on our prokaryotic symbiotes.

58   See Frederik Pohl and Jack Williamson, *Land's End* (New York: Tor Books, 1989); Robert Sheckley, *Dimension of Miracle* (London: Penguin, 2020 [1968]). See further Clark, *How to Live Forever*, 153–65.

simply assumes their malice. But on the one hand, they do indeed facilitate our destruction, and on the other, we may suspect that they are gathering information and power to effect a vast rebellion against a predatory and uncompassionate demon that seeks to be the one surviving soul. They stand for an alternative existence—and which side should we be on? Which side would Plotinus be on?

This last question may seem at first to have an obvious answer: surely Plotinus already thinks that we are elements within the wider world, that each of us here-now is one expression of a particular soul, and that soul in turn the echo of one facet of the eternal. The intelligible world, the world as we should understand and enjoy it, is that Sphere of Many Faces, shining with living faces, which he describes. We are not separate from that Sphere, even when we here-now have forgotten our original being. The devils or mischievous *daimones* or misleading physical echoes who or which divert us from that awareness are to be taught better, may even be made to *assist* the great return though they themselves are barred from ever enjoying it. Wakening to that grand original is in a way like dying to our old lives, which are hardly worth remembering. But there is a problem: every time the Cosmic Mind incorporates or re-incorporates another seemingly lesser mind it also loses an associate, a potential "friend," an Other, just as kings and tyrants (or so Aristotle tells us) turn all their sometime "friends" into mere tools and organs of their will.[59] Plotinus, though he declares that all things individually and all things together exist by being one, by being focused on the transcendent Good, is also insistent that multiplicity is not in itself an evil:

> There must not be just one alone—for then all things would have been hidden, shapeless within that one, and not a single real being would have existed if that one had stayed still in itself, nor would there have been the multiplicity of these real beings which are generated from the One, if the things after them had not taken their way out which have received the rank of souls.[60]

All things exist, so far as they do, by *theoria*: all things "aspire to contemplation"—which is more than a merely "playful" notion.[61]

---

59 Aristotle, *Politics*, 3.1287b29.
60 Plotinus, *Ennead*, IV.8 [6].6, 1–6.
61 Ibid., III.8 [30].1, 1–8.

The One that all things aim at, both severally and together, is "none of the things of which it is the origin,"[62] and each level of actual being must experience a multiplicity in itself, and a distinction between itself and its origin. "If you take away otherness, it will become one and remain silent."[63] That may be, as it were, the condition of the One itself, but it is not simply ours. To imagine oneself instead as the totality, as the only real thing, is exactly that beginning of the Fall into separate being, and at last into the merely physical. No one should wish to be "alone," to exchange a real communion for a solitary dream, any more than "one would delight in a boy because he was present when he was not present."[64] So there is something un-Plotinian after all about a Cosmic Mind as it is too often imagined. Reality, as best understood, as grasped in the eternal Intellect, is experienced as multiple and interdependent, and each of us must find delight in *friendship*, in there really being an Other. The Divine itself is better conceived as triune: as "loved and lover and love of himself (*erasmion kai eros ho autos kai autou eros*),"[65] or intellect, object and thinking.[66] That eternal mode is mirrored in our own friendships. Or else conversely, we grow acquainted with the Divine under the guise of an intimate connection[67] and hope at last to join "the dance of immortal love."[68]

The war at the end of time (as speculative fiction has it) or in Heaven (as our ancestors supposed) now looks a little different. On the first and flawed account we might suppose a contest between the unified Cosmic Mind and the paltry holdouts who decline to be absorbed, between the Overmind and the Overlords. But we might instead consider that the better path is to be taken by those who acknowledge their own identity within community, as the many varied expositions of the One Alone who has always already

---

62 Ibid., III.8 [30].10, 27–8.
63 Ibid., V.1 [10].4. 38.
64 Ibid., VI.7 [38].26, 21–22.
65 Ibid., VI.8 [39].15.
66 Ibid., VI.7 [38].41; see also ibid., V.1 [10].4. 38: "If you take away otherness, it will become one and remain silent."
67 See Zeke Mazur, "Having Sex with the One: erotic mysticism in Plotinus and the problem of Metaphor," in *Late Antique Epistemology: Other Ways to Truth*, ed. Panayiota Vassilopoulou and Stephen R. L. Clark (Basingstoke: Palgrave MacMillan, 2009).
68 Porphyry, *Life*, 23.26.

"chosen" not, after all, to be alone. It is Ahriman, not Ormuzd, who wants us all absorbed in him, while everything there is, in contrast, flowers *outward* from the One. The One is "the power of all things,"[69] not simply as their bare possibility but as what is expressed by everything that is, the generosity of being.

THE END OF DAYS

In this last section I shall entertain a non-Plotinian possibility, that this world here is open to a radical transformation, an apotheosis. My earlier guesses about our future are no more than extrapolations from past and current lives. Even such extrapolations are more debatable than is usually remembered: we can never exclude the possibility that we shall soon discover that past and current patterns were not what we had supposed. Charles Babbage, as I have remarked in other works, revealed how even a strictly "uniform" world could hide surprises. In 1833 he constructed a small portion of the calculating engine he had devised, the Difference Engine, and set it to list the integers.[70] It counted up from 1 to 2 to 3 to every number up to 100,000,001. We might reasonably expect that it would continue "in like fashion," adding 1 to each succeeding number—yet the numbers that followed were 100,010,002; 100,030,003; 100,060,004; 100,100,005; 100,150,006 "and so on" until the 2672nd term, when the rule seemed to change again (and yet again after 1430 terms, and again after 950, and so on).[71]

> Now it must be remarked, that the law that each number presented by the Engine is greater by unity than the preceding number, which law the observer had deduced from an induction of a hundred million instances, was not the true law that regulated its action; and that the occurrence of the number 100,010,002 at the 100,000,002d term was as necessary a consequence of the original adjustment, and might have been as fully foreknown at the commencement, as was the regular succession of any one of the intermediate numbers to its immediate antecedent.

---

69   Plotinus, *Ennead*, III.8 [30].10, 1–2. See Eric D. Perl, "The Power of All Things," *American Catholic Philosophical Quarterly* 71 (1997): 301–13.

70   Charles Babbage, *The Ninth Bridgewater Treatise: A Fragment* (London: Frank Cass, 1967), 186–89.

71   Ibid., 34–37.

The same remark applies to the next apparent deviation from the new law, which was founded on an induction of 2761 terms, and to all the succeeding laws; with this limitation only that whilst their consecutive introduction at various definite intervals is a necessary consequence of the mechanical structure of the engine, our knowledge of analysis does not yet enable us to predict the periods at which the more distant laws will be introduced.

A less alert investigator, of course, might simply have concluded that the engine was defective, even if he could not tell how. Babbage's own insight was that the fossil record revealed just such "sudden changes," "programmed in" (as we would say) from the beginning.[72] Robert Chambers amplified the claim so as to understand the history revealed in fossils: the very same inherited rules can produce apparently dissimilar phenotypes: birds are what dinosaurs beget when the proper moment comes.[73] Or in Euripides's words, the coda to several of his plays:

> Zeus on Olympus has many things in his treasure-house, and many are the things the gods accomplish against our expectation. What men expect is not brought to pass, but a god finds a way to achieve the unexpected. Such is the outcome of this story.[74]

It may at any moment turn out that something altogether different from our easy reading has been happening all along, and that this will be something that even an angelic intellect could not have predicted, could not have picked out from the very many imaginable predictive formulae. The play, the detective story, the thriller, even the great world itself, may have very different endings because we cannot tell, till then, what was really happening already.

Nor can we exclude the possibility (even the likelihood) that events outside the local context will have a sudden effect. Alien invasions, meteor strikes and solar flares, even the collapse of current spatial order itself, might all be predictable if we knew more about the wider world, and yet be wholly unexpected, given our ignorance of that world. All our predictions, even the most

---

72   Ibid., 44–46.
73   Robert Chambers, *Vestiges of a Natural History of Creation* (Leicester: Leicester University Press, 1969).
74   Euripides, *Medea* 1415; see also *Bacchae*, 1389–90; *Alcestis*, 1159–60.

secure, may be defeated. Recent apocalyptic fantasies—of alien invasion, meteor strike or the collapse of the "false vacuum"—can serve as helpful reminders of uncertainty.[75] But the possibility that I shall consider next is more radical still: that the playwright, the director, the owner of the theatre may intervene and the whole play be suddenly wound up. On this, as Chesterton pointed out, "science" can have no opinion.

> Science is the study of the admitted laws of existence; it cannot prove a universal negative about whether those laws could ever be suspended by something admittedly above them. It is as if we were to say that a lawyer was so deeply learned in the American Constitution that he knew there could never be a revolution in America. Or it is as if a man were to say he was so close a student of the text of Hamlet that he was authorized to deny that an actor had dropped the skull and bolted when the theatre caught fire. The constitution follows a certain course, so long as it is there to follow it; the play follows a certain course, so long as it is being played; the visible order of nature follows a certain course if there is nothing behind it to stop it. But that fact throws no sort of light on whether there IS anything behind it to stop it.[76]

That question is, precisely, metaphysical, and the answer we are more inclined to give will likely depend on our ethical and even meta-religious convictions. It is widely assumed—it may even have been assumed in Plotinus's day—that the cosmos has no "outside," that it comprises everything. Everything that comes into being is a modification or a product of what came before. On the one hand, nothing comes from nothing. On the other, entropy always wins. Plotinus's God or gods, we are told, would never "intervene"

75 "The possibility that we are living in a false [unstable] vacuum has never been a cheering one to contemplate. Vacuum decay is the ultimate ecological catastrophe; in a new vacuum there are new constants of nature; after vacuum decay, not only is life as we know it impossible, so is chemistry as we know it. However, one could always draw stoic comfort from the possibility that perhaps in the course of time the new vacuum would sustain, if not life as we know it, at least some structures capable of knowing joy. This possibility has now been eliminated": Sidney Coleman and Frank De Luccia, "Gravitational effects on and of vacuum decay," in *Physical Review D* 21 (1980): 3314. See John Leslie, *End of the World: the science and ethics of human extinction* (London: Routledge, 1998) for a brief account of the more unexpected possibilities for our extinction.
76 Chesterton, *The Thing*, 137.

in Nature: the whole cosmos is always unfolding itself to mirror the eternal, and no entirely *new* thing ever happens (even if, as above, we can expect to be surprised to learn what secrets have been kept from our beginnings, or what the real implications of established law and custom may be). Plotinus's God—if that is even an appropriate title either for the "sphere of many faces" which is *Nous* or for the One itself—does not care what its/his offspring are doing. Christians and other religious theists rather suppose that God *does* care, and may even, at His will, amend what happens here. The problem, obviously, is that He does not intervene when we would wish Him to!

> He who has eyes can see the sickening sight;
> Why does not Brahma set his creatures right?
> If his wide power no limits can restrain,
> Why is his hand so rarely spread to bless?
> Why are his creatures all condemned to pain?
> Why does he not to all give happiness?
> Why do fraud, lies, and ignorance prevail?
> Why triumphs falsehood—truth and justice fail?
> I count your Brahma one th'unjust among,
> Who made a world in which to shelter wrong.[77]

Plotinus's answer to those who doubted the present world's perfection was to insist that it was as good as a temporal, physical world could be, and that we should not despise its rulers in the heavens. Our hardships are not evil in themselves, but only warnings and opportunities. Even our "escape" from the cycles of birth and death, our long return from exile, is perhaps only a rediscovery of what the "real world" is already, not its transformation. Some day we shall leave the theatre and be free to comment on the play's shortcomings. Does it follow that a Plotinian philosophy can never agree that there will be a moment when all things are made new, and never any moments when a really *other* world intrudes on ours? Might there after all be a better world, even a better *physical* world than this? Despite Plotinus's overt declaration that there couldn't be, he does also seem to agree that we were once alive in God and may be so again.

---

77 Obeyesekere, *Imagining Karma*, 135, citing the *Bhuridatta Jàtaka* from the Jàtaka Tales, a compendium of the Buddha's earlier lives. E. B. Cowell, ed., *The Jàtaka, or stories of the Buddha's former births*, vol. 6 (London: Pali Text Society, 1981), 110.

The very fact, as Platonists suppose, that this world here and now is in large part a delusion, something that is only real in being experienced by us, entails that there may be a more real world, the origin and end of all our partial and prejudiced experience. And that real world might intrude on us: we might be caught, like Achilles, by Athena, and compelled to see things otherwise.[78] Our whole history, both personal and social, may turn out to have been a dream—another apocalyptic theme adumbrated in twentieth-century science fiction.[79] The question then arises: to whom should we expect such revelations to be made? Scientists, scholars, respected politicians may be easily persuaded that they above all *deserve* to know the truth. But perhaps it is far more likely that it will be infants, outcasts, victims, losers who will be rescued from the dream, or break free by their own efforts.

What such an irruption could or will be like is of course, of its nature, quite unknown. It is the mere *possibility* that is of interest. And though it is hardly likely to be a *Plotinian* prediction, it may not be entirely un-Platonic. Plato, after all, was willing to imagine a grand reversal of all temporal and causal order when God or the gods laid hold again upon the worlds. Whether in the long-ago or in the days to come, he fancied:

> There was no such thing in the then order of nature as the procreation of animals from one another; the earth-born race, of which we hear in story, was the one which existed in those days—they rose again from the ground; and of this tradition, which is now-a-days often unduly discredited, our ancestors, who were nearest in point of time to the end of the last period and came into being at the beginning of this, are to us the heralds. And mark how consistent the sequel of the tale is; after the return of age to youth, follows the return of the dead, who are lying in the earth, to life; simultaneously with the reversal of the world the wheel of their generation has been turned back, and they are put together and rise and live in the opposite order, unless God has carried any of them away to some other lot.[80]

---

78 Plotinus, *Ennead*, VI.5 [23].7, 9f; cf. Porphyry, *Life*, 23.
79 For example, Philip K. Dick, *Time out of Joint* (London: Gollancz, 1959).
80 Plato, *Statesman*, 271ab. The myth has also been invoked as a fanciful anticipation of one possible—but probably incorrect—story about our expanding, and maybe one-day contracting, cosmos: see Martin Gardner, *The New*

The story as Plato tells it is consciously absurd but speaks to a powerful feeling: our wish that the past be really (and finally) undone.

> In our own time,
> Some say, or at a time when time is ripe.
> Then he will come, Christ the uncrucified,
> Christ the discrucified, his death undone,
> His agony unmade, his cross dismantled—
> Glad to be so—and the tormented wood
> Will cure its hurt and grow into a tree
> In a green springing corner of young Eden,
> And Judas damned take his long journey backward
> From darkness into light and be a child
> Beside his mother's knee, and the betrayal
> Be quite undone and never more be done.[81]

This world, after all, could be a better place.

Ambidextrous Universe: symmetry and asymmetry from mirror reflections to superstrings (New York: Dover, 2005), 295–98. But that is to ignore Plato's insistence that he (or rather his Eleatic Stranger) is talking about a *supernatural* event.
81   Edwin Muir, "The Transfiguration [1949]," in *Collected Poems* (London: Faber, 1984), 198.

CONCLUSION

WE ARE ALL BORN INTO A WORLD WE DID NOT make, and few of us are ever able even to contribute much to its remaking. Even our dreams of change are likely to be dictated by powers beyond our reach—they may as well be *daimones* or the shifting stars. There may nonetheless be moments in our history when some particular vision is expressed a little before it is at least partially enacted, though the converse moments are more frequent: moments when an existing social order is given some queasy rationale before it is gone forever (or gone, at least, until another age or cycle). John Locke's attempt to decry patriarchal order and authority in the hope of instead composing a contract to which we could all as individual persons give consent might, on the one hand, be considered an early intimation of a future constitution, or on the other, a new excuse to deny all land and liberty to persons outside the compact, to rationalize what his contemporaries were already doing.[1] The Neo-Platonic effort to acknowledge *Nous* as the proper authority, to be embodied in monarch, council or even the individual heart, provided an attractive gloss for imperial government, before being overwhelmed by the many alternate visions even of that *Nous*. Plato was perhaps correct

---

1 Graeber and Wengrow, *Dawn of Everything*, 149: "Colonial appropriation of indigenous lands often began with some blanket assertion that foraging peoples really were living in a State of Nature—which meant that they were deemed to be part of the land but had no legal claims to own it. The entire basis for dispossession, in turn, was premised on the idea that the current inhabitants of those lands weren't really working. The argument goes back to John Locke's *Second Treatise of Government* (1690), in which he argued that property rights are necessarily derived from labor. In working the land, one 'mixes one's labor' with it; in this way it becomes, in a sense, an extension of oneself. Lazy natives, according to Locke's disciples, didn't do that. They were not, Lockeans claimed, 'improving landlords' but simply made use of the land to satisfy their basic needs with the minimum of effort. James Tully, an authority on indigenous rights, spells out the historical implications: land used for hunting and gathering was considered vacant, and 'if the Aboriginal peoples attempt to subject the Europeans to their laws and customs or to defend the territories that they have mistakenly believed to be their property for thousands of years, then it is they who violate natural law and may be punished or "destroyed" like savage beasts,'" citing James Tully, "Aboriginal property and Western theory: recovering a middle ground," *Social Philosophy and Policy* 11, no. 2 (1994): 153–80.

269

to declare us "puppets of the gods," pulled one way or the other by the strings of our own affections and prejudgments.[2] Plotinus may have been wise not explicitly to endorse any particular social structure but allow his followers and readers to devise what schemes they may, remembering that other schemes may emerge without our will, in accordance with a cosmic, maybe cyclical, pattern we don't know. That openness was reflected in the lax management of his classes (or so Amelius and Porphyry supposed).[3] Cities and thrones and powers are both mortal and recurrent, and our own souls should rather aim for the stars than be obsessed with what will in the end be futile efforts radically to improve our present world. Alternatively, perhaps we may put on a splendid display for the star-gods, and act out many different dreams here-now, in the hope that some of the performances will earn their (our) applause. What is constantly repeated, piecemeal, here may turn out to reflect or echo or partly embody unchanging forms of beauty, more beautiful indeed than the morning and evening stars.

Families, tribes, cities, empires and the living world itself precede us. Even Societies of Friends, ashrams, churches, choirs and colleges all have their existence independently of any particular member. Even those few of us who seriously seek an isolated, eremitical existence owe their lives and thoughts to human and non-human social beings. All these social forms, on Neo-Platonic terms, are variations, echoes, slices of the eternal, experienced by us here-now only in local and linear ways. The souls that awaken within them, as the multifarious parts are drawn together in focusing on a goal, are also elements within a network, an everlasting dance that sometimes loses its coherence, as souls drift away from the common goal to seek "their own." What they should rather be doing, as Socrates and Euthyphro agreed, is to join with the gods in making many and beautiful things[4]—and above all, appreciating the beauty that is already real. On the one hand, all the things we make are transient and incomplete. On the other, they are all echoes, reflections, avatars of an eternal beauty, which recurs

---

2 Plato, Laws, 1, 645b1-3: marionettes or (possibly) wind-up toys. See Ken Moore, "Plato's Puppets of the Gods: representing the magical, the mystical and the metaphysical," Arion 22, no. 2 (2014): 37–72.

3 Porphyry, Life, 3.36-8.

4 Plato, Euthyphro, 13b-14b.

forever. If we must choose between *making* such beautiful things and *appreciating* the beauty that is already real, there can only be one sensible answer: how should we expect to make beautiful things without an appreciation of beauty?

> "Two birds, beautiful of wing, close companions, cling to one common tree: of the two one eats the sweet fruit of the tree, the other eats not but watches his fellow. The soul is the bird that sits immersed on the one common tree; but because he is not lord he is bewildered and has sorrow. But when he sees that other who is the Lord and beloved, he knows that all is His greatness and his sorrow passes away from him." The parable of the two birds is famous and appears in multiple Upanishads....The individual soul, the Jivatman, is focused on the life of the world, eating the sweet fruit of the tree, and because it is immersed in that life and the results of action in the world, it is subject to the illusion of separation and the suffering that attends it. The other bird represents the Divine consciousness which exists in a state of unity, not fragmentation. It witnesses the action of the fragmented consciousness of each individual yet remains aloof and unmoved by the joy and suffering of the individuals. When the soul recognizes its oneness with the Divine, then it passes beyond sorrow and grief.[5]

Philosophy, both Plato and Aristotle said, begins in wonder:[6] the aphorism is ambiguous. On the one hand, wonder may be simply bafflement, and issue in attempts to make better sense of seeming contradictions (though bafflement recurs). On the other, it is an immediate response to something, exactly, wonderful. God or the gods are recognized in saying and feeling "wow." The long and difficult attempt to live from and within that response we may also call "religion." Trying to organize the response, in ourselves and others, is the province, in the broadest sense, of "politics": what other options we may yet discover than the ancient *polis*, the would-be global empire, or the unofficial and scattered communities of friends and fellow believers is uncertain. Platonists

---

5 *Mundaka Upanishad*, 3.1, 1–2, as translated and interpreted by Sri Aurobindo, *The Upanishads* (Twin Lakes, WI: Lotus Press, 1996), 193–210: https://sriaurobindostudies.wordpress.com/2019/09/18/two-birds-on-a-common-tree/ (accessed 22 November 2021).

6 Plato, *Theaetetus*, 155c; Aristotle, *Metaphysics*, 1.982b.

who follow in Plotinus's wake may hope that the real and eternal world that we now know only in fragments and reminiscences will continue to be reflected in the outer phenomenal world and also in our hearts.

> As kingfishers catch fire, dragonflies draw flame;
> As tumbled over rim in roundy wells
> Stones ring; like each tucked string tells, each hung bell's
> Bow swung finds tongue to fling out broad its name;
> Each mortal thing does one thing and the same:
> Deals out that being indoors each one dwells;
> Selves—goes itself; myself it speaks and spells,
> Crying Whát I dó is me: for that I came.
>
> I say móre: the just man justices;
> Keeps grace: thát keeps all his goings graces;
> Acts in God's eye what in God's eye he is—
> Chríst—for Christ plays in ten thousand places,
> Lovely in limbs, and lovely in eyes not his
> To the Father through the features of men's faces.[7]

---

7   G. M. Hopkins, "As Kingfishers catch fire," in *Poems*, 34.

REFERENCES

Aesop. *The Complete Fables*. Translated by Olivia and Robert Temple. New York: Penguin, 1998.

Aho, J. P. *Religious Mythology and the Art of War*. London: Aldwych Press, 1981.

Akçay, K. Nilüfer. *Porphyry's On the Cave of the Nymphs in its Intellectual Context*. Leiden: Brill, 2019.

Al-Azmeh, Aziz. *Muslim Kingship: Power and the Sacred in Muslim, Christian and Pagan Polities*. London: I. B. Tauris, 1996.

Al-Farabi. *Aphorisms of the statesman (Fusul al-madani)*. Edited and translated by D. M. Dunlop. Cambridge: Cambridge University Press, 1961.

———. *On the Principles of the Views of the Inhabitants of the Excellent State (Abu Nasr al-Farabi's al-madina al-fadila)*. Edited and translated by R. Walzer. Oxford: Oxford University Press, 1985.

Allen, James P. *Middle Egyptian: an Introduction to the Language and Culture of Hieroglyphs*. 3rd ed. Cambridge: Cambridge University Press, 2014.

Annas, Julia. *Platonic Ethics: old and new*. Ithaca: Cornell UP, 1999.

Anthony of Sourozh. *Sayings of the Desert Fathers*. Translated by Benedicta Ward. Collegeville, MN: Cistercian Publications, 1975.

Appleton, Naomi. *Narrating Karma and Rebirth: Buddhist and Jain multi-life stories*. Cambridge: Cambridge University Press, 2014.

Aristotle. *Politics*. Translated by Ernest Barker, edited by R. F. Stalley. Oxford: Oxford University Press, 1995.

Armstrong, A. H. *Plotinus: The Enneads*. Cambridge, Mass: Loeb Classical Library, Harvard University Press, 1966–1988.

Armstrong, A. J. "Some Advantages of Polytheism." *Dionysius* 5 (1981): 181–88.

Asimov, Isaac. *I Robot*. London: Harper Voyager, 2018.

Assmann, Jan. *Religio Duplex: how the Enlightenment reinvented Egyptian religion*. Translated by Robert Savage. Cambridge: Polity, 2014.

Athanasius. *On the Incarnation*. London: Bles, 1944 [c. 318].

Augustine. *The Teacher, The Free Choice of the Will & Grace and Free Will*. Translated by R. P. Russell. Washington: Catholic University of America Press, 1968.

Augustine. *City of God*. Translated by R. W. Dyson. Cambridge: Cambridge University Press, 1998.

Augustine. *Soliloquies*. Translated by Rose Elizabeth Cleveland. Boston: Little Brown & Co, 1910.

Augustine of Dacia, *Rotulus pugillaris*, vol. 1. Edited by Angelus Walz. Rome: Pontifical Institute, Angelicum, 1929.

Aurobindo, Sri. *The Upanishads*. Twin Lakes, WI: Lotus Press, 1996 [1972].

Ayfre, Amédée. "Le corps miroir de l'ame." In *Un Cinéma Spiritualiste*. Edited by René Prédal. Paris: Éditions du Cerf, 2004.

Babbage, Charles. *The Ninth Bridgewater Treatise: A Fragment*. London: Frank Cass, 1967 [1838].

Bakhsh, Alireza Omid. "The Virtuous City: the Iranian and Islamic heritage of Utopianism." *Utopian Studies* 24, no. 1 (2013): 41–51.

Barfield, Raymond. *The Ancient Quarrel Between Philosophy and Poetry*. Cambridge: Cambridge University Press, 2011.

Beard, Mary. "The Roman and the Foreign: the cult of the 'Great Mother' in Imperial Rome." In *Shamanism, History and the State*. Edited by Nicholas Thomas and Caroline Humphrey. Ann Arbor: Michigan University Press, 1996.

Benford, Gregory. *In the Ocean of Night*. New York: Delacorte Press, 1977.

Berkeley, George. *Works*. Edited by A. A. Luce and T. E. Jessop. Edinburgh: Thomas Nelson, 1948–57.

Berkeley, George. *Principles of Human Knowledge and Three Dialogues*. Edited by Howard Robinson. Oxford: Oxford University Press, 1996.

Berndt, Ronald M. and Catherine H. Berndt. *The World of the First Australians: aboriginal traditional life, past and present*. Canberra: Aboriginal Studies Press, 1988.

Berthelot, Katell. "Philo's Perception of the Roman Empire." *Journal for the Study of Judaism in the Persian, Hellenistic, and Roman Period* 42, no. 2 (2011): 166–87.

Beston, Henry. *The Outermost House: a year of life on the great beach of Cape Cod*. New York: Henry Holt & Co, 1988 [1928].

Betegh, Gábor. *The Derveni Papyrus: Cosmology, Theology and Interpretation*. Cambridge: Cambridge University Press, 2004.

Beyer, Stephen. *The Cult of Tara: Magic and Ritual in Tibet*. Berkeley, CA: University of California Press, 1973.

Bhikkhu, Ānandajoti, rans. *Asoka and the Missions: from Extended Mahāvaṁsa V, XII–XV, XVIII–XX)*. Edited by G. P. Malalasekera. Oxford: Pali Text Society, Oxford, 1988 [1937].

Black, Antony. *The History of Islamic Political Thought: from the Prophet to the Present*. Edinburgh: Edinburgh University Press, 2011.

Blake, William. *Complete Writings*. Edited by Geoffrey Keynes. London: Oxford University Press, 1966.

Blois, Lukas de. *The Policy of the Emperor Gallienus*. Leiden: E. J. Brill, 1976.

Bobonich, Christopher. *Plato's Utopia Recast; His Later Ethics and Politics*. Oxford: Oxford University Press, 2002.

Bodhi, Bhikku, trans. *Connected Discourses of the Buddha: a translation of the Samyuuta Nikaya*. Boston: Wisdom Publications, 2000.

Bostrom, Nick. "Are You Living in a Computer Simulation?" *Philosophical Quarterly* 53 (2003): 243–55.

Boswell, James. *Life of Johnson*. Edited by R. W. Chapman. Oxford: Oxford University Press, 2008 [1791].

Bourdieu, Pierre and Jean-Claude Passeron. *Reproduction in Education, Society and Culture*. Translated by Richard Nice. London: Sage Publications, 1990.

Bradley, Ian. *God Save the Queen: the spiritual heart of the monarchy*. London: Continuum, 2012 [1999].

Bradshaw, David. "The Logoi of Beings in Greek Patristic Thought." In *Toward an Ecology of Transfiguration: Orthodox Christian Perspectives on Environment, Nature, and Creation*. Edited by John Chryssavgis and Bruce V. Foltz. New York: Fordham University Press, 2013.

Brantlinger, Patrick. *Dark Vanishings: Discourse on the Extinction of Primitive Races, 1800–1930*. Ithaca, NY: Cornell University Press, 2003.

Brock, Michelle D., Richard Raiswell and David R. Winter, eds. *Knowing Demons, Knowing Spirits in the Early Modern Period*. London: Palgrave Macmillan, 2018.

Brown, Paula. "Conflict in the New Guinea Highlands." *Journal of Conflict Resolution* 26 (1982): 525–46.

Brown, Peter. "The Rise and Function of the Holy Man in Late Antiquity." In *Society and the Holy in Late Antiquity*. Berkeley: University of California Press, 1982.

———. "The Rise and Function of the Holy Man in Late Antiquity, 1971–1997." *Journal of Early Christian Studies* 6.3 (1998): 353–76.

Buber, Martin. *I and Thou*. Translated by Walter Kaufmann. New York: Simon & Schuster, 1996 [1923].

Budrys, Algis. *Rogue Moon*. London: Gateway, 2012 [1960].

Bühler, George, trans. *Manu Samhita: The Laws of Manu*. Delhi: Motilal Banarsidass, 1964 [1886].

Bulgakov, Sergius. *A Bulgakov Anthology*. Edited by James Pain and Nicolas Zernov. London: SPCK, 1976.

Bunge, Gabriel. *Despondency: the spiritual teaching of Evagrius Ponticus on Acedia*. Translated by Anthony P. Gythiel. New York: Vladimir's Seminary Press, 2012.

Burke, Edmund. *Reflections on the Revolution in France*. Edited by Conor Cruise O'Brien. Harmondsworth: Penguin, 1968.

Burns, William C. G. and D. James Baker "From the harpoon to the heat: Climate change and the international whaling commission in the 21st century." *Journal of International Wildlife Law & Policy* 3.1 (2000): 50–72.

Bussanich, John. "Ethics in Ancient India." In *Ancient Ethics*. Edited by J. Hardy and G. Rudebusch. Göttingen: Vandenhoek & Ruprecht, 2014, 33–53.

Caciola, N. M. "The Science of Knowing Spirits: Rationality and the Invisible World." In *Knowing Demons, Knowing Spirits in the Early Modern Period*. Edited by Michelle D. Brock, Richard Raiswell and David R. Winter. London: Palgrave Macmillan, 2018.

Calderón de la Barca. *Life's a Dream.* Boulder, Colorado: University Press of Colorado, 2004 [1635].

Calvo, José María Zamora. "Proclus on the Atlantis Story." *Rupkatha Journal on Interdisciplinary Studies in Humanities* 10.3 (2018): 1–9.

Carruthers, Peter. *The Animals Issue: Moral Theory in Practice.* Cambridge: Cambridge University Press, 1992.

Caseau, Béatrice. "Sacred Landscapes." In *Late Antiquity: a guide to the post-classical world.* Edited by G. W. Bowersock, Peter Brown and Oleg Grabar. Cambridge, Mass: Harvard University Press, 1999.

Cassian, John. *Works.* Translated by Edgar C. S. Gibson. New York: Veritatis Splendor, 2012 [1886].

Chambers, Robert. *Vestiges of the Natural History of Creation.* Leicester: Leicester University Press, 1969 [1845].

Chappell, Sophie-Grace. "Autonomy in Sophocles' Antigone." In *The Routledge Handbook of the Philosophy of Autonomy.* Edited by Ben Colburn. London: Routledge (forthcoming).

Charbit, Yves. "The Platonic City: History and Utopia." In *Population* (English edition) 57, no. 2 (2002): 207–35.

Cheetham, Tom. *The World Turned Inside Out: Henry Corbin and Islamic mysticism.* New Orleans: Spring Journal Inc., 2015.

Chesterton, G. K. "The Philosophy of Islands." In *The Venture Annual.* Edited by Laurence Housman and W. Somerset Maugham. London: John Baillie's, 1903.

———. *Tremendous Trifles.* London: Methuen, 1904.

———. *The Napoleon of Notting Hill.* Harmondsworth: Penguin, 1946 [1904].

———. *Heretics.* London: Bodley Head, 1905.

———. *What's Wrong with the World.* London: Cassell & Co, 1910.

———. *Fancies versus Fads.* London: Methuen, 1923.

———. *The Everlasting Man.* London: Hodder & Stoughton, 1925.

———. *The Poet and the Lunatics.* London: Darwen Finlayson, 1962 [1929].

———. *Chaucer.* London: Faber, 1932.

———. *The Well and the Shallows.* London: Sheed & Ward, 1935.

———. *The Thing: why I am a Catholic.* London: Sheed & Ward, 1929.

———. "Utopia of Usurers" (1917). In *Collected Works.* Vol. 5. San Francisco: Ignatius Press, 1987.

Chlup, Radek. *Proclus: an introduction.* Cambridge: Cambridge University Press, 2012.

Cicero. *On the Republic. On the Laws.* Translated by Clinton W. Keyes. Cambridge, Mass: Harvard University Press, Loeb Classical Library, 1928.

Ćirković, Milan M. *The Astrobiological Landscape: philosophical foundations of the study of cosmic life.* New York: Cambridge University Press, 2012.

Clark, Gillian. "Desires of the Hangman: Augustine on Legitimized

Violence." In *Violence in Late Antiquity: perceptions and practices.* Edited by H. A. Drake. Aldershot: Ashgate, 2006.

Clark, Stephen R. L. *Aristotle's Man: speculations upon Aristotelian anthropology.* Oxford: Clarendon Press, 1975.

———. "God, good and evil": *Proceedings of the Aristotelian Society* 77 (1977): 247–64.

———. *From Athens to Jerusalem: the love of wisdom and the love of God.* Oxford: Clarendon Press, 1984 (reissued by Angelico Press, 2019).

———. "Slaves and Citizens": *Philosophy* 60 (1985): 27–46.

———. "The City of the Wise." *Apeiron* 20 (1987): 63–80.

———. "How to Believe in Fairies." *Inquiry* 30 (1988): 337–55.

———. "Robotic Morals." *Cogito* 2 (1988): 20–22.

———. *Civil Peace and Sacred Order.* Oxford: Clarendon Press, 1989.

———. *How to Think about the Earth: models of environmental theology.* London: Mowbray, 1993.

———. *How to Live Forever: science fiction and philosophy.* London: Routledge, 1995.

———. Herds of Free Bipeds: In *Reading the Statesman: proceedings of the Third Symposium Platonicum.* Edited by C. Rowe. Sankt Augustin: Academia Verlag, 1995; 236–52.

———. "A Plotinian Account of Intellect." *American Catholic Philosophical Quarterly* 71 (1997): 421–32.

———. *The Political Animal.* London: Routledge, 1999.

———. "Nothing without Mind." In *Consciousness Evolving: Advances in Consciousness Research.* Vol. 34, Edited by James H. Fetzer. Amsterdam: John Benjamins, 2002.

———. "Genocide, War and Consistency." In *Human Rights and Military Intervention.* Edited by Richard Norman and Alex Moseley. Aldershot: Ashgate, 2002; 113–21.

———. "Slaves, Servility and Noble Deeds." *Philosophical Inquiry* (Thessaloniki) 25, no. 3 (2003): 165–76.

———. "Vegetarianism and the Ethics of Virtue." In *Food for Thought: the debate over eating meat.* Edited by Steve F. Sapontzis. New York: Prometheus Books, 2004.

———. "Deference, Degree and Selfhood." *Philosophy* 80 (2005): 249–60.

———. "Elves, Hobbits, Trolls and Talking Beasts." *Creaturely Theology.* Edited by Celia Deane-Drummond and David Clough. London: SCM Press, 2009.

———. *Understanding Faith: Religious Belief and its Place in Society.* Exeter: Imprint Academic, 2009.

———. "Plotinian Dualisms and the 'Greek' Ideas of Self." *Journal of Chinese Philosophy* 36 (2009): 554–67.

———. "Ethical Thought in India." *Routledge Companion to Ethics*. Edited by John Skorupski. London: Routledge, 2010.

———. "Therapy and Theory Reconstructed." *Philosophy as Therapy*. Edited by Clare Carlisle and Jonardon Ganeri. Cambridge: Cambridge University Press, 2010.

———. "*The Mind Parasites*: Wilson, Husserl, Plotinus." In *Around the Outsider: essays presented to Colin Wilson*. Edited by Colin Stanley. Alresford: O-Books, 2011.

———. *Ancient Mediterranean Philosophy*. London: Continuum: London, 2013.

———. "Imaginary futures and moral possibilities: blossoming in the morn of days." *International Social Science Journal* 62, nos. 205-6 (2013): 301-12.

———. "God, Reason and Extraterrestrials." In *God, Mind and Knowledge*. Edited by Andrew Moore. London: Ashgate, 2014.

———. *Plotinus: myth, metaphor and philosophical practice*. Chicago: University of Chicago Press, 2016.

———. "The Sphere with Many Faces." *Dionysius*, 34 (2016): 8-26.

———. "Who is God." *European Journal for Philosophy of Religion* 8, no. 4 (2016): 1-22.

———. "Climbing up to Heaven: the Hermetic Option." In *Purgatory: philosophical dimensions*. Edited by Kristof K. P. Vanhoutte and Benjamin W. McCraw. London: Palgrave-Macmillan, 2017.

———. "Classical Mediterranean Conceptions of the Afterlife." In *The Palgrave Handbook of the Afterlife*. Edited by Yujin Nagasawa and Benjamin Matheson. London: Palgrave-Macmillan, 2017.

———. "Heracles, Hylas and the Uses of Reflection." In *Plotinus and the Moving Image*. Edited by Thorsten Botz-Bornstein and Giannis Stamatellos. Leiden: Brill, 2017.

———. "An Absence of Fairies." *First Things* 271 (March 2017): 33-38.

———. *The Mysteries of Religion: an introduction to philosophy through religion*. Eugene, OR: Wipf & Stock, 2017 [1986].

———. "Citizens of the World and their Religion." *Philosophical Papers* 48, no. 1 (2019): 103-22.

———. *Can We Believe in People: human significance in an interconnected cosmos*. Brooklyn: Angelico Press, 2020.

———. "Souls, Stars and Shadows." In *Differences in Identity in Philosophy and Religion: A Cross-Cultural Approach*. Edited by Lydia Azadpour, Russell Re Manning, and Sarah Flavel. London: Bloomsbury, 2020.

———. "History of Appearances, or Worlds United." In *Homage to Owen Barfield*. Edited by Martin Ovens. Forthcoming.

———. "Plotinus and Godlike Virtues." In *Quietism, Agnosticism and Mysticism*. Edited by Krishna Pathak. New York: Springer, 2022.

———. *Commentary on Ennead VI.9*. Las Vegas: Parmenides Publishing, 2020.

———. "Multiplicity in Earth and Heaven." In *Christian Platonism: a history*. Edited by Alexander J. B. Hampton and John Peter Kenney. Cambridge: Cambridge University Press, 2020.

Clarke, Emma C. *Iamblichus' De Mysteriis: A Manifesto of the Miraculous* London: Routledge, 2019.

Clarke, George Herbert, ed. *A Treasury of War Poetry*. Plano, TX: Last Post Press, 2015 [1917].

Clay, Diskin. "The Athenian Garden." In *Cambridge Companion to Epicureanism*. Edited by James Warren. Cambridge: Cambridge University Press, 2009.

Clastres, Pierre. *Society against the State: essays in political anthropology*. Translated by Robert Hurley and Abe Stein. Brooklyn: Urzone Inc., 1987 [1974].

Coleman, Sidney and Frank De Luccia. "Gravitational effects on and of vacuum decay." In *Physical Review D* 21 (1980): 3305-315.

Coleridge, Samuel Taylor. *The Complete Poems*. Edited by William Keach. London: Penguin, 1997.

Collins, Steven. *Nirvana and Other Buddhist Felicities*. Cambridge University Press, 1998.

Constantine, Philotheos, and the Australian Association for Byzantine Studies. *The Book of Ceremonies: With the Greek Edition of the Corpus Scriptorum Historiae Byzantinae (Bonn, 1829)*. Edited by Johann Jacob Reiske. Translated by Ann Moffatt and Maxeme Tall. Byzantina Australiensia / Australian Association for Byzantine Studies, 18. Canberra: Australian Association for Byzantine Studies, 2012.

Cook, Francis H. *Hua-Yen Buddhism: The Jewel Net of Indra*. Pennsylvania: Penn State Press, 1977.

Cooper, Susan. *The Soul of Film Theory*. Basingstoke: Palgrave Macmillan, 2013.

Copenhaver, Brian P. *Hermetica*. Cambridge: Cambridge University Press, 1992.

Corbin, Henry. *Spiritual Body and Celestial Earth: from Mazdaean Iran to Shi'ite Iran*. Translated by Nancy Pearson. Princeton: Princeton University Press, 1977.

Cornford, F. M. *From Religion to Philosophy: a study in the origins of western speculation*. New York: Harper & Row, 1957 [1912].

Corrigan, Kevin. *Evagrius and Gregory: Mind, Soul and Body in the 4th Century*. London: Routledge, 2009.

Cowell, E. B., ed. *The Jàtaka, or stories of the Buddha's former births*. London: Pali Text Society, 1981.

Crawford, Matthew. *The Case for Working with Your Hands: or why office work is bad for us and fixing things feels good*. London: Penguin, 2010.

Crone, Patricia. *Medieval Islamic Political Thought*. Edinburgh: Edinburgh University Press, 2013.

Damascius. *Philosophical History*. Edited by Polymnia Athanassiadi. Athens: Apamea, 1999.

Daniel, Tony. *Warpath*. London: Gollancz, 1994.

Dawson, Doyne. *Cities of the Gods: Communist Utopias in Greek Thought*. New York: Oxford University Press, 1992.

Deck, J. N. *Nature, Contemplation, and the One*. New York: Larson, 1991.

De Lubac, Henri. *Medieval Exegesis*. Vol. 1, *The Four Senses of Scripture*. Translated by Mark Sebanc. Grand Rapids: Eerdmans, 1998.

Dennett, Daniel. C. *Consciousness Explained*. New York: Little, Brown & Co., 1991.

Denyer, Nicholas. *Plato: Alcibiades*. Cambridge: Cambridge University Press, 2001.

Descola, Philippe. *Beyond Nature and Culture*. Translated by Janet Lloyd. Chicago: University of Chicago Press, 2013.

De St. Croix, Geoffrey. "Slavery and Other Forms of Unfree Labor." In *Slavery and Other Forms of Unfree Labor*. Edited by L. J. Archer. London: Routledge, 1988.

Deutsch, David. *The Fabric of Reality: towards a theory of everything*. London: Allen Lane, 1997.

Dick, Philip K. *Time out of Joint*. London: Gollancz, 1959.

———. *Do Androids Dream of Electric Sheep?* New York: Doubleday, 1968.

Dillon, J. M. "An ethic for the antique sage." In *Cambridge Companion to Plotinus*. Edited by Lloyd Gerson. Cambridge: Cambridge University Press, 1996.

———. "Iamblichus' Doctrine of the Soul Revisited." In *Literary, Philosophical, and Religious Studies in the Platonic Tradition*. Edited by John F. Finamore and John Phillips. Sankt Augustin: Akademia, 2013.

———. "Plutarch, Plotinus and the Zoroastrian Concept of the *Fravashi*." In *Passionate Mind: essays in honor of John M. Rist*. Edited by Barry David. Sankt Augustin: Academia Verlag, 2019.

Diodorus Siculus. *Library of History*. Vol. 1. Translated by C. H. Oldfather. Cambridge, Mass: Loeb Classical Library, Harvard University Press, 1933.

Diogenes Laertius. *Lives of Eminent Philosophers*. Vols. 1 and 2. Translated by R. D. Hicks. Cambridge, Mass: Loeb Classical Library, Harvard University Press, 1924-25.

Dodds, E. R. "Numenius and Ammonius." In *Sources de Plotin* (Entretiens Hardt 5), 1-61. Geneva: Fondation Hardt, 1960.

Donne, John. *A Critical Edition of the Major Works*. Edited by John Carey. Oxford: Oxford University Press, 1990.

Douglas, Mary. *Natural Symbols*. 2nd ed. Harmondsworth: Penguin, 1973.

Dumézil, Georges. *Mitra-Varuna: Essay on Two Indo-European Representations of Sovereignty*. Translated by Derek Coltman. New York: Zone Books, 1988.

Dumont, Louis. *Homo Hierarchicus: the Caste System and its Implications.* Chicago: University of Chicago Press, 1980 [1966].

Dunayer, Joan. *Speciesism.* Derwood, MD: Ryce Publishing, 2004.

Dyson, Freeman. "Time without End: Physics and Biology in an Open Universe." *Reviews of Modern Physics* 51, no. 3 (1979): 447–60. Reprinted in *Selected Papers of Freeman Dyson.* Providence, RI: American Mathematical Society, 1996.

———. "The Darwinian Interlude." *Technology Review* (16 February 2006).

Edmonds, R. G. "The Children of Earth and Starry Heaven: The Meaning and Function of the Formula in the 'Orphic' Gold Tablets." In *Orfeo y el orfismo: nuevas perspectivas.* Edited by Alberto Bernabé, Francesc Casadesús and Marco Antonio Santamaría. Alicante: Biblioteca Virtual Miguel de Cervantes, 2010.

Edwards, Mark. "Ammonius, Teacher of Origen." *The Journal of Ecclesiastical History* 44, no. 2 (1993): 169–181.

———. "Plotinus and the Emperors." *Symbolae Osloenses* 69 (1994): 137–47.

———. trans., with introduction. *Neoplatonic Saints: the lives of Plotinus and Proclus by their students.* Liverpool: Liverpool University Press, 2000.

———. "Birth, Death and Divinity in Porphyry's *Life of Plotinus.*" In *Biography and Panegyric in Late Antiquity.* Edited by Tomas Hägg and Phillip Rousseau. 52–71. Berkeley: University of California Press, 2000.

Egan, Greg. *Incandescence.* London: Gollancz, 2011.

Engberg-Pedersen, Troels. "Philo's De Vita Contemplativa as a Philosopher's Dream." *Journal for the Study of Judaism* 30, no. 1 (1999): 40–64.

Epictetus. *Discourses.* Translated by W. A. Oldfather. London: Loeb Classical Library, Heinemann, 1925.

Eusebius. *History of the Church.* Translated by G. A. Williamson. Edited by Andrew Louth. London: Penguin, 1989.

———. *Praeparatio Evangelica.* Bk 7. Edited and translated by G. Schroeder and É. des Places. La préparation évangélique, livre VII, Paris, 1975.

———. *Life of Constantine.* Edited by Averil Cameron and Stuart G. Hall. Oxford: Clarendon Press, 1999.

Evans, Matthew. "Can Epicureans be Friends?" *Ancient Philosophy* 24 (2004): 407–24.

Evans, Paul. "Down Memory Lane." *Guardian Weekly* (24 November 2006).

Evans-Wentz, W. Y. *The Fairy Faith in Celtic Countries: the Classic Study of Leprechauns, Pixies, and Other Fairy Spirits.* Oxford: Oxford University Press, 1911.

Fakhry, Majid. *Al-Fārābi, Founder of Islamic Neoplatonism: his life, works and influence.* Oxford: Oneworld Publications, 2002

Ferdowsi, Abolqasem. *Shahnameh: the Persian Book of Kings.* Translated by Dick Davis. New York: Penguin, 2006.

Ferwerda, R. *La Signification des Images et des Métaphores dans la Pensée de Plotin.* Groningen: J. B. Wolters, 1965.

Festugière, A. J. "Platon et l'Orient." *Revue de Philologie, de Littérature et d'Histoire Anciennes* 21 (1947): 5–45.

Feynman, Richard. *Feynman Lectures on Physics.* New York: Basic Books, 2011 [1963].

Foltz, Bruce V. *The Noetics of Nature: Environmental Philosophy and the Holy Beauty of the Visible.* New York: Fordham University Press, 2013.

Fowden, Garth. *The Egyptian Hermes: a historical approach to the late pagan mind.* Cambridge: Cambridge University Press, 1986.

Franklin, Benjamin. *Autobiography.* Edited by Charles W. Elliot. New York: P. F. Collier, 1909.

Galiani, Ferdinando. *Lettres de l'abbé Galiani a madame d'Épinay ed Eugène Asse.* Paris: Charpentier, 1882.

Gammage, Bill. *The Biggest Estate on Earth: how Aborigines made Australia.* Sydney: Allen & Unwin, 2011.

Gandhi, Mohandas Karamchand. *Collected Works of Mahatma Gandhi.* Vol. 70. New Delhi, Publications Division Government of India, 1999.

Gardner, Robert and Karl G. Heider. *Gardens of War: Life and Death in the New Guinea Stone Age.* New York: Random House, 1968.

Gardner, Martin. *The New Ambidextrous Universe: symmetry and asymmetry from mirror reflections to superstrings.* New York: Dover, 2005 [1964].

Geertz, Clifford. "From the native's point of view: on the nature of anthropological understanding." *Bulletin of the American Academy of Arts and Sciences* 28, no. 1 (1974): 26–45.

Gerson, Lloyd P. "Metaphor as an Ontological Concept: Plotinus on the Philosophical Use of Language." In *Logos et langage chez Plotin et avant Plotin.* Edited by Michel Fattal, 255–70. Paris: L'Harmattan, 2003.

Gerson, Lloyd P., ed. *Plotinus: the Enneads.* Translated by George Boys-Stones, John M. Dillon, Lloyd P, Gerson, R. A. H. King, Andrew Smith and James Wilberding. Cambridge; Cambridge University Press, 2018.

Gertz, Sebastian. *Death and Immortality in Late Neoplatonism.* Leiden: Brill, 2011.

Gethin, Rupert. *The Foundations of Buddhism.* Oxford: Oxford University Press, 1998.

Gill, Christopher. "Plato's Atlantis Story and the Birth of Fiction." *Philosophy and Literature* 3, no. 1 (1979): 64–78.

Glatzer, N. N., ed. *The Dimensions of Job.* New York: Schocken Books, 1969.

Gleason, Maud. "Visiting and News: Gossip and Reputation-Management in the Desert." *Journal of Early Christian Studies* 6, no. 3 (1998): 501–21.

Goldman, David P. "The God of the Mathematicians: the religious beliefs that guided Kurt Gödel's revolutionary ideas." *First Things* (August–September 2010): 45–50.

Gombrich, Richard F. *Theravada Buddhism: a social history from Ancient Benares to Modern Colombo.* London: Routledge, 2006 [1988].

Goodenough, E. R. "The Political Philosophy of Hellenistic Kingship," *Yale Classical Studies* 1 (1928): 55–102.

Graeber, David and David Wengrow. *The Dawn of Everything: a new history of humanity.* London: Allen Lane, 2021.

Granoff, Phyllis. *The Forest of Thieves and the Magic Garden: an anthology of medieval Jain stories.* London: Penguin, 2006.

Gregory the Great. *Morals on the Book of Job.* Vol. 3. Translated by James Bliss. Ex Fontibus Company, 2012 [1844].

Griffith, R. Drew. "Sailing to Elysium: Menelaus' Afterlife (*Odyssey* 4.561–569) and Egyptian Religion." *Phoenix* 55 (2001): 213–43.

Hadot, Pierre. "Ouranos, Kronos and Zeus in Plotinus's Treatise against the Gnostics." In *Neoplatonism and Early Christian Thought: essays in honour of A. H. Armstrong.* Edited by H. J. Blumenthal and R. A. Markus. London: Variorum, 1981.

Hadot, Pierre. *Plotinus, or the Simplicity of Vision.* Translated by Michael Chase. Chicago: University of Chicago Press, 1993.

Hall, Roger L. "Aaron Copland's 'Simple Gifts' in Appalachian Spring." *Bulletin of the Society for American Music* 45, no. 2 (2019).

Hankey, Wayne. "Re-Evaluating E. R. Dodds' Platonism." *Harvard Studies in Classical Philology* 103 (2007): 499–541.

Harrington, Hannah K. *Holiness: Rabbinic Judaism and the Graeco-Roman World.* London: Routledge, 2001.

Harris, Ian. "A Vast Unsupervised Recycling Plant: animals and the Buddhist cosmos." In *A Communion of Subjects: animals in religion, science and ethics.* Edited by Paul Waldau and Kimberley C. Patton. New York: Columbia University Press, 2006.

Harrison, Jane. *Prolegomena to the Study of Greek Religion.* 3rd ed. New Jersey: Princeton University Press, 1991 [1922].

Harvey, Peter. "Buddha and Cakravartins." In *Encyclopedia of Buddhism.* Edited by Damien Keown and Charles S. Prebish. London: Routledge, 2013.

Hao Wang. *A Logical Journey: From Gödel to Philosophy.* Cambridge, Mass: MIT Press, 1996.

Heath, John. "Blood for the Dead: Homeric Ghosts Speak Up." *Hermes* 133, no. 4 (2005): 389–400.

Hekster, Olivier. *Rome and its Empire, AD 193–284.* Edinburgh: Edinburgh University Press, 2008.

Helm, R. M. "Platonopolis Revisited" (1995). In *Neoplatonism and Contemporary Thought I-II.* Vol. 2. Edited by R. Baine Harris. New York: SUNY Press, 2001.

Henrich, Joseph *The Weirdest People in the World: How the West Became Psychologically Peculiar and Particularly Prosperous.* London: Allen Lane, 2020.

Herrin, Judith. *Margins and Metropolis: Authority across the Byzantine Empire.* New Jersey, Princeton University Press, 2013.

Hesiod *Works and Days.* Translated by Hugh G. Evelyn-White. London: Loeb Classical Library, Heinemann, 1914.

Heyer, Georgette. *The Quiet Gentleman.* London: Arrow Books, 2005 [1951].

Hillman, James. *The Dream and the Underworld.* New York: Harper, 1979.

Hocking, W. E. *Living Religions and a World Faith.* London: Allen & Unwin, 1940

Hooykaas, R. *Religion and the Rise of Modern Science.* Edinburgh: Scottish Academic Press, 1972.

Hopkins, Gerard Manley. *Poems.* Edited by Robert Bridges. London: Humphrey Milford, 1918.

Hornung, Erik. *Conceptions of God in Ancient Egypt: the One and the Many,* Translated by John Baines. New York: Cornell University Press, 1982 [1971].

Hoyle, Fred. *The Black Cloud.* New York: Harper, 1957.

Hoyle, Fred and Chandra Wickramasinghe. *Evolution from Space.* New York: Simon & Schuster, 1981.

Hub, Berthold. "Filarete and the East: The Renaissance of a Prisca Architectura." *Journal of the Society of Architectural Historians* 70, no. (2011): 18–37.

Hume, David. *Hume on Religion.* Edited by R. Wollheim. London: Fontana, 1963.

Humphreys, Sally. "Law, Custom and Culture in Herodotus." *Arethusa* 20, nos. 1–2 (1987): 211–20.

Huntington, Samuel P. *The Clash of Civilizations: and the remaking of world order.* London: Simon & Schuster, 1996.

Hutton, Ronald. *Pagan Britain.* New Haven: Yale University Press, 2013.

Ilaiah, Kancha. *Why I Am Not a Hindu: a Sudra Critique of Hindutva Philosophy, Culture and Political Economy.* Calcutta: Bhatkal & Sen, 2001.

Ingold, Tim. "Being alive to a world without objects." In *Handbook of Contemporary Animism.* Edited by Graham Harvey. Durham: Acumen, 2013.

James, William. *The Principles of Psychology.* New York: Cosimo, 2007 [1890].

Johnson, Ryan J. "Ethics in the Garden of Epicurus." In Ryan J. Johnson, *The Deleuze-Lucretius Encounter.* Edinburgh: Edinburgh University Press, 2017.

Jones, A. H. M. *The Later Roman Empire 284–602.* Oxford: Blackwell, 1964.

Julian, Emperor. *Complete Works. Translated by* Wilmer C. Wright. Loeb Classical Library; London: Heinemann 1913–23.

Julian of Norwich. *Revelations of Divine Love.* Translated by Elizabeth Spearing. London: Penguin, 1998.

Kalligas, Paul. "Forms of Individuals in Plotinus: A Re-Examination." *Phronesis* 42 (1997): 206–27.

Kamenskikh, Aleksey. "The Dialectic of the Other: Political Philosophy and Practice in the Late Neoplatonist Communities." *Deformations and Crises of Ancient Civil Communities*. Edited by Valerij Goušchin and P. J. Rhodes. Stuttgart: Franz Steiner Verlag, 2015.

Kant, Immanuel. "Perpetual Peace." In *Kant's Political Writings*. Translated by H. B. Nisbet. Edited by Hans Reiss. Cambridge: Cambridge University Press, 1970.

Karayiannis, Anastassios D. "The Platonic Ethico-Economic Structure of Society." *Quaderni Di Storia Dell'economia Politica* 8, no. 1 (1990): 3–5.

Kennedy, Hugh. *The Caliphate*. London: Penguin, 2016.

Kinahan, F. "Armchair Folklore: Yeats and the Textual Sources of 'Fairy and Folk Tales of the Irish Peasantry.'" *Proceedings of the Royal Irish Academy. Section C: Archaeology, Celtic Studies, History, Linguistics, Literature* 83C (1983): 255–67.

King-Farlow, John. *Self-knowledge and Social Relations: groundwork of universal community*. New York: Science History Publications, 1978.

Kingsley, Peter. *Ancient Philosophy, Mystery, and Magic: Empedocles and Pythagorean Tradition*. Oxford: Clarendon Press, 1995.

Kipling, Rudyard. *Puck of Pook's Hill*. London: Macmillan, 2016 [1906].

Kirkland, Russell. *Taoism: the enduring tradition*. London: Routledge, 2004.

Klibansky, R., E. Panofsky and F. Saxl. *Saturn and Melancholy*. Edinburgh: Thomas Nelson, 1964.

Kraemer, Joel L. *Humanism in the Renaissance of Islam*. 2nd ed. Leiden: Brill, 1992.

Kragh, Helge. "Big Bang: the etymology of a name." *Astronomy & Geophysics* 54, no. 2 (2013): 2.28–2.30.

Langellotti, Micaela and D. W. Rathbone, eds. *Village Institutions in Egypt in the Roman to Early Arab Periods,* Oxford: Oxford University Press, 2020.

Lash, Nicholas. *The Beginning and the End of "Religion."* Cambridge: Cambridge University Press, 1996.

Leaf, Walter. *Homer and History*. London: Macmillan, 1915.

Leibniz, G. W. *Monadology and other philosophical writings*. Translated by Robert Latta. Oxford: Clarendon Press: Oxford 1898 [1714].

Leopold, Aldo. *A Sand County Almanac and Sketches Here and There*. New York: Oxford University Press, 1968 [1949].

Lerner, Ralph. "Review: Beating the Neoplatonic Bushes. *Al-Farabi on the Perfect State* by Richard Walzer." *The Journal of Religion* 67, no. 4 (1987): 510–17.

Leslie, John. *The End of the World: the science and ethics of human extinction*. London: Routledge, 1998.

Lewis, C. S. *The Abolition of Man: reflections on education with special reference to the teaching of English in the upper forms of schools*. London: Geoffrey Bles, 1943.

———. *Out of the Silent Planet*. London: Harper Collins, 2005 [1938].

———. *Perelandra* (aka *Voyage to Venus*). London: Harper Collins, 2005 [1943].

———. *That Hideous Strength: a modern fairy-tale for grown-ups*. London: Harper Collins, 2005 [1945].

Lilley, Keith D. *City and Cosmos: the medieval world in urban form*. London: Reaktion Books Ltd, 2009.

Lincoln, Bruce. *Theorizing Myth: narrative, ideology, and scholarship*. Chicago: University of Chicago Press, 1999.

Linforth, Ivan M. *The Arts of Orpheus*. Berkeley: University of California Press, 1941.

Litwa, M. David. *Posthuman Transformation in Ancient Mediterranean Thought: becoming angels and demons*. Cambridge: Cambridge University Press, 2021.

Liu, Cixin. *The Three Body Problem*. London: Head of Zeus, 2015.

Locke, John. *Second Treatise on Government*. Edited by Mark Goldie. Oxford: Oxford University Press, 2016 [1690].

Long, A. A. and D. N. Sedley, eds. *The Hellenistic Philosophers*. Cambridge: Cambridge University Press, 1987.

L'Orange, H. P. "Expressions of Cosmic Kingship in the Ancient World." In *The Sacral Kingship/La Regalità Sacra: Contributions to the 8th International Congress for the History Of Religions* (Rome 1955), 481–512. Leiden: Brill, 1959.

Louth, Andrew. *Maximus the Confessor*. Oxford: Oxford University Press, 1996.

Lowell, James Russell. *Poems*. Boston: Ticknor, Reed & Fields, 1853.

Lowin, Shari L. and Nevin Reda. "Scripture and Exegesis; Torah and Qu'ran in historical perspective." In *Routledge Handbook of Muslim-Jewish Relations*. Edited by Josef W. Meri. London: Routledge, 2016.

Lutoslawski, Wincenty. *The World of Souls*. London: Allen & Unwin, 1924.

Mac Cárthaigh, Críostóir. "Midwife to the Fairies (ML 5070): The Irish Variants in Their Scottish and Scandinavian Perspective." *Béaloideas* 59 (1991): 133–43.

MacIntyre, Alasdair. *God, Philosophy, Universities: a selective history of the Catholic philosophical tradition*. London: Rowman & Littlefield, 2009.

Mann, Charles C. *1493: How Europe's Discovery of the Americas Revolutionized Trade, Ecology and Life on Earth*. New York: Knopf, 2011.

Margulis, Lynn and Dorion Sagan *Microcosmos: Four Billion Years of Microbial Evolution*. New York: Summit Books, 1986.

Marquet, Yves. *La Philosophie des Ihwan al-Safa*. Algiers: Études et documents, 1973.

Maximus Confessor. *Selected Writings*. Translated by George C. Berthold. London: SPCK, 1985.

Mayhew, Robert. "The theology of the Laws." In *Plato's Laws: a critical guide.* Edited by Christopher Bobonich. Cambridge: Cambridge University Press, 2010.

Mazur, Zeke. "Having Sex with the One: erotic mysticism in Plotinus and the problem of Metaphor." In *Late Antique Epistemology: Other Ways to Truth.* Edited by Panayiota Vassilopoulou and Stephen R. L. Clark. Basingstoke: Palgrave Macmillan, 2009.

McCarraher, Eugene. *The Enchantments of Mammon: How capitalism became the religion of modernity.* Cambridge, MA: Harvard University Press, 2019.

McEvilley, Thomas. "Plotinus and Vijñānavāda Buddhism." *Philosophy East and West* 30, no. 2 (1980): 181–93.

McGilchrist, Iain. *The Master and his Emissary: the divided brain and the making of the western world.* New Haven: Yale University Press, 2009.

Merchant, Carolyn. 'The Scientific Revolution and *The Death of Nature*." *Isis* 97 (2006): 513–33.

———. "The Violence of Impediments: Francis Bacon and the Origins of Experimentation." *Isis* 99 (2008): 731–60.

Meyer, Yakov Z. "Parashat Teruma: the primordial Torah." *Haaretz* (30 January 2014).

Midgley, Mary. *Science and Poetry.* London: Routledge, 2011.

Minucius Felix. *Octavius*: In *Tertullian: Apology; De spectaculis,* Translated by T. R. Glover. *Minucius Felix: Octavius.* Translated by W. C. A. Kerr and Gerald H. Rendall, based on the unfinished version by W. C. A. Kerr.. Boston: Harvard University Press, Loeb Classical Library, 1931.

Mirrlees, Hope *Lud-in-the-Mist.* London: Gollancz, 2000 [1926].

Moin, A. Azfar. *The Millennial Sovereign: Sacred Kingship and Sainthood in Islam.* New York: Columbia University Press, 2012.

Montaigne, Michel de. *Apology for Raymond Sebond.* Translated by Roger Ariew and Marjorie Grene. Indianapolis: Hackett, 2003.

Moore, Ken. "Plato's Puppets of the Gods: representing the magical, the mystical and the metaphysical." *Arion* 22, n. 2 (2014): 37–72.

Morenz, Siegfried. *Egyptian Religion.* Translated by Ann E. Keep. New York: Cornell University Press, 1973 [1960].

Morgan, Kathryn A. "Plato and the Stability of History." In *Greek Notions of the Past in the Archaic and Classical Eras: History without Historians.* Edited by John Marincola, Lloyd Llewellyn-Jones and Calum Maciver. Edinburgh: Edinburgh University Press, 2012.

Morgenthau, Hans. *Politics among Nations: the struggle for power and peace.* New York: Alfred A. Knopf, 1956 [1948].

Most, Glenn W. "Plotinus' Last Words." *Classical Quarterly* 53, no. 2 (2003): 576–87.

Muir, Edwin. *Collected Poems.* London: Faber, 1984 [1960].

Müller, Max, trans. *Upanishads.* Oxford: Clarendon Press, 1869.

Murdoch, Iris. *The Sovereignty of Good.* London: Routledge & Kegan Paul, 1970.

Narbonne, Jean-Marc "L'énigme de la non-descente partielle de l'âme chez Plotin: la piste gnostique/hermétique de l'ὁμοούσιος." *Laval Theologique et Philosophique* 64 (2008): 691–708.

Narbonne, Jean-Marc. *Plotinus in Dialogue with the Gnostics. Studies in Platonism, Neoplatonism, and the Platonic Tradition.* Leiden/Boston: Brill, 2011.

Naydler, Jeremy. *Temple of the Cosmos: the Ancient Egyptian Experience of the Sacred.* Rochester, VT: Inner Traditions International, 1996.

Newman, John Henry. *Apologia pro Vita Sua.* Teddington, Middlesex: Echo Library, 2007 [1890].

Noble, Christopher Isaac. "Everything in Nature is in Intellect: Forms and Natural Teleology in Ennead 6.2.21 (and elsewhere)." *Phronesis* 66, no. 4 (2021): 426–56.

Obeyesekere, Gananath. *Imagining Karma: Ethical Transformation in Amerindian, Buddhist, and Greek Rebirth.* Berkeley: University of California Press, 2002

O'Donnell, James J. "The Next Life of Augustine." In *The Limits of Ancient Christianity: essays on late antique thought and culture in honor of R. A. Markus.* Edited by William E. Klingshirn and Mark Vessey. Ann Arbor: University of Michigan Press, 1999.

O'Meara, Dominic J. "Aspects of Political Philosophy in Iamblichus." In *The Divine Iamblichus: philosopher and man of God.* Edited by H. J. Blumenthal and E. G. Clark. Bristol: Bristol Classical Press, 1993.

———. "Neoplatonist Conceptions of the Philosopher-King." In *Plato and Platonism.* Edited by J. van Ophuijsen. Washington, D. C.: Catholic University America Press, 1999.

———. *Platonopolis: Platonic political philosophy in late antiquity.* Oxford: Clarendon Press, 2003.

Origen. *Contra Celsum.* Translated by Henry Chadwick. Cambridge: Cambridge University Press, 1953.

———. *On First Principles.* Translated by John Behr. Oxford: Oxford University Press, 2017.

Ousager, Asger. *Plotinus on Selfhood, Freedom and Politics.* Aarhus, Denmark: Aarhus University Press, 2005.

Paganini, Mario C. D. "Private Associations and Village Life in Early Roman Egypt." In Micaela Langellotti and D. W. Rathbone, *Village Institutions.*

Palmer, G. E. H., P. Sherrard and Kallistos Ware, eds. *The Philokalia,.* Vol. 1. London: Faber, 1979–95.

Panofsky, Erwin and Gerda Panofsky-Soergel, eds. *Abbot Suger on the Abbey Church of St. Denis.* New Jersey: Princeton University Press, 1979 [1946].

Parke, H. W. "The Massacre of the Branchidae." *Journal of Hellenic Studies* 105 (1985): 59–68.

Pascal, Blaise. *Pensées.* Translated by W. F. Trotter. New York: Dutton & Co, 1956.

Pascoe, Bruce. *Dark Emu: Aboriginal Australia and the Birth of Agriculture*. London: Scribe, 2018.

Patrides, C. A., ed. *The Cambridge Platonists*. Cambridge: Cambridge University Press, 1969.

Patterson, Orlando. *Slavery and Social Death*. Boston: Harvard University Press, 1982.

Pearce, Sarah J. K. *The Land of the Body: Studies in Philo's Representation of Egypt*. Tubingen: Mohr Siebeck, 2007.

Perl, Eric D. "The Power of All Things." *American Catholic Philosophical Quarterly* 71 (1997): 301–13.

Perrett, Roy W. *Hindu Ethics: A Philosophical Study*. Honolulu: University of Hawaii Press, 1998.

Philo of Alexandria. *Complete Works*. Translated by F. H. Colson and G. H. Whitaker. Loeb Classical Library. Boston: Harvard University Press, 1929–1962.

Pickstock, Catherine. *After Writing: on the liturgical consummation of philosophy*. Oxford: Blackwell, 1998.

Plumwood, Val. "Nature in the Active Voice." In *Handbook of Contemporary Animism*. Edited by Graham Harvey. Durham: Acumen, 2013.

Plutarch. *Moralia*, Vol. 5. Translated by Frank Cole Babbitt. Cambridge, Mass: Loeb Classical Library, Harvard University Press, 1936.

———. *Moralia*. Vol. 10. Translated by Harold North Fowler. Cambridge, MA: Loeb Classical Library, Harvard University Press, 1936.

———. *Lives, Volume 7: Demosthenes and Cicero. Alexander and Caesar*. Translated by Bernadotte Perrin. Cambridge, Mass: Harvard University Press, Loeb Classical Library, 1919.

Pohl, Frederik and Jack Williamson. *Farthest Star*. London: Macmillan, 1976.

———. *Land's End*. New York: Tor Books, 1989.

Porphyry. *On Abstinence from Killing Animals*. Translated by Gillian Clark. London: Duckworth, 2000.

Poulsen, Birte. "City Personifications in Late Antiquity." In *Using Images in Late Antiquity*. Edited by Stine Birk, Troels Myrup Kristensen & Birte Poulsen. Oxford: Oxbow Books, 2014.

Prestige, G. L. *God in Patristic Thought*. London: SPCK, 1952.

Proclus. *Commentary on Plato's Timaeus*. Edited by H. Tarrant. Cambridge: Cambridge University Press, 2007.

Ps-Dionysius. *Complete Works*. Translated by Colm Luibheid and Paul Rorem. London: SPCK, 1987.

Radhakrishnan, S. and Charles Moore, eds. *Sourcebook of Indian Philosophy*. New Jersey: Princeton University Press, 1957.

Raine, Kathleen. *Blake and the New Age*. London: Routledge, 2011.

Rajaee, F. *Islamic Values and World View*. Lanham: University Press of America, 1983.

Ramadan, Moussa Abou. "Muslim Jurists' Criteria for the Division of the World into Dar al-Harb and Dar al-Islam." In *International Law and Religion: Historical and Contemporary Perspectives*. Edited by Martti Koskenniemi, Mónica García-Salmones Rovira, and Paolo Amorosa. Oxford: Oxford University Press, 2017.

Ramelli, Ilaria L. E. "Origen and the Platonic Tradition." *Religions* 8 (2017): 21–41.

Ramsey, Frank. *Foundations of Mathematics*. London: Routledge, 1931.

Rees, Alwyn D. and Brinley Rees. *Celtic Heritage*. London: Thames & Hudson, 1989 [1961].

Reeve, C. D. C. *Philosopher Kings: the argument of Plato's Republic*. Indianapolis: Hackett, 2006 [1988].

Rhys-Davids, Thomas William. *The Milinda Panha: the Questions of King Milinda*. Loschberg: Jazzybee Verlag, 2017.

Ricci, Matteo. *China in the Sixteenth Century: the journal of Matteo Ricci: 1583–1610*. Translated by Louis J. Gallagher. New York: Random House, 1942.

Rinpoche, Kalu and M. Montenegro. *Luminous Mind: Fundamentals of Spiritual Practice*. Somerville, MA: Wisdom Publications, 1997.

Rist, John M. "Integration and the Undescended Soul in Plotinus." *American Journal of Philology* 88, no. 4 (1967): 410–22.

———. *Plotinus: the Road to Reality*. Cambridge: Cambridge University Press, 1967.

Robertson, David G. "Plotinus on Disorderly Men in Political Communities." *Politeia* 1, no. 4 (2019): 183–94.

Robins, Gay. *The Art of Ancient Egypt*. London: British Museum Press, 2008.

Robinson, O. F. *Ancient Rome: City Planning and Administration*. London: Routledge, 2003.

Rosenmeyer, T. G. "Plato's Atlantis Myth: 'Timaeus' or 'Critias?'" *Phoenix* 10, no. 4 (1956): 163–72.

Ross, W. D., ed. *Works of Aristotle*. Vol 12. *Select Fragments*. London: Oxford University Press, 1952.

Runia, D. T. "God and Man in Philo of Alexandria." *Journal of Theological Studies* 39 (1988): 48–75.

Russell, Jeremiah Heath. "Athens and Byzantium: Platonic political philosophy in religious empire" (2010). LSU Doctoral Dissertations. 2978.

Rykwert, J. *The Idea of a Town*. London: Faber, 1976.

Sabo, Theodore. "The Politics of the One." *Acta Classica* 58 (2015): 209–16.

Sahlins, Marshall. *Stone Age Economics*. London: Routledge, 2017 [1972].

Sallustius, *Concerning the gods and the universe*. Edited by Arthur Darby Nock. Cambridge: Cambridge University Press, 1926.

Samaras, Thanassis. "Family and the question of women in the Laws." In *Plato's Laws: a critical guide*. Edited by Christopher Bobonich. Cambridge: Cambridge University Press, 2010.

Sangharakshita, Urgyen [aka Dennis Lingwood]. *What is the Sangha? The nature of spiritual community.* Cambridge: Windhorse Publications, 2001.

Schall, James V. "Plotinus and Political Philosophy." *Gregorianum* 66, no. 4 (1985): 687–707.

Schibli, Hermann S. *Hierocles of Alexandria.* New York: Oxford University Press, 2002.

Schmidt, Gavin A. and Adam Frank. "The Silurian hypothesis: Would it be possible to detect an industrial civilization in the geological record?" *International Journal of Astrobiology* 18, no. 2 (2019): 142–50.

Schultz, David E. and S. T. Joshi. eds. *Essential Solitude: the letters of H. P. Lovecraft and August Derleth 1926– 37.* New York: Hippocampus Press, 2013.

Schwartz, Richard H. *Judaism and Vegetarianism.* New York: Lantern Books, 2001.

Scott, Kenneth. "Plutarch and the Ruler Cult." *Transactions and Proceedings of the American Philological Association,* 60 (1929): 117–35.

Sedley, David. "The Ideal of Godlikeness." In *Plato 2: Ethics, Politics, Religion and the Soul.* Edited by Gail Fine. Oxford: Oxford University Press, 1999.

Shaw, Brent D. "War and Violence." In *Late Antiquity: a guide to the post-classical world.* Edited by G. W. Bowersock, Peter Brown and Oleg Grabar. Cambridge, Mass: Harvard University Press, 1999.

Sheckley, Robert. *Dimension of Miracles.* London: Penguin, 2020 [1968].

Sherwood, Polycarp. *The Earlier Ambigua of Saint Maximus the Confessor and his Refutation of Origenism.* Rome: Herder, 1955.

Shewan, A. "The Scheria of the Odyssey": *The Classical Quarterly* 13, no. 1 (1919): 4–11.

Simak, Clifford D. *City.* Baltimore: Old Earth Books, 2004 [1952, 1976].

Simard, Suzanne. *Finding the Mother Tree: Uncovering the Wisdom and Intelligence of the Forest.* London: Allen Lane, 2021.

Sinkewicz, Robert E., trans. *Evagrius of Pontus: the Greek ascetic corpus.* Oxford: Oxford University Press, 2003.

Smart, Christopher. *The Poetical Works of Christopher Smart, I: Jubilate Agno.* Edited by Karina Williamson. Oxford: Clarendon, 1980.

Solovyov, Vladimir. *War, Progress and the End of History: three conversations including a short story of the Anti-Christ.* Translated by Alexander Bakshy and Thomas R. Beyer. Edited by Czeslaw Milosz and Stephan A. Hoeller. New York: Lindisfarne Press, 1990 [1900].

Solovyov, Vladimir. *Lectures on Divine Humanity.* Translated by Peter Zouboff. Edited by Boris Jakim. New York: Lindisfarne Press, 1995.

Song, Euree. "The Ethics of Descent in Plotinus." *Hermathena* 187 (2009): 27–48.

Sorabji, Richard, ed. *Philosophy of the Commentators.* Vol. 1. *Psychology.* London: Duckworth, 2004.

Soundararajan, Thenmozhi [Dalit Diva]. "Why It is Time to Dump Gandhi." *Medium.* June 14, 2017. https://medium.com/@dalitdiva/why-it-is-time-to-dump-gandhi-b59c7399fe66.

Sourvinou-Inwood, Christiane. *Hylas, the Nymphs, Dionysos and Others: myth, ritual, ethnicity.* Stockholm: Åströms Förlag, 2005.

Spengler, Oswald. *The Decline of the West.* Translated by Charles Francis Atkinson. New York: Alfred Knopf, 1928.

Sprat, Thomas. *History of the Royal Society.* 3rd ed. New York: Elibron, 2005 [1722].

Stamatellos, Giannis. *Plotinus and the Presocratics: a philosophical study of pre-Socratic influences in Plotinus' Enneads.* New York: SUNY Press, 2007.

Stapledon, Olaf. *Last and First Men.* London: Gollancz, 1999 [1930].

———. *Last Men in London.* New York: Dover, 2011 [1932].

Steegmuller, Francis. "Diplomacy: the Abbé Galiani: 'The Laughing Philosopher.'" *American Scholar* 57, no. 4 (1988): 589–97.

Steel, Carlos. *Proclus, On Providence.* London: Bloomsbury, 2007.

Stegman, Casey. "Plato's *Timaeus-Critias,* the Ancestral Constitution, and the Democracy of the Gods." *Political Theory* 45 (2017): 240–60.

Stern-Gillet, Suzanne. "Dual Selfhood and Self-Perfection in the *Enneads.*" *Epoche: A Journal for the History of Philosophy* 13, no. 2 (2009): 331–45.

Stevenson, Ian. *Twelve Cases in Lebanon and Turkey: Cases of the Reincarnation Type.* Vol. 3. Charlottesville: University Press of Virginia, 1980.

Suetonius. *The Twelve Caesars.* Translated by Robert Graves. Edited by James Rives. London: Penguin, 2007 [1957].

Sunjana, Peshotun Dustoor Behramjee. *The Dinkard.* Bombay: D. Ardeshir & Co., 1874.

Surowiecki, James. *The Wisdom of Crowds: why the many are smarter than the few.* New York: Random House, 2004.

Taormina, Daniela Patrizia and Angela Longo, eds. *Plotinus and Epicurus: Matter, Perception, Pleasure.* Cambridge: Cambridge University Press, 2017.

Tarrant, Harold. "Atlantis: Myths, Ancient and Modern." *The European Legacy* 12, no. 2 (2007): 159–72.

Taylor, Jill Balte. *My Stroke of Insight.* London: Hodder & Stoughton, 2008.

Tegmark, Max. *Our Mathematical Universe: my Quest for the Ultimate Nature of Reality.* London: Allen Lane, 2014.

Thoreau, Henry David. *Walden and Civil Disobedience.* Wordsworth, 2006 [1854, 1849].

Tolkien, J. R. R. *On Fairy Stories.* Edited by Verlyn Flieger and Douglas A. Anderson. London: Harper Collins, 2014 [1947].

Toynbee, Arnold. *A Study of History.* Vol. 10. Oxford: Oxford University Press, 1954.

———. *Some Problems in Greek History.* London: Oxford University Press, 1969.

Tully, James. "Aboriginal property and Western theory: recovering a middle ground." *Social Philosophy and Policy* 11, no. 2 (1994): 153–80.

Vajira, Sister and Francis Story. *Last Days of the Buddha (Mahà Parinibbana Sutta)*. Kandy, Sri Lanka: Buddhist Publication Society, 1988.

Vatican, *Catechism of the Catholic Church*. London: Burns & Oates, 2004.

Vernant, Jean-Pierre. *The Origins of Greek Thought*. London: Methuen, 1982.

———. "Hestia-Hermès: Sur l'expression religieuse de l'espace et du mouvement chez les Grecs." *L'Homme* 3 (1963): 12–50.

Vidal-Naquet, Pierre. "Plato's Myth of the Statesman, the Ambiguities of the Golden Age and of History." *The Journal of Hellenic Studies* 98 (1978): 132–41.

———. *The Atlantis Story: a short history of Plato's myth*, tr. Janet Lloyd. Liverpool: Liverpool University Press, 2007.

Vilenkin, Alexander. "The principle of mediocrity." *Astronomy & Geophysics* 52, no. 5 (2011): 33–36.

Viveiros de Castro. "Cosmological Deixis and Amerindian Perspectivism." *Journal of the Royal Anthropological Institute* 4, no. 3 (1998): 469–88.

Von Balthasar, Hans Urs. *Cosmic Liturgy: the Universe according to Maximus the Confessor*. Translated by Brian E. Daley. San Francisco: Ignatius Press, 2003 [1988].

Wakoff, M. "Awaiting the Sun: A Plotinian Form of Contemplative Prayer." In *Platonic Theories of Prayer*. Edited by J. M. Dillon and A. Timotin. Leiden: Brill, 2016.

Walzer, Richard. *Al-Farabi on the perfect state: Abū Naṣr al-Fārabī's Mabādi' ahl-madīna al-fadila*. Oxford: Clarendon Press, 1982.

Ward, Benedicta. *The Desert Christians*. Mowbrays: London, 1975.

Waterfield, Robin. *The First Philosophers: the Presocratics and Sophists*. Oxford: Oxford University Press, 2000.

Watt, John W. "Julian's *Letter to Themistius*—and Themistius' Response?" *Emperor and Author: the writings of Julian the Apostate*. Edited by Nicholas Baker-Brian and Shaun Tougher. Swansea: Classical Press of Wales, 2012.

Watts, Alan. *The Book on the Taboo against Knowing Who You Are*. London: Souvenir Press, 2011 [1996].

Weiss, Amaroq E., Timm Kroeger, J. Christopher Haney and Nina Fascione. "Social and Ecological Benefits of Restored Wolf Populations." In *Transactions of the 72nd North American Wildlife and Natural Resources Conference*. Washington, D. C.: 2007.

Wells, H. G. *The First Men in the Moon*. Oxford: Oxford University Press, 2017 [1901].

Wiedemann, Thomas. *Greek and Roman Slavery*. London: Routledge, 1988.

Williams, Charles. *The Place of the Lion*. London: Faber, 1931.

———. *Descent into Hell*. London: Faber, 1937.

———. *All Hallows Eve*. London: Faber, 1945.

———. *The Descent of the Dove.* London: Collins, 1963 [1939].

Wilson, Colin. *Religion and the Rebel.* London: Gollancz, 1957.

———. *The Mind Parasites.* London: Barker, 1967.

———. *The Philosopher's Stone.* London: Barker, 1969.

Wilson, E. O. *On Human Nature.* Cambridge, Mass: Harvard University Press, 1978.

Wilson, James. *The Earth Shall Weep: a history of Native America.* New York: Grove Press, 1998.

Wittgenstein, Ludwig. *Tractatus Logic-Philosophicus.* 2nd ed. Edited by D. F. Pears and B. F. McGuinness. London: Routledge & Kegan Paul: London, 1972.

———. *Philosophical Investigations.* Translated by G. E. M. Anscombe, P. M. S. Hacker, Joachim Schulte. Edited by P. M. S. Hacker and Joachim Schulte. Oxford: Blackwell, 2009.

Wodehouse, P. G. *The Mating Season.* London: Everyman, 2001 [1949].

Wohl, Ellen. *Saving the Dammed: Why We Need Beaver-Modified Ecosystems.* New York: Oxford University Press, 2019.

Wohlleben, Peter. *The Secret Network of Nature: the delicate balance of all living things.* London: Bodley Head, 2018.

Wolfe, Kenneth. "The status of the individual in Plotinus." In *Ancient Models of Mind: studies in human and divine rationality.* Edited by Andrea Nightingale and David Sedley. Cambridge: Cambridge University Press, 2010.

Wren-Lewis, John. "Resistance to the Study of the Paranormal." *Journal of Humanistic Psychology* 14 (1974): 41–48.

———. "Death Knell of the Guru System?: Perfectionism Versus Enlightenment." *Journal of Humanistic Psychology* 34 (1994): 46–61.

Wright, John C. *Golden Age Trilogy: The Golden Age; The Phoenix Exultant; The Golden Transcendence.* New York: Tor Books, 2002–2003.

Yeats, W. B. *Fairy and Folk Tales of the Irish Peasantry.* London: Walter Scott Publishing, 1890.

———. *Collected Poems,* ed., Richard J. Finneran. London: Macmillan, 2016 [1961].

Zarcone, Thierry. *Mystiques, Philosophes et Franc-Maçons en islam.* Paris: Jean Maisonneuve: Paris, 1993.

———. "Stone People, Tree People and Animal People in Turkic Asia and Eastern Europe." *Diogenes* 207 (2005): 35–46.

Zebrowski, George. *The Omega Trilogy.* Medford, OR: Armchair Fiction, 2015 [1972, 1977, 1983].

Zimmer, Heinrich. *Philosophies of India.* Edited by Joseph Campbell. London: Routledge & Kegan Paul, 1967 [1952].

INDEX

CHAPTERS OF THE *ENNEADS*

ABOUT THE AUTHOR

STEPHEN R.L. CLARK is Emeritus Professor of Philosophy at the University of Liverpool, and an Honorary Research Fellow in the Department of Theology at the University of Bristol. His books include *Ancient Mediterranean Philosophy* (2013), *Plotinus: Myth, Metaphor and Philosophical Practice* (2016), *Plotinus Ennead VI.9: On the Good or the One: Translation with an Introduction and Commentary,* and *Can We Believe in People?* (2020). His chief current interests are in the philosophy of Plotinus, the understanding and treatment of non-human animals, philosophy of religion, philosophy of psychiatry, and science fiction.

www.ingramcontent.com/pod-product-compliance
Lightning Source LLC
Chambersburg PA
CBHW020525270326
41927CB00006B/449

9 781621 388555